INTREPID
WOMEN

INTREPID WOMEN

CANTINIÈRES AND VIVANDIÈRES OF THE FRENCH ARMY

Thomas Cardoza

Indiana University Press

BLOOMINGTON AND INDIANAPOLIS

This book is a publication of

Indiana University Press
601 North Morton Street
Bloomington, Indiana 47404-3797 USA

www.iupress.indiana.edu

Telephone orders   800-842-6796
Fax orders   812-855-7931
Orders by e-mail   iuporder@indiana.edu

♾ The paper used in this publication meets the minimum requirements
of the American National Standard for Information Sciences—Permanence
of Paper for Printed Library Materials, ANSI Z39.48-1992.

Manufactured in the United States of America

Library of Congress Cataloging-in-Publication Data

Cardoza, Thomas, date
Intrepid women : cantinières and vivandières of the French army /
Thomas Cardoza.
p. cm.
Includes bibliographical references and index.
ISBN 978-0-253-35451-8 (cloth : alk. paper) 1. Women and the military—France—History.
2. Women and war—France—History. 3. Army spouses—France—
History. 4. Camp followers—France—History. 5. France. Armée—
Military life—History. I. Title.
UB21.75.C37 2010
355.0082′0944—dc22
2009037114

1 2 3 4 5   15 14 13 12 11 10

To

THOMAS WAGSTAFF and JOHN BOYLE
for inspiring me to become a historian

and to

GUNTHER ROTHENBERG and JOHN TALBOTT
for making me one

The cantinières of our regiments are really intrepid. One sees them in the most exposed positions; they hear the whistle of the shells and bullets without flinching.

—General Boniface de Castellane, Commander, Third Infantry Division, 1832

Contents

Acknowledgments

A book of this type depends even more than usual on the support, feedback, assistance, and prior work of a great many people. First and foremost, I thank my wife, Cheryl, and our children for living with this project over the course of many years, many research trips, and much absence on my part. My wife also reviewed the manuscript and made many suggestions for improvement. I owe a large debt of gratitude to Professor Gunther E. Rothenberg of Purdue University for helping me to find and define this topic as well as for mentoring, material and intellectual support and guidance, criticism, and, most of all, for friendship. This is his book as much as it is mine.

I also need to thank my editor at Indiana University Press, Robert Sloan, who saw something valuable in this work that others missed. His willingness to publish this book took some courage, particularly in these difficult economic times. His assistant, Anne Clemmer, has been consistently helpful, knowledgeable, and professional, in addition to being delightful to work with. My copy editor, Shoshanna Green, did sterling work correcting errors and clarifying ambiguities. The book is much stronger because of her work.

Many academics at one point or another read and commented on all or some of the manuscript, and to them I owe many thanks. Professor Margaret Darrow of Dartmouth University provided invaluable assistance with matters of interpretation and context, and made the final book much stronger than it would have been. Professor Alan Forrest of the University of York also read the manuscript and offered a great deal of helpful advice; without him, this would be a much poorer book. Professors J. E. Talbott, Patricia Cohen, Catherine Nesci, and Michael Osborne of the University of California, Santa Barbara, all read early drafts of the manuscript and provided important suggestions. I also owe thanks for comments and criticism to Professor Eleanor Hancock of the Australian Defence Force Academy at the University of New South Wales, Professor Karen Haggeman of the University of North Carolina, Chapel Hill, Professor Jane Rendall of the University of York, and Professor James Martin of Marquette University for their reviews of various portions of the manuscript. I received a great deal of constructive criticism and moral support from the editors of *War and Society* and *Paedagogica Historica*. It goes without saying that the anonymous peer reviewers retained by Indiana University Press corrected errors of fact and interpretation, and offered many helpful suggestions.

Due to the peculiar nature of the sources and research involved, this book was a long time in the making, and numerous people helped support and fund that research. I owe special thanks to the archival staff of the Service historique de l'Armée de terre (now the Département Armée de terre) at Vincennes, especially Madame Guéna-Edith, for their friendly, courteous, and professional assistance. Likewise, the staff and director of the Bibliothèque de l'Armée de terre in the Château de Vincennes went far above and beyond the call of duty in providing me assistance, particularly during my visit in September 2000. The French Army Museum at the Hôtel des Invalides gave me aid and comfort at every turn, and in particular the Service photographique, the Société des amis du Musée de l'armée, and the staff of the Bibliothèque du Musée de l'armée were outstanding in their efforts. Cécille Gallais of the Service photographique was particularly helpful and patient. The Réunion des musées nationaux and its American agent, Art Resource, provided me with excellent help in acquiring images. I am particularly grateful to Ms. Márta Fodor for constantly exceeding my expectations. Likewise, the permissions department of the New York Public Library was extremely helpful and efficient, processing my requests with lightning speed. I am extremely grateful to the Musée du Château du Versailles, and I can only inadequately express my thanks to Valéry Bajou for her constant and generous efforts on behalf of this project. I would also like to thank M. Jean Rivière of Les petits frères des pauvres for his generous assistance in obtaining original images. Every French departmental archive offered some assistance, but I owe a particular debt of gratitude to the Archives départementales des Doubs, the Archives départementales des Vosges, and the Archives départementales du Val d'Oise for their assistance. The Archives départementales des Ardennes, especially Solange Bidou, provided me with inestimable service. The staff of the Musée de la Légion d'honneur was truly *formidable* in the help they provided me, and I need to particularly single out Christine Minjollet for her intrepid efforts on my behalf. The guides of the Musée des chasseurs at Vincennes were extremely helpful and friendly. In particular I thank Chasseur Gilles for the gift of his time and his friendship. Madame Luce Larcade also helped with her prior published research and helpful correspondence. I would be remiss if I did not thank the Interlibrary Loan staffs at the University of California, Santa Barbara, and the University of California, San Diego, for their constant and often trying work on my behalf. Without them, this work would have been impossible. I owe particular thanks to Jim Buffon of UCSB. Likewise, I owe a debt of gratitude to the Boston Athæneum Library for access to its rare book collection, and to librarians Neil Siegel, John Fitzsimmons, and Sherry McGee of Truckee Meadows Community College (TMCC) for their help, advice, and encouragement. The library of the University of Nevada, Reno, was also of great assistance. The Public Information Office at TMCC was also a tremendous help. I especially want to thank Kyle Dalpe, Tim Ill, Brandie Davis, and Tracy Mentzer for their help and advice in processing images for this book, as well as for their patience and sense of humor.

During the time I worked on this book I received funding or other support from many sources. The Regents of the University of California provided me funding in the form of a number of grants, including a Humanities Special Fellowship and a Humanities Research Grant. The History Associates at UCSB also provided generous funding. The Interdisciplinary Humanities Center at UCSB, the Minda de Gunzburg Center for European Studies at Harvard University, the German Historical Institute of Washington, D.C., and the Institute for the Arts and Humanities at the University of North Carolina, Chapel Hill, all provided funding for travel and research for this project, for which I am extremely grateful. I wish to especially thank the Kavli Institute for Theoretical Physics in Santa Barbara, in particular Ms. Deborah Storm and Dr. David Gross, for providing me with a place to work and with invaluable moral support. Likewise, the faculty and staff of Eleanor Roosevelt College at the University of California, San Diego, provided me with crucial resources and support, as did the Theodore Geisel Library at UCSD. The staff of the History Department at the University of California, Santa Barbara, gave me a great deal of support in my work. I would particularly like to thank Darcy Ritzau and Catherine Salzgeber. Likewise, I owe thanks to Professor Tsuyoshi Hasegawa for his sage advice and genuine friendship. Finally, I owe a great debt of thanks to my many friends and family members over the years who listened patiently to my conversations about cantinières and who kept me going when things were difficult: you helped more than you will ever know.

To thank everyone who has gone before me in the fields of military history, women's history, and (much more unusually) the intersection of the two would be too vast a task to undertake. Anyone reading through the bibliography and notes of this book will see what a long list that is. However, it is worth noting that without the prior work of scores of historians across several continents and several centuries, this work would not have been possible. While this book is based in large part on previously unpublished and unstudied archival materials, its larger context and many of its details and interpretations owe their existence to the work of those who have gone before me. I only hope that my own work will be as helpful to those who come after me.

INTREPID
WOMEN

Introduction

I N THE AUTUMN OF 1805, in the midst of Napoleon's victorious Austerlitz campaign, a detachment of the French Seventh Hussar Regiment
was in trouble. Attacked by vastly superior numbers of Russian troops,
the men of the Seventh fought desperately to avoid being overrun. They
fought not only for their own lives, but for the safety of a family: their
cantinière, Madeleine Kintelberger, and her six children. For Hussar Josef
Kintelberger, this was a very personal fight; his wife and children were not
abstractions, safely tucked away at home, but all too real flesh and blood
on the hilltop with him and his comrades. Cossacks made rushes at the
position, and a rain of iron shot and howitzer shells fell on the hapless
French. The Kintelberger children sheltered behind the ammunition cais-
sons of the accompanying horse artillery to avoid the hail of fire. Unfortunately, a caisson exploded nearby from a direct hit, and Josef heard the
screams of his children as the flames and debris blinded them. Those were
perhaps the last sounds he heard, for a cannon ball struck and killed him
immediately afterward. His wife, six months pregnant and fighting by his
side, saw him killed, then felt a cannon ball slam into her arm, nearly sev-
ering it just below the shoulder.

The Cossacks closed in for the kill, but found to their surprise that
the pregnant woman with the dangling and bloody arm was full of fight.
Wielding a sword expertly, she fought off her mounted attackers, suffering multiple lance and sword wounds herself in the process. It looked as
though her heroic stand might buy the time needed for French troops
to strike back and rescue her and her children. The Cossacks, never noted
for standing toe to toe with regular troops, were concerned that a French
counterattack might retake the hill, yet they wished to capture this woman

alive. They finally drew pistols and shot her in the leg. Kintelberger continued to fight, so they shot her in the other leg, dropping her to the ground. The Cossacks then bundled her and her wounded children onto their ponies and escaped. Her right arm was amputated in captivity, and soon afterward she gave birth to twins in a Russian prison, despite her thirteen wounds. The rest of her stay in Russian captivity is undocumented, but in 1806 she was repatriated following the cessation of hostilities. After being returned to the French troops in Germany, Kintelberger and her children traveled to France in a luxury coach provided by General Jean Rapp, and in 1809 she was granted an extraordinary pension by Emperor Napoleon himself, who was deeply impressed by her remarkable heroism.[1]

Nevertheless, despite her almost unbelievable courage and suffering, today Madeleine Kintelberger is totally forgotten. She appears in no history books, no monument reminds us of her deeds, and even in her own country she remains completely unknown. Moreover, while some people remember that women known as vivandières and cantinières once served with French combat troops, there exists no comprehensive history of their service. In fact, most people remain totally ignorant of their existence, and even many professional historians have never heard of them, or have an incomplete or even mistaken idea of their history. The truth is that women served as official (and for a time uniformed) auxiliaries of the French army from 1793 until World War One, and in less regular but nonetheless officially sanctioned capacities long before that. The French army of the eighteenth century made extensive use of two types of female auxiliaries: vivandières (sutlers), who sold food and drink to the troops, and blanchisseuses (laundresses), who washed the men's uniforms. Nor were they alone. While the French vivandières (and later cantinières) had the most regular situation and the longest history, women campaigned with every European army in some capacity or other in the early modern period.[2] Nevertheless, while some passing (and usually inaccurate) mentions were made of these women in some older military histories, for the most part history has ignored them and their remarkable stories until recently. Instead, historians have focused most of their attention on the dramatic but numerically tiny number of women who served in the ranks as soldiers, often disguised as men. The less exciting but more numerous women who provided logistical support have received far less coverage, yet they were vital to the operation of early modern armies.

In a groundbreaking article in *Signs* in 1981, Barton Hacker asked about the female members of early modern armies, "Who are these women?"[3] Though thousands of women routinely traveled with European armies,

Hacker's initial "reconnaissance" found that existing scholarship was rare, and he concluded that more work was needed. In the intervening decades, there have been some explorations of women's roles in European armies of the period, and these have been increasing in frequency and importance in recent years.[4] However, apart from occasional brief (and often inaccurate) references in more general works and a few short articles in French, the subject of the French military auxiliaries known as vivandières and cantinières has been largely ignored.[5] This is particularly troubling because tens of thousands of women served in these roles, many of them in uniform and many of them in combat. In fact, when reading reports, commendations, and memoirs written by French officers, the adjective one most often finds used to describe these women is "intrepid." That, and the striking boldness, courage, and even recklessness that many of these women displayed on battlefields around the world for more than a century, gave this book its title.

Women and armies have been closely linked throughout history. Whether as soldiers, camp followers, prostitutes, laundresses, sutlers, nurses, or army wives, women have traveled and lived with armies for thousands of years, and they often outnumbered the male soldiers they traveled with. Right up to the late eighteenth century, a strong tradition existed of women serving in and with military formations. Many of these served in disguise as soldiers, but the very nature of their service makes an exact count impossible. Obviously, only those women who were discovered have left a traceable historical record, and often even that is very tenuous and incomplete. Their narratives were usually written by men, who focused on the moment of discovery rather than on the women's prior service. Ultimately, their stories became mere curiosities: intriguing but largely peripheral footnotes to what was, after all, a men's business. However, thousands of other women served openly in official or semi-official capacities, and these women were for a long time studiously ignored by most historians, or else marginalized as generic "camp followers," with all the connotations of prostitution and illegality that term has wrongly come to imply. These women were essential to the functioning of early modern armies, but from the mid-seventeenth century onward, there were clear signs of a movement to fully professionalize and masculinize armed service.[6] These efforts remained partial and tentative, however. In France, Louis XIV moved to reduce dramatically the presence of women with the army, yet he could not eliminate them entirely because, as John Lynn wrote, "they filled too many essential roles."[7] During the nineteenth century, the support roles formerly filled by women began to be assigned to male soldiers, and most western armies moved to exclude women from military participation. France, as we shall see, took a very different path, continuing to use women in support roles until the early twentieth century. Indeed, the time span between the abolition of female auxiliaries in 1906 and their restoration (albeit in a different form) during the First World War consists of less than a decade. When one considers that some cantinières served up to and even into the First World War, the interval becomes even shorter and even more of an anomaly. This suggests that the widespread idea that women's participation in war is somehow new to the twentieth century is not just misguided: it is patently false.

When I first proposed this project, several people counseled me against it, arguing that if no one else had written a history of cantinières, it must mean that no documents existed. This turned out to be untrue, but the problems of researching nineteenth-century military women proved to be indeed formidable. This was due to several factors. Few cantinières before 1850 were literate, so most left no records of their own concerning their experiences. Even those who were literate came from social backgrounds that did not encourage the writing and publishing of memoirs. Therefore, like most poor people of the period, cantinières left few records in their own words other than requests for pensions or other government benefits. The surviving evidence dictates that much of the cantinières' history be told through regulations, legislation, and the official correspondence of relatively high-ranking men in the War Ministry and the army, but this is balanced as much as possible by battle and daily life narratives told in the words of cantinières and of the common soldiers whose lives (and deaths) they shared.

Another problem is rooted in the structure of the French language itself. French uses masculine and feminine noun forms, but in any mixed group of masculine and feminine, the masculine plural always applies to the group as a whole. The army employed both male and female sutlers at various times: vivandiers and vivandières, cantiniers and cantinières. Given French grammar rules, however, a mixed plural of vivandiers and vivandières would always be termed "vivandiers," for example, even if the group included twenty women and one man. This is yet another way that women's military participation has been covered over, and since the fault lies with the gendered construction of the language itself, it is difficult to compensate for.

Despite this, extremely rich document deposits might have existed had the French army and the War Ministry chosen to keep records on cantinières as they did for male soldiers. Sadly, the army's recordkeeping on cantinières was spotty at best, and the War Ministry's procedures were only marginally better. Since all decisions on individual cantinières were made at a regimental level by the Council of Administration or by commanding officers, recordkeeping was a matter for individual units. Usually, regiments did not keep detailed or complete records on cantinières. Women were issued identification certificates (*patentes de cantinière*) that they themselves retained, and in the small family of the regiment, everyone knew that Madame X was authorized to be one of the unit's cantinières. Records passed to the War Ministry only in certain circumstances, usually serious criminal activity, outstanding bravery, requests for pensions, or death when the unit could not be located. Even then, the War Ministry did not keep records scrupulously, and many were lost or destroyed over the years.

This last point is perhaps the most significant hurdle in researching military women. Military records are usually organized in such a way that a cursory examination of finding guides and indexes turns up no trace of cantinières or of women in general. The structure by which records are catalogued often leaves no place for women, so that the records that do exist are hard to find and scattered. The idea that women are a legitimate subject of study in military history is a fairly new one, and there are some who still do not accept it. Archival records are usually not indexed in such a way that one can easily find records on cantinières. Rather, material relevant to women has often been classified in ways that hide the presence of women from the casual researcher.

In this case, I found significant stores of records at the Service historique de l'Armée de terre at Vincennes (now the Département de l'Armée de terre of the consolidated Service historique des armées, and referred to as AT in the notes). In the Xs series (non-combatants), I found two cartons of cantinière records, uncatalogued and only marginally organized at best. Many still bore unbroken wax seals from the eighteenth century, while almost all were still fastened in bundles with string, pins, or paper crimps that obviously dated to the time of their arrival at the Ministry of War. Some bore what appeared to be bloodstains or other damage. A few of these records (those near the top) had been examined by casual researchers, but the vast majority had not.[8] Additional information pertaining to cantinières was scattered throughout the official publications of the Ministry of War, acts of the Legislature, deliberations of higher military bodies such as the Conseil supérieur de guerre (Supreme War Council), in the Artillery Archives, in the annual *inspections générales* of individual units, and in assorted cartons on diverse topics in a variety of series. Though I queried every French departmental archive, limitations of time precluded a visit to every one for in-depth searches. Several yielded isolated (but often important) documents, but I suspect that many more lie hidden due to the structure of the cataloguing system. The vast majority of departmental archives claimed to have no documents whatsoever pertaining to women with the army, but only careful and in-depth research on the spot would be able to confirm this. Such research for all the departments would be the work of at least one lifetime.

This same problem also manifests in most of the published primary and secondary sources on the French army. Cantinières sometimes appear in these works (especially the primary sources), but their presence is often taken for granted, and it is usually not indexed or explained. Indexes in works published before 1970 rarely include entries for women, cantinières, vivandières, wives, or any other category that might make searching easier, and even recent works in military history often do not recognize or index women and their service. Therefore, finding published references to cantinières is often tedious and time-consuming, since it involves carefully reading every page of every book, and women have therefore been largely erased from French military history.

A few notable exceptions exist. Anyone who takes the trouble to read extensively in the primary literature of the eighteenth- and nineteenth-century French army will find many mentions of cantinières. This is particularly true of letters, diaries, and accounts written soon after an event. In some cases, cantinières appear only briefly, mentioned in an off-hand way that illustrates how ordinary and commonplace it was to see women with armies.[9] In others, where the authors were of a more descriptive bent, there is extensive discussion of cantinières and their daily lives.[10] One source combines both approaches: an assumption that cantinières need no description, and an irresistible desire to chronicle their activities. Writing in the late 1860s, Emile Gaboriau stated, "It is unnecessary to describe the cantiniere in her glory; that is to say, at the head of her regiment on review days, arrayed in full uniform, her glazed cap perched jauntily over one ear and her little cask on her back. Every one knows her traditional jacket, coquettish short skirt, trousers with scarlet stripes, and her fantastic boots."[11] This neatly summarizes the dual nature of many primary sources on the subject, but most assume familiarity without providing the detail that Gaboriau revels in.

Likewise, a careful look at the paintings and sketches of Antoine Watteau or Horace Vernet, among many others, shows abundant pictorial evidence. However, most secondary sources either ignore these women completely or marginalize them to such an extent that no true picture of their lives can be found. Some sources, such as Arlette Farge's *Les fatigues de la guerre,* discuss the paintings in great detail, yet utterly miss the significance of the women because the authors were apparently unaware of the very existence of official female auxiliaries with the army.[12] Instead of explaining the unexpected presence of women in camp, on the march, and on the battlefield, many authors try instead to explain them away, further distorting our historical understanding of this phenomenon.

Despite these problems, a rich fund of data does exist. It includes the personnel dossiers at the French army archives, army regulations on cantinières, and the memoirs, diaries, and letters of soldiers and officers who served with cantinières. The surviving evidence is weighted heavily toward regulations and official documents, meaning that much of this book is devoted to examining how the government and army perceived cantinières, rather than how they perceived themselves. This is therefore an institutional history at least as much as it is a social history. However, I have tried my best, within the limitations of the evidence, to find the voices of the cantinières, both individually and collectively. Because of the lacunae that exist in the more traditional documents, I have also made extensive use of music, artwork, advertisements, and museum artifacts in my attempt to recreate the lives of these forgotten women. In this respect, the artifacts and art on display at the Musée de l'armée in Paris were particularly useful, but I have encountered paintings of cantinières in many unexpected places, including shop windows, a private museum in Atlanta, a flea market in Paris, and an E-bay auction in which an unsigned oil painting of a cantinière recently sold for almost 1,250 Euros. Even more promising for the future of research into the subject, the explosion of digitized historical sources over the last year or two has opened up previously undreamt-of vistas for historians. Some archives, museums, and libraries have begun ambitious projects of digitizing and putting online a variety of sources: books, documents, and images. One of the leaders of this movement is the New York Public Library with its superb digital collections, which make materials in a variety of media quickly available to researchers regardless of time of day or distance. Although French archives and museums have been slow to digitize, the Musée de la Légion d'honneur has created an excellent search engine, Léonore, which allows researchers to at least make preliminary searches without going through the usual process of contacting museum staff or traveling to Paris. The Archives nationales have digitized a number of documents, though their search engine, ARCHIM, leaves a great deal to be desired. One of the most promising and indeed revolutionary online research tools, though, is Google Books. This service allows researchers to search for key words in millions of books, many of them long out of print and available only at a few select research libraries. The possibilities for people researching obscure and often unindexed topics are enormous. Instead of spending days reading a likely book, only to find that it contains no useful information, one can simply do a Google Book search to find in seconds any relevant material. The recent agreement between Google and a consortium of authors and publishers to make in-copyright but out-of-print books available online for a fee offers to expand these possibilities greatly. Of course, this approach has its potential pitfalls. The breadth and depth of historical knowledge one can gain about one's period by simply reading broadly risks being replaced by a sharply focused but potentially very narrow knowledge of the research subject gained by highly selective reading. However, with proper caution, this service has the potential to revolutionize the study of military women, a topic hitherto crushingly difficult to research in breadth in the many extant published primary works.[13]

For all the problems of evidence, the surviving sources provide several clear themes. Perhaps the most salient is the recurring struggle over how to define military women and their service. Were they *militaires,* as the women themselves believed, and therefore entitled to recompense for their service in the form of a retirement pension? Or were they civilian *employées,* as the War Ministry maintained from 1792 onward, and therefore entitled to nothing? This was a major point with serious implications. Aside from the money involved, if cantinières were *militaires,* then they served the nation as soldiers. Given the explicit connection Republican governments made between military service and citizenship, this would make them citizens, eligible to vote and to hold office. This could in turn undermine male dominance in the rest of society. Even leaving the question of citizenship aside, *militaires* earned pay and, in their old age, retirement pensions. Cantinières never demanded pay, but they did demand retirement pensions in recompense for their service, and pensions for tens of thousands of women would have amounted to significant sums. Perhaps more ominous for male control of society, they also would have represented a large number of women who were financially independent through state subsidies.

Whether fiscal or social conservatism was the cause, the War Ministry never relented on this point after the French Revolution. Despite all evidence to the contrary, the Ministry refused to grant women any status other than that of civilian *employée.* Just as stubborn, cantinières never gave up believing that they were soldiers and therefore integral parts of their regiments and of the army. This tension between cantinières and the

War Ministry over the nature of their service remained a central theme throughout the period of this study. Another pervasive theme was the tension between the army's need for female auxiliaries and its discomfort with the presence of numbers of civilian women with the troops. Despite its distaste for the widespread presence of women on campaign, the War Ministry recognized a clear need for those women's presence through most of the eighteenth and nineteenth centuries. However, the Ministry could never countenance making women officially members of the army any more than it could dispense with their services. The army's relationship with its female auxiliaries was, then, a long-term relationship of convenience, and while it went on for more than a century, it ended as soon as the War Ministry no longer saw a need for it.

I chose to arrange my chapters chronologically, roughly by political regime, though this does not purport to be a comprehensive account of French politics.[14] Much of this work is really about the institutional history of cantinières and looks at the changing attitudes of different regimes toward cantinières, so this approach seemed the most appropriate. Each regime, from the Bourbon monarchy to the Third Republic, had a unique relationship with the army, a relationship that was codified and often shaped by legislation and military regulations. Given the volatile nature of French society and politics in the years of this study, a strong interest in the organs of power and coercion was necessary if a regime hoped to survive. The major changes in the everyday lives of French cantinières were for the most part not gradual evolutions but sudden transformations imposed from above by the War Ministry, often but not always at the behest of its political masters. Each successive regime made its mark on the army as it sought to ensure its own continued existence, and the chapter organization of this work reflects that. The sole exception was the Second Republic, whose short and embattled existence left it with no time or resources for major reorganization of the army.[15]

The first chapter examines the immediate origins of the cantinières by looking at the sutlers (vivandières) and laundresses (blanchisseuses) of the old Royal Army in the period 1700–1789. Major foci include defining the basic duties and daily life of the vivandières and examining how the War Ministry viewed their service. The chapter shows that vivandières in the Royal Army did not own their businesses in their own right, but were subject to the near total control of their husbands. However, the War Ministry did view them as serving their country and rewarded them on occasion with financial payments irrespective of their husbands' service. On the whole, however, the War Ministry viewed vivandières with mistrust and suspicion, often with good reason. Few archival sources on military women survive for the period before 1789, so this chapter more than any other makes use of published primary and secondary sources to supplement the relatively small number of surviving archival documents.

Chapter 2 explores the dramatic changes the French Revolution brought to the army as a whole and to vivandières in particular. It examines the changing legal status and increased combat participation of these women as the army and the Republic struggled to define themselves and their relationship while at the same time fending off mortal enemies at home and abroad. A key turning point was the Law of April 30, 1793, which legalized military participation for vivandières and blanchisseuses while at the same time criminalizing it for almost all other women. Although most women were banned from the armies, vivandières gained economic emancipation and became free to own and run their own businesses, over which their husbands now had little or no control.

Chapter 3 examines the substantial changes that occurred under Napoleon Bonaparte, especially in the areas of widows' pensions and in marriage and recruiting patterns. It also analyzes the more active combat roles of vivandières (increasingly referred to as cantinières during this period) as warfare became more intensive and costly than during earlier periods. Another important element is the de facto elimination of blanchisseuses and their replacement by an all-purpose "cantinière," who combined the functions of blanchisseuse and vivandière. The Napoleonic era is particularly rich in sources, allowing a degree of depth and detail regarding daily life that is unattainable for earlier periods. Therefore, this chapter also focuses on the patterns of daily life, families, and the sometimes profitable or heroic, but often tragic, results of battle.

Chapter 4 analyzes the period 1814–1848, and therefore covers a wide spectrum chronologically, politically, and geographically. The restored monarchy tried to return to the pre-1789 division of female military labor between vivandières and blanchisseuses, but Charles X's own attempt at overseas glory, the invasion of Algeria, resulted in an expansion of women's roles and a return to the all-purpose cantinière of the Napoleonic period. Ultimately, the French war in Algeria was responsible for introducing two key aspects of the nineteenth-century cantinières' existence: the creation of quasi-official uniforms, and the rationalization of military regulations concerning women.

The fifth chapter covers what has been called the "Golden Age of Cantinières"—the Second Empire of Napoleon III, from 1852 to 1870.[16] It focuses on the daily life, recruiting patterns, and battlefield roles of cantinières at the zenith of their service, as well as the development and acceptance (both official and popular) of their increasingly elaborate uniforms. The chapter gives special attention to the decoration of cantinières for battlefield heroics, as well as their use by artists as decorative symbols, as advertising icons, and as fashion plates.

Finally, chapter 6 covers the years from the founding of the Third Republic in 1870 until World War One, but it focuses on the gradual elimination of cantinières during the period 1875–1906. It argues that cantinières were eliminated almost incidentally as part of two separate currents of French military reform: one political, aimed at the destruction of the old professional army and the substitution of a republican citizen army; the other professional, aimed at increasing the efficiency and uniformity of the army. Their nexus was their mutual abhorrence of alcohol and alcoholism, and the cantinières were finally eliminated because of their role as providers of liquor, the only role that remained to them by the early twentieth century. However, the chapter also discusses the strong probability that a growing fear of liberated women and a perceived breakdown in gender roles influenced or even inspired the suppression of this group of women who lived outside the normal restrictions placed on members of their sex, while the conclusion discusses in an exploratory and admittedly speculative manner the possible repercussions to French army effectiveness caused by the absence of cantinières during World War One.

Writing in 1932, historian Louis Gosselin stated that the cantinières had left behind "only a silhouette, although one desires a completed portrait."[17] A thorough search of archival records turned up a surprising amount of information on cantinières: not as much as one would hope, but enough to form a clear idea of their origins, lives, and deaths. This study is an attempt to provide not just a silhouette, but as full a portrait as possible.

CHAPTER I

An Uncertain Existence

Vivandières in the Royal Army

WOMEN WERE NO STRANGERS TO ARMY LIFE in the early modern period, and long before the government of the French First Republic formalized women's service in 1793, vivandières and other women worked with the French royal army on an ad hoc but extensive and officially recognized basis. During the seventeenth century, wives, sutlers, laundresses, and prostitutes traveled with armies. In addition, numbers of women served in disguise as soldiers. The irregular nature of most women's presence with armies made authorities nervous. By the mid-eighteenth century, women's roles in the French army had been regularized as laundresses (blanchisseuses) and sutlers (vivandières). Blanchisseuses were soldiers' wives authorized to take in laundry and needlework in their company. Seven to ten blanchisseuses usually accompanied an infantry regiment, and the fees they charged for their services supplemented their husbands' pay. The task of vivandières, on the other hand, was to sell supplementary food and drink to the soldiers, since the supply system rarely filled all their needs. This was a much more lucrative trade. Civilian entrepreneurs had long accompanied French armies on campaign and continued to do so in the eighteenth century. However, vivandières were different because they had distinct and direct ties to the regiment with which they served. While they were civilians, they were married to soldiers in their regiment, and there is evidence that both the vivandières themselves and the War Ministry considered them as servants of the crown, not simply as camp followers. While female sutlers had long been a part of French military life, the unique nature of army life and warfare in the mid-eighteenth century gave vivandières a special place in the early modern French military system.

The French army prior to 1789 was very different from the more modern armies of the First Republic. The idea of a national citizen army had not yet arrived, and soldiers represented not citizens serving their country, but the poorest and least respected members of society. Desertion was common, and this fact alone dictated much of the structure and behavior of the contemporary armies.[1] Most major European armies of the eighteenth century were similar in that common soldiers were recruited, often unwillingly, from the dregs of society. Criminals, the destitute, and those who needed to escape problems in civilian life often filled the lower ranks.[2] Fritz Redlich characterized eighteenth-century armies as being composed of "the picked-up riff-raff, the duped lambs, and the victims of an abominable recruiting system."[3] In France this was less true, as large numbers of otherwise reputable sons of peasants and artisans served.[4] The French army still treated common soldiers harshly, though, and the French recruiting system was subject to abuse, especially during wartime. Recruiters were paid by the head for new recruits, and used almost any means to fulfill their quotas.[5] In Paris, the soldier's social status was accurately reflected in the signs reading "No lackeys, dogs, or soldiers" posted in cafés and public parks, and most parents were reluctant to allow their daughters to marry a soldier.[6] Because the official ideology considered soldiers untrustworthy, military discipline was harsh. Minor offenses merited thirty lashes, being broken on the wheel, or running the gauntlet of the entire regiment. Capital punishment was less common, but was still inflicted for a wide variety of offenses, especially desertion. One captain noted laconically in his diary that a deserter "had his head broken," while two soldiers convicted of stealing some handkerchiefs were hung.[7] Jean Chagniot has pointed out that in practice deserters often were simply sent back to their units and charged with extra years of service, but the death penalty could be and was enforced if superiors wanted to make an example.[8] In any case, adding years of service was a heavy penalty for any soldier desperate enough to risk death in order to desert in the first place.

Poor pay and living conditions also plagued the soldiery. Soldiers were paid so poorly that they often spent their spare time working odd jobs on the civilian market in order to buy food. For example, soldiers drew pay and rations for only thirty days per month, so on the thirty-first they went without food unless they could pay for it.[9] Presumably they purchased meals from local civilians or from their vivandières, who must have done good business on these days. This practice, discontinued after 1789, continued in other Old Regime states, such as Prussia, into the nineteenth century.[10] But even on the other thirty days (and in the five months without a thirty-first), French soldiers struggled. A third of their daily pay went to pay for their rations: twenty-four ounces of bread. All other dietary supplements, such as meat, vegetables, or fruit, as well as tobacco, salt, or wine, came out of the pitifully small remainder, as did fees to the blanchisseuse and the barber.[11] Soldiers invariably had to work odd jobs to pay for their subsistence. As Gunther Rothenberg wrote, "French soldiers hoped for garrison duty in Brest, where 'everyone could find a job,' and prayed to be delivered from 'the plague and famine of service at Bergue and Graveline.'"[12] Among the Paris garrison in the 1760s, up to three quarters of the enlisted men worked civilian jobs. Conditions often led to poor health as well. One private wrote that the "poor diet, miserable quarters, and damp air" of the barracks made him chronically ill for years, while "it would be impossible to explain to what point I suffered from lack of money, and to what extremities poverty reduced me."[13]

Soldiers were not allowed to marry without permission from the regiment's colonel, and these permissions were kept to an absolute minimum in order to avoid "breeding beggars and vagabonds."[14] In addition, barracks were cramped, unheated, and dirty, while entry into military hospitals was considered by most soldiers to be the equivalent of death.[15] One French officer wrote during the Seven Years' War, "Recruiting takes place in remote parts of the provinces. . . . [The recruits] are sent to the army, ill clad and exhausted by the long march, in February and March. . . . They are given the uniforms of dead men, they are made to share rooms with older soldiers, several of whom have just come out of the hospitals. . . . The young soldiers, whom winter sentry duty fatigues, are overcome, fall sick, and often a fourth of them die before the campaign starts."[16]

All this occurred before the actual fighting began. Once the soldiers encountered the enemy, the closely ordered linear battle tactics of the period routinely resulted in casualty rates of 30 to 50 percent in a single day. Large-caliber lead musket balls and iron cannon shot produced hideous wounds, and those who did not have a limb removed by the impact often had it amputated in crude field hospitals. More likely, the wounded suffered horribly on the battlefield until they died of shock or exposure. There was a justifiable fear that soldiers aiding the wounded might not return to the firing line until after the battle, so soldiers were absolutely forbidden to break ranks to aid their wounded comrades.[17]

Because of these conditions, desertion was common, and could quickly debilitate an army on campaign if not checked.[18] One solution was to keep armies in the field closely concentrated, so that individual soldiers had no opportunity to desert. When on campaign, a good commander did his best "to convert his army into a mobile prison: he kept close march discipline . . . and he observed special precautions when soldiers were marching through woods and villages."[19] In practical terms this had several consequences. One was that armies moved slowly, encumbered by a great deal of baggage and by the necessity to reduce straggling. Another was the heavy toll from disease as tens of thousands of people and animals crowded into small camps, since smaller camp perimeters were easier to guard. A third consequence was the difficulty of foraging for food. Foraging for fodder was a group activity that could be closely guarded and controlled, but foraging for food required soldiers to travel in many small groups, and for the groups to split up further to search individual dwellings. The opportunities for desertion were so great that foraging for more than fodder proved unworkable except in extreme circumstances.[20] Therefore, soldiers had to be kept in camp between marches, and the boundaries of the camp heavily guarded by reliable troops. Passage beyond a line drawn closely around the encampment was considered desertion, and punishable by death.[21]

In order to feed their soldiers on campaign, eighteenth-century armies set up elaborate supply services using civilian contractors. The expense was enormous, and since ammunition and fodder took precedence, food for the common soldier was the lowest priority. Food shortages were everyday occurrences, and even officers suffered from hunger while on campaign.[22] Soldiers who marched all day over poor roads were often tortured by hunger or thirst and driven to leave the camp in search of sustenance.[23] Since they faced the imminent prospect of death in battle anyway, harsh punishments could not always deter them. The only way to take away the temptation was to provide the goods soldiers needed in camp. In the French army, this was the function of the vivandier, a soldier given the privilege of selling food, drink, and sundries such as wig powder and shoe polish to the soldiers of his regiment. Each regiment had eight vivandiers, who held a monopoly on this commerce within the regiment.[24]

The lucrative nature of this privilege meant that most vivandiers were senior non-commissioned officers, though simple privates sometimes exercised the profession. These men had military duties that occupied much of their time, so their ability to run a canteen and to sell their wares was limited. This was where their wives came in. Vivandiers always received the rare permissions to marry, and so their wives became "vivandières." Albert Babeau has written that many commanders refused to allow soldiers "to tie themselves to a woman who would augment their needs without augmenting their resources."[25] If this was so, it certainly did not apply to vivandiers and their wives. Vivandiers married because they could not fully exploit the economic benefits of their positions without wives. A wife could legally leave camp to buy (or steal) goods for sale, since she posed no desertion risk. Even vivandiers were denied this privilege. She could also cook, sew, and run a canteen during her husband's time on duty. Thus the vivandier and the vivandière divided the business responsibilities according to their own skills and abilities, and both husband and wife were needed to run a successful business. In this respect, vivandières' work was no different from that of most other poor eighteenth-century French women, who shared responsibilities with their husbands in the store, farm, or workshop.[26] The husband owned the business and was its nominal and legal head, but the vivandière did most of the physical labor.

The vivandière fulfilled a major economic function for her husband and for the army, yet the Royal Army lacked a comprehensive set of regulations or guidelines for vivandières. Rather, like the later armies of the Republic and Empire, it regulated vivandières in an ad hoc fashion, publishing new regulations in response to specific problems or abuses. In this way, it defined the vivandière's responsibilities and ideal attributes negatively, by outlining behaviors and practices that were proscribed. Vivandières were ipso facto required to be the wives of vivandiers, and legitimate (rather than informal or de facto) marriages were required. Apart from that, there were no universal requirements. Rather, requirements varied from colonel to colonel, just as many other standards did. As for the War Ministry, it assumed that vivandières would be troublesome and morally suspect, but tolerated them because of the vital services they provided. Ideally, a vivandière would pay her taxes, practice monogamy or at least refrain from prostitution, and would not steal, smuggle, spy, or run games of chance. However, there were no examinations, interviews, or requirements for proof of good conduct. The Royal Army paid much attention to punishing abuses, but none to preventing them by screening potential vivandières.

Women who became vivandières came from various backgrounds, but certain generalizations hold true. First, like the soldiers they lived with, vivandières came from the very lowest social strata. Daughters of peasants were the majority, but some daughters of the urban poor and of rural artisans also followed the army. Many were daughters of soldiers, born and bred in the army, while foreigners, orphans, and foundlings accounted for large numbers of vivandières. The majority of the Royal Army's vivandières were illiterate, though exact figures are impossible to determine. Ages at first marriage varied between eighteen and twenty-five, with the average being twenty-two, significantly lower than for poor French women in general.[27] Husbands were usually significantly older than their brides, often by ten or even twenty years. This was a function of the system that awarded most of the marriage permissions to senior corporals and sergeants, since they were more able to support a wife, as well as more likely to have influence in the regiment.

That most vivandières came from rural backgrounds is hardly surprising, given the overwhelmingly rural nature of eighteenth-century France. They were baptized in places like La Bassée, Bayonne, Valenciennes, and L'Isle du Rhin, the daughters of farm laborers and of small-town artisans such as bakers and glassblowers.[28] Their places of birth tended disproportionately to the frontier provinces, especially the north and east. A woman was most likely to meet a soldier there, because the frontiers were more heavily garrisoned than the interior, and during wartime units on campaign passed through constantly. In fact, André Corvisier's research identified a *"France militaire"* consisting of the northern and eastern provinces, and it was here that most soldiers found their brides.[29]

Foreign volunteers were another major source of new vivandières. The Bourbons made special exceptions to the normally strict marriage rules for foreign volunteers, mostly Swiss, Irish, and Germans, and foreign soldiers enlisting in the service of the French kings often brought their wives along. For example, when Johann Eulen and Katerina Sauvart married in Bonn in 1777, they immediately set out on an eight-day trek west to France, where the two joined the Seventy-seventh Regiment, Johann as a simple soldier, Katerina as a blanchisseuse.[30] On the other hand, Josef Pisetky and Katerina Boos from the Palatinate waited six years to marry, until Josef had enough seniority to obtain a vivandier position, allowing his wife to avoid washing clothes and exercise the more lucrative profession of vivandière.[31]

Foundlings, orphans, and illegitimate children also followed the army. Due to steadily rising food prices, the number of abandoned children in France shot up dramatically during the eighteenth century, increasing by more than twenty times from 1670 to 1770.[32] Alone and unwanted, many of these children eventually found their way into the army. For example, vivandière Marie Pierrette was "born of unknown parents" in Avignon in 1757. Abandoned at birth and raised in an orphanage, she needed little incentive to marry a soldier like Louis Hoccard of the Beaujolais Regiment. For Marie, the army offered a sense of security and family that her earlier life lacked.[33]

Finally, the army itself provided a breeding ground for new vivandières, making the system to a certain extent self-perpetuating. For women born into the military, it was an easy and logical choice to marry a soldier and become a vivandière. Certainly it was an easier and more familiar path than stepping out into the uncertain world of civilian life. Marie Lepère was the daughter of a soldier and a blanchisseuse. Born into the army in 1773, she moved with her family to Calais after her parents' retirement. At age nineteen, she returned to the army by marrying Louis La Roche and becoming a vivandière.[34] Considering her family background, nothing could have been more natural. Catherine Campagne was born in the army in 1767, daughter of a vivandière and a sergeant. She became a vivandière in 1783 at age sixteen, and served thirty-one years until her retirement in 1814.[35] Another daughter of the army later became famous as "Marie Tête-de-Bois." She was born at the Hôtel des Invalides in Paris to a retired military family in 1765. Orphaned at an early age, she married a drummer of the French Guards stationed in Paris and became a career vivandière, following the army until her death at Waterloo in 1815.[36]

Given the hazards of military life, many vivandières lost husbands during their careers. When a woman was widowed, she could either leave the army or remarry in order to retain her position. The terrible economic pressures in eighteenth-century France caused by rising prices and over-population meant that most women preferred to stay in the familiar and relatively secure military community, and remarried rather than face an uncertain life as a civilian. Remarriage rates in the Royal Army remained high, reaching 100 percent in the Piedmont Regiment.[37] As long as a widowed vivandière remarried a vivandier, she could retain her position, though it is unclear from surviving sources whether her intended was granted the title of vivandier or whether she was compelled to marry the new vivandier. There were no regulations covering this situation, and undoubtedly the procedure varied according to circumstances and the whim of the regiment's colonel.

Marriage led naturally enough to children, and although army life was hard, most vivandières bore and raised children while they practiced their trade. Since vivandières tended to marry early, while late marriage was one of the most common contraceptive methods of the period, vivandière fertility was fairly high compared to that of civilian women.[38] An examination of surviving records shows vivandières with from one to six children at the time of the mothers' retirement, with an average of about two children per vivandière.[39] However, this does not include children who had reached adulthood. It also does not include stillbirths or children who died while their mothers served, and, given conditions of the time, these numbers must have been considerable. Infant mortality rates among French civilians were approximately 250 per thousand. During wartime and during changes of garrison, vivandières' children suffered through conditions that most civilian children did not, so it is likely that infant mortality was higher in the army. Nevertheless, vivandières continued to have children, who grew up in the military world of barracks, marches, and bivouacs.

Childbirth, a difficult job in the best of times, was complicated for vivandières by conditions in the army. Those women who gave birth in barracks were relatively fortunate, but the French army was often on campaign, and conditions in the field could be terrible. As historian André Corvisier wrote, "The children of soldiers were born in the most diverse conditions. If François Louis Courias was born around 1701 at the Invalides, Nicolas Clément was 'born in a thicket, on campaign in Flanders, child of the Picardie Regiment,' around 1680, and Philippe Boisseron was 'born on campaign, during the war,' around 1702. Their places of birth were strewn along the route of the regiment."[40] Corvisier's examples are as sweeping as they are understated. Giving birth "in a thicket, on campaign in Flanders" might entail anything from a quiet birth attended by fellow vivandières to an agonizing and lonely ordeal in blazing heat, pouring rain, or snow. Certainly bearing children involved greater potential hardships and difficulties for a vivandière than for most civilian women.

Once the children were born, the parents baptized them and chose godparents. The regiment was a close-knit group, and the godparents were almost always a soldier and a vivandière, or sometimes more than one. In February, 1749, Marie Offman, vivandière to a dragoon regiment, gave birth to twins while in garrison at Caen. Little François-Marie was named after his godfather, drummer François-Marie Decourt, while the second son was christened Boniface after his godfather, dragoon Boniface Duclerq. Two vivandières, Marie Jefrain and Jeanne Freulat, were the godmothers. Occasionally, one of the godparents was a civilian female relative, and very rarely both godparents were civilians, but for the most part, vivandières and their families were cut off from civilian society. Draftees rarely returned home, and while the nominal length of service was eight years, enlistment often resulted in a life sentence of military service. For most, the regiment functioned as their extended family.[41]

Family life in the army followed the patterns of campaigning and revolved around work. In peacetime barracks, vivandières were forbidden to ply their trade, as it would put them in competition with local merchants. Therefore, families with children got by as best they could, often engaging in unauthorized commerce out of sheer economic necessity. In camp, the vivandière would set up her tent and operate her canteen with the help of her children, while blanchisseuses would stake out a clothes-drying area and find a source of water. Mothers carried infants with them in slings or

packs as they worked, and often nursed while working as well. Slightly
older children helped their mothers carry water, hang clothes, fetch firewood, cook, and serve drinks: the same tasks they would have performed
in civilian life.[42] Far from being a burden to the army, vivandières' children
actively supported it as cooks, foragers, and musicians. In short, French
army camps were alive with children's activities, and these activities contributed materially to the maintenance of the army.

More metaphorically, older children fed the army by furnishing new
generations of soldiers and vivandières. This was no small contribution, as
these were children born and bred in the army. They were familiar with
drill and with military codes of conduct and discipline, and they were
accustomed to the harsh conditions of military life, making them excellent
recruits. Since they already understood the rhythms and unwritten con-
ventions of camp and barracks, there was no "breaking in" period such as
was necessary with civilian recruits. Boys who had been born in the army
also knew how to handle weapons and had grown up with the military
ethos of duty, honor, and bravery instilled in them from birth. All officers agreed that so-called enfants de troupe made excellent soldiers and
were prime candidates for promotion.[43] The War Ministry recognized this
officially in 1766 when it authorized putting enfants de troupe on the pay
and ration rolls at age six. The system was expanded in 1786 and 1788.[44] In
practice, most regiments counted the boys' service to have begun at birth,
which more accurately reflected their real term of service.[45] This of course
had major benefits in terms of seniority of rank and the size of retirement
pensions, should the child survive that long.

Male children usually started as drummers, and eventually found their
way into the ranks of the regiment's soldiery. This was the path followed
by Jean-Pierre Leytier, the son of a sergeant and a vivandière. Similarly,
vivandière Marguerite Pisetky's three sons all became troopers in the Ester-
hazy Hussars, while Catherine Sabatier's three sons all became infantrymen
in her regiment.[46] Older female children assisted their mothers, learning
their trade and living in daily contact with hundreds of soldiers. Civilian
life was unknown to them, and they often became career vivandières when
they reached fifteen to eighteen years of age.

While the vivandières' daily life included looking after their children,
their chief focus was on business. The primary official means for making money was to sell food, drink, tobacco, and sundries to the soldiers.
Drink usually meant alcohol of some kind, and food would be whatever
vivandières could find, primarily cheese, poultry, meat, and soups. A number of other possibilities for commerce also existed, all of them illegal and

therefore potentially lucrative. Whether it was smuggling, fencing, or gambling, some vivandières were willing to go beyond "respectable" business in order to augment their incomes, and their mobility as part of an army on the move often made this easier.

On the march, Royal Army vivandières traveled at the rear of the army with the artillery, baggage wagons, and supplies. Regulations allowed them one pack horse each, but established vivandières usually owned a large wagon instead. Although vivandières were under the supervision of the wagonmaster, this abuse was widespread and was apparently tolerated in most instances. If it slowed the march of the army as a whole, it materially increased the comfort of the very men who were charged with enforcing the rules. The wagon was loaded with foodstuffs, barrels of wine and brandy, a tent, cooking equipment, children, and all the family's material possessions. It was also a convenient hiding place for items looted along the way or bought from freebooting stragglers. There was often a goat tethered and walking behind, while a chicken or two might occupy a cage on the back. Newly joined vivandières might go on foot with a few goods on their backs or with their wares in baskets loaded on a mule or pack horse.

Marches themselves were arduous, and when rain turned the roads to mud or the summer heat became excessive, soldiers could collapse and die of exhaustion during routine army movements.[47] One French captain wrote of conditions in June of 1762: "A heavy rain all day long, the roads are difficult. . . . It was necessary to construct a large number of bridges and even cross two marshes with long causeways. All these works were done well for good weather and an army of 20,000, but since the army is 100,000 and the weather very bad, . . . all the bridges broke, the routes have become impassable, the columns find themselves stuck, [and] each one arrived as he could in the greatest disorder."[48] Such were conditions for the soldiers at the front of the column. For the vivandières traveling at the rear of the army and following the heavy equipment, road conditions could be horrendous. The preceding troops, horses, and wagons would have churned the roads into almost impassable quagmires, making any forward movement virtually impossible. The captain's laconic comment that "as for the equipment trains, they remain stuck in the mud" barely hints at the suffering, the exertion, and the exhaustion of those trapped in the rear.[49] Even in good weather, roads turned to dust under the tramping of hundreds of thousands of feet and hooves, and the resulting cloud choked, blinded, and parched the throats of soldiers, officers, and camp followers alike. However, bad road conditions also offered vivandières good business opportunities. Brandy sold well during cold or wet weather, and in summer heat, soldiers with dry, parched throats would pay high prices for a glass of beer or wine.

Upon arrival in camp, the vivandières set up their tents. They would be part of a vast tent city, since the Royal Army housed all its soldiers under tents in the field, and an army's officers would have thousands of hangers-on in the form of lackeys, entertainers, and consorts.[50] The vivandière's tent was different, though, since it acted as a social center for the soldiers of the regiment: a place to drink, smoke, and talk. Once the tents were up, vivandières started their fires and began cooking. Soups were the most common fare, since they were easy to make from ingredients on hand and were less labor-intensive than roasted or fried meats. However, a large part of vivandières' business was in supplying the demand for more luxurious foods like sausage, cheese, eggs, and meat. Vivandières who kept chickens or a goat were especially well equipped to engage in this trade, and their customers were often officers. One captain during the Seven Years' War complained that when bad weather held up the vivandières, food became scarce and very expensive if it could be had at all, suggesting that vivandières were absolutely crucial to keeping the French army fighting.[51] As necessary as food was, though, vivandières did a booming business in luxuries as well; all the while that they cooked and served food, they also served drinks and tobacco to all who could pay.

These were the officially sanctioned activities, but some vivandières took part in a burgeoning illegal economy as well. Smuggling was a favorite, since cheating the tax collectors or "tax farmers" was considered just and morally defensible among the poorer classes from which the vivandières came. Because of the Old Regime's numerous internal trade barriers and its complicated series of taxes and exemptions, a unit changing garrison or marching to war could easily pass through one or more "tax zones." The possibilities for profit were great, especially when dealing with the many differences in the gabelle (tax on salt). If a regiment were stationed in an area where the gabelle was low, and transferred to an area where it was high, soldiers could buy salt at low prices and carry it to their new garrison, where they could sell it for a substantial profit. Differences between and even within provinces in the application of the gabelle made this a common practice.[52] The trick, of course, was to avoid the tax farmers, who would exact the tax upon entry to the new province, making the whole exercise futile.[53] Since vivandières had both capital and hauling capacity, they were naturals for smuggling, and the farmers paid close attention to them especially. As early as 1717, the minister of war issued a regulation that "women following the regiments who are convicted of defrauding the

[tax] farmers will be condemned to the lash in addition to the confiscation of their goods."[54]

A similar regulation from 1720 forbade vivandières from "holding any gaming table in the camp or near it, on pain of being sent to the galleys."[55] Gambling was a popular pastime for soldiers trapped in camp, and many vivandières capitalized on this by running games of chance in addition to selling drinks. Prostitution was another of the illegal ways that a vivandière, or indeed any woman, could earn a living in the army. From the reign of Louis XIV on, the War Ministry looked on prostitution as a serious problem, and some of the regulations are shocking in their brutality. In 1687, Louis ordered that prostitutes found with the armies have their noses and ears mutilated in a desperate measure to halt their trade.[56] Less severe, but still harsh, was the treatment prescribed by the regulation of May 6, 1720: "One will not suffer in the camp nor in its environs any public girl nor any of a bad character, and will punish by whipping those who are recognized, and they will be conducted to prison to pass the rest of their lives."[57] The regulations saw the woman as the problem, since no punishments were prescribed for men caught with prostitutes. This was typical of French military regulations throughout the eighteenth and nineteenth centuries, in which women appeared as an element of disorder and a cause of disciplinary problems. Combat soldiers were expensive and scarce commodities, and the army preferred not to punish them when it could punish a militarily "useless" woman instead. Certainly the virulence and repetition of the regulations on prostitution suggest that they were largely ineffective, and that prostitutes found ready access to most military units. Jean Chagniot has extensively documented the pervasiveness of prostitution among the guard regiments stationed around Paris. In these cases, the women were imprisoned and then banished from Paris for "bothering the soldiers."[58]

It remains an open question how closely the army enforced these rules in wartime, or how many vivandières participated in these illegal trades. Given the social background of the typical vivandière, and the omnipresent demand for female sexual partners in a mostly male camp environment, it seems possible that some vivandières participated in prostitution. However, the extent of the trade and its exact nature will probably never be known with certainty, and the numbers of vivandières involved, if any, were certainly quite small. What is certain is that no evidence of vivandières being punished for prostitution exists, suggesting that two separate groups of women existed around the army camps, and that vivandières and prostitutes were mutually exclusive. Certainly many vivandières ran gambling tables, as this was a long-standing tradition and one that continued long after the collapse of the Bourbon monarchy, but while much unsubstantiated speculation has swirled around the issue of vivandières' possible involvement in prostitution, the total lack of any surviving evidence implies that these women did not engage in the sex trade.

Whatever their activities, vivandières presented an interesting picture as they worked. For the most part, visual evidence suggests that French vivandières during this period wore the same loose dresses, sabots, and bonnets they would have worn had they stayed in their villages.[59] There were few of the distinguishing uniform or quasi-uniform pieces worn later by nineteenth-century cantinières. This also held true for blanchisseuses, who could not afford to "dress up" on their meager earnings. John Lynn has recently suggested that "the wearing of military dress in the field would later be associated with cantinières, but it seems to have been more generalized earlier."[60] However, this statement needs some qualification regarding the French army. Lynn cites three sources for this statement, none of them French. Existing visual references for the French army from this period always show vivandières dressed in civilian garb. There may indeed be art that shows an occasional vivandière wearing an odd uniform piece, but this appears not to have been general practice in the French army of the period. Moreover, even the wearing of occasional "cast-off uniform jackets" does not in any way equate with the elaborate, officially sanctioned, and quite literally "uniform" costume of nineteenth-century cantinières. In the French army at least, women continued to dress as civilians during this period. The vivandière's concession to utility was her pocketed apron, which she used to hold coins and glasses while she worked. Some vivandières occasionally affected a more extravagant dress. Dumonchelle's painting *La vivandière* shows a woman in a fancy dress gown, fur-lined slippers, and a plumed hat. She also keeps a small, well-groomed dog on a leash. In manner and in appearance, she is more like a noblewoman than a peasant, but the brandy flask slung over her shoulder and the burning city in the background give away her profession as explicitly as the painting's title does.[61] The rarity of this example implies that this woman's dress was unusual, and the burning city in the painting's background suggests that her finery was freshly looted. Such looting was common practice.[62] Thus, it is more likely that she was trying it on and soon sold it than that she habitually dressed in that impractical fashion. On the whole, visual evidence suggests that French vivandières during the Old Regime continued to dress like peasants, and personal distinguishing marks were few and subtle.

The official attitude of the royal government toward vivandières was mixed. On the one hand, the War Ministry saw vivandières and lower-class women in general as sources of indiscipline and disorder. This attitude can best be summed up by a detail from de Bonnelles' *Ordonnances militaires*. Looking in the index under "v" one reads: "Vivandière, see contraband." From the War Ministry's point of view, any women following the army were potential prostitutes, smugglers, spies, and looters, and at the very least they contributed to road congestion during marches. But in the field, vivandières were a vital part of the Royal Army's supply system, which in turn was fundamentally linked to the army's discipline. Eliminating vivandières could threaten the very cohesion of the army itself by increasing incentives for desertion, which often reached startling proportions even in relatively good times. It would also alienate the very men on whom the maintenance of army discipline depended the most—the senior noncommissioned officers who often served as vivandiers, and who therefore profited in multiple ways from the vivandière system. Therefore, official policies toward vivandières remained a curious combination of reward and punishment, tolerance and mistrust.

The War Ministry's view of vivandières expressed itself in a number of regulations designed to discourage crime and disorder. Some, such as prohibitions on vivandières' selling or even possessing printed cloth, were aimed at protecting specific royal revenues and privileges. Others prevented more loosely defined disorder, such as a 1768 regulation forbidding "soldiers' wives, valets, wagons, or horses" from mixing with the troops on the march or upon entry into a new garrison, ordering them instead to "march all together a hundred paces behind [the column]."[63] The risk of congestion and confusion was partly the inspiration for this regulation, since any disorder greatly increased possibilities for desertion. Perhaps more importantly, though, it prevented soldiers and their wives from passing back and forth any contraband, and made the job of the tax farmers easier by keeping the two groups distinctly separate before and during the customary searches. In another attempt to maintain speed and order on the march, the War Ministry ordered that each infantry battalion or cavalry regiment could have only two vivandière wagons, "each pulled by four good horses."[64] Limiting the number of wagons reduced road congestion, while mandating "four good horses" ensured that overloaded and under-harnessed vivandière wagons did not disrupt the march by moving too slowly or becoming stuck, provided that the women followed the regulations.

Military officials also feared that vivandières could become liabilities when in proximity to the enemy. For example, one officer wrote disparagingly after the battle of Holzminden in 1757, "All the army made a retrograde movement. The valets, vivandières, and surgeons who were spectators took fright, set themselves to crying '*sauve qui peut!*' and fled."[65] However, these "camp followers" had good reason to run, as they were mostly unarmed and would be considered fair game for pillage, rape, or murder by the enemy. In addition, they could not look to the French army for protection, since "when they got in the way, the military police simply cut their traces and left them to their own devices."[66] In any case, the example makes clear that accusations of indiscipline and cowardice, if generally applicable, were also made regarding the many male camp followers.

Vivandières were more than just potential road hazards or battlefield impediments, though. They also represented for the high command a "bad element" that encouraged the soldiers' tendencies toward licentiousness and debauchery. This led one regimental colonel to write that "the fifteen or twenty women who follow each regiment give more trouble than four times that many soldiers."[67] In this, vivandières were subsumed into the larger fear of the lower classes in general and of soldiers and their women in particular. Certainly there were some grounds for concern, as evidenced by couples like Michel Daunay and Charlotte Bracq, who successively joined and deserted no fewer than five Royal Army regiments between 1765 and 1775.[68] But couples like this were the exception rather than the rule. Vivandières were not paragons of virtue, but neither were they necessarily criminals. They were working-class women surviving in a harsh and often brutal environment.

Punishment for vivandières who did transgress regulations was no less brutal than for the soldiers, though it was sometimes applied less systematically. When a vivandière mistakenly roused the entire French army near Krumbach after she "dreamed she saw the enemy," she was not punished.[69] On the other hand, vivandières caught stealing, cheating customers, or receiving stolen goods were forced to run the gauntlet before being cast out of the regiment.[70] Punishments like this were apparently still not enough to deter soldiers and vivandières alike from breaches of discipline, but most vivandières avoided openly antagonizing the military authorities. Nevertheless, the equality with which the French army punished vivandières and soldiers shows that the Royal Army saw vivandières as integral parts of the military structure, rather than as outsiders.

Despite some examples of official hostility, the War Ministry continued to hold vivandières' services to be absolutely necessary to the functioning of the army. After all, the War Ministry also distrusted private soldiers and used brutal discipline and extensive regulations to control their behavior, yet no one suggested that the army rid itself of privates. Likewise, for all its fear and mistrust, the Royal Army never considered eliminating vivandières. On the contrary, the War Ministry recognized the indispensable nature of vivandières' contributions to the army's maintenance and even granted special consideration to individual vivandières, while at the same time taking active steps to control military women's behavior.

Louis XIV was the first French monarch to place all soldiers' wives under the authority of the military code, in 1706.[71] However, it was not until 1761 that any systematic attempt was made to classify and register all camp followers, and even this applied only to one field army. On campaign in Flanders that year, Marshal de Soubise ordered that "vivandières, bakers, and merchants following the army will wear on their clothing a plaque of white iron, where will be written: vivandière, or baker, or merchant following the army of France." Though this method was primitive, it marked a first step toward keeping track of all non-military personnel, while at the same time acknowledging that they were "militarily of very great importance."[72] The problem, from Soubise's perspective, was not morals but security. Preventing enemy spies from circulating in the camp among the general bustle of civilian contractors was a top priority when on campaign, and this was the object of the order. This and other regulations continued to recognize the importance of vivandières, and indeed the barrage of military laws concerning women is a measure of just how important their continued presence with the armies was; without them, the army could not function.

The commander of Fort de Pierre at Strasbourg, Baron de Maes, even submitted a proposal to the Ministry of War for the official incorporation of women into the French Army, since "there have always been women in the army, and having neither bread nor pay, they live at the expense of the soldier." De Maes proposed a complement of eight women per company (seventy-two per regiment) who would cook, carry water, and serve as nurses, rendering thereby "the greatest of services."[73] In exchange they would receive army pay and rations. It is not clear how this plan would have affected the status of vivandières, though certainly their near monopoly on female company would have been broken. Very likely it would have meant the end of vivandières as they existed, but the War Ministry rejected the proposal, and de Maes remained an unappreciated visionary.

The real official recognition for vivandières came in the form of financial aid for retired vivandières. Whereas later governments insisted that cantinières deserved no pension because they were not soldiers, the Old Regime openly acknowledged vivandières' military contributions and rewarded them. Though the government did not give women pensions as such, it did provide cash payments that represented considerable sums for women of the lower classes. When Madame Andierne, a widow and retired vivandière, wrote to the minister of war in 1776, she received a prompt and positive response, along with a *gratification* (one-time payment) of 150 livres. Writing from the War Ministry to the controller-general, the Count de Saint-Germain wrote, "I cannot refuse myself the honor of assuring you that she merits regard for the difficult position in which she finds herself," especially "in consideration of the frequent services that she rendered to the army during the last war and notably by her bravery."[74] Saint-Germain argued for a payment based not on the husband's service but on Mme Andierne's own service as a vivandière. Neither her letter nor the internal War Ministry memos mentioned her husband's service at all, focusing instead on her own career. They show that when it really mattered—in matters of finance—the Old Regime saw vivandières as serving the state and therefore deserving of recompense.

Evidence shows that Mme Andierne's experience was not isolated. Barbe Mangin of the Lyonnais Regiment received a similar *gratification* of 150 livres in 1777. Widowed and encumbered with six children at age thirty-nine, she had little hope of remarriage. She existed on the charity of the Lyonnais officers until the government granted her aid at their request. Marguerite Renaut, the widow of a simple soldier and mother of nine, received only eighty livres, but she did not have the backing of high-ranking officers as Barbe Mangin did, nor a record of distinguished service in the Seven Years' War, as did Mme Andierne.[75] Even eighty livres was a considerable sum for the time, and could have made Marguerite Renaut an attractive bride to a cash-starved groom, given the importance of dowries in eighteenth-century peasant marriages.[76] Thus, while the monarchy did not directly provide for retired vivandières' long-term subsistence, it did give them enough money to make them attractive marriage partners despite their sometimes advanced age and numerous children. Of course, this royal charity would end abruptly with the French Revolution. Once French subjects of the king became French citizens under the law, the rules for monetary rewards for service would become much more stringent and uniform. As long as the king could arbitrarily grant *gratifications,* though, vivandières had open to them a route to official recognition that the new equality under the law of the later Republican governments would close.

The final legacy of the Old Regime vivandières was a mixed one. They firmly established the vivandière as a military type, and the existence of female sutlers in the French army remained unchallenged for almost a century after the French Revolution. They lived a life of travel and adventure that other peasant women could never hope to equal, and made a tangible contribution to French military efforts. However, they also achieved a reputation for being elements of disorder, a reputation that their detractors later used to eliminate women from the army entirely. Nevertheless, concerted opposition to the legitimate presence of women in the army was far in the future in the eighteenth century, and the vivandière was one of the "types" of the Royal Army as much as the noble officer or the grizzled old sergeant. When revolution came in 1789, it overthrew the army's aristocratic structure, but the vivandières not only retained their position, they made tremendous gains in independence and autonomy.

CHAPTER 2

"Absolutely Necessary"

*Vivandières in the Armies of the
French Revolution*

THE FRENCH REVOLUTION of 1789 brought about the disintegration of the Royal Army, and the resulting changes dramatically altered the conditions of service for vivandières. Fully one-third of French soldiers deserted during the early stages of the Revolution, and many who remained became undisciplined and unreliable. The supply system that supported the army on campaign also broke down as the whole structure of the absolute monarchy that supported it collapsed. In this atmosphere of chaos, France went to war in 1792 with Austria, Prussia, Spain, and Sardinia, and the Revolutionary armies swelled to unprecedented size to meet the demands of war on several fronts. The breakdown of the Royal Army's supply system and the increase in size of the army under the Republic meant that vivandières and other entrepreneurs were essential to keeping the soldiers fed. Whereas the vivandière's function in the Royal Army was to prevent desertion by providing goods for sale in camp, the role of the vivandière during the Revolution was to help supply large, mobile armies that often lived by foraging in enemy country. To a certain extent, this was the same function, but whereas it was very closely circumscribed and controlled in the Royal Army, in the armies of the Revolutionary era both vivandières and common soldiers had much more individual freedom of movement. In spite (or perhaps because) of this, the French army saw an important role for women who fulfilled the roles of foragers, cooks, and sutlers and who therefore allowed the soldiers to concentrate on more martial matters. Despite this importance, though, the French government continued to view Revolutionary vivandières with suspicion and mistrust. While acknowledging their importance to the army, the governments of the First Republic saw women with the army as agents of disorder, and

sought to limit their numbers and control their activities through legislation. For the most part, these attempts failed. The services that vivandières
provided were in such high demand, and the pressures of the continuous wars were so great, that it proved impossible to effectively control the
army's vivandières. These women, who continued to come mainly from
poor rural families, defied the government's directives with the help of sympathetic soldiers and officers. The life of a vivandière was a hard one, much
harsher and more dangerous than in the old Royal Army. And while the
French Revolution opened hitherto unparalleled opportunities for vivandières, it also ended the monarchy's practice of officially rewarding them
for their own service. Instead, under the new pension laws, they could
claim widows' pensions based only on their deceased husbands' service; the
irregular nature of many military marriages therefore meant that large
numbers of retired or widowed vivandières finished their lives in the very
misery they had sought to escape by following the army. While their service would be more independent of their husbands, their security in old
age would be directly dependent on their husbands' service, not their own.

The French army underwent major changes in the years 1789–1793. The
emigration of noble officers in the early years of the Revolution meant
that promotion from the enlisted ranks was rapid and common. Out of
9,500 officers serving in 1789, more than six thousand left the country in
1791–1792.[1] The effects on the army are hard to overstate: with mass aristocratic desertions, thousands of new officers had to be promoted from the
ranks.[2] Therefore, the French army after 1792 was unique compared to its
European counterparts of the time due to its much less class-ridden structure and much more egalitarian spirit. In addition, as many enlisted men
deserted during the upheavals of 1789–1792, new volunteer citizen-soldiers
replaced many of the unwilling veterans of the Old Regime. The army
absorbed the new volunteers in successive waves in 1791, 1792, 1793, and
1794, finally amalgamating one regular army and two volunteer battalions
into "demi-brigades" and eliminating the old royal title of "regiment" in
1794 in order to foster a more republican spirit. The new government also
saw (male) soldiers as brave defenders of the nation, not as criminal mis-
fits. Initially at least, the government and many soldiers saw bearing arms
in defense of the nation as a privilege, not an onerous imposition. A soldier convicted of crimes was far less likely to be beaten or shot than to be
"stripped of rank and expelled from the unit as unfit to bear arms for their
Patrie."[3] Due to the voracious demand for manpower during wartime, this
idealistic attitude did not survive beyond 1793, but it exercised a powerful
influence during the army of the Republic's formative period. The nature

of discipline changed, and with it much of the character of daily military life as it had been under the Bourbons. Soldiers were no longer kept prisoner in camps and barracks, and arbitrary imposition of harsh punishments for minor offenses ended. From 1790 to 1793, the volunteer battalions even elected their own officers, and these officers were understandably reluctant to enforce harsh discipline. After 1793, discipline became stricter, but the French army continued to be far less rigid and formal in its discipline than other European armies throughout the Revolutionary and Napoleonic wars, maintaining a relatively egalitarian spirit until 1814.[4]

Along with these changes, the French army grew in size, and from 1792 onward it was engaged in constant warfare on several fronts. Especially after the National Convention voted the *levée en masse* in 1793, the government placed the whole nation and all its citizens at the disposal of the war effort. This resulted in hitherto unheard-of numbers of soldiers under arms: the army grew from 130,000 to more than 500,000 soldiers in just eighteen months.[5] The Revolutionary government was hard-pressed to equip and supply such large forces, and consequently the French army began a policy of living off the land, or foraging. This allowed the government to concentrate on providing weapons and ammunition, while the armies found their own food and fodder. As long as the armies were on French soil, foraging was generally forbidden, though not in rebel areas such as the Vendée in western France. Once in foreign countries, however, the French soldiers were given wide latitude to find what they needed, and the depredations of French armies ruined many towns and villages.

Given this state of affairs, vivandières became more important than ever. Foraging broke down unit cohesion and discipline, and slowed the movement of units. It also had limits. Soldiers could only carry so much, and since French armies after 1789 lacked extensive baggage trains, it proved difficult to accumulate supplies when on the move. Vivandières, on the other hand, could forage on their own without seriously affecting a unit's combat strength. Since most had a wagon or at least a pack animal, they could store and transport more requisitioned goods than soldiers could, reselling them to the troops at a later time for a profit and ensuring a fairly steady supply of food. Since the soldiers paid for this food with their own money, this form of supply effectively cost the government nothing.

The government of the National Convention recognized the importance of vivandières, calling them "absolutely necessary" to the maintenance of the army.[6] At the same time, it feared the presence of women in the camps as conducive to bad morals among the soldiers. The leaders of the Revolution claimed to be more interested in moral and ideological purity than in utility, so under the Republic a vivandière had to be the legitimate wife of a soldier in the unit, and Councils of Administration routinely required applicants to provide a marriage certificate. She must also "behave as a true Republican," show "honor and probity," and "never cease to demonstrate she is of good morals, and lives an irreproachable life."[7] It is open to question to what degree these requirements were actually enforced in the field, but examples of their strict enforcement do exist. After 1794, however, the zeal with which the armies enforced these standards declined markedly as the army became increasingly separate from French civil society. Informal marriages and "immoral" behavior became more common and accepted, though by no means universal, among soldiers and vivandières alike.

The French Revolution also brought a reaction against privilege and arbitrary authority in the army. In 1793, during its most radical phase, the government of the National Convention instituted a new, more democratic and more direct method of selecting vivandières. This method probably began with the first volunteer battalions in 1790, as it was the equivalent of the method by which soldiers elected their own officers. Since Republican soldiers were meant to be soldiers and not businessmen and petty tyrants, vivandier positions were eliminated. A woman no longer became a vivandière by marrying a vivandier. Instead, she applied for a position directly to the battalion or regiment's Council of Administration, which was authorized by the Ministry of War to make all decisions regarding admissions and dismissals. This marked an important turning point in the history of vivandières. From 1793 they were legally no longer simply the female helpers of the vivandiers, but officially recognized in their own persons. They held their posts on their own, not through their husbands, and this fruit of the Revolution lasted throughout the next century, even while France denied civilian women property rights and equality with men. One officer even recalled that a vivandier of his regiment married a vivandière in 1793, "so as not to sink below his station" by losing his former position.[8] The power and independence that vivandières held, while limited in scope, was very real.

Successful applicants received a *patente,* or certificate of permission to follow the army. These were often merely crude, handwritten papers drawn up in the field and bearing the signatures of the Council's members below a short paragraph stating that the named woman had permission to follow that unit as a blanchisseuse, vivandière, or cantinière. More elaborate versions bore the woman's physical description as well as her place of birth, age, and husband's name and rank. After 1793, some army commanders even had special forms printed up, which had spaces for all relevant information.

The fact that commanders would go to this trouble is again indicative of both the sheer numbers of women involved and their importance to the army.

The French army also continued to employ blanchisseuses. Holdovers from the Royal Army, blanchisseuses continued to wash and mend uniforms during the years 1789–1799, though there was increasing crossover between the trades, partly because government regulations changed, partly because the army's rigidly defined hierarchical structure broke down. Many nominal blanchisseuses exercised the functions of vivandières, and many vivandières took in washing as well. As early as 1793, the trend was toward a single position that incorporated all of the "female" military support functions. This is illustrated by changes in designation on the women's official papers. Many women's *patentes* gave their positions as "vivandière or blanchisseuse," "blanchisseuse-vivandière," or similar variations.[9]

Throughout the Revolutionary period, most vivandières came from the same background as those of the Old Regime. In fact, many of the Revolutionary vivandières were veterans of the Royal Army or their daughters, but major changes in military recruiting practices also changed the makeup of the new generation of vivandières. The cohort of new vivandières during 1792–1799 came mostly from peasant families, though the new prestige of volunteer military service attracted a few daughters of the lower bourgeoisie. These remained the exception, however, and the biggest changes to the vivandière cadre were the increased number of urban women, especially from Paris, and increased geographical diversity, though the frontier departments continued to supply an inordinately large proportion of vivandières. Leaving aside those older women who joined volunteer battalions along with their husbands, surviving records suggest that the average age at first marriage was also younger than during the Old Regime, with most new vivandières for whom we have records starting their careers between ages seventeen and twenty-two.

Exactly why women became vivandières remains difficult to pin down, as they rarely wrote down their thoughts. In most cases, we can only infer motivation from what we know of the women's circumstances and actions. Pension applications offer additional clues, but they must be carefully parsed for exaggerations or outright falsehoods. Certainly some women became vivandières in order to remain near a husband or lover, but economic considerations also played a large role, as did familiarity in the case of daughters of the regiment, and perhaps also a thirst for adventure in many women who would otherwise never have traveled more than twenty miles from their homes. And of course the patriotism that swept France in the years 1792–1793 certainly drew women as well as men to the colors. Many women, in fact, openly enlisted as soldiers and fought in the ranks until the National Convention outlawed the practice in 1793.[10]

Whatever their motives, the vast majority of Revolutionary vivandières continued to come from poor rural families. Daughters of agricultural day laborers, farmers, and small-town artisans were the rule. As in earlier times, many married after meeting a soldier whose unit was garrisoned in the area. While a large number of vivandières joined volunteer battalions along with their spouses, making their own contributions to the citizen army, even during the height of the volunteer era women in frontier areas were still more likely to become vivandières by a ratio of approximately 2:1. This was partly because frontier departments fielded more volunteer battalions than interior provinces, but also because many of the volunteer units from the interior did not start with vivandières. Instead, they picked them up in the war zone as they became familiar with the French military system. Regular army units also continued to form a large proportion of the army as well, and these recruited vivandières almost exclusively from their places of garrison or while on campaign, usually along or outside the frontiers during 1792–1799.

Marie Elizabeth Peter is a good example of a vivandière recruited from the frontier peasantry. Born in Hagenau in the department of Haut-Rhin on September 21, 1768, she met Étienne Bory when his cavalry regiment passed through her village in 1793. Bory was a forty-three-year-old sergeant of carabiniers, a career soldier since 1768. Marie was twenty-four, the illiterate orphaned daughter of Alsatian peasants. Neither had strong ties to French civilian society, and when they married in June of 1793 only soldiers of Étienne's regiment were present as witnesses. Marie served as "vivandière or blanchisseuse" of the First Regiment of Carabiniers until Étienne's death in 1794.[11] Anne Petry was born the same year as Marie Peter in nearby Villageneuf. She married Joseph Donnet, an infantryman of the Sixty-eighth Demi-brigade, in 1793 and became a blanchisseuse, serving for four years and bearing a child who became an enfant de troupe.[12]

Many other women joined the army as members of local volunteer battalions. Marianne Ressouce was born in Mende in the department of Lozère in south central France. She joined a volunteer battalion with her husband, who died soon after being amalgamated into the Forty-eighth Demi-brigade. In 1793, she remarried Corporal Antoine Boyer in the department of Nord. Boyer was a career soldier, serving since 1777. Three lieutenants of the unit witnessed the civil marriage, and Marianne continued to exercise the function of blanchisseuse until 1795, when she left after

losing her second husband and her children to disease in Holland.[13] Félicité Hequette and Jean Dionkre were another volunteer couple. Both were
agricultural day laborers from the village of Dix in the department of
Nord. They married in 1791 and joined the Twenty-seventh Battalion of
National Volunteers in 1793. When Jean was killed at Le Cateau only two
months later, Félicité lost her taste for military life and returned home.[14]

Other traditional sources continued to supply vivandières during the
Revolution, but the patterns of recruitment were already changing by 1791.
Foreign volunteers and their wives were no longer an important category
of recruits. With a wave of patriotism bringing in volunteers, and with the
introduction of nationwide conscription of a citizen army, the First Republic could obtain all the recruits it needed. However, as the French armies'
victories took them abroad in the late 1790s, French soldiers began to
marry Dutch, German, Swiss, and Italian women, who then followed the
army, either officially as vivandières or unofficially as illegal camp followers. For example, Sergeant Jean Billers of the Twenty-third Demi-brigade
married Kristina Conrad in Obermöschel, Switzerland, in January 1798. She
served as a vivandière in the French army until 1812.[15] Marrying a French
soldier sometimes caused serious problems for a non-French woman, and
often led to her being cut off from her family and her home. Ann André
of the town of Lens in the Austrian Netherlands found that her family
would not speak to her after she married a French soldier and served as a
vivandière in the Seventh Demi-brigade. When her husband was killed,
she returned to Lens but found herself ostracized, and had to turn to the
local French prefect for assistance.[16]

Among French women, the dispossessed, the rootless, and the orphaned
continued to supply a large proportion of vivandières. Marie Pierrette was
"born of unknown parents" and abandoned in Avignon in 1757, part of
the growing tide of infant abandonment in eighteenth-century France.[17]
Growing up poor, she married Seraphin Rozier, a laborer and native of
Avignon. The two joined a battalion of volunteers, where Marie served
first as blanchisseuse and later as vivandière.[18] Sophie Barrau was the illegitimate daughter of Françoise Barrau and a local notable in Valler (Loire
Inférieure). Neither her mother, her grandmother, nor her godparents could
sign her birth certificate, and her father, though known, was not named.
Born the twelfth of January, 1775, Sophie received enough financial support from her father to survive until she married at age eighteen. Her husband, Claude Bachelet, was a grenadier in the Eighty-fifth Demi-brigade
and four years her senior. She served as blanchisseuse until Claude's death
in Italy in 1795.[19]

Women living away from home also became vivandières in large numbers. Without close family ties and usually able to obtain only menial work
for low wages, these women often saw military service as an attractive alter-
native to spinsterhood and poverty. Marie Gourau was born in 1771 in St.
Martin du Linet in the department of Mayenne. In 1789, she moved to the
city of Craon, where she lived with relatives while working as a domestic
servant. There she met Sergeant Louis Sicard of the Sixty-seventh Infantry
Regiment. On 27 Thermidor, Year II (1794), Marie and Louis were married in a civil ceremony with five soldiers of his unit as witnesses. None
of Marie's family attended the wedding, suggesting that they were either
unhappy with her choice of husband or ignorant of the proceedings.[20]
Nonetheless, Marie served the next nine months as vivandière, staying on
to give birth to a daughter just six days after Louis was killed by Vendéean
rebels near Fougères.[21] Likewise, Marguerite Léger was born in 1770 in
Maubeuge, the daughter of a washerwoman and a plasterer. She moved to
Gercy to work as a dressmaker, and in 1797 she met and married Pierre
Boldevin, a soldier on leave in his home town. Marguerite served as a cav-
alry vivandière until her death in battle in 1807.[22]

While Marie Gourau and Marguerite Léger both lived and worked in
the regions of their birth, many poor provincial women migrated to Paris
to find work. Marie Bathis traveled to Paris from Dieuze in Lorraine. She
married Jean Simon on September 21, 1792, the same day he enlisted as a
corporal in the First Republican Battalion of Paris. She followed the battalion to war unofficially, and in February 1793 she officially became a
vivandière. Jean was killed in May, but Marie remarried a career soldier and
served until 1796, when she lost her second husband.[23] Similarly, Françoise
Bailleul moved to Paris from a small hamlet in the Department of Nord
when she was nineteen. In 1793, she married Corporal Joseph Moulin of
the Thirty-eighth Demi-brigade. Françoise served first as blanchisseuse and
then as vivandière, even after Joseph's death in Italy in 1800.[24]

One unusual pattern among new vivandières during the early 1790s
was the increase in older women. The tremendous increase in the size of
the army and the great number of older volunteers meant many women
started careers as vivandières in their thirties, forties, or even fifties. These
were wives of older volunteers or conscripts, and often married couples
enlisted together rather than be separated. Péronne Branche and her husband were both forty-six when they volunteered in June 1793. Marie Bathis
was thirty-nine when she began her career in a volunteer battalion the same
year, and Ann Horr was over fifty when she began serving. The upsurge in
volunteerism and the truly national character of the French army, at least

during 1792–1794, meant that many middle-aged women had an opportunity to start careers as vivandières, an opportunity that was rare or non-
existent in earlier and later professional armies. Another new development
in the volunteer battalions was the spectacle of entire families joining
together. Such was the case of the Devrez family of Douai, who served
from 1792 to 1802, "the father as fusilier, the mother as vivandière, Dominique, the son, as drummer, and two little girls as blanchisseuses."[25]

The military family of the Revolutionary armies was very similar to
that of the old Royal Army, but while vivandières continued to bear children, on the whole they bore fewer children than their predecessors. Most
women who were vivandières during the years 1789–1799 bore at least one
child, and many bore two or more. Surviving pension applications under
the First Republic suggest that more than 90 percent of vivandières applying for widows' pensions claimed at least one living child, and 38 percent
claimed two or more children. Of course, given the limited nature of surviving documentation, we cannot draw firm conclusions from this data. In
addition, these statistics provide only a snapshot of childbearing patterns,
since they do not include children who died before the mother's retirement
or women who died before claiming a pension. However, they do show
a decline in the average number of children from the Royal Army to the
army of the Republic, with republican vivandières having an average of 1.7
living children upon retirement as opposed to an average of 2 in the Royal
Army. One plausible explanation is that the higher incidence of battle and
the harsher camp conditions after 1792 produced both a lower fertility rate
and a higher infant mortality rate. In any case, most vivandières continued
to bear and raise children, and these children often stayed with the army
for their entire lives.

Children's existence in the army retained many familiar features from
the Old Regime, but was also radically different. Boys tended to enroll as
enfants de troupe and become musicians and ultimately private soldiers.
Girls helped their mothers with the business and often married soldiers,
many young women going on to become vivandières themselves. The insu-
lar nature of the regimental family continued, with units caring for children of vivandières collectively in case of the parents' deaths. In some ways
this impulse to care for one's own was even stronger than before, since the
number of battle deaths was much higher than under the Old Regime due
to the greater intensity of warfare under the Revolutionary system. The
massive influx of volunteers in the years 1791–1793 diluted this sense of a
separate military society, but by 1796 the army of the Republic had once
again become a largely professional army with its own identity separate

from civil society. It was standard practice for regiments to adopt male orphans, though young girls were usually sent to relatives or to orphanages. For example, Jeanne Delforge was able to place her son as a drummer after her husband's death, but could find no place for her seven-year-old daughter.[26]

A child's life in the Revolutionary armies was harsher and less secure than it had been in the Royal Army. Units moved quickly, fought often, and carried little in the way of shelter or baggage. Prior to 1789, the long days and weeks of encampments in barracks and in guarded tent cities had at least provided children of Royal Army vivandières with a relatively stable environment. Under the Republic, they learned to move with the unit, to stay out of the way, and to be useful. Those who survived into puberty faced service in the ranks if male, and constant sexual challenges if female, brought on by a perception among some soldiers that single women in the regiment were sexually available.[27]

Life with the Revolutionary armies was certainly not idyllic. Loss of fathers was routine, while mothers also often died or were wounded. Even if they avoided battles, the children themselves suffered from the same disease and exposure that killed far more soldiers than did combat throughout the eighteenth and nineteenth centuries. Living in the crowded, unsanitary conditions of army camps and exposed to the elements, children often did not reach adulthood. A typical example, Marianne Boyer of the Forty-eighth Demi-brigade lost her husband Antoine and all her children to epidemics in Holland in the Year III (1795).[28] The son of Marie Laroche of the Seventy-first Demi-brigade found himself even further afield when his father died of fever in St. Domingue (Haiti). Already an enfant de troupe drawing military pay and rations at age three, young Louis faced an uncertain future. He and his mother survived a harrowing sea voyage back to Europe, landing at Cadiz to escape the English blockade. From there they traveled overland more than a thousand miles to Marie's native town of Abbéville, an exceedingly arduous journey in the eighteenth century.[29] In some cases, children found themselves abandoned to the care of the unit. When Anne Donnet of the Sixty-eighth Demi-brigade lost her husband in Germany in Year IV, she stayed with the Second Battalion as a blanchisseuse in order to support her four-year-old son. After less than two years, though, she placed him as an enfant de troupe in care of the battalion and returned to her village, leaving him to be raised as a soldier.[30] The pay and rations of an enfant de troupe were a valuable addition to the family income, and many women found themselves unable to support their children once they returned as widows to civilian life. In such cases, poor widowed vivandières often chose to leave their young sons in the army. Other children were more fortunate: their mothers found new husbands. Young Thérèse Réné never knew her biological father, killed four months before her birth. But less than two months before the birth her mother remarried a sergeant in the Ninety-first Demi-brigade, who raised Thérèse as his own daughter. In this case, at least, advanced pregnancy was not an obstacle to remarriage.[31]

Constant warfare and rapid movements made the child's world in the Revolutionary armies chaotic, uncomfortable, and dangerous. The new emphasis on seeking out decisive battles and the relative abundance and cheapness of conscript manpower meant that fathers died more often in combat than in earlier times. On the other hand, the French government offered orphans' and widows' pensions for the first time, and these at least ameliorated life after army service. Ultimately, the child of a vivandière and a soldier faced a life of danger and uncertainty, and faced an early introduction to violent death, but the hardships and dangers involved did little to deter women from becoming vivandières, or from actively continuing their careers during and after pregnancy. As a means of earning a living and supporting a family, vivandière positions remained highly sought after.

In order to provide for her family or even to keep herself alive, the vivandière had to operate her business successfully. This business was essentially the same as it had been in the Royal Army—to provide food, drink, and a gathering place to the unit's soldiers as a means of limiting the incentives to desertion.[32] However, changes in French military practice also changed the vivandière's basic function. Under the Republic, French armies often campaigned without tents and the large baggage trains necessary to carry them. This meant that armies could move faster, but it also forced the soldiers to "bivouac," or sleep in the open regardless of the weather, often with only overcoats for cover. The general lack of tents in the Revolutionary armies made the vivandière's tent far more important than before as a comfortable gathering place and as a shelter. Even officers frequented the vivandières' tents, something that was unusual before the Revolution, since Old Regime officers had their own spacious accommodations. This change was partly due to the more humble birth of most Revolutionary officers, and partly due to the allure of a warm meal and a drink served under a roof. To soldiers who marched, ate, and slept in the open exposed to the weather, the value of spending time under shelter cannot be overestimated.

In addition to the loss of the tents, the relaxation of march and camp discipline had far-reaching effects on the army. Though looting was still technically illegal and punishable by death, the Revolutionary governments could not afford to supply their large armies, and from 1796–1799 the Directory, in particular, used foreign wars as a relatively cheap means of feeding and supplying large numbers of French soldiers who would otherwise be hungry and idle at home. In this atmosphere, vivandières became expert foragers and fences in order to keep their businesses supplied. While this was also a common practice in the Royal Army, it became far more widespread and officially tolerated during the Revolution. A whole vocabulary arose from the practice. Vivandières engaged in *chapardage* ("pinching," or more figuratively, "scrounging"), and rather than "steal," they "found" items. They also became experts at the art of extricating themselves from trouble (*se débrouiller*), whether it came in the form of outraged locals or overzealous military officials.[33] In some cases, enterprising vivandières turned their talents for extralegal profit-making against the War Ministry itself. For example, Anne Jumier of the Thirteenth Dragoon Regiment lost two husbands in battle between 1797 and 1800. She successfully drew widow's pensions for both of them at the same time, even while remarrying and continuing to serve with her regiment.[34] This was entirely in keeping with the prevailing attitude that those at the bottom could engage in small frauds, since those at the top were engaging in enormous ones. As one soldier put it, he was merely "taking my example from Messieurs the Commissaries of War."[35]

"Scrounging" provided not only goods to sell but the means to carry them as well. Many Old Regime vivandières started out following the regiment on foot, moving up to a pack animal and later a wagon or cart when finances allowed it. Prior to 1789, the highly disciplined nature of marching and camping in the Royal Army meant that marauding in search of goods and vehicles to plunder was difficult and sometimes impossible, and the War Ministry under the monarchy enacted a whole range of regulations designed specifically to prevent soldiers' wives from plundering while on the march. During the Revolution, however, the need to feed the armies cheaply and without long supply lines led the French armies to adopt a very relaxed attitude toward "foraging." In this environment, horses, donkeys, carts, and wagons were readily available at no cost, either by capture from the enemy or through "requisition" from civilians.

The diary of quartermaster Charles François provides a good example. In the middle of Prairial, Year III (June 1796), the Army of the North suffered from serious food shortages. At the same time, the amalgamation of two demi-brigades brought into François' company "an old German sergeant coming out of the *Régiment de Suède*" and his pretty eighteen-year-old wife. François used government funds he had embezzled to purchase

her a brandy barrel, an apron, and a set of glasses. Obtaining for her a
patente de vivandière, François then set out to equip "his" vivandière in
style. He "procured" a light wagon for her and used his authority as quartermaster to "requisition" two horses from a rich Dutch farmer, so his
vivandière "could now buy in bulk."[36] François made a nighttime foray
toward the enemy lines, killed an Austrian sentry, and brought back a fine
cavalry horse for his new girlfriend as well. In exchange for his rather lavish gifts, we can assume that she shared her profits with him, and François
was quite clear that she shared her favors as well. François' memoirs have
to be treated with some caution. He comes across as a braggart, and some
of his tales (including this one) may well have been embellished, especially
in the area of sexual exploits. Nevertheless, pillage and theft of government
property were widespread, and the story is plausible enough in its broader
outlines.

None of this emphasis on theft and scavenging was unique to the Revolutionary period. What was new was the massive scale of brigandage and
its general acceptance as a military necessity and even as a patriotic duty.
Peasants and townspeople who resisted vivandières' foraging efforts often
met with harsh punishment from the soldiers of the women's units.[37] Most
soldiers considered obstructing a vivandière in her foraging as a crime, and
indeed many vivandières carried with them an official army warrant authorizing them to buy at reasonable prices "any and all merchandise of which
they have need."[38] Using this legal sanction (and armed and escorted as
well), they effectively forced local populations to provide them with cheap
food and drink, then resold it at a profit to the soldiers.

Others received their "license to steal" in a more genteel fashion. While
most vivandières were attached to field units, technically every military
post was eligible to have a canteen (*cantine*) and hence a "cantinière." The
earliest known official use of the term "cantinière" was in the Year II (1794)
in the Army of the Western Pyrenees. The assistant director of the Grand
parc d'artillerie (central artillery depot) asked the Council of Administration "to have a cantinière at the Grand parc, so that she could procure the
subsistence necessary for the artillery employees who arrive daily and at
all hours of the night."[39] Due to the great numbers of employees, and "the
difficulty there is in procuring food, given its high price," the Council
approved his request and petitioned the commander of the army, General
Muller. Muller not only provided permission, but he provided a cantinière
as well, Madame Leroux. She had a well-placed relative in charge of "general expenses" as well as "miscellaneous services" in the Ministry of War's
supply division, which probably allowed her to sell government supplies

furnished illegally by her relative with the connivance of the general or of his staff, a common arrangement.[40] This sort of high-level involvement reflected a continuing interest in profiteering throughout the period of this study.[41] Officials with good connections were eager to control sedentary cantinière posts whenever they were both lucrative and safe, while they left the dangerous itinerant posts to poor soldiers' wives.

Although routine business dominated the vivandière's daily life, battles were important events that could bring great profit or loss. While a vivandière could conceivably earn a small fortune in one day of combat, she could also lose all her goods or even her life. In the old Royal Army, vivandières doubtless braved enemy fire from time to time, but there are no surviving documented examples. Partly because of strict discipline in the ranks, partly because she had no patriotic feelings or perceived stake in the nation, the Old Regime vivandière stayed back with the baggage trains during battles. Even had she gone forward, the non-commissioned officers charged with maintaining order would never have allowed men to break ranks to eat and drink. Prevailing military doctrine made even the slightest breach of discipline unthinkable, and so the soldiers fought and died unaided. Under the Republic, both factors changed, making battlefield heroics an optional but common and highly respected aspect of the vivandière's work.

Republican tactics and the philosophy underlying them made the vivandière's battlefield role possible. Rather than moving across the battlefield in straight, carefully laid out lines with sergeants behind them enforcing strict discipline, French Revolutionary armies attacked in what contemporary observers described as "hordes" or "swarms." Though some modern historians contest these labels, the French armies did move in looser, less structured formations, and a soldier who took a moment to quaff a glass of wine or a shot of brandy proffered by a vivandière was not considered a criminal or a shirker.[42] Therefore, on the demand side there was a sudden opening for vivandières' business on the battlefield itself. Moreover, soldiers would pay far more for a drink in the midst of a battle than under other circumstances, and the lure of quick money tempted many vivandières to risk their own safety for increased profit. The peculiar psychology of the battlefield played an important role here. A soldier facing imminent death cared little if a drink cost one franc or five, since money would mean little if he were killed. In addition, conditions for soldiers were difficult. Marching and fighting under a hot sun was thirsty work. The dust and powder smoke that covered eighteenth-century battlefields like a dense fog burned their throats, as did the gunpowder left in their mouths from biting paper musket cartridges. In such situations, soldiers would often be desperate for a drink once their own limited supply ran out. Finally, since an infantry-man's job often consisted of holding ground by standing for hours under artillery fire as those around him were killed or maimed, alcohol helped steady his courage under the terrible ordeal.[43] These factors made battle days potentially very lucrative for the vivandière willing to take risks. For example, during the siege of Bergen-op-Zoom in 1794, some soldiers of the Fourth Battalion of National Guards built a fine hut for winter quarters. Their vivandière offered to buy it out of her proceeds from supplying the troops under fire. She offered two hundred francs, a huge sum in those circumstances, and one payable only by someone who possessed literally more money than she knew what to do with.[44] On the other hand, some commanders took steps to limit the prices vivandières charged. General Debrun of the Army of the Ardennes issued orders on 4 Vendémiaire, Year III, that vivandières and other sutlers could sell goods at no more than a 33 percent markup. Debrun wrote that he was "justifiably indignant at such guilty proceedings on the part of individuals who, forgetting that they are only with the soldiers of liberty to aid them, instead make of them the victims of their shameful and criminal greed."[45] There was a general understanding among many officers that vivandières existed not to make a profit but to keep the troops supplied. In that context, price-gouging was not only unjust, but treasonous as well. Neither the War Ministry nor the Convention legislated an army-wide price limitation, but local regulations like Debrun's provided some brake on prices. However, it proved impossible to adequately regulate vivandières' prices. Rather, the most effective control proved to be their own sense of fairness and the rapport they established with their units. Vivandières who consistently overcharged were not popular, and could be expelled or simply left in the lurch by their units.

In addition, the revolutions in politics and in civic culture may have begun to change the vivandières' motivation. While many Revolutionary vivandières were long-term professional holdovers from the Royal Army, many others were volunteers with considerable élan. To these women, holding back during a battle may have seemed unpatriotic, and the possibilities for financial gain can only have supplemented their own desire to contribute to victory. Even some of the old-timers must have seen and reacted to the change in the spirit that motivated French soldiers in the years 1792–1794, though it is impossible to judge how many or to what extent. What is certain is that vivandières increasingly entered into battle with their units, bringing up food and drink, carrying ammunition, aiding the wounded, and even firing weapons themselves. This more intensive battlefield engagement fixed the vivandière positively in the sentiments of the army and of the nation, but it also led to increased casualties and new questions about the state's formal relationship with female auxiliaries.

Volunteer vivandière Angélique Brévilier of the Seventh Hussars provides one example of the results. Assisting her unit in combat near Celestat on 7 Ventôse, Year II, she was struck by an Austrian howitzer shell. The explosion removed her left leg at the thigh and filled her right leg with shrapnel, which, according to a military doctor, still remained four months later, causing her "horrible suffering."[46] Vivandières entering combat also risked capture. Volunteer vivandière Suzanne L'Abbé of the First Battalion of the Mayenne was captured along with her husband in the winter of 1792. Although they continued to hold her husband, the Austrians quickly repatriated Suzanne as a civilian, a sign that they did not yet fully understand the nature of Revolutionary warfare or the military importance of vivandières.[47] This generous attitude toward captured vivandières did not last, though. French women soon found themselves treated no differently than male prisoners, once the extent of their military contributions became clear, and this treatment continued into the Napoleonic era. For example, when the Spanish transferred French prisoners to the island of Cabrera in 1809, all female camp followers were released, except for the cantinières, who went into permanent captivity with their units.[48] Not only volunteers went into combat. Elizabeth Chauvet of the Eighth Demi-brigade was a long-term vivandière who served the kings of France before serving the Republic. She was wounded while participating in close combat in Italy in late Vendémiaire, Year V. Fighting at her husband's side, she received a musket ball in the right arm, rendering it permanently unusable, while her husband was mortally wounded.[49]

However dramatic these actions were, the French army and government did not recognize these women as heroines. In fact, the War Ministry even rejected Angélique Brévilier's requests for a pension on the grounds that she was not a soldier and could not therefore request an invalid's pension, and her husband was not dead, so she could not request a widow's pension. The Ministry's formal response stated that "the law of 28 Fructidor is not applicable to Citoyenne Pélletier [her maiden name]," and a marginal note by a functionary reminded his subordinates that the sole benefit accorded her was a socket for a wooden leg available from the Hôtel des Invalides. The leg itself and any other associated expenses were left to Angélique and her husband, and the functionary specifically warned her against returning to his office to press her case.[50]

If Angélique Brévilier did not merit special consideration for her actions, then who did? Two women who received unusual attention provide an idea of the kind of female military heroine the Republic wanted. She would be brave and resourceful, but would limit herself to the "sister of mercy" role. Rather than taking lives, she would save them, and thereby stay within the bounds of accepted Republican womanhood. While soldiers in battle valued tough female fighters, and indeed several *femmes soldats* received public acclaim, vivandières as heroines for public consumption had to meet a different set of standards.

In May 1795, Jeanne Marie Girard of the Forty-fifth Demi-brigade was a passenger aboard the warship *Cazira* during a battle with a British squadron off Corsica. Jeanne's husband was soon killed, but Jeanne spent the eight hours of battle aiding the wounded under fire, bringing them drinks, washing and dressing wounds, and comforting the dying. After the battle, the captain of the *Cazira* wrote a letter to the minister of war praising her actions and asking that she receive special consideration for her pension request. Likewise, the Representative of the People in Toulon arranged for public fêtes for Jeanne, as well as luxury travel accommodations for her journey home. There was no talk of her continuing the struggle or avenging her husband. Instead, she received public acclaim in Toulon and a generous widow's pension before returning to the obscurity of her native Lyon.[51]

A later and much more celebrated case involved Marie Dauranne, vivandière of the Fifty-first Demi-brigade. On March 12, 1797, her unit was crossing the Piave River near Ospedaletto, Italy. Two soldiers fell into the water and none of the men on the scene could or would save them: few Frenchmen of the time knew how to swim. Dauranne leapt into the river and rescued both men. One witness wrote in his diary, "the courage that this woman showed for these brave grenadiers on this day merited her a gold medal . . . with these words engraved 'first quantinière [*sic*] of the army.'"[52] Dauranne was decorated by General Bonaparte, acclaimed by the Directory, and featured in government bulletins. Like Jeanne Girard, the traits she showed that won her acclaim were courage and the irrepressible will to save lives. The nurturing, mothering side of the vivandières' nature was the side the Republic glorified, in keeping with Republican ideas about women and their place in society. One of the key concepts of Republican ideology was that only men were true citizens, and that military service to the state validated a man's citizenship. If women were acknowledged as giving military service to the state, would that require the state to grant them full privileges of citizenship? Beyond that, most French men saw the place of women as in the home, caring for children and nurturing future (male) citizens. The idea of women as killers who fought like men (and perhaps instead of men) was frightening to them. Therefore, vivandières who saved lives through nurturing were turned into heroines, while vivandières who took lives were kept shrouded in obscurity.

Had Dauranne saved the two men by single-handedly killing several of the enemy, it is unlikely that she would have gained national fame. As it was, her act of lifesaving gained her a short-lived celebrity. Afterward, she passed quickly from the limelight, and her fate is unknown. Most likely she died on campaign, as there is no record of her after she received the medal in July. However, her memory long exercised a certain fascination in France, and newspaper articles appeared occasionally into the twentieth century reminding later readers of her achievement: a heroic but safe model for Republican women to emulate.[53]

It is true that a few women who enlisted as soldiers became popular heroes and received government recognition. However, these were rare exceptions, and by the late 1790s this type of behavior was both illegal and almost non-existent. The number of women who served as actual soldiers was tiny, and they had effectively disappeared by the time Napoleon seized power. In specific times and places, for its own reasons, the government could recognize their military service, in part because female soldiers were so rare. Vivandières, on the other hand, numbered around five thousand at any given time: to honor and promote their combat exploits would have implications far beyond occasionally recognizing a *femme soldat* who was, after all, statistically insignificant. Therefore, while *femmes soldats* were occasionally rewarded for combat exploits, vivandières, as the housewives of the army, were publicly rewarded during this period only for actions that safely fit the government's view of ideal feminine behavior.

Despite the risks and lack of official recognition, women continued to exercise the profession of vivandière in large numbers, and many of them paid with their lives, though few of their deaths were officially recorded. Official army policy called for deaths of "civilian employees" to be reported only to their battalion or regiment. Most combat units did not keep accurate records, and those that did often lost them while on campaign. The death notices for employees only went to the Ministry of War if the reporting hospital could not find the unit in question. This meant that the Ministry only received records on a vivandière's death if she died in a military hospital after her unit had moved on and become embroiled in battle or destroyed. One such instance brought us the death certificate of a woman known only as "Citoyenne Gauthier of the Fourth Battalion of Federals."

Unknown to anyone except the other volunteers of her battalion, Gauthier took fever and stayed behind at a military hospital in Nord Libre in the Year III, dying nine days later surrounded by strangers who were ignorant even of her Christian name.[54]

Even though relatively few vivandières received the praise of the Republic or its armies, the Republic did recognize their usefulness. Women in general, however, came under intense scrutiny as potential threats to military discipline and efficiency. This scrutiny reached its climax under the National Convention in the spring of 1793. The Convention sent out Representatives on Mission to report on military matters and to act as political officers for the armies. Technically they were co-equal with military commanders, but their political clout often made them the true authorities. These Representatives wrote fiery letters to Paris and even invoked the Law of Suspects in their effort to rid the army of unauthorized women. Meanwhile, the potentially lucrative nature of vivandière positions and the extreme hardships suffered by civilian women living alone continued to drive the numbers of women with the army beyond official limits. Many units had two or three times the allotted number of women, and regulations reminding units of the limits came out with monotonous regularity. Yet there was never any serious talk of banning vivandières outright. Most efforts were confined to keeping vivandières' numbers under control and to expelling unauthorized camp followers. While the Ministry of War saw women in general as a threat to the efficiency of the armies, it saw vivandières in proper numbers as an asset, albeit one in need of constant monitoring.

The presence of women with the army was not a serious issue for the Republic's authorities until the National Convention voted on March 8, 1793, to allow soldiers to marry without the permission of their officers. This law reflected the general change in ideology already discussed, in which the Republican soldier was regarded as a free man. As a "defender of the patrie," he should enjoy at least equal rights with those who were not under the colors, and the idea of forbidding a free man to marry simply because he was serving the nation seemed arbitrary and unfair. However, the number of legitimate wives following the army swelled to unprecedented numbers as thousands of soldiers exercised their new freedom, and as women fled poverty and economic dislocation to be with their husbands at the front. In addition, girlfriends and prostitutes also flocked to the armies under cover of the new permissiveness. As one Representative on Mission wrote from the Army of the North, "this law brings with it a problem which is in urgent need of reform. We must fix the number of women who may follow the army; they are there in such great numbers that they slow the march of troops, consume much, and occupy a great number of wagons destined exclusively for the transport of baggage and supplies."[55] A month later, Representative Jean Defrenne wrote to the minister of war, also from the Army of the North, "The great number of women who follow the army is frightening; they are so many mouths infinitely expensive to the republic, above all at a moment when it is only with difficulty and with much money that the armies are provisioned."[56]

Delacroix's and Defrenne's arguments were based solely on practical military grounds, but Representative Pierre Gudolle also injected a moral note in his letter of April 27. "The battalions of volunteers are followed by twenty to twenty-two wagons, and these wagons are so filled with women, with cradles, and with children that there remains no place for the sick or the soldiers' equipment. Elsewhere, I learn that eighty gendarmes were followed by fifty to sixty women, of whom more than one had morals discordant with the pure village women with whom they were housed."[57] Lazare Carnot, who exercised an immense influence on the army, took a harsher approach to the presence of women with the army. Writing to the Convention from Dunkirk, he stated,

> A terrible disease is destroying our army; it is the flock of women and of girls that follows them; there are as many of them as of soldiers; the barracks and camps are engorged with them; the dissolution of morals has reached its limit. The women debilitate the troops and destroy by the illnesses they bring ten times more men than the fire of the enemy. We do not doubt that this is the principal cause of the weakening of courage. It is imperative that you make on this point a law of the greatest severity. The abuse is not easy to destroy. We, your deputies, may not be able to do so without the authority of a very strong and very menacing law. . . . We insist on this point, because the army is lost if you do not apply the promptest remedy to this principle of dissolution.[58]

Carnot's impassioned discourse placed the blame for the army's failures squarely on the women who followed it, and his letters had a great influence on the Convention. Six days later he wrote, "Rid us of the whores who follow the army and everything will go well."[59]

Reacting to such demands, the Convention voted on April 30, 1793, to ban all "useless women" from the armies. The law included in its proscription all women serving as soldiers in combat units as well as all female camp followers, so the patriotic female soldier was banned along with the prostitute. The only exceptions to the new law were that each infantry battalion and cavalry regiment could have four blanchisseuses and an unspecified number of vivandières, with the proviso that each general should keep only those vivandières that "they believe absolutely necessary for the needs of their divisions."[60] The law further required that all "legal" women register with the military authorities and carry an identification plaque to be displayed at all times. While this law was clearly arbitrary and unfair to some women, it just as clearly acknowledged the importance of vivandières by declaring their services to be "absolutely necessary" to the functioning of the army. Moreover, the law failed to keep women away from the troops. Although such outrageous abuses as three thousand women following 350 soldiers no longer continued, many women found ways to stay with their men, and the complicity of the soldiers and their officers was widespread.[61] After all, from their perspective, the members of the Convention had their wives with them, so how could the Convention deny soldiers the same right? Besides, as Alan Forrest argued, "military commanders had every interest in ensuring that their soldiers were given a modicum of creature comforts wherever this was compatible with the basic discipline of regimental life."[62] Many units inflated the number of vivandières that were "absolutely necessary," while some commanders printed up fill-in-the-blanks "Certificates of Usefulness to the Army" for soldiers' wives.[63] Although one French historian has argued that the ban was totally ineffective, it did in fact reduce the number of women traveling with the armies, although the very nature of the problem makes precise measurement impossible.[64] However, numerous means of evasion as well as some outright defiance prevented the law from being as "strong and menacing" as Carnot would have liked, and after Thermidor the army became increasingly insulated from civil society and from government control. The law did have the effect of stranding large numbers of homeless women and children throughout northern France, since families leaving the armies on the frontier were often unable to pay for travel to distant homes. Carnot himself recognized this and set up extralegal machinery to identify and aid these families, "of whom the majority are in indigence."[65]

Perhaps the most telling outcome of the law of April 30 was the continual outpouring of orders and regulations to limit the number of women with the army, which showed the overall ineffectiveness of the Convention's original decree. In September 1793, General Houchard's "Order to the Army of the North to Restore Discipline" threatened soldiers' wives caught riding in supply wagons with being "painted black, paraded [naked] in front of the camp, and sent home."[66] In January 1794, Minister of War Bouchotte sent out a reminder "that the wives of general officers and of all other officers are subject to the exclusion," suggesting that those in positions of authority were openly flouting the law.[67] This, of course, would only have encouraged the common soldiers to do the same. In October 1794, Representative of the People Boursault in Brest attacked "the scandalous number of *citoyennes* who follow the army in violation of the law that keeps them away." Boursault even went so far as to invoke the Law of Suspects against women who failed to leave, warning that "only blanchisseuses and vivandières prominently carrying the plaque of their profession will be retained."[68] Four years later in the Army of Italy, General Bonaparte was still issuing orders to limit the number of women in his units, suggesting that little had changed.[69] Clearly, soldiers and their wives were persistent in their disregard of the ban, and far more women traveled with the armies than were authorized.

While the army tolerated vivandières, it had a long history of trying to solve problems of discipline by punishing women rather than the soldiers themselves. This continued to be the case under the Republic, when women were arrested or publicly humiliated for following the army while the soldiers who sheltered them went unpunished. From a commander's perspective, women were easily expendable where discipline was concerned, but combat soldiers were not. An excerpt from the diary of a private soldier of the Ninety-sixth Demi-brigade shows the extent to which officers often viewed women's presence as corrosive of morals and discipline.

Our marauders entered a château and took the silverware and sold it to a cantinière who had the misfortune to receive these objects. And the master of the château who saw the soldiers dispose of these items in the woman's apron mounted his horse and arrived at the riverbank and found the colonel and showed him the receiver of the stolen items and the mark of his silverware and the quantity. All that verified, the cantinière was condemned to be shaved and placed on her donkey totally naked, and to parade before the front of the regiment; and eight soldiers led the donkey, and this unhappy woman trembled on this donkey without a stitch on! And the owner of the silverware asked for her to be pardoned and cried! It was heartrending to see. But the soldier laughs at everything. The unfortunate woman, exhausted from fatigue in this position, let loose everything on the back of her donkey, and the soldiers who led the victim front and back didn't want to continue their service because the odor didn't suit them. They threw the donkey and the woman into the River Po, "to wash them," they said, and then they pulled them out. And the woman was chased from the regiment and the seigneur of the château gave her a purse and he cried sincerely.[70]

Certainly, the woman in question knew the goods were stolen, so she had a degree of responsibility. The soldiers also probably stole them with the express intention of fencing them through the cantinière, though, even in the complete absence of women, the troops would undoubtedly have found other buyers. On the other hand, the soldiers committed their crime of their own volition, in accordance with the prevailing moral code among private soldiers. The cantinière, for her part, was also partaking in the technically illegal but practically sanctioned trade in looted goods. That she alone was punished reflects the military necessity of preserving combat strength, but it also suggests a view that somehow she as a woman was the corrupting influence. Delacroix's statement that "the great number of women who follow the army is frightening" and Carnot's admonition to "rid us of the whores who follow the army and everything will go well" find an echo here. If there were problems with the troops' behavior, many commanders and officials thought it was the fault of the women who traveled with them. On the other hand, commanders sometimes shared blame for problems more equitably, especially where drunkenness was concerned. A September 1794 circular to battalion commanders charged "that the intemperance of a large number of soldiers and the cupidity of the cantinières of the army is occasioning serious problems. To bring about a prompt remedy, it suffices to remind defenders of the patrie that temperance is a civic virtue, and that in practicing it they not only conserve their health, but they multiply the force of the army."[71] This decree equitably shared blame among both soldiers and cantinières, but it was an exception. It appears that far more often, vivandières faced blame and expulsion from the unit for any malfeasance, even when soldiers were not punished.

Whether it occurred voluntarily or not, the vivandière's separation from her unit was usually painful, though instances like the one above in the Ninety-sixth Demi-brigade were comparatively rare. Many women chose to stay with the army as long as they could, since it offered a kind of security civilian life did not. Therefore, most vivandières ended their service when either they or their husbands were killed or disabled. A number of vivandières left when their husbands retired, but during the emergency years of 1792–1799 voluntary retirements were rare. All French soldiers were effectively on indefinite enlistments until after the peace of Amiens in 1802, and virtually no one was discharged unless unfit for service. Of those women who were killed in battle or died of disease, little more need (or can) be said. They remain for the most part anonymous victims of the wars. Since they were not officially soldiers, the Ministry of War did not record their deaths. At best we have a name, as in the case of "Citoyenne

Gauthier," but in most cases no record remains. A widow, however, some-times left copious records, and she often found that her husband's death was just the beginning of her troubles. First she faced the choice of staying with the army or leaving. She could remarry within the unit and remain a vivandière, or she could retire and take her chances in a depressed civil-ian economy. Some women did not get to make this choice themselves. For example, when Charlotte Daunay's layabout husband Michel was cap-tured on July 12, 1793, the Seventh Battalion of Paris dismissed her imme-diately, not even waiting until the next day to turn her out. One reason may have been the couple's bad reputation. Michel was a habitual deserter and bounty jumper, and Charlotte was his accomplice. Very likely, the two represented the kind of bad moral influence that military regulations were designed to curb. Another reason may have been Charlotte's advanced age. At sixty, she was extremely old for the time and not a likely candidate for remarriage.[72] In fact, women over fifty-five were likely to be dismissed when they lost their husbands, but this was by no means universal. There were women who remained vivandières as elderly widows in violation of the law, enjoying a status akin to that of a kindly grandmother to the men of the unit. The esteem in which the men held an individual vivandière seems to have been the deciding factor in most cases.

Those who did remarry stayed with the unit as though nothing had changed, and in some cases later claimed pensions for both husbands. Those who left the army faced an uncertain future. They often found themselves far from home, and often they had broken their ties with their original families by marrying a soldier. Those who could do so usually returned to their own or their husbands' birthplace to live with relatives. Depending on their knowledge of the law, many applied for a government widow's pension, the very existence of which marked a radical change from pre-Revolutionary policies toward widows. The Old Regime offered no such pensions. As we have already seen, some widowed vivandières received one-time *gratifications* in recognition of their service to the monarchy, but widows had no legal right to support, and no right to be vivandières except through their husbands' position. Because of this, remarriage rates of Royal Army vivandières were very high (approaching 100 percent in most units), since leaving the army often meant leaving behind all financial security. The Revolutionary governments, on the other hand, gave some thought to caring for their soldiers' widows. The law passed by the National Assem-bly on August 3, 1790, specifically included pensions for widows of French soldiers. However, this was in direct conflict with what Isser Woloch de-scribed as one of the principal tenets of Revolutionary ideology—"that

pensions were to be based solely on services rendered and were purely personal."[73] Therefore, the Assembly created a *pension alimentaire* for widows.
The underlying logic was that this was welfare rather than a pension, but
that the husband earned by his service the right of the widow to feed herself. The 1790 law established the principle of widows' pensions, but it was
not until June 4, 1793, that the government actually implemented the details, and by this time, a new and more radical government—the National
Convention—was in power. The growing number of casualties left numerous widows and orphans, and the government's failure to provide for them
was a major embarrassment. As one observer commented, "Not a week
passed without a crowd of emaciated women and children dressed in tatters
coming to offer the Convention the heart-rending spectacle of their tears
and their nudity."[74] The Convention passed a new law that gave a widow
up to one-half her husband's pay, but not less than 150 francs nor more
than a thousand. In addition, she had to prove she was in need of support.
This had a profound leveling effect, since even a new recruit could leave his
wife a reasonable (though still inadequate) sum of 150F a year, while even
a long-serving officer could not leave a pension of more than a thousand.

A year later, at the urging of the Committee for Public Safety, the Convention voted a new law of 13 Prairial, Year II (1794), that substantially
increased pension payments. This law made widows' pensions three hundred francs, regardless of the husbands' rank, with a supplement of fifty
francs for each year of the husband's military service. Even the widow of a
new volunteer could now gain a pension sufficient to feed herself, but since
most vivandières were married to long-term soldiers, they tended to receive
more generous pensions than the average widow. This law proved expensive, however, and by the law of 8 Fructidor, Year VI, the more parsimo-
nious (and decidedly less egalitarian) Directory trimmed widows' pensions
back to a minimum of one hundred francs, with the actual amount based
on the husband's rank and length of service. Under the new law, widows
of long-service professionals received spartan but adequate pensions, while
those whose husbands served only briefly found the pensions difficult if
not impossible to live on.

Obtaining a pension was a bureaucratic nightmare. In practice, the War
Ministry's Bureau of Pensions required a birth certificate for both spouses,
a marriage certificate, a certificate of non-divorce from the woman's commune of residence, a certificate of indigence from the woman's commune
of residence, and the husband's certificate of death. For many poor, illiterate women far from home, whose only residence was a mobile combat
unit, these requirements were difficult or impossible to meet. In practice,

it often took a year or more to assemble documents from various civil and military entities. A widow would then send them to the Ministry of War, where they would wait in a backlog that at times reached ten thousand cases.[75] Any discrepancies in the documents, often due to different phonetic spellings or use of a nickname, resulted in demands for clarification and regularization. Few people outside the Ministry of War were aware of the extent of the documentation required, and because of this, virtually all pension requests were initially incomplete. Thus, a woman could easily wait two or three years for her application to be processed, only to receive a letter detailing the array of documents required to complete it. This would be followed by another long wait. Marguerite Pain, vivandière of the Second Battalion of Mayence, needed documentation from her unit, but she could only write to the War Ministry, "I do not know at this time where the battalion is."[76] She eventually received a pension, but it took two years to assemble the required documents, given the poor state of communications and the constant movement of her unit. Other women were unable to document their pension requests and received no pension. For instance, former vivandière Jeanne Leytier had eight exchanges of letters with the War Ministry concerning the complexities of documenting her case. Eventually she was reduced to writing to the minister of war and begging for a chance to work as a blanchisseuse, as she was totally unable to support her children outside the army.[77]

The worst hardships fell on women who were elderly and without good personal connections. Such widows were more likely to be thrown out by their units, and less likely to have easy access to their birth and marriage certificates. Most had been born and married under the Old Regime, sometimes without legal or religious sanction. Many career vivandières had not seen their birthplace in thirty or forty years, and it is possible that they could not remember precisely where they had been married in an army on the move. Moreover, many had served for years under a system that did not grant pensions and did not expect meticulous documentation, so keeping track of such things would have been alien to them, meaning they often possessed no papers whatsoever. Another problem was that their advanced age made them unattractive to the men who could help them or not as they saw fit. Often, younger women received preferential treatment that was denied the elderly. As one observer commented, "the prettiest widows and daughters saw all the difficulties fall before them; the others continued to suffer."[78]

Foreign vivandières also had problems documenting their claims. Many German women served as vivandières in the Royal Army and continued their service under the Revolution. When they found themselves widowed under the new regime, they faced a difficult and sometimes impossible struggle to obtain suitable documentation for the War Ministry, reflecting perhaps a prejudice against foreigners who had served the Bourbons and now claimed the rights of French citizens. Katerina Eulen and her husband Johann had served in the French army since 1777, but when he was killed by Vendéean rebels in the Year III (1795), Katerina found herself unable to obtain a pension despite eighteen years of service.[79] Jeanne Leytier was another German woman who ran into unforeseen obstacles. Leytier was a Hanoverian who had married a Frenchman in 1782, serving fifteen years with the Fourth Regiment of Chasseurs à Cheval. Though she produced abundant documentation, the Ministry ignored her application for three years. She wrote eight letters to the minister and two to the legislature over that period, before she finally received a pension of two hundred francs.[80] Persistence sometimes paid off. In a rare surviving internal memo, the minister's secretary wrote to the head of the Pension Bureau complaining of Leytier's constant letters and all but ordered him to grant her a pension. "She ceaselessly paints to me her misery and the deplorable state to which she is reduced. I can only, my dear colleague, recommend she merits your interest in her case."[81] In this case at least, unusual pressure won a pension for a deserving widow, but it is worth noting that it took her until 1800 to receive it, by which time the more sympathetic Napoleon Bonaparte was in power.

Pressure of a different kind was often a prerequisite for a speedy and favorable resolution of pension claims, and the right support could prove decisive. For example, Péronne Branche claimed to be a vivandière of the Twenty-third Infantry Regiment and the wife of a volunteer killed in the Year II. However she had no marriage certificate, relying instead on the sworn testimony of two illiterate *laboreurs* who allegedly witnessed the marriage. The dates on her husband's death certificate and her son's birth certificate conflicted, and her whole documentary case was riddled with inconsistencies. Nevertheless, she had the strong support of Deputy Balmaire of the Convention, and his political clout gained her a pension despite the flimsy nature of her claim.[82] Marie Leroux was another woman whose political connections bolstered her successful pension application. After her husband's death, she received strong support for her pension application from her brother-in-law, an official in the Ministry of War. Even so, it took two years before she received her money.[83] Many women with stronger claims but without powerful benefactors found their applications denied.

These examples show the extent of the bureaucratic delays women faced in obtaining pensions, but they also show that the government refused vivandières pensions of their own. All the various pension laws granted pensions to a soldier's widow based on the husband's service, not the wife's. Therefore, women like Angélique Brévilier who were maimed without losing their husbands received no aid whatsoever. In addition, a woman who served many years as a vivandière but who remarried several times might find that her last husband had fewer years of service than she did. In cases like this, she received a pension only for his shorter length of service. A number of women challenged this aspect of the law, writing for pensions based on their own service rather than that of their husbands. Marianne Boyer was a blanchisseuse with the Forty-eighth Demi-brigade when her second husband, Antoine, died in the Year III. She wrote the minister of war that she deserved a pension because she had "made six campaigns as blanchisseuse, and so been useful to my country."[84] This type of claim might well have earned her a *gratification* under the monarchy, but under the Republic the very idea of a blanchisseuse "serving" was unacceptable. She received her answer on the standard printed form, which stated that "The Citoyenne _____, born the _____, department of _____, widow of Citizen _____, has the right to a pension of _____, in recompense for the services of her husband."[85] The form itself imposed its own logic on the pension process: with no place on the form for women's service, women's service could have no legitimacy. Only the husband's service counted, and the War Ministry refused to even discuss challenges to this rule.

On the whole, vivandières' experience during the Revolution was decidedly mixed. On the one hand, the chaos and tumult of the years 1789–1794 provided many women with unprecedented opportunities owing to the increased size and new structure of the French army. A very few women amassed considerable fortunes, and many others found a way out of the terrible economic distress affecting the lower classes. The job also provided a patriotic means for a family to answer the call of the nation while keeping itself together. Finally, the very existence and nature of the vivandières' position was regularized and enshrined in law by the decree of April 30, 1793, and maintained for more than a century. On the other hand, the Republic's emphasis on caring for its dead and wounded defenders bypassed vivandières, who were eligible for aid only if their husbands died, and then only after a long and tortuous process. This was especially significant because under the Republic vivandières increasingly came under fire, and the number of vivandières killed and wounded in battle increased significantly. The peace and quiet of garrison life in the Old Regime all but disappeared, and vivandières were constantly on campaign. In short, the years of war and revolution from 1789 to 1799 provided many new opportunities but offered many new perils as well. During those years, though, the government recognized vivandières' usefulness in supplying the troops, and their presence in the army, hitherto legally tenuous at best, became regular and legal. The Law of April 30, 1793, that drove "useless women" from the army also gave vivandières a strong and enduring legal basis, and for the next century, no one would imagine a French army on campaign without its female auxiliaries.

CHAPTER 3

Expanded Opportunities

Cantinières in the Armies
of Napoleon

NAPOLEON BONAPARTE'S ACCESSION TO POWER in 1799 and the founding of the First Empire in 1804 were mixed blessings for the army's cantinières. Napoleon's attention to the welfare of the army and his penchant for autocratic rule above the law meant that cantinières sometimes received augmented pensions that the First Republic would never have granted. The increased scale of warfare under Napoleon also expanded the number of cantinière positions and created more opportunity for plunder. On the other hand, Napoleon's constant wars and his ruthless use of his armies subjected cantinières to hardships and dangers on a scale unheard of under the Republic. In particular, guerrilla wars of occupation in Italy, the Tyrol, and Spain entailed new dangers to soldiers' families, and the terrible retreat from Russia in 1812 became the graveyard of the cantinière corps as well as of Napoleon's veteran soldiers. Even without these notable exceptions, the increased scale, frequency, and intensity of battles and the development of an unwritten convention that cantinières belonged on the battlefield during combat resulted in growing numbers of female casualties, yet the Empire created no mechanism for compensating the wars' female victims. While cantinières both benefited and suffered from Napoleon's unique mixture of paternalism and ruthless ambition, on the whole they ended his reign in worse condition than they began it.

The same economic forces that existed in earlier years continued to push many of the same kinds of civilian women into the ranks of the cantinières. These forces were aggravated by Napoleon's Continental System, which sought to exclude British goods from Europe in order to force Britain to make peace, but which badly damaged the French economy. Many of the Empire's vivandières served the Republic as well, but by 1810, the cantinière ranks were increasingly composed of foreign women and hereditary canti-nières: women who were born in the army and knew nothing of civilian life. This was a consequence of the professionalization of the army, its Imperial nature, and its isolation from civilian society.

For the historian, the Napoleonic period stands in contrast to earlier and later periods for a number of reasons. One is the sheer volume of doc-umentation. Many Napoleonic soldiers published memoirs in the years after Napoleon's death, and their popularity helped build the Napoleonic legend. The flood of posthumous memoirs, diaries, and letters published around the centennial of the First Empire made Napoleon's era one of the best documented periods in French history. Many of these publications helped shed light on the daily life of the soldiers and on their interactions with cantinières. Another important change from the period of the early Republic was that under Napoleon, the French army assumed a strong sense of professionalism and became detached from French civilian society. Living for years in foreign countries and feeling more attachment to their units than to their country, French cantinières tended to be long-service professionals, with no life outside the army. They married long-service sol-diers, many of whom had served continuously since the 1770s, and they raised children who followed their parents' careers in the army. While this insularity had existed in the Royal Army, it was even more pronounced under the Empire, and it stood in stark contrast to the legions of volunteer vivandières and their citizen-soldier husbands of the early Republic. The de facto tolerance of unmarried cantinières also distinguished the Empire from the Republican and Restoration governments, which emphasized legit-imate marriage. Finally, the changing nature of warfare made cantinières even more important under Napoleon than they had been in previous wars; armies increasingly traveled without tents or baggage and relied on forag-ing for supplies, a continuation of a trend started under the First Repub-lic, but taken to new heights under the First Empire.

The Law of April 30, 1793, remained the official regulation governing vivandières and cantinières under the First Empire, but it was modified by the Consular Decree of 7 Thermidor, Year VIII (1800). This decree main-tained vivandières, but also reminded commanders of the limit of four women per battalion and two per cavalry squadron. It also closed a loop-hole in the 1793 law that allowed a set number of women as blanchisseuses, but any number of women to be kept as vivandières, a loophole that had been much abused. The new decree specifically limited units to a total of four women, regardless of their function. Because of this limitation, units tended to combine the functions of vivandière and blanchisseuse, using titles like "vivandière-blanchisseuse," "blanchisseuse et vivandière," or increasingly "cantinière." For the next century, this shift in terminology caused confusion, as even the War Ministry could not decide if the women were "vivandières," "cantinières," or "blanchisseuse-vivandières."[1] For example, Jeanne Billers' *patente* from General Ney's division in the Army of the Rhine hedged by calling her a "blanchisseuse or vivandière," while Marguerite Dimel received a *permission de vivandière et blanchisseuse.*[2] Certainly, blanchisseuses still served, but on paper at least, there was a growing tendency to dispense with them as part of the maximum four women allowed. Under the old law, with its strict limit of four blanchisseuses but its large loophole allowing unlimited vivandières, it made sense to keep the blanchisseuses in order to augment the number of wives who could legally stay with the unit, and doing so cost nothing. Under the new law, it made sense to conflate roles into a multipurpose "cantinière." Circumstantial evidence suggests that blanchisseuses who remained were often "unofficial," such as Mme Angot, whose colonel referred to her as a "femme de troupe" of the Sixty-seventh Infantry Regiment, leaving her actual legal status highly ambiguous.[3]

The decree also ordered brigadier generals to make decisions about which women to retain if there was an excess, a tacit admission that far more women were present with the armies than were authorized. Commanders were to choose "women of good manners, married to soldiers or non-commissioned officers on active service, recognized as the most active, the most useful to the troops, and whose conduct and morals are the most regular." Women denied places would be given travel allowances and sent home. They were forbidden to approach within four leagues of the army, on pain of being punished as prostitutes. "As for the women who are authorized to remain following the units and the headquarters, they have no right to any pay or rations. The inspectors of revues will do no more than furnish a register of identity of their age, of their profession, and of their appearance. They will deliver to each one of them a certified extract of this register; this extract will serve as a security card in the zone of the army."[4] Once again, the War Ministry had weighed in and made it clear that these women were civilians and not soldiers. Cantinières' only reward from the state would be a pension if their husbands were killed in battle. Otherwise, they were left to their own devices to feed, clothe, and equip themselves.

The social background of cantinières in the Napoleonic era was humble, as it had always been. Official records show daughters of bakers, soldiers, plasterers, and peasants, as well as orphans. Few were literate. Most were married to senior non-commissioned officers, and many began their careers under the Republic and continued to serve under the Emperor. One woman who started during the early days of the Revolution but continued into the Empire was Marie Elisabeth Peter. She was an orphan from Hagenau (Bas-Rhin) who married Corporal Etienne Bory of the First Regiment of Carabiniers in 1790.[5] Another holdover from the days of the Republic was Marguerite Léger, a plasterer's daughter from Maubeuge (Nord). After leaving home to work in Gercy as a dressmaker, she married Sergeant Pierre Boldevin in 1796 and served as cantinière of the Sixth Regiment of Cuirassiers until she was killed in action in 1807 near Thorn in Poland.[6] Jeanne Conrad, a Swiss peasant's daughter, came later to the profession, but still served under the Directory, Consulate, and Empire. She married a sergeant of the Twenty-third Demi-brigade in 1798 and served as a cantinière until 1812.[7] Marie Pierrette of the Forty-eighth Infantry Regiment was a foundling from Avignon who married Sergeant Louis Hoccard in 1798.[8]

Not all cantinières of the First Empire were holdovers from the army of the Republic, though. As the old cohort of Revolutionary vivandières died or retired, younger women filled their places. One such was Jeanne Demonay, a peasant woman from Aurelle (Mont-Blanc). Leaving her mountain village for domestic service in Turin, she met and married Nicholas Gerard, a private in the Fifteenth Infantry Regiment, in July 1801. She became a cantinière and served until his death in 1807.[9] Daughters of cantinières also remained important sources of new blood. Elizabeth Haros of the Thirty-sixth Infantry Regiment was typical. Born in the army at an unknown date, her mother and grandmother were vivandières and her father was a career sergeant who died in retirement.[10]

The actual formalities of becoming a cantinière varied from unit to unit and over time, but the only real requirements were that the woman be married to a soldier in the unit she served and that she have the permission of the unit's Council of Administration. Legally, all cantinières were required to be the legitimate wives of soldiers, but this was not uniformly enforced in the years 1796–1814, though it was in earlier and later periods. Instead, cantinière marriages under the Empire tended to be quick and informal. Many units accepted mutual verbal consent as proof of marriage, especially when women who were already cantinières remarried. In his memoirs, Sergeant Bourgogne of the Imperial Guard recalled an instance when he "took a wife" during the retreat from Moscow.

> I caught sight of a woman dressed in a soldier's cloak, looking curiously at me. . . . I asked her who was with her, and she said no one; that since the

day her husband was killed she had been alone, but that if I would take her under my protection, she would take good care of me. I consented at once.[11]

However, the two became separated in the retreat, and Bourgogne was soon single again. "I made several inquiries about my 'wife,' as I so badly wanted the change of linen she had promised me, but I never saw her again, and so I found myself bereft both of her and my knapsack."[12] Bourgogne witnessed another episode that is more typical. A drunken soldier accused an old cantinière of having not been married to her late husband. "Not married! Not married! Haven't I been with him nearly five years, ever since the Battle of Eylau, and I'm not married?"[13] Relatives who later sought information on their Napoleonic cantinière ancestors could often only tell researchers at the War Ministry archives that "she was a cantinière, married in the army," meaning that no marriage license existed.[14] In addition, not all widowed cantinières remarried immediately, even unofficially. One old sergeant during the Russian campaign said of a "widowed" Spanish cantinière, "She is a good woman: ask the others—no one dares say anything else. She had a fancy for a sergeant, who was to have married her; but he was murdered by a Spaniard in Bilbao, and until she has chosen someone else she must be taken care of."[15] She never actually married in the first place, but had nevertheless served as a cantinière in the French army from Saragossa to Smolensk. A male protector in the regiment and a professed intent to marry was often enough, especially in Spain where enforcement of regulations of all kinds was extremely lax, and many generals traveled with wives, mistresses, and even prostitutes. The rank and file understandably followed suit.[16]

Widows were also the subject of many extra-legal exceptions. Sometimes this was a temporary humanitarian gesture intended to last only until the widow could secure a pension. When Joseph Angot of the Sixty-seventh Infantry Regiment was killed at Wagram in July 1809, the regiment kept his wife and two children under its wing. The colonel of the Sixty-seventh personally solicited a pension from the War Ministry, and Madame Angot left the unit once she had received a means of subsistence.[17] Sometimes the exception was more permanent, as was the case with Madame Daubigny. A long-term cantinière, she was widowed in 1804 when she was forty-seven years old. Physically unable to continue the tough job of cavalry cantinière, she asked the War Ministry for help, and received a lucrative sedentary post as cantinière of the Rue de Grenelle barracks in Paris in recompense for her long service. She retained the post until 1817 though she never remarried.[18] In many cases, however, widows served permanently with their regiments on campaign. Marie Hoccard was still serving as a blanchisseuse for the Forty-eighth Infantry Regiment in 1811, five years after the death of her legal husband.[19] Most likely, she had "remarried" unofficially in the fashion of the times, and therefore was at least nominally still qualified to remain with the unit. The unofficial nature of her remarriage had the added advantage of allowing her to claim a widow's pension. The incidence of fraud and embezzlement in the French army was enormous, and the un-official remarriage in combination with a widow's pension was a relatively easy way for couples to increase their income at the state's expense. Less suspect but in some ways more irregular was the case of Catherine Sabatier. A soldier's daughter and a career cantinière since 1792, she was widowed at least twice in Spain and spent two years in Spanish prisons before making a dramatic escape in 1810. Her father and two husbands were killed in battle and she had two sons serving as soldiers. At age forty-five she knew nothing of civilian life, and in 1812 she received a special dispensation as a widow to be cantinière of the Third Division's headquarters.[20]

More problematical were the hundreds or perhaps thousands of foreign women who joined the French armies as cantinières during the many for-eign campaigns. Units picked up local cantinières in every country they passed through. Just as non-French soldiers were scattered throughout the nominally French units of the Grand Army, foreign cantinières were legion in the French army. Spaniards, Hungarians, Italians, Croats, Germans, Dutch, Portuguese, and Poles, these women were often not legal spouses, and were not even French citizens, so few official records remain of them. Bourgogne described one such couple, a Hungarian cantinière and a ser-geant of the Chasseurs of the Guard, not as husband and wife but as "the best friends possible."[21] Theophilus Conneau was a the product of a mixed French-Italian marriage, claiming that "my father came to Italy with the Republican conquering army under General Bonaparte and married my mother in Niece (Piedmont), who followed him on many campaigns, till the Emperor Napoleon abdicated and was sent to the Island of Elba."[22] Conneau was born in Florence in 1808, so his father was probably gar-risoned there, but the details of his childhood remain unclear. We do know his father was killed at Waterloo, and that his mother was left with six chil-dren. This suggests that Madame Conneau and her children traveled with the army for approximately fifteen years: an impressive length of career in such a violent time. Particularly large numbers of Spanish women followed the French armies as well, the product of the extended French occupation of Spain. Some were prostitutes, but a good many were hitherto respectable women attracted to the free lifestyle of the military camps, and sincerely convinced that their soldiers planned to marry them.[23] John Elting wrote that "thousands of them, whether from want or the lure of something new in their narrow, superstition-bound lives, took Frenchmen as their partners."[24] While this is pure speculation, it does raise important issues. Like many French women, foreign camp followers often fled from desperate poverty, especially in Spain, where the protracted guerrilla war devastated the economy and made food scarce. Then again, an affair with a French soldier and a life as a cantinière may have seemed exotic and exciting. To women brought up under strict religious and familial controls, the coming of the French army could mean an unparalleled opportunity to break free from traditional bonds. As one French soldier wrote of the Spanish and Portuguese women who followed his unit in large numbers, "They were quite free and were very attracted by this new type of life."[25] Whatever their motivations, by 1812 there were many foreign women serving in French units, and though they left few official records, they performed the same roles as their French counterparts.

For all the apparently casual nature of cantinière marriages, it would be a mistake to view them all as loveless marriages of convenience. Certainly, there were relationships without love, but many cantinières and their husbands shared deep emotional bonds. Unfortunately, loss or the threat of loss of a spouse often was the catalyst that caused chroniclers to record these feelings. For example, a cantinière of the Eighty-first Infantry braved heavy fire all day at Waterloo, but, as one soldier wrote, "then, her husband had his head taken off by a cannon ball, and she left us in tears."[26] Raymond de Fezensac recalled a drummer from the Seventh Light Infantry Regiment who performed "a feat of the most sublime devotion" for his wife during the bitter retreat from Moscow.

> His wife, cantinière of the regiment, fell sick at the start of the retreat. The drummer drove her as long as he had a cart and a horse. At Smolensk, the horse died. Afterward he pulled the cart himself and carried his wife as far as Wilna. Arriving in this city, she was too sick to go farther, and her husband stayed on to be a prisoner with her.[27]

This devotion was often mutual. One Bavarian sergeant remarked that his wife brought him food under heavy artillery fire in Russia. "We were surprised at her boldness, and the officers called out to her to inquire how she had escaped the hail of shot and shell in which she could so easily have been wounded or killed. 'If my husband is hit,' she said, 'I must look after him, on campaign just as much as at home.'"[28] Likewise, when a company of the Fourteenth Light Infantry fought its way out of a guerrilla ambush in Italy, one officer recalled that his cantinière "carried her husband, who was wounded in the leg, more than two leagues on her back."[29] Philippe Girault's wife showed her devotion in a less spectacular but no less effective way. Girault, a musician in the Ninety-third Infantry Regiment, suffered from recurrent fevers. His wife Lucille spent a great deal of her time nursing him back to health during outbreaks of cholera and typhus, and her care saved his life on several occasions.[30]

Being the cantinière's husband meant that a soldier was well provided with food, drink, and sex, all three of which the cantinière might or might not provide to others as well. Cooking for her family entailed little extra work, since the cantinière invariably cooked food in quantity for sale to the soldiers. However, while cooking in garrison was hard work, cooking in the field could be grueling. Finding suitable food was only the first step. The cantinière also had to procure dry firewood or attempt the frustrating and smoky task of lighting a fire with green wood. Cooking involved simply roasting, frying, or boiling the food over an open fire. All cantinières carried a small assortment of saucepans and frying pans, placing them (and thus their husbands) at a distinct culinary advantage over most soldiers, who often resorted to skewering meat on the ends of their swords or bayonets and thrusting them into a fire. In this respect, the cantinière's ability to cook multi-course meals in real pots made being her husband an attractive proposition. Napoleon's long forced marches meant that troops often arrived at a destination too physically exhausted to cook, even if they had the time and equipment to do so, and a hot meal could fetch exorbitant prices under the right circumstances. Having a wife with a wagon, food supplies, cookware, and perhaps even a stock of dry wood was a decided benefit.

The cantinière also provided her husband with copious amounts of alcohol, which played an important role in military life. Most soldiers had to pay for it, and the more difficult alcohol was to procure, the more expensive it became. Some husbands simply enjoyed their prosperity, but others used it to ingratiate themselves with their superiors. At Borodino, Trumpeter Lejeune of the Eleventh Chasseurs à Cheval brought some of his wife's brandy to his officers as a gift. Brandy was in such short supply at the time that nearby French soldiers were looting Russian corpses of the bottles of the "frightful beverage" they carried into battle. Later, during the retreat from Moscow, Lejeune allowed Colonel Biot to ride in his wife's wagon, which Biot described as "encumbered with sacks of flour, sugar, coffee, etc."[31] On the whole, being a cantinière's husband provided excellent benefits, and women who were widowed had their pick of replacements.

Like the extent of their marital devotion, cantinière's sexual habits during this period are difficult if not impossible to accurately assess from surviving sources. Clearly, they were not celibate. They were all married, legitimately or otherwise, and the large number of children they bore attests to their sexual activity. Less easily answered are questions about the extent of their sexual relations outside marriage. Captain Elzéar Blaze hinted that pretty cantinières slept with virtually everyone in the unit, but offered no evidence.[32] The few modern authors who have included cantinières in their works have often passed on similar allegations as fact. The author of one popular French work wrote, "Without changing battalions, some of these fierce amazons passed easily from one man to the next on the condition that their rank would increase. Others, like Madame Thérèse, dubbed 'Sans-Gêne' ["No Problem"], acted as intermediaries for decidedly immoral marriages!"[33] There may indeed have been cantinières who moved from man to man, as well as cantinières who ran prostitution rings, but no verifiable records remain either of their existence or of their suppression. Prostitutes, of course, abounded in and around the armies, and some cantinières may have sold sex as well. Again, however, not a single piece of evidence exists to support this assertion, with one singular exception. Denis Smith claims that "canteen women" stranded with French prisoners of the Spanish on the desert island of Cabrera routinely prostituted themselves to the many male prisoners there. However, Smith apparently relies on a single source, Philippe Gille, for his rather sweeping assertions. Smith himself admits that the source "must be treated with scepticism," and it is well worth noting that none of the other Cabrera memoirists mention prostitution, though Guillemard does mention a makeshift theater where several cantinières worked as actresses in order to earn their keep—a far safer and more respectable solution to the problem of staying alive among thousands of men. A further problem is that Smith never uses the words "cantinière" or "vivandière," and his descriptions make it plain that he is not entirely clear who these women were or what their function in the French army was.[34] Finally, the French soldiers and cantinières on Cabrera were in desperate straits from thirst, starvation, and disease with no hope of relief or rescue. These were extreme conditions, which hardly represented ordinary circumstances for an army, or routine duty for cantinières. The existence of prostitution among the cantinière corps, therefore, remains a possibility, but as a widespread phenomenon it is unlikely at best, and if it existed at all, it was most likely quite rare.

What is certain is that some cantinières appeared to value fidelity above the opportunity for multiple sexual partners that army life provided, and were careful to guard their virtue, making sure that they were among those "whose conduct and morals are the most regular."[35] One good example of such care occurred after a party in the ruins of Moscow in 1812, when a cantinière of the Chasseurs of the Guard returned home at 4:00 AM.

> As she left, the Sergeant of the Guard on police duty, seeing a strange lady in the street so early, and thinking he had found a prize, went to her and tried to take her to his room. But Mother Dubois, who had a husband, and moreover had drunk a good deal of punch, dealt the sergeant such a vigorous blow to the face that she knocked him completely over.[36]

Other cantinières were not so monogamous. One was a cantinière of the Fourteenth Light Infantry Regiment, Catherine Beguin, whose husband "was not very tickled in the area of his wife's virtue," but she gained the respect of her unit because of her bravery in battle.[37] Another was "Marie," cantinière of the Chasseurs of the Young Guard. Sergeant Bourgogne wrote that she was known for her generosity and care for the wounded, and "in addition to these good qualities, Marie was pretty. She had a number of friends too, and her husband was not jealous."[38] Neither of these examples involve or imply prostitution, merely promiscuity. It would be as much of a mistake, though, to view cantinières as promiscuous or as prostitutes as it would be to view them all as chaste. None of these anecdotes can necessarily pass as typical. Rather, they represent a range of responses to the complicated issue of a woman's sexuality in an almost exclusively male world. What is clear is that vague allegations of prostitution among cantinières cannot be supported with conclusive evidence, and that alone is fairly damning. While some cantinières may have been promiscuous, they were not prostitutes, and many were devoted and monogamous spouses.

Quite naturally, considering cantinières' sexual activity, children continued to be a large part of their lives. Virtually all Napoleonic cantinières had at least one child, with surviving documents suggesting that two to four were average. Many had more, though, and Madeleine Kintelberger of the Seventh Hussar Regiment had eight, two of them born in Russian captivity.[39] Children were so commonplace in eighteenth-century army life that few soldiers even mentioned them in their memoirs. They formed part of the background of sights and sounds that contemporaries took for granted in army camps. Artists, however, often painted them, and they appear as details or background in countless period paintings and sketches, playing or helping their cantinière mothers with chores.[40]

Pregnancy and childbirth rarely made cantinières unfit for duty. Rather, they were just normal events to be dealt with, whether in camp or in battle. Certainly, neither soldiers nor cantinières viewed childbirth as extraordinary, even when it occurred in combat as a woman carried out her duties. When one cantinière gave birth on the battlefield at Marengo, a grenadier standing near her allegedly shouted, "Hey, Marie! You dropped something!"[41] Another cantinière gave birth during the Battle of Heilsberg in 1807, washing the baby with one hand and pouring drinks with the other.[42] Childbirth often consisted of leaving the marching column at the last moment to deliver the baby by the roadside. The mother and the child would then mount up and keep moving, so as not to be left behind.[43] This imposed haste could have tragic results, but most women and their children held up well. German artist Albrecht Adam witnessed an encounter in 1812 between Prince Eugene and a cavalry cantinière. The woman had given birth on the march and was nursing the newborn infant on horseback, while the attentive father rode alongside in the heat of the Russian summer. The prince, used to much more pampered women, was so fascinated that he stayed and talked with the couple for some time, then gave them a gold florin as a parting gift.[44] Madame Dubois, a cantinière of the Chasseurs of the Imperial Guard, was less fortunate. She gave birth to a baby boy by the roadside in temperatures of −20C during the retreat from Moscow, and the child soon froze to death. Soldiers gave him a hasty burial, and Dubois moved on to avoid the pursuing Russians.[45] Some suffered even worse fates. A general in the Russian army pursuing the French saw a cantinière "who had just given birth and had expired next to her dead infant."[46] Nor did childbirth take place only on campaign. One cantinière captured in Spain gave birth on a Spanish prison hulk in Cadiz harbor, and later raised her twins on the barren prison island of Cabrera. Since her husband was dead, the other prisoners adopted the twins and helped care for them, even using the island's sole donkey to carry their cradle about.[47]

Life in the field was harsh even in the best of circumstances. In winter, or in extreme cases like the retreat from Moscow, it could be brutal on children, who nevertheless accompanied their parents. One French civilian fleeing Moscow in 1812 wrote that "women were obliged to keep their children warm by covering them in a pelisse, and wept tears of despair."[48] But persistence and hard work sometimes paid off. Colonel Fezensac wrote of a cantinière's seven-month-old baby who survived the retreat from Moscow on a diet of icicles made of horse's blood. The mother crossed the Berezina River on horseback in icy water up to her neck, balancing the baby on her head with one hand and holding the reins with the other. Both mother and

baby returned safely to France.[49] Sometimes more than nurturing was necessary. In such instances many cantinières were willing to do whatever was
required. At the chaotic crossing of the Berezina, a cantinière who was
trapped at the waist by the ice was "holding her child above the water and
begging the pity of passers-by, that they might save the child. Another,
whose children were in danger of being crushed [by the mob of panicked
soldiers], seized a musket and, animated by her maternal instinct, sought to
defend them."[50] In 1809, the War Ministry attempted to force all cantinières'
sons to stay with regimental depots, but as the above examples illustrate,
many women continued to keep their children with them.[51] Maintaining
the family intact routinely took precedence over army regulations.

Though children of cantinières led a harsh life, it was not all misery. The
soldiers of the regiment adopted the children as their own, and the children thus gained a variety of interesting tutors, protectors, and friends.
As one cantinière put it, "Those great guys! [*Les bons lurons!*] There isn't
one soldier in the regiment who doesn't act as father to my children, since
they are used to seeing them, to caressing them, and to playing with them
during halts."[52] While young, the children had ample time for play, and as
they grew older they performed various tasks to aid their mothers and, by
extension, the army.

Finally, the army provided cantinières' sons with employment as enfants
de troupe. Enfants de troupe were a long tradition in the French army, one
that Napoleon reaffirmed in 1801.[53] From age two to sixteen, they could
collect rations, pay, and a uniform allowance: important financial bonuses
to struggling military families.[54] Eligibility was strictly limited to boys who
were the product of "the legitimate marriage of a woman attached to the
unit as a blanchisseuse or vivandière, with a defender of the patrie currently in service or died of his wounds during wartime."[55] The young boys
were brought up in the regiment by several tutors, old soldiers of proven
bravery, skill, and moral character who were hand-picked by their officers.
The boys were taught to read, write, and handle arms, but this education
had a price: enfants de troupe were required to enlist at age sixteen.[56] Many
served first as drummers and then as soldiers in the regiment. Others served
as musicians of various types, especially as trumpeters. However, the army
paid particular attention to training them in "crafts useful to the army," so
that they could serve as *ouvriers* and eventually as *maîtres ouvriers*.[57] This
strong emphasis on providing skilled workers for the army agrees with
Frederick Schneid's assessment of Napoleonic recruiting practices. Schneid
argues that there was a "purposeful method to Napoleonic conscription,"
since French armies had an insatiable appetite for skilled workers such as

cobblers, gunsmiths, bakers, and blacksmiths, which "allowed Napoleon to conduct war on the strategic level in a manner to which other European armies were unaccustomed." Because of this, "conscription was carried out with a careful regard for those persons with special skills that would enable the army to achieve this relative logistical independence."[58] This could work particularly well in the case of cantinières' sons, since the army already had a supply of potentially skilled workers on hand, and placed great importance on training them. Bred from birth in the regiment, enfants de troupe made excellent recruits, and in bearing and raising them, cantinières performed a valuable service for the army. In fact, enfants de troupe knew no other life than the army, and some found it impossible to leave, no matter what the benefits. Philippe Girault told of an old friend who was born in the army and raised as an enfant de troupe. As an adult he met and married a wealthy woman with landed estates, a city home in Nancy, and numerous servants. He retired to live the life of a country gentlemen in his twenties, but was restless outside the army. Eventually, he told his wife he was going hunting, rode off, and enlisted as a common soldier. His wife and commanders entreated him to return, but he was steadfast, visiting his wife only once, under protest and escorted by gendarmes. As he told Girault, "only the soldier's life suited him; he could only be happy in the regiment."[59]

Although raising children was an important part of their lives, vivandières were first and foremost businesswomen, and they displayed a wide range of temperaments in their business dealings. While there were some who took advantage of the soldiers at every turn and never gave away the slightest sip to the needy, others combined a certain pragmatic business sense with fierce patriotism, loyalty to the unit, and a feeling of compassion and generosity to the unfortunate. Business dealings with soldiers were usually carried out through a system of mutual consent in which the soldiers grumbled about high prices but paid anyway. Cantinières and soldiers were interdependent. Cantinières could rarely supply themselves in the field without the active help of the soldiers, and soldiers could never carry enough food and drink to last them through the lean times between purchases or pillages. Given this situation, cantinières who were truly mean-spirited and selfish seldom lasted long. Philippe Girault described the fate of an unpopular cantinière in 1809. When a wagon carrying a regimental cantinière and Girault's pregnant wife plunged into the Danube, a soldier swam out and rescued Madame Girault. As for the other cantinière, who was standing on the wagon seat and calling for help as the wagon drifted downriver, "since she was not well loved in the regiment, no one wanted

to get wet to go get her."[60] This illustrates the very real consequences cantinières faced if they mercilessly exploited their captive clientele.

One common complaint against the conduct of cantinières was that they
overcharged in difficult times. This complaint usually came from officers
rather than enlisted men, who generally shared the same social background
and values as the cantinières. The concept of a "just price" in a theater of
war was a difficult one to adjudicate. A great number of factors could affect
the availability of commodities like brandy or meat, both for the seller and
for the consumer. In an area heavily looted by one or more armies, supply
became a major difficulty for cantinières, and prices rose. They rarely ran
completely out of brandy, at least, always keeping a reserve on hand. However, during the retreat from Moscow, those who survived lost everything,
including their wares, and conditions in Poland in 1806–1807 were so bad
that many cantinières were hard-pressed to resupply themselves. Likewise,
during the campaign in France in 1814, one captain thought the fact that
the cantinières were without brandy important enough to note in his
diary.[61] Nevertheless, many cantinières had no qualms about charging high
prices for questionable goods in times of scarcity, especially when the customers were perceived to be wealthy, and some officers complained bitterly. Lieutenant Jacques de Norvins had this to say about a cantinière he
encountered in Poland in 1807 when General Grouchy wanted to buy him
a drink:

> He brought me to a cart where a horrible vivandière washed the baby she
> had just given birth to with one hand while with the other she poured an
> unspeakable beverage into pewter goblets. After getting up the courage to
> drink it despite its strange color and its taste, since the torment of thirst is
> insupportable, we could see that the baby's bath had not been elsewhere. . . .
> Since this liquor without a name was not susceptible to any price, the good
> mother asked for and received six francs: she gave it for two sous to soldiers,
> and screwed over those with epaulettes, especially those with stars.[62]

Another lieutenant, Octave Levavasseur, wrote in more general terms.
"All the money acquired or pillaged by the soldiers went to the vivandières.
These women, exploiting the penury of food and the abundance of cash,
sometimes sold a little glass of brandy for as much as twenty francs."[63] Given
that both these complaints were made during the bitter winter campaign
in Poland in 1807, the position of the cantinières becomes more understandable. In a wild, poor, roadless, and inhospitable countryside, dealing
alternately with ice and knee-deep mud, cantinières were hard-pressed to

stay supplied, especially with liquor. As one old veteran soldier sympa-
thetically wrote of the cantinière's succor, "That cost a bit sometimes, but
money is only good for procuring necessities. The moment one cannot
exchange it for bread, gold is worth no more than iron."[64]

As these examples show, vivandières' primary commodity was alcohol,
usually brandy or "eau de vie" as it was commonly known. In fact, the very
term "water of life" suggests the distilled spirit's importance in the era. It
represented a safe, unpolluted beverage that one could drink with confi-
dence, and it contained alcohol, which gave the drinker a pleasant buzz
and constituted "liquid courage." More colloquially, soldiers referred to its
cruder forms as "casse-poitrine," "rogomme," or "chien-chien," all of which
referred to the effects it could have on the drinker. Vivandières also carried
wine and beer, but hard alcohol was the most sensible investment when on
campaign, simply because it could be carried more compactly and served
more easily. Cantinières used *tonnelets,* small wooden barrels of about a
gallon capacity, to dispense liquor to soldiers, saving bottles of better quality for officers with more money.[65]

Food was another commodity in which Napoleonic cantinières did a
great trade. A beginning cantinière on foot could hope only to carry her
tonnelet strapped across her chest and two or three glasses, but once she
moved up to a pack animal, and eventually to a cart or wagon, she could
afford to carry victuals of all sorts. One cantinière of the Grenadiers of the
Guard, Mother Dubois, managed to stock sought-after white bread even
in the depths of Russia.[66] A more standard stock of food included several
varieties of sausage, cheeses, bread, and wild game, as well as the occasional
pig, cow, goat, or chicken. Captain Elzéar Blaze described the load of a
pack horse as sausages, cheeses, and barrels, all "carefully balanced" around
the seated cantinière, while Albrecht Adam's 1812 drawing of a nursing cantinière showed her horse draped with cooking utensils and sacks of supplies, with a goat tethered to her saddle.[67] At about the same time, another
German artist sketched a relatively poor French cantinière on a horse with
almost no baggage but with two goats tied to the horse's tail.[68] French army
surgeon Charles Cadet de Gassicourt described a more prosperous vivandière's wagon in 1809 as follows: "A captured horse, very skinny, ate its
oats in its harness. A large barrel of white wine, two little barrels, three
sacks, and several pots composed the load of the little cart."[69] As these examples suggest, cantinières varied considerably in their means, but all of
them cooked and sold hot meals, especially on the day of a battle, when
ordinary arrangements for distribution and cooking of rations broke down.
For example, at Wagram, food and drink were largely unavailable at night

except from cantinières.[70] This scarcity led to price increases, but most soldiers were only too happy to pay. As one officer noted,

> A well-apprised cantinière always had a small reserve for the officers; she kept it for the Big Days, which doubled or tripled the importance of the service. What happiness, when one finds oneself on a plowed field, wet to the bones, and believing one has to go to sleep without supper, to encounter around a good fire a slab of ham or a bowl of hot wine, or better yet both, which would certainly be worth a lot more![71]

Not every cantinière was greedy, though. Some were more motivated by devotion to their regiment than to profit. As Sergeant Bourgogne said of one his cantinières, "Marie was a good sort, thinking nothing of herself, retailing her goods to the soldiers—to those who had no money as well as to those who had."[72]

As her common name under the First Empire suggests, the cantinière kept a canteen as one of her primary functions. On the march or on the battlefield, this would often consist only of the wagon or cart itself, with the cantinière dispensing drinks while standing in front of her vehicle or seated upon it. She could, if necessary, arrange a barrel of wine on the rear of the vehicle so that she could serve large numbers quickly. In camp, the canteen took on a less temporary nature, and the cantinière set up a large tent as a social center for the unit. Like the armies of the First Republic, Napoleon's armies carried no tents for shelter while on campaign, except for higher-ranking officers. Instead, French soldiers simply slept in the open in all sorts of weather. Not carrying tents or taking time to set them up allowed armies to travel faster. It also meant that any adverse weather left the soldiers miserably exposed to the elements. Outside of the Emperor's household, there were few tents except for those of the cantinières, so their importance as places of shelter is hard to overstate. Each cantinière's tent served as a gathering point and social center for the men of her unit, and cantinières did excellent business when the army camped for any period of time.[73] The canteen could even be organized as a restaurant and hold as many as a hundred drinkers, smokers, and gamblers.[74] In this way, cantinières provided for basic human needs such as food, shelter, comfort, and socialization. In an environment where all of these were scarce, it is little wonder they did so well financially, even if they often lost everything and lived out their retirement in poverty.

In garrisons in towns or cities, the canteen could become more elaborate, usually involving a rented, requisitioned, or abandoned building. In these cases, cantinières could offer their customers everything from drinks to excellent meals, and could serve them on real tables as well, as in the establishment of Esther, a cantinière of the Imperial Artillery Park in Vilna.[75] One French sergeant noted the ability of his regiment's cantinières to "get into good quarters," even in difficult circumstances.[76] When forced to live wretchedly in the field near Moscow, they complained bitterly against the emperor. A cavalry officer heard the regimental cantinières asking, "'When will he keep his promise, lounging around over there [in Moscow] with his Guard, leaving us here to die of cold and hunger?' 'Yes,' interrupted another. 'This Napoleon who promised us a mountain of gold and a beautiful country for winter quarters, he'll keep his promise no doubt when it is too late and we are long dead.'"[77]

Cantinières also acted as bankers. They were often the only members of a unit with ready cash to lend, and French officers were notorious for living beyond their immediate means. The cantinières' investment strategy took several factors into account. Loaning money to officers was a risk since they might be killed, in which case the debt would have to be written off. However, in war zones many cantinières saw a far greater risk in keeping large amounts of cash on their persons, since they were constantly at risk of being robbed by French stragglers or by enemy light cavalry. As one officer put it, "The risk of seeing several insolvent debtors die was for them less to fear than the Cossacks and bands of stragglers who often relieved them of their cash."[78] Cantinières protected their assets by loaning them out, using the interest from the survivors to pay for the losses from the dead.

Interestingly enough, enlisted men often gave money to their cantinières to hold for them during battle, fearing they might otherwise lose it if wounded and pillaged. Throughout the Napoleonic wars, soldiers as well as local peasants moved across the field during and after a battle, stripping the dead and the wounded alike of clothing and valuables, and the robbing of prisoners was considered a right of war. This was a widely accepted practice that offered soldiers the chance to make considerable sums, and thus provided a powerful motivation for fighting.[79] Because of this practice, many soldiers felt their cash would be safer in a cantinière's cart than on their persons. This provided cantinières with an interest-free supplement to other earnings, and allowed them to loan the same money out at interest to officers. If a debtor died, the loan was a loss, but if a depositor died, the money was forfeited to the cantinière, providing a balance. Speaking of her "investors," one cantinière laughed, "The good fellows! . . . I am their depository, often even their heir."[80]

Cantinières also served as fences for soldiers who looted civilian dwellings or enemy baggage trains. Pillaging was endemic in the Napoleonic
armies of all nations, and no primary account fails to turn up accounts of
outrageous license. Since looted goods were often heavy or cumbersome
and since carrying them at all entailed some risk of punishment, most soldiers were only too glad to trade them to a cantinière in exchange for a
drink or a meal. In this way, cantinières could come to possess a great variety of plundered goods, which they could later sell to civilian merchants.[81]
Despite the obvious risks, pillage was in fact the Napoleonic cantinières'
primary means of resupply, at least while in the field. Under the Republic,
vivandières of units on French soil received warrants that allowed them to
buy from civilians at reasonable prices "any and all merchandise of which
they have need," which was pillage thinly disguised by legal sanction.[82] During the First Empire, cantinières rarely bothered with such warrants. They
and the soldiers of their units simply took by force or coercion what they
needed from civilians in the war zone. French soldiers referred to all foreign
civilians as "peasants," regardless of their actual status, and viewed pillage
as almost a sacred right. Cantinières were active along with the soldiers,
and their pillaging activities were often even more extensive.

One officer witnessed a scene at Moscow where an armed cantinière
stationed herself at the city gate as civilian refugees fled. "With her wild
and sharp eye she surveyed the fugitives; then she searched all among them
who looked to her as if they might be carrying money or provisions."[83]
Similar behavior gave birth to a north German proverb that "it is better
to have four French soldiers [quartered in the house] than one Bavarian
soldier, but better ten Frenchmen than one Frenchwoman!"[84] Speaking
of the Russian Cossacks who robbed so many cantinières in 1812–1814,
Captain Blaze described them as "thieves who stole from other thieves."[85]
Cantinières did in fact run great risk of being robbed themselves. Stragglers might easily be tempted to prey on a cantinière separated from her
unit, and enemy troops nearly always robbed those they found. Sergeant
Bourgogne found one cantinière killed, stripped naked, and robbed during
the retreat from Moscow, though whether by Russians, French, or allied
troops was uncertain. He himself robbed another cantinière of a frying pan
so that he could cook his frozen food.[86] Sometimes even organized troops
from a neighboring unit robbed a cantinière, usually when there was some
dispute over prices involved.[87]

But pillaging does not imply that cantinières were a bad influence on
the army. Rather, they entered into a military society in which pillage was
not only common but viewed as justifiable and necessary. Although corps

and army commanders issued endless interdictions against pillaging and executed numerous individuals, the officer corps as a whole turned a blind eye toward the crime, and acknowledged it as a necessity in enemy countries during wartime.[88] In general, they preferred to see their men fed and clothed than to see regulations carried out, and in this sense, cantinières were helping the army, not hurting it. The common soldiers were even better disposed toward pillage and pillagers, and indeed it was often the soldiers themselves who supplied the cantinière with her goods. As one woman said,

> Everything that composes my baggage and my provisions didn't cost me one sou. The regiment gave it to me; it is the *grognards* who took my part at the last pillage, and it is to the *grognards* that I will sell these same provisions. They will find it just to pay because they did not take the trouble to conserve them and to transport them.[89]

This illustrates another of the cantinière's roles: transport provider. In the above case, private soldiers gave their cantinière stolen goods they could not carry, knowing that in a few days they might be glad to buy them back. In closer-knit units, cantinières sometimes allowed soldiers to use space in their wagons free of charge. The Grenadiers of the Imperial Guard used Madame Dubois' cart to carry alcohol and a huge silver punch bowl they had stolen. However, Madame Dubois did not always live up to the trust they put in her, as happened after the grenadiers brewed five barrels of homemade beer during a stay in Vitebsk. "On August 13 when we left the town, we still had two barrels of beer left; we put them under the care of Mother Dubois, our cantinière. The happy idea then occurred to her of staying behind and of selling the beer for her own profit to the men who were following us, while we, in the sweltering heat, were nearly dead of thirst."[90]

The ideas of ownership and of theft were somewhat flexible in the armies of Napoleon. Since goods were lost, found, abandoned, and seized by (or from) the enemy on a daily basis, and since owners died frequently and in large numbers, the line between "theft" and legitimate "scrounging" was often blurred. For example, in 1813, General Pajol's personal carriage was abandoned on the Leipzig highway during a Cossack attack. Some time later, Colonel Biot, the general's aide, spotted the carriage in Mainz. Inside, "sitting gravely and escorted by three or four sappers, a buxom vivandière was enthroned." When Biot demanded the return of the carriage, the vivandière insisted that "because they had found it abandoned on the highway, it was their legitimate property."[91] Biot eventually resorted to force, summoning a squad of infantry to eject the woman and her friends from the carriage. It is worth noting, though, that a lowly vivandière felt comfortable arguing with a full colonel simply because she felt that justice was on her side. Only *force majeure* decided the issue against her.

Contrary to modern expectations, neither Colonel Biot nor Mother Dubois' regiment took revenge. Biot saw the woman's point, but also knew that military law (and rank) was on his side. He did not punish the woman for theft; he merely ejected her from the carriage. Though they did not express the idea of a "transport fee" as explicitly as the anonymous cantinière above, the soldiers in Dubois' regiment obviously viewed the whole transaction as just. They had loaded the beer on Dubois' cart, she had sold it for her own gain, and that was that. She had outwitted them in a time-honored tradition of French peasants that was devious but understandable.[92] In fact, Mother Dubois and her regiment got along famously after the theft. Two months later, when the men threw a costume ball in Moscow using stolen clothes, they invited Mother Dubois. For a costume they handed her "a beautiful Russian national dress, and true to her trade, and knowing the full value of the clothes she wore (silk brocade in gold and silver), she went off without a word."[93] However inconvenient Dubois' larcenies may have seemed, the soldiers valued her as an inveterate scrounger, for they knew they were as likely to benefit as to suffer from her talent. This is not to say that soldiers always forgave cantinières. It was possible to push the troops too far, and Dubois clearly walked a very fine line. Girault's example of the cantinière left to drift down the Danube is evidence of what could happen to cantinières who stepped over that line.

Though officers were in a better position to exercise control over any items left with their cantinière for transport, some cantinières had an independent spirit that could lead them to defy even officers when plunder and profit were concerned. Captain Jean-Baptiste Barrès of the Chasseurs of the Guard stored a stock of provisions in his cantinière's cart during the Leipzig campaign, but went hungry anyway when the cantinière abandoned the unit in the rugged Bohemian mountains and purloined Barrès' supplies.[94] Instead of relying on his cantinière for transport, Surgeon-Major Louis Lagneau of the Second Regiment of Grenadier-Conscripts took no chances. He requisitioned her wine barrels so he could stock his ambulance with pillaged food and drink for the retreat from Moscow, allowing him "to live very well until Vilnius."[95]

This shows the extent to which cantinières were de facto members of the unit and subject to its control. Although legally their vehicles and goods were private property, the unit could and did requisition them when necessary. This sort of requisition took place only under extreme circumstances, such as the disasters of 1812 in Russia. For instance, when Colonel Pelet of the Forty-eighth Infantry Regiment could no longer ride or walk due to his wounds during the retreat from Moscow, his soldiers commandeered a cantinière's cart to transport him. Yet Pelet did not take the cart from the woman; he merely had her drive him, and "because I had nothing better to do to chase away my black thoughts, I set myself to chat with her in my best Polish."[96] When another cantinière of his regiment offered him her scarf as a bandage, Pelet went so far as to promise her payment for a replacement, though the woman refused to accept it.[97] Thus even in extreme circumstances officers usually recognized cantinières' proprietary rights; even so, some cantinières insisted on putting the welfare of their unit and its soldiers above their own profit and ownership by freely offering personal property to the men of their unit at no cost.

Despite the patchwork of traditions, precedents, unwritten rules, and assorted regulations, cantinières' duties and privileges as members of the regiment were never systematically defined before 1832, meaning that the entire Napoleonic period was one of ad hoc improvisation when it came to these women. Legally, cantinières' only duties were to be registered with the military authorities and to obey relevant military commands. Though the laws authorizing their existence did not specifically stipulate it, there was an understanding that they also had a duty to sell food and drink at reasonable prices, yet living with a combat unit on campaign raised more serious issues. Cantinières cared for the wounded during and after a battle, but not all entered the actual zone of fire. Cantinières could and did stay well behind the lines during combat. When Captain Parquin saw a fellow cavalry officer haunting the wagon of the Thirteenth Chasseurs' cantinière during the Battle of Salamanca, he remarked sarcastically, "You can rest easy, the cannon balls will not come this far to trouble you."[98] On the other hand, a cantinière of the 108th Infantry Regiment who always went into battle with the soldiers chided her more timid sisters "for not daring to do what she did."[99] Those who accompanied their regiments in attack and defense earned the respect and admiration of the soldiers. For example, the officers and men of the Fourteenth Light Infantry Regiment admired Catherine Beguin because she "was active, alert, jovial, indefatigable on the march, and intrepid under fire."[100] Nor was she the exception. Women fought and died in every major Napoleonic battle, and cantinières represented a large proportion of them. The emperor seems to have inspired a strong sense of devotion to the regiment and to the army, and a willingness to sacrifice among women and men alike.

Most cantinières restricted themselves to aiding the wounded and to distributing food and drink under fire rather than actually fighting in the ranks. However, cantinières could and did defend themselves when menaced, and evidence suggests that some habitually fought in the ranks, seeing themselves more as soldiers than as auxiliaries. In either case, casualties were often the result. After the French disaster at Leipzig, Colonel Biot wrote, "The road was covered with wounded vivandiers [the term covers both sexes], infantrymen, and cavalrymen."[101] And at Krasnoy in 1812, Colonel Pelet of the Forty-eighth Infantry Regiment lost both his remaining cantinières; one was killed outright, the other had her thigh pierced by a musket ball.[102] Other women, like blanchisseuse Elisabeth Chauvet, preferred to fight hand-to-hand with the enemy rather than to stay behind and watch.[103] Marie Tête-de-Bois served as a cantinière in the army of the Republic, then throughout the Imperial period in the Imperial Guard. One of her officers wrote, "Her place on a day of battle was at the most perilous point. . . . Marie knew how to fire her musket and follow up with a bayonet thrust."[104] Marie enjoyed fighting, and died in one of the last combats of the Guard at Waterloo. Most cantinières, though armed, only fought when necessary to defend themselves. Nevertheless, they were often excellent fighters, as many a would-be robber or captor found out. Madeleine Kintelberger, whom we met in the introduction to this book, was one such woman. Her assailants were surprised at the ferocity of the pregnant, wounded cantinière's resistance, and so was the Cossack who tried to rob the cantinière of the Neuchâtel Battalion when she fell behind the column after the battle of Leipzig. Sensing easy prey, the Cossack approached, whereupon the cantinière "produced her pistol and shot him out of the saddle. She rejoined the battalion mounted on the Cossack's horse, to the applause of all the column."[105]

Even cantinières who did not fight played important roles on the battlefield. Thirst could rapidly cripple a unit on the battlefield, leading to sluggish responses, poor morale, or even desertion and surrender.[106] One captain of the 108th Infantry Regiment later wrote, "Many cantinières were as brave as old grenadiers. My company's cantinière, Thérèse, carried brandy to the soldiers in the midst of cannon balls and bullets: she was wounded twice."[107] At Austerlitz, the cantinières of the Fourth Infantry and Twenty-sixth Light Infantry were noted for their actions when they "vied with each other to distribute brandy to the soldiers under fire, responding to those who offered money, 'You can pay me tomorrow!'"[108] Likewise, Catherine Baland of the Ninety-fifth Infantry Regiment charged forward at the battle of Chiclana when her unit engaged a British regiment. According to General Lejeune, she passed out drinks to the soldiers, saying to them "in a bright encouraging tone, 'Drink, drink my brave fellow; you can pay me tomorrow.' She must have known when she saw so many men falling around her that most of her debtors would not answer the roll-call the next day."[109] In the same vein, Elzéar Blaze wrote of Thérèse, "Don't believe that the hope of gain made her face these dangers. It was a sentiment more noble, because on battle days she did not ask for money."[110] Similar heroism gained recognition for a cantinière during the Polish campaign of 1807. When the Russian army launched a surprise attack on Marshal Ney's corps on June 5, the Fifty-seventh Infantry Regiment stood heavily outnumbered. One of the regiment's cantinières, Madame Cazajus, "in the heat of the action, brought free drinks to the skirmishers and carried away the wounded. She was told several times to retire, but she persisted in staying," despite "a hail of bullets" striking the position.[111]

Just as cantinières gained praise for bringing drinks under fire, they also gained a reputation as nurses. Eventually, it was considered one of a cantinière's duties to comfort the wounded and aid the surgeons, if not during a battle then certainly after it was over. This angel of mercy aspect of the cantinière's duties came to be more dominant as the nineteenth century progressed and as the public perception of women's place in society changed, but it was in its formative years during the First Empire and different women embraced it in different ways. Cantinières used their carts or wagons to carry the wounded, especially officers. This was particularly noteworthy during the disastrous retreat from Russia in 1812, when keeping hold of any kind of vehicle and team was a major accomplishment in itself. Captain Saur of the Eighth Chasseurs lost most of his thigh to a cannon ball near Moscow and his doom seemed certain. His friend later recalled,

> His return to France was almost a miracle. He was saved by the care and devotion of a cantinière of the regiment, who laid him in her cart. She succeeded in surmounting all the obstacles, all the privations, all the dangers of the retreat, and in bringing him back to his home.[112]

Cantinières were as likely to aid the sick, injured, or exhausted on the march as in battle. Nicolas Taunay witnessed one cantinière caring for a frostbitten soldier in the Alps in 1808, while "Mother Saracen" of the Fifty-seventh Infantry Regiment routinely put her wagon at the disposal not only of the wounded, but of soldiers exhausted from marching as well.[113] As a Dutch general in the French army recalled, in an often cruel male world, the cantinières "were much more human than we, and in the midst of indescribable suffering, gave testimony of their compassion and concern."[114]

Cantinières also cared for the wounded on the battlefield under fire. Sergeant Bourgogne described Mother Dubois' younger counterpart, a Belgian named Marie who served as cantinière in his regiment for four years:

> In every one of our battles she had shown herself most devoted in helping the wounded. One day she herself was wounded; it did not prevent her from going on with her help, careless of the risks she was running, for the bullets and the grape-shot were falling all around her.[115]

At Leipzig, Marie was finally hit seriously, though not fatally. She went on to fight in the defense of France in 1814 and at Waterloo, where she was taken prisoner. Likewise, Louis-Jacques Romand of the Eighty-first Infantry Regiment was wounded at Waterloo and witnessed the extraordinary efforts of his cantinière to care for the wounded even though she "received numerous bullets in her clothes that fortunately did not wound her."

> During the heat of the action, which didn't frighten her in the least, she did not content herself with thinking of her personal safety—other cares occupied her instead. She went from rank to rank to distribute brandy to the unfortunate wounded. . . . I myself received some from her hand. . . . She stayed on the battlefield until nightfall, always keeping the same sang-froid, the same attention for the wounded.[116]

And at Borodino a young Spanish cantinière of the Sixty-first Infantry Regiment took part in the fighting at the Great Redoubt, bandaging the wounded and giving them brandy until a Russian bullet smashed her hand. Soldiers carried her to the rear and the emperor's personal surgeon tended her wound.[117]

Sometimes cantinières had to act more aggressively to succor the wounded. Joséphine Trinquart, cantinière of the Sixty-third Infantry Regiment, saw her battalion commander wounded and about to be captured by two Cossacks; she killed both of them with a bayonet and used one of their horses to bring him back to the battalion.[118] A cantinière of the Twenty-sixth Infantry Regiment proved less violent but no less determined. When General Simon was badly wounded and captured at Busaco, his valet could not cross British lines to care for him since the British sentries shot at him each time he tried. According to General Marbot, the exasperated cantinière then loaded her donkey with medical supplies and crossed the battlefield, saying, "Let us see if the English are brave enough to kill a woman."[119] The English let her through and she tended the general for several days before returning to her unit.

Though the cantinière of the Twenty-sixth fared well, capture by the
enemy was a constant hazard for anyone traveling with the armies. During
Napoleon's wars, many French women languished in allied prison camps,
or on the notorious floating hulks of Portsmouth and Cadiz. These last
came mostly from the war in Spain, particularly from the infamous surrender of an entire French army at Bailén in 1808, which gave more than
fifteen thousand French soldiers and more than a hundred cantinières to
the enemy. Conditions in prisons of the era were harsh beyond imagining,
but most observers concluded that the women held up better under adver-
sity than the men did. Madeleine Kintelberger survived the loss of an arm,
multiple wounds, a trip through Russia in winter, and captivity on the
steppes for eight months, all while pregnant with twins, which she successfully delivered.[120]

Conditions on the Spanish prison hulks were even worse. Old ships without masts floating in the harbor at Cadiz, the hulks contained at times more
than fifteen thousand prisoners, with no sanitation and virtually no food or
water. One French sailor who spent time there wrote, "Of fourteen thousand that we had been, there were only eight thousand left, of which half
had scurvy and dysentery, the other half only scurvy. These two illnesses,
with their auxiliary typhus, made our hulks a terrifying tableau of destruction and of death."[121] The dead rotted where they lay, as the prisoners were
forbidden to throw them overboard. Food was so scarce that the French
quickly killed and ate their own pet dogs.[122] Henri Ducor noted, "It was
only the soldiers' wives and cantinières who held up well. It was a remarkable fact that we had several hundred with us, and that not one of them
was sick."[123] Instead of dying in droves, the cantinières generally occupied
themselves with nursing the sick and the dying. There were no wares to sell
on the hulks, so their usual profession was irrelevant. Ducor wrote that one
widowed cantinière was "consecrated day and night to the service of the
sick." Even giving birth to twins on board and taking care of them "did not
hinder her from seizing with alacrity every opportunity of making herself
useful to the prisoners when the poor state of their health required care."[124]

Once the French prisoners were transferred from the hulks to the deso-
late island of Cabrera in the Balearics, conditions improved slightly, but
new challenges arose. Trapped with thousands of men in desperate conditions, cantinières found new opportunities but also faced unwanted harassment. François Billon spent time as a prisoner at nearby Mahon. He wrote,

All the feminine population, composed of servants and old hags, offered no
attractions to this agglomeration of captives, with their coppery skin and

sordid clothing. A cantinière nevertheless made something of an exception to this group. Marguerite, with her big black eyes, would have passed for the Venus of Lazaret. Her adorers sometimes concentrated in a crowd so numerous around this divinity that, to clear out her temple, the goddess armed herself with a shovel and a broom.[125]

By the time Billon was transferred to Cabrera in late 1811, he reported that "four or five women made up all the feminine personnel of the island, and four or five thousand men were all more or less in love with them."[126] Cantinières therefore found themselves the only women that thousands of men had any hope of ever seeing. Occasionally this uncomfortable position could be turned to advantage. More than a year earlier, Robert Guillemard remarked that there were about twenty French, Italian, and Spanish cantinières on Cabrera when he arrived, suggesting that the number of women dropped dramatically from 1810 to 1811, though whether they escaped, were released, or died is unclear. He opened a theater and hired two pretty young women to play in his acting troupe. The theater proved an immense success, largely due to the allure of the actresses, and all concerned made a handsome profit.[127]

Conditions were appalling for most prisoners, however, and this led some to attempt escape. Madame Barreau of the Twenty-sixth Infantry was freed from a British hulk when the British government decided to return her to France as part of a prisoner exchange. She offered to smuggle her husband back to France with her in a large trunk. He was afraid and refused, so Madame Barreau took a French naval officer with her instead. "The escape succeeded thanks to the imperturbable sang-froid of the vivandière, while the fearful husband stayed on the hulk."[128] In a more desperate attempt, a cantinière and her sergeant husband participated in seizing the prison hulk *Argonaute* in Cadiz harbor. The prisoners, inspired by desperation, killed their guards, cut the anchor cables, and drifted the hulk toward shore in the dark, while English ships and Spanish shore batteries fired at them. The sergeant was cut in half by a cannon ball during the attempt, but the woman "got ashore with little more than a few rags of clothing."[129] Joseph Sabatier and his wife Catherine made a similar escape from the Cadiz hulks in 1810. Though they lost everything, they quickly reestablished themselves with their old regiment.[130]

Other cantinières were less fortunate, especially in areas of guerrilla activity. In Spain and Italy, French soldiers and cantinières who fell into the hands of the guerrillas were tortured and murdered.[131] Captain Parquin recalled a Spanish guerrilla leader known as "the curé," who disemboweled captured cantinières and left them by the roadside.[132] Likewise, Captain François wrote that he saw soldiers and cantinières alike, "ripped open from the groin to the stomach and with their breasts cut off."[133] The French army, used to relatively docile local populations, found it diffi- cult to adjust to anti-partisan warfare, and when traveling in small groups the soldiers often fell into ambushes. Jean-Baptiste Barrès recalled a few grenadiers and a cantinière who dropped behind, stopping in a village to pass the night. Next day, a guide led them into a prepared ambush; "there they were all murdered with refinements of cruelty."[134] Even outside the normal areas of guerrilla activity, peasants outraged by French army requi- sitioning or motivated by xenophobia sometimes attacked isolated detach- ments. Elzéar Blaze recalled going fishing with his comrades in a pond near Peterswald in Prussian Poland in 1807. Instead of fish, they pulled up the bodies of thirty-seven French soldiers and a cantinière, all murdered with hatchet blows and weighted down to sink to the bottom. They surrounded and searched the village, and upon finding French uniforms and weapons, "thirty-eight inhabitants of Peterswald were shot, and the village was burned to the ground."[135] It is worth noting that while the villagers murdered thirty-seven French soldiers, the French reprisal included thirty-eight vil- lagers: as far as Blaze and his men were concerned, cantinières were an in- tegral part of the French army, and the murder of a cantinière demanded vengeance.

For all the hazards involved in the job, many Napoleonic cantinières survived to retire. Some left the army because their husbands were killed, some because they themselves were disabled, and some due to old age. Often their final official act was to apply for a pension, and it was only then that many cantinières learned the true nature of their unofficial sta- tus. One of the biggest material losses cantinières suffered under Napoleon came in his revision of the pension laws in 1803. Prior to that date, the Directory's law of Fructidor, Year VI, had provided for a minimum pen- sion for widows of one hundred francs, and the law covered the wives of all soldiers who died on duty.[136] This law resulted in pensions that averaged 154F a year for all widows.[137] While still first consul, Napoleon ordered an investigation of all civil and military administrations, and the inspector's report on widows' pensions was reassuring: "The women are only a light obligation. There is little that needs to be done here. It suffices to see that the law of 14 Fructidor, Year VI, is scrupulously executed."[138] In 1803, how- ever, Napoleon embarked on a cost-cutting measure that drastically reduced widows' legal pension benefits. The new law of Floreal, Year XI, reduced the minimum annual pension amount to sixty francs, and paid pensions only to women whose husbands died in battle or died of wounds within six months. Since disease was by far the leading cause of death in all armies, most widows were now de facto ineligible for pensions. Even those who were eligible often received such tiny awards that they could not live on them, let alone support families. The average pension award for all widows under the new law was 219F, but for widowed cantinières the average was much less: a mere 107F a year, according to surviving records.[139] The discrepancy was due to the higher pensions paid to widows of officers, while cantinières were by definition married to enlisted men, whose widows received less money under the new law. Like the Republic before it, the Empire refused to recognize service as a cantinière as military service, and women were therefore not given military pensions except as widows of male soldiers.

Still, an integral part of the Napoleonic pension system was the extra-legal power of the emperor himself, and a few cantinières benefited from this. Just as the Bourbon kings had granted extraordinary bonuses to deserving widows, Napoleon liked to show special favor to certain individuals, in contrast to his miserly pension policy. An Imperial memorandum stated, "Military pensions are disbursed by the War Ministry according to rules prescribed by the laws. The lists are presented for approval to the emperor, who signs and occasionally augments them."[140] This meant that whatever the law read, Napoleon could and did grant pensions where no marriage existed or increase pensions on the basis of merit. While few cantinières benefited from his largesse, Madeleine Kintelberger was a notable exception. She lacked any real documentation of her marriage (it may well have been unofficial), but her heroic exploits and her terrible wounds inspired the emperor to grant her a widow's pension. The report from the head of the Pension Bureau argued that although "this unfortunate woman doesn't have a single one of the supporting documents required by the law," he recommended "the delivery of a report to the emperor to propose the award of a pension of 150F instead of the sixty-one that would come to her according to the law."[141] Even this was inaccurate. In order to qualify for her sixty-one-franc pension, she would have had to produce all the necessary paperwork, which she did not have. So, in reality, Kintelberger was facing the prospect of no pension at all. Instead, she received her 150F pension, as well as a supplementary fifty-franc emergency payment to support her until the paperwork could be completed. This was unheard of for the wife of a common soldier, but the heroic circumstances surrounding her capture and the strong support of General Rapp and Marshal Kellerman were enough to overcome her total lack of documentation.

Most widows were not so lucky. While Napoleon awarded 450F to Madame Rigollet when her husband died in Spain, and 225F to Madame Monthion when her husband died in Germany, many cantinières received nothing.[142] Elisabeth Chauvet, widow of two soldiers and herself seriously wounded in Italy, received no pension, since neither husband qualified as having been killed in battle, and Elisabeth's long years as a cantinière did not count as military service.[143] Even when widowed cantinières had proper documentation, it often took years to receive their pensions. Marie Hoccard was cantinière of the Forty-eighth Infantry Regiment when her husband was killed in 1807. She stayed on with the unit until she turned fifty-two in 1809. She then applied for a pension, but it took two more years for the War Ministry to process her application, during which time she claimed to be without resources.[144] Julie Huin of the Nineteenth Infantry Regiment faced even longer delays. Her husband died in 1802, and she applied for a pension in 1804. She did not receive her award of 122F until 1809, seven years after her husband's death.[145] The interminable paperwork for widows' pensions became legendary enough for Balzac to have a Napoleonic officer's widow still waiting for her pension in 1819 in *Père Goriot*. As Madame Vauquer says to the unfortunate woman, "Government departments never do come to the end of their red tape."[146]

Ultimately, the size of a pension and the speed with which the request was processed were largely determined by the importance of the woman's supporters. If the emperor himself felt moved, or if some other important personage acted on behalf of a widow, she could be assured of a speedy and positive outcome. Madeleine Kintelberger had two important officers plead her case, while the Imperial prefect of the Department of the Ourthe wrote three letters in support of Ann Horr's pension request.[147] Both women received their pensions quickly. Regimental commanders could also usually obtain quick action if they lent their influence to a widow's cause. The colonel of the Sixty-seventh Infantry Regiment wrote to the minister of war, "I call then all of the attention of Your Excellence to the situation of Madame Angot and her two children," and Angot received her pension in less than a year.[148] Those without influential supporters often waited years to receive little or nothing.

Not all cantinières ran into difficulties upon retirement. Some retired peacefully on their earnings and never figured in official pension records. One cantinière boasted, "With the money I've earned, I could set myself up with a place in the city," and many probably did so.[149] However, there is no way to tell how many Napoleonic cantinières retired comfortably, precisely because they were the least likely to leave any government records.

Many left the army in some hardship and returned either to their own or their husband's place of birth. When Boniface de Castellane was en route to Fontainebleau in 1809, he passed through a small village where he ran into an old acquaintance. "At the last post, a woman hugged me around the neck. It was Madame Dubois, wife of a sergeant, who fed us at Modena and Cremona. Her husband was dead, and this ex-cantinière had established herself at Chaily, her birthplace."[150] Castellane's use of the term "established herself" suggests the woman was running a business and therefore had done well as a cantinière, but he gave no further details. Elzéar Blaze related a happier story of a cantinière and her sergeant husband. When he was promoted to officer's rank, his wife gave up her cantinière's job, in keeping with her new status. The two lived out their years happily drinking and singing.[151]

Still, despite the happiness of a few, the First Empire ended unhappily for most cantinières. Those who braved the last battles in France received no pensions, no thanks, and no security. Marie Tête-de-Bois lost her husband of twenty years and her only surviving son in the final battles before Paris, where she herself was seriously wounded, but the deposed emperor could give her nothing, and the Bourbons were hardly likely to reward a fanatical Bonapartist.[152] Many never lived to see the final defeat. Napoleon's wars left millions dead across Europe, and numbers of them were cantinières, though the exact figures will never be known. Though cantinières had unparalleled opportunities for plunder and profit, they suffered from disease, wounds, peasant reprisals, imprisonment, loss of loved ones, and death from Portugal to Russia, and from Denmark to Egypt. Even if Napoleon wished to reward his most humble followers, after his defeat he could no longer do so.

Despite these rather dark personal prospects, however, cantinières as a group made a major achievement during the First Empire, even if as individuals they rarely reaped any long-term rewards. By their devotion, generosity, and bravery under fire, cantinières made a permanent place for themselves in the French army. Many of the men who served as junior officers from 1805 to 1814 served at the highest levels of command well into the 1850s, and their positive recollections of cantinières helped assure continuance of cantinières' service. Laurent de Gouvion-Saint-Cyr, who saw several of his closest friends rescued by generous cantinières in the retreat from Moscow, served as minister of war under Louis XVIII, and Lieutenant Boniface de Castellane, who fondly remembered Madame Dubois and the hot meals she served to him in his youth, became a Marshal of France and the trusted adviser to Napoleon III. These and other senior officers helped establish a firm tradition of cantinière service, and their published memoirs planted a positive image of cantinières in the public mind. France's collective memory apparently forgot the pillaging, the robbery, and the price-gouging that also characterized cantinières. Half a century later, young French officers who had not yet been born when Napoleon I abdicated consciously compared their own cantinières to the positive legends that came out of the wars of the First Empire.[153] While the French army underwent drastic reorganization and reduction in the years after Napoleon's downfall, cantinières remained an active and vital part of French military life until 1906, and subsequent war ministers regarded them as essential to the functioning of the army.

But how essential were they? Cantinières were valuable parts of the French military system of the late eighteenth and early nineteenth centuries. They supplemented the army's rudimentary logistics system, provided essential laundry and sewing services, and helped to prevent desertion by providing in camp what soldiers might otherwise desert to obtain: food, drink, tobacco, and female companionship. Their willingness to dispense alcohol to soldiers under fire also had a real military benefit. Since the role of the infantry in particular was often simply to stand firm under artillery fire, the ready availability of brandy helped keep men from breaking in situations where their natural instincts would have urged them to run. Cantinières also bore and raised children accustomed to army life, children who almost always followed their parents' footsteps into military careers. Especially in times when new soldiers were in demand, this contribution of high-quality recruits was extremely valuable to the army. So was the shelter that the canteen tents provided, if only temporarily, to the officers and men of the regiment. Some cantinières fought alongside the soldiers as well, and while this did not greatly augment the firepower of a given unit, it did provide a morale boost to those soldiers tempted to run from the enemy, and it showed a fierce devotion to duty beyond what was legally expected of cantinières. Finally, cantinières and their children provided a genuine family atmosphere in their regiments, which undoubtedly helped foster unit cohesion and build morale.

Taken together, these contributions to French military effectiveness were significant if not always precisely quantifiable. There is no doubt that cantinières represented valuable assets for Napoleonic field commanders, even if their unruly side presented some problems. Certainly, the armies could have replaced them with military or civilian male counterparts, although this would have involved a great deal of reorganization and disruption. In a purely theoretical sense, cantinières may not have been essential to the functioning of the army, as the Law of April 30, 1793, claimed. However, contemporaries believed them to be so, and historically that fact has much significance, as does the practical reality of their situation. In a largely male military world, soldiers, commanders, and politicians alike saw a widespread and vital role for women.

Christian Wilhelm von Faber du Faur, *In der Gegend von Semlewo
den 28. August 1812*. Note that this cantinière participating in the invasion of
Russia is dressed as a civilian woman, and not in distinctive military uniform.
Cantinière uniforms did not become widespread until the 1830s. She does have a
tonnelet, and the flamboyant top hat with a large colored scarf was typical of
cantinières of the First Empire. The goats tethered to the tail of her horse
constitute a mobile food supply.

Charles Joseph Henri Courtois d'Hurbal (1802–1876), *Prise d'Anvers*
(*The Capture of Antwerp*). Oil on canvas, 1832. The final stages of the assault
on the citadel. Close-range artillery fire lands in the French trenches. In the
center, a surgeon operates next to an artillery position. To the left,
a cantinière helps a wounded soldier

Musée du Château de Versailles et du Trianon.
PHOTO: Réunion des musées nationaux/Art Resource, N.Y.

Prise d'Anvers, detail. A cantinière bandages a wounded soldier's foot while under fire in a front-line trench. Note that a shell has just exploded behind her, knocking over the gabions and leaving red-hot coals in the crater. Her tonnelet is natural wood with the back end painted red. Her skirt is red, and her uniform jacket is dark blue. She wears a red scarf around her black hat.

Musée du Château de Versailles et du Trianon.
PHOTO: Réunion des musées nationaux/Art Resource, N.Y.

Edouard Moreau (1825–1878), *Soldier in Algiers*. Oil on canvas, c. 1845. This
chasseur à pied and his cantinière wife show the close resemblance between the
official regimental uniform and the feminine version patterned on it. Her tonnelet
is royal blue with gold trim and gold inscription. Its carry strap is decorated
with a hanging gold chain suspended from two gold hunting horns: the symbol
of the Chasseurs à Pied. Her uniform is dark blue. Note her white lace collar,
red and black cravat tied in bows, and wedding ring.

Musée de l'armée, Paris (Inv. 6777; Ec 338).
PHOTO: Réunion des musées nationaux /Art Resource, N.Y.

Horace Vernet (1789–1863), *Mme Bru, cantinière*. Oil on canvas, 1837.
Officially attributed to Edouard Moreau, this painting is signed "H.V. 1837"
and exhibits a very different style from Moreau's. Vernet traveled in North Africa
around this time, and was known to take an interest in cantinières. Mme
Bru is from the Seventh Hussar Regiment, so her equipment includes spurs and
a riding crop. Her tonnelet is red with gold lettering, her skirt and uniform jacket
are green with red accents, and her trousers are red with green accents. She wears
the brimmed *marinier* hat common to cantinières of the period.

Musée de l'armée, Paris (Inv. 1484; Ea 292).
PHOTO: Réunion des musées nationaux/Art Resource, N.Y.

Horace Vernet (1789–1863), *Siège d'Anvers* (*Siege of Antwerp*). Oil on canvas, 1840.
Marshal Gérard, in the presence of the Ducs d'Orléans and Nemours (center),
gives his orders for the attack on the citadel, December 22, 1832. To the left,
soldiers drink and warm themselves around a fire. To the right, a cantinière tends
to wounded soldiers (see detail).

Musée du Château de Versailles et du Trianon (Inv. MV2016).
PHOTO: Réunion des musées nationaux/Art Resource, N.Y.

Siège d'Anvers, detail. A cantinière (possibly Antoinette Mouron) aids the wounded as the final preparations for an assault are made, December 22, 1832. Her tonnelet is red, white, and blue. Her uniform jacket is dark blue, and her skirt and trousers are red with blue trim. She wears a black hat with the regimental number in gold, and a soldier's waterproof cape. She also wears a civilian lace bonnet under her hat against the cold. Two enfants de troupe (probably her sons) kneel to the left, watching the battle. Note that the wounded soldiers all head to her for help; she is effectively the regimental first-aid post. She holds a brandy bottle in her right hand, and the soldier standing in front of her is just tipping his glass to drink.

Musée du Château de Versailles et du Trianon (Inv. MV2016).
PHOTO: Réunion des musées nationaux/Art Resource, N.Y.

Roger Fenton (1819–1869), Crimean War: "Incidents of camp life." A French cantinière outside Sevastopol, Russia, in 1856. The first war photographer, Fenton was interested in cantinières and took several pictures of them. Note the exaggeratedly slim waist, probably the result of a corset purchased in the shops at Kamiesch. She wears earrings and carries a purse, but not a tonnelet. Under her lace cuffs is an undershirt of a very striking pattern. She holds a riding crop in her left hand, which is badly scarred on two fingers—evidence of her prior service in battle.

Musée d'Orsay, Paris.
PHOTO: Réunion des musées nationaux/Art Resource, N.Y.

Cantinière's tonnelet, 137th Infantry Regiment of the Line. 1870.
This tonnelet belonged to Mme Chevrau. It is painted in red, white, and
blue stripes, and is decorated with the regimental crest and number as well as
numerous flags. Mme Chevrau's name and position are hand-painted diagonally
at the lower left. This tonnelet is extremely unusual for its two compartments
with double taps and fill caps, allowing the cantinière to carry and dispense two
types of beverage. Whether these were two entirely different drinks or merely
two grades of the same beverage is unknown. The eye hooks at the top are
attachment points for a carry strap.

Musée de l'armée, Paris (Inv. Gb587; 9293).
PHOTO: Réunion des musées nationaux/Art Resource, N.Y.

Cantinière's tonnelet, Second Regiment of Voltigeurs of the Imperial Guard. Second Empire (1852–1870). With its single tap and elaborate artwork, as well as the cantinière's name boldly painted across the front, this tonnelet is much more representative than that of Mme Chevrau. The property of Mme Froideveaux, it carried brandy most if not all of the time.

Musée de l'Armée, Paris (Inv. Gb584; 186).

Image d'Épinal: Cantinière of the Imperial Guard, circa 1860. This
image was found in a Parisian flea market. At some point in the late
nineteenth century, someone carefully cut the image of this woman from
a larger lithograph, hand-cut a red velvet matte, then glued and sealed
the image into a gilt frame. This showed a strong desire to have an image
of the cantinière, but only her, without the soldiers of her unit who
were part of the original lithograph. Her tonnelet is red and white, while
her uniform is blue with red trim. She wears a black bearskin shako
with red plume and trim.

Author's collection.

DUBONNET

Dubonnet advertisement from *L'illustration,* 1939. This ad shows a "historical" progression of cantinières, projecting the women (and Dubonnet) as far back as ancient Greece. It also shows a medieval woman pouring a drink for a knight, and cantinières of the Old Regime, the First Empire, the Second Empire (most likely the Crimean War), and a colonial campaign of the Third Republic. The poem offers a theme common to ads using cantinières to sell food and beverages: that cantinières of all people know quality products, and that if they used a brand, a civilian consumer could count on its being a good product. The ad also shows a continuing fascination with and nostalgia for the era when women marched with their regiments, suggesting perhaps a general dissatisfaction with the lack of comfort in the new, all-male army. For more examples of cantinière art and advertising, visit http://www.cantinieres.com.

Author's collection.

CHAPTER 4

"Useful and Necessary"

Cantinières and the Constitutional Monarchies

FTER NAPOLEON I'S ABDICATION IN 1814, the restored Bourbon monarchy reduced the size of the French army dramatically. Opportunities for women to serve as cantinières became correspondingly rare. Coupled with the large number of experienced job seekers, this created fierce competition for the available positions. With the notable exceptions of the Hundred Days, the Spanish campaign of 1823, and a minor intervention in Portugal during its civil war, the French army undertook no active service for more than fifteen years. Even when French armies invaded Algeria in 1830 and fought continual low-intensity wars against guerrilla forces, the numbers of combatants remained small, as they did during France's brief intervention in Belgium in 1832. Given this sharply reduced military establishment and the lack of actual field service, it is little wonder that even those interested in the history of cantinières have ignored the period of the Bourbon Restoration and the July Monarchy. Nonetheless, though dull in comparison to the glory of the First Empire before it and the glitter of the Second Empire after it, the era of the constitutional monarchies was an important period for cantinières, and one that merits careful study. After all, it was the radical revolutionaries of the Convention who shaped the modern cantinière tradition in 1793, while the wars of the First Empire had given a distinctly Bonapartist tinge to that tradition. For the restored Bourbons to have retained cantinières at all was a testimony to a strongly perceived need for their services, strong enough to outweigh a considerable tradition of service to treasonous causes. Rather than eliminating cantinières as relics of the Age of Revolution, the Bourbon regime retained them in numbers proportional to the new reduced army, and this alone suggests that the government saw them as important

military assets. The monarchy did make one significant change; it reinstated the Old Regime title of "blanchisseuse," all but wiped out in practice
by the regulations of 1793 and 1801. The new Bourbon regime also tended
to revert to the usage of "vivandière"—with all its Old Regime connotations—rather than the more modern "cantinière" that had become common during the Empire. However, the older term was more prevalent in
official documents than in common usage, especially among Napoleonic
veterans. Women continued to play an important role in the daily sustenance of the new Royal Army, and on those rare occasions when that army
marched to war, its female auxiliaries went with it.

One of the first acts of the newly restored Bourbon monarchy in 1814
was to disband much of Napoleon's army. Thousands of officers with long
careers were placed on half-pay and retired. Many more common soldiers
were let go without recompense of any kind. While this policy resulted in
some mutinies, for the most part it was handled peacefully. The French
army was soon only a shadow of its former self. Cantinières were among the
many "licenciés," as the discharged personnel were called, and the government provided no recompense whatsoever for their service. This reduction
was necessary if France was to pacify the victorious allies and move back
to a peacetime military establishment, but it led to a great deal of grum-
bling and discontent, particularly among the now unemployed soldiers and
their wives. Those soldiers who remained in uniform also chafed at the lack
of respect they received from the new government and from their new aristocratic officers, many of them émigrés who had served France's enemies
during the recent wars.

Thus, when Napoleon returned from exile in March 1815, he found many
of his old soldiers ready to support his cause. Commanders who remained
loyal to the king often found their junior officers and soldiers unwilling to
follow orders.[1] Some cantinières were among the returned emperor's most
enthusiastic supporters, and in several cases they helped carry the common
soldiery into the Bonapartist camp. Guillaume de Peyrusse described one
of the more memorable sights amidst the general acclaim for Napoleon at
Grenoble, site of a crucial early test of the emperor's viability. All the cantinières of the city's garrison marched out to meet the emperor, singing a
song of their own composition, "Nous avons des pommes / pour le Roi de
Rome."[2] Napoleon himself was uncertain of the outcome of his adventure
until after his triumphant entry into Grenoble, saying, "As far as Grenoble
I was nothing but an adventurer. At Grenoble I was a prince."[3] Meanwhile,
in different parts of France, each soldier and each regiment had to decide
whether to join with the emperor or to oppose him. Many cantinières

showed steadfast loyalty to the emperor, and some acted aggressively and effectively to aid his cause. One soldier described a scene near Lyon on the thirteenth of March when his unit heard of Napoleon's return:

> Some laughed, some cried. On all sides there were frenetic outpourings of emotion, felicitations given and received a thousand times. The vivandières, elated by so much enthusiasm, no longer sold liquor, they gave it away and so fanned the flames.[4]

Thus, in at least two of Napoleon's crucial early encounters with Royal Army troops, the women of the regiments did what they could to push the troops over to the Imperial cause. Later, when the Imperial armies reassembled, many cantinières returned to Paris, some from outside France's borders, to join the emperor's cause once again. Many of these women fought later at Waterloo, and a good number were killed, wounded, or captured.[5] Marie Tête-de-Bois was one example. Left destitute by the restoration and forced to work as a laundress in Paris, she eagerly returned to the colors in 1815 and received a position as cantinière in the Imperial Guard. She was wounded at Fleurus in the thick of the first fighting, but continued to serve. Once defeat was imminent at Waterloo, she preferred death in the final stand of the Old Guard rather than a return to France in disgrace.[6]

Such actions could not escape the notice of the Bourbons. After Louis XVIII returned to Paris in June 1815, the War Ministry set about transforming the army by renewing the enforced retirement of soldiers and civilian employees. The decree of June 18, 1815, concerning civilian employees gave half-pay pensions only to male employees, and only to those of fairly high rank. Cantinières were to receive nothing.[7] At the same time, the army let go of large numbers of cantinières incidentally when it disbanded numerous French regiments after Napoleon's second abdication. Along with thousands of soldiers, hundreds of cantinières suddenly found themselves unemployed, unwanted, and under suspicion. They received no severance pay, travel money, or any other form of assistance, and for some, this was as much of a hardship as any they had endured on campaign. Many of these women had known no life other than with the army, which may have explained why such women as Marie Tête-de-Bois were willing to die in hopeless combat rather than try surviving in civilian life. Even those who were originally born civilians had often served for ten or twenty years and had lost all contact with their former lives. Many were also foreigners, and some, like Madeleine Kintelberger, could barely speak French. Trapped in the heart of France with no money and no friends outside the army, these reluctant civilians had to try to make a living in a strange and often hostile environment where poverty was already endemic and jobs scarce. In some monarchist parts of France, notably the south and west, the so-called "White Terror" offered another danger. Royalist mobs dispensed vigilante justice to those who had served Napoleon, and it was often unwise to admit to having been part of the Imperial army.[8]

In units that still existed, the army dismissed cantinières who were loyal to Napoleon and replaced them with women of known monarchist sympathies. This was generally carried out by local garrison commanders, but the competition for cantinière posts was so fierce that the concerned parties often brought their cases before the minister of war. For example, at the end of 1815, Madame Maire, cantinière of the Fort de Goux at Besançon, lost her post to Madame Charlet. Madame Maire had been a cantinière under Napoleon, while Madame Charlet was the recently widowed wife of a royalist officer. The director of engineers at the fort, Colonel Marion, defended Madame Maire in a letter to the minister of war. He claimed that she had been the victim of false rumors impugning her loyalty, and argued that she was in fact loyal to the king.[9] Ultimately the minister sided with Madame Maire, who was reinstated, but the implications of the case were serious. First of all, political loyalties were now a factor in choosing and expelling cantinières. Moreover, if Madame Charlet's claim had set a precedent, cantinières might have been drawn not from common soldiers' wives but from officers' widows. The shift in social status, and therefore in political sympathies, would have been enormous, seriously lowering the prestige and social status of the officer corps. This would have been an unsatisfactory arrangement for the enlisted soldiers as well, since they could hardly be expected to socialize comfortably with the wife of an officer, and their own wives would lose the opportunity to serve in the posts. In these ways, this change went against all tradition, and the War Ministry probably rejected it for that very reason, though it is most likely that the implied drop in officers' wives' status was the decisive factor. Madame Daubigny of the Rue de Grenelle Barracks in Paris was less fortunate than Madame Maire. Given her sedentary post in 1804 by Napoleon as a reward for her loyal service as a cavalry cantinière, Daubigny lost her job in 1817 when a regiment of the Royal Guard came to the barracks with their own royalist cantinière. Madame Daubigny was the widow of a sergeant and had a son in the Regiment of Chasseurs de Berry. She had served faithfully in her post for thirteen years, and for another decade before that as vivandière, but she was also sixty years old and politically suspect. She appealed to the minister of war, but in vain, and the Guard turned her out.[10]

Many women who had received pensions from Napoleon or from the Republic also lost these in 1815 as part of a general reduction of pensions granted under the Empire. Marie Dieulevant was a cantinière until 1807, when her husband was killed and she received a pension from the emperor. In 1815, the new government revoked her pension. Unable to obtain any help by mail, she made the long journey from Grenoble to Paris, where she begged for help from various government officials. She was sixty-nine years old and supported two children. The monarchy was not interested in her service to Napoleon, however, and she received nothing.[11] Likewise, Marie Bory was the widow of a sergeant and vivandière of the First Regiment of Carabiniers until her husband's death. After Waterloo, the Bourbons eliminated the pension she had received from Napoleon since 1804, and she too was reduced to begging for help. At fifty, she had three sons serving in the army, owed three months' back rent, and had pawned or sold even her furniture and clothing to pay her bills. However, the War Ministry once again refused to honor her pension for service under governments it considered treasonous and illegitimate.[12]

Women first applying for their pensions in the opening years of the Restoration also faced a strange quandary. They were applying to the monarchy for recompense for their services to the monarchy's enemies. This required a certain vagueness of language as well as delicate phrasing, and even so, women often lost their appeals. Catherine Sabatier, who served as cantinière for thirty-one years for three governments, tried to obtain a pension immediately after being discharged from the French army in 1815. Her letter to the king stated that she had "three sons serving in the Royal Army" without mentioning that they had all served Napoleon before that. It related that "she lost two husbands and her father killed in battle," but never once used the words "Empire," "Republic," "Napoleon," or "Revolution." In effect, the letter from Catherine Sabatier and the supporting letter from the commander of the Bordeaux garrison worked on a concept of service to the state through the army that assumed she had some higher loyalty to the nation beyond that of any particular government. Such pragmatism was necessary for women to serve as they did in an era of constant warfare and political instability, and in this sense Sabatier's careful language simply reflected her own truth. It also paralleled Sabatier's personal life. She had served successively the Old Regime, the Republic, and the Empire, living the hard life of a cantinière for more than three decades. She had loved and lost at least two husbands, and marriage took on a higher meaning that transcended any individual husband, just as the state took on a higher meaning that transcended any individual government. In effect, Catherine

Sabatier was loyal to the army, regardless of what government directed it, and she was a faithful wife, regardless of who her husband was. Despite her rhetoric, the War Ministry denied her pension request, although the sympathetic garrison commander gave her fifty francs from his own pocket.[13]

This atmosphere of revenge did not last long, however. By 1818, the mood at the War Ministry had mellowed considerably, and Gouvion-Saint-Cyr's accession to the post of minister of war in 1819 helped accelerate the change. A Napoleonic veteran with positive memories of cantinières, Gouvion-Saint-Cyr went out of his way to help women obtain or regain places with the army. While his successors repudiated this policy, nothing like the toughness of the years 1815–1816 returned. Instead, the Bourbon War Ministry dealt with issues as they arose, and the army's cantinières served drinks, cooked food, and washed clothes peacefully in garrison. With no wars to fight, cantinières stayed in barracks and had little need for the elaborate traveling gear of their recent past. Except for a brief interruption in 1823, this pattern continued until 1830.

Despite the scarcity of positions and the sometimes hostile attitude of the War Ministry, many women sought appointments as cantinières or blanchisseuses, but few received them. The small size of the army meant that there were far fewer posts available than there had been under Napoleon. Women who held the few available posts passed them down to their daughters, so that many of the cantinières who later served the Second Empire were born in army canteens during the 1820s, '30s, and '40s.[14] But the appeal of the jobs continued, and may have been stronger in some ways now that prolonged peace seemed likely. Chances for pillage were rare, but the new army offered stability, safety, and relative comfort compared to the life of the bivouac under Napoleon. In addition, there were thousands of unemployed cantinières waiting to fill the few available posts. Indeed, demand was so high that many women sought to bypass the crowds by applying for jobs directly to the minister of war or even to the royal family.

For example, Madame L'Archevêque was born in the Royal Army in 1782 and began serving as a blanchisseuse in 1792. She married a soldier and served as cantinière of the Ninety-second Infantry Regiment until 1815, though her husband died in 1814. Finding herself suddenly cashiered after Waterloo and with two children to support, she asked not for a pension but for a position as blanchisseuse with one of the newly organized legions, a position "she so well merited for her thirty years of service." She received a sympathetic response, but the war minister could not place her in her desired position. He did offer to place her two children as enfants de troupe, "if she was married legitimately to Sergeant L'Archevêque and if it is true that she finds it impossible to provide subsistence for her children."[15]

After Gouvion-Saint-Cyr took over the War Ministry in 1819, his desire to help former cantinières in need became a factor. When Madame Decker wrote to him in 1819, she was the widow of a sergeant, an ex-cantinière, and the mother of six. One of her sons served in the Legion of the Tarn et Garonne, and she wished to serve there as a blanchisseuse in order to support her other children. Gouvion-Saint-Cyr wrote to the legion's commander in the misleadingly polite language of the Old Regime, "I can only invite you to have regard for the demands of this *militaire,* if nothing is opposed to it."[16] His use of the word *militaire* instead of *employée* is particularly intriguing; it suggests that he saw cantinières as regular and legitimate members of the army. He took an active interest in numerous other cases, but he lost his position in 1820 due to political intrigues, and his successor remained aloof from such matters, seeing Gouvion-Saint-Cyr's behavior as "interfering in the details of the interior administration of units."[17]

Women who waited until after the White Terror to reapply for lost pensions also received a fairer hearing. Jeanne Billers served as vivandière in the Twenty-third Demi-brigade starting in the Year V, and went on to serve the Empire until 1812, when her husband was killed in Russia. She wrote to the War Ministry in 1820 asking for a reinstatement of her widow's pension of 150F, which the government had discontinued in 1815. Able to prove her legitimate marriage, her service, and her husband's death with a well-documented application, she took advantage of the new mood of tolerance to press her case. The war minister hesitated at first, consulted the minister of finance, and finally obtained the king's permission for the renewed pension.[18]

The massive dislocation caused by military cutbacks and the difficulty in obtaining or retaining pensions meant that cantinières in the first half of the nineteenth century tended to be either old-timers or their daughters. Some new cantinières still came from civilian backgrounds, but they were comparatively rare. Most were either born in the army or were ex-cantinières desperately seeking an escape from poverty through return to the familiar military life. These latter women tended to join the army in the first five years after Waterloo, though some of them stayed on into the second half of the century. Interestingly, the French army apparently incorporated Spanish women as cantinières during the Spanish campaign of 1823. Theophilus Conneau, a slave trader imprisoned at Brest in 1833, met two "Spanish women, wives of musicians of the corps who having heard that several Spaniards had been incarcerated in the tower, had availed

themselves of the opportunity to visit their countrymen. These two Cat-
alonian women had married in this regiment when the Duc d'Angoulême
marched with French troops into Barcelona and had followed their husbands ever since."[19] Thus, even in an era that saw fierce competition
among French women for cantinière posts, even the most minor of foreign
interventions brought in at least some foreign-born cantinières. This suggests that armies on campaign had not only a very high need for women's
services, but a concomitantly low propensity to follow established peacetime channels in obtaining them.

Escape from poverty was a powerful motive for many would-be cantinières. Madame Decker was widowed and burdened with five young
children to support. Having known only army life before 1815, she was at
a disadvantage in the civilian work force. She begged the colonel of her
son's legion to hire her as a blanchisseuse so she could "support the existence of her numerous family with her work."[20] Many of the women trying to obtain commissions were the wives of new volunteers or draftees,
but the same motives often drove them. Living alone while their husbands
served in the army imposed emotional and financial burdens on them, and
they hoped both to support themselves and to be near their husbands.
Geneviève Bouquet was the wife of a draftee and applied for a position as
"blanchisseuse or vivandière" in the Fourth Regiment of the Royal Guard.
She had a three-month old son and felt the need "to put myself to work
to provide for his nourishment."[21] Françoise Verier was also the wife of a
draftee. She argued that she needed a cantinière position not to escape
poverty but to support her husband. "I don't pretend at all, Monseigneur,
to be a burden to my husband. A soldier cannot come to the aid of his
wife. On the contrary, my intentions in making myself close to him are to
do the most possible to soften his lot by my work."[22]

Letters such as these make clear that cantinière posts were still highly
sought after. For new civilian women to break into the few available posts,
drastic action was often necessary. In some cases, soldiers refused to enlist
unless their wives were made cantinières. Celestine Gressier's husband
joined the Legion of the Lower Seine with the explicit understanding that
his wife would be a cantinière. Soon afterward, the legion's colonel replaced her with another woman. Celestine would not give up, though: she
wrote to the minister of war in 1819, and he had her restored to her place.[23]

The assorted intrigues, agreements, pleas, and influence-peddling vary in
their details, but they all point to one conclusion: that in a time of scarcity
of positions, women and their male protectors fought with determination
to obtain or keep jobs as cantinières. Certain political considerations played

their part as the Bourbons tried to assure the loyalty of the army, but the key point is that even after the army's defeat in battle, even after the horrors of guerrilla war in Spain and the terrible frozen retreat from Russia, French women still coveted cantinière and blanchisseuse posts. The army's small size and the lack of battle casualties kept the number of available posts small until 1830, and this, combined with the large numbers of unemployed ex-cantinières seeking positions, assured that there would be sharp disagreements over who would serve. Once the French army was actively on campaign again and the older generation of women died out or found other careers, more opportunities became available, though conditions of service in Algeria were considerably less attractive than those of service in a peacetime garrison in France.

The French invasion of Algeria in 1830 was intended to be a temporary punitive expedition that would gain popularity for the government of Charles X and distract the French public from domestic political issues, but the Revolution of 1830 swept Charles from his throne within days of the army's successful attack on the city of Algiers. After much deliberation, the new government of Louis-Philippe decided to remain in Algeria and to conquer and pacify the country. This decision had far-reaching effects on many aspects of French society, including the cantinière corps. The realization that a French army would be in Algeria more or less permanently made it apparent that army wives would want to be with their husbands, and the government soon took action to make this possible. More important in the long term, the creation of the Army of Africa resulted in a separate military society in Algeria that was French in origin but that had its own unique outlook, moral code, and culture, and often saw itself as above the law.[24] At the same time that this separate military entity was developing, the overall number of cantinière posts increased, and the stigma of having supported Napoleon lessened and eventually disappeared.

The Algerian conflict was small compared to the wars of Napoleon I, but though it was not a glorious war in the grand European tradition, it was the only war the French army had, and for better or for worse it was the background against which military careers were played out in the years 1830–1854. It featured some pitched battles and sieges, but mostly it involved the employment of regular French troops against highly mobile guerrilla armies. At times, the French faced first-class leaders and troops, such as Abd el-Kader and his regular forces. Mostly, however, the French fought against tribesmen who were highly skilled in ambush and close combat, but whose understanding of larger military principles was limited. Unfortunately for the French, their own military leadership and doctrine proved hopelessly inadequate to the pacification of a hostile country, and France suffered numerous setbacks and defeats in the early years of its involvement in Algeria. Only the innovative and brutal leadership of Thomas Robert Bugeaud in 1841–1848 allowed the French to dominate their enemies, but even this did not win their love, only their submission.

The first years of the French effort in Algeria were marked by failure and stagnation. From 1830 to 1841 the French adopted a policy of garrisoning fortified camps and towns, leaving the initiative largely to their Algerian enemies. When the French did take the offensive, they employed large, sluggish columns encumbered with heavy artillery, and baggage wagons that had poor mobility in Algeria's rugged mountains and deserts. Infantrymen carried extremely heavy loads, and hundreds died or were incapacitated by heat stroke and inadequate medical care.[25] Pack animals were entrusted to Algerian mercenaries who often deserted at the first sign of trouble, and disease, demoralization, and suicide were rampant among the troops. Under these circumstances, the French suffered a series of defeats, notably the disastrous Battle of the Macta River in 1835 and the abortive attack on Constantine in 1836.[26] In the first, a French force of 2,500 under General Trézel was surrounded and badly mauled by a native force led by Abd el-Kader. The French were hampered by poor leadership, weak discipline, and a large and cumbersome supply and artillery train that became almost immobile in the difficult terrain. The survivors fled in panic, making this one of France's worst defeats. The next year, a winter expedition to Constantine had to turn back due to bad weather and lack of supply, leaving the hungry French soldiers to retreat through snowy mountains over poor paths. Hundreds died of hunger, exposure, and disease.[27]

However, in 1841 Thomas Bugeaud became governor-general of Algeria. Bugeaud's early military career involved anti-guerrilla operations in Spain in the years 1807–1814, and he applied the lessons he learned there to Algeria. Bugeaud abandoned many of the fortified camps, thus freeing more troops for offensive operations. He also eschewed cumbersome columns with baggage and artillery that were more suitable for European warfare than for guerrilla operations in the Algerian wilds. Instead, he formed troops into small flying columns devoid of heavy artillery or transport. Rations were carried by mules, and the mules were handled by French volunteers. Bugeaud's strategy was to substitute speed, surprise, mobility, high morale, and individual firepower for numbers. The results were impressive, and these remained the tactics of the French army for the rest of its stay in Algeria.[28] With a French army again engaged in ongoing operations, French cantinières once again rode into battle with their canteen carts or pack horses, aided the wounded, sold drinks, fought with the enemy, and were themselves killed and wounded.

As if in recognition of the changing situation, the new regime of Louis-Philippe set out in its early years to redefine the duties and structure of the army, including cantinières. In March 1831, the War Ministry ordered that wives and children of military personnel were to be given free passage to Algeria on French ships, an indication that the government already viewed the Algerian occupation as permanent even at this early date.[29] But while this was an important (and welcome) regulation for soldiers' families, orders issued the following year proved more important still. The king and his war minister set out to rationalize the whole legal structure concerning women and children in the army. As the minister put it in April 1832, "I realized that it was indispensable to bring together the numerous decisions handed down over the last thirty years on this matter, and to make such changes as experience renders necessary."[30] The new regulations, issued April 14, 1832, fixed the number of "blanchisseuses-vivandières" and enfants de troupe allowable in each regiment, battalion, squadron, or detached company of each arm. Notably, now that the army was actively on campaign again, the separate blanchisseuse was once again eliminated in favor of an all-purpose female auxiliary. The limit was four women per infantry battalion, and one per cavalry squadron. Even disciplinary companies (penal units) were allotted four women each, while certain companies of veterans could have up to eight. The regulation stated that "the number of women attached to each unit must never exceed that determined by Article I. Commanders will not grant any marriage permission that would result in this complement being exceeded."[31] This is noteworthy since it implies that the July Monarchy saw it as the right of *all* army wives to find employment with the army. This was a new concept that not even the Convention had considered— that soldiers and their wives had a right to be together, and that the army therefore had a duty to employ the wives. Whereas the Convention had affirmed the soldier's right to marry but denied his wife's right to be with him, and the Directory, Consulate, and Empire had denied both rights, the July Monarchy denied the soldier's right to marry but insisted that those who did should have their wives with them, and that those wives should "be useful to the regiment."[32] Whether this represented a growing recognition of the importance of the family or merely the practical considerations of fighting a prolonged overseas colonial war is debatable. However, like so much of the legislation of 1832, it marked a distinct break with the recent past, and showed that the July Monarchy was serious about making important and far-reaching military reforms.

Ambiguities in the April 14 ordinance led to a clarification from the minister of war only four days later. He had received numerous requests concerning specific applications of the law, indicating that many more women were serving as cantinières than the regulation allowed. The minister made it clear that the king had no wish to throw women out on the street, as the Convention had done in 1793 and the Bourbons had done in 1814–1815, but he also made clear that commanders were under no obligation to fill their allowed complement of women. "The ordinance is not at all retroactive. Women who are found to exceed the number determined may be kept on, but they will have no right to either lodging in military buildings or bedding." While this was lenient beyond precedent, the minister was not anxious to see the army become a haven for women.

> Only women useful and necessary to the well-being of the troop can be admitted. Commanders are moreover to understand that there is no obligation to fill the complement of blanchisseuses-vivandières, nor enfants, and that in all cases where they assure adequate service without attaining the limit, their duty will be accomplished.[33]

Having settled on numbers and requirements, the minister then turned to duties and responsibilities. New regulations for armies on campaign had not seemed urgent under the Bourbons, when campaigning was decidedly the exception. After 1830, however, with campaigning in Algeria a constant reality, the War Ministry issued a comprehensive set of regulations in May 1832.[34] In keeping with its mission to group together past regulations and to improve upon them, the new ordinance for the first time laid out in one place the responsibilities and duties of military women. Women who wished to "exercise any profession whatsoever following the army" would have to apply to the commander of the military police, who would issue them a *patente*. "They are obliged to prove their good conduct and their talents."[35] Regimental cantinières could effectively bypass this system by obtaining a *patente* directly from their regiment's council of administration, but those serving as cantinières to a headquarters could not. All cantinières would receive a metal plaque with their job designation and their *patente* number. They were required to wear this plaque prominently on their persons and have another plaque giving this information and their unit number on any vehicle they used.

But unlike earlier regimes, the July Monarchy did not lose interest once it had dealt with the screening and licensing of cantinières. The new ordinance went so far as to ensure the utility of cantinières to the troops and the exclusion of bad influences by regulating cantinières' conduct on the job. The military police and headquarters staffs were charged to ensure that "the comestibles and liquids that the vivandières and cantinières supply are always of good quality, in sufficient quantity, and at the lowest possible price. They will take into account in this last regard the favorability of the circumstances and locality for provisioning."[36] Although the last line provided some flexibility in pricing, here for the first time was an army-wide regulation laying out business guidelines for cantinières. Senior officers' memories of the outrageous prices some cantinières charged under the First Empire no doubt inspired this provision.

The widespread involvement of the First Empire's cantinières in pillaging and trafficking in stolen goods inspired another change to the cantinière regulations. Commanders were ordered to make frequent searches of all non-military vehicles accompanying their units "to prevent them from transporting other objects than those which they should contain." Without saying the word "pillage," this clause clearly aimed at preventing cantinières from becoming mobile clearing houses for stolen goods as they had during the First Empire. As if to leave no doubt about who the culprits were, the regulation ordered "battalion commanders, adjutant-majors, and adjutants to be especially charged with using severity in this regard against their units' cantinières."[37]

Those who transgressed the rules were subject to severe punishment. Cantinières who defrauded soldiers were subject to confiscation of their goods, suspension of their *patentes,* and expulsion from the army, "none of which would protect them from making restitution, nor from other punishments they could incur for fraud." Unauthorized cantinières and prostitutes (which the army often saw as one and the same) also received some attention. Any women found following the army without authorization "will be taken before the provost of the division, who, after having condemned them, will impose a fine of fifty francs and send them from the army, without protecting them from any punishment more severe if it is judged that they introduced themselves there with bad intentions."[38]

It is difficult to judge to what extent the French army carried out the letter of this law. In Algeria at least, pillage became so institutionalized that it became almost impossible to prosecute those responsible. Indeed, under Bugeaud's leadership, the theft or destruction of Arab property became an integral part of French strategy, making heroes out of those who were thieves and vandals.[39] Few records on cantinières have survived from the 1830s, but those that have suggest that troops in the field were more interested in assuring their own comfort (and hence that of their cantinières) than in scrupulously observing regulations. For example, in 1836 the minister of war wrote to the military intendants of a number of "flagrant abuses" of the military supply system. Among them were the provisioning of blanchisseuses, cantinières, and their children with rations and fodder during military marches.[40] In 1839, the minister forbade sergeants' wives from serving as "vivandières or blanchisseuses." This prevented sergeants from ordering men to purchase non-essential supplies or from coercing men into not reporting price-gouging and any other illegal business practices of their wives.[41] However, while no record exists of this regulation being repealed, it is clear that it was not followed in practice. Wives of sergeants continued to serve throughout the nineteenth century and into the twentieth, and the army as a whole appears to have simply ignored this regulation, as well as others that prohibited wives of soldiers in specific positions or ranks from acting as cantinières.

But bad influences continued, and not all of them came from sergeants' wives. Madame Romieu of the Thirtieth Coastal Artillery Company, stationed in Toulon, provided a case in point. The illegitimate wife of a professional draft replacement and malingerer, she proved to be a troublesome influence in her unit.[42] Her origins are unknown. The War Ministry knew only that "she is a cantinière who followed Gunner Romieu, and who has constantly turned him from his military duty, to the point where he no longer renders any useful service to the unit, and he is even dangerous by his example of immorality and by his statements against his superiors, which have brought him frequent punishments." Gunner Romieu himself brought disparagement from his commanders because his three enlistments between 1828 and 1840 were all as a paid replacement for draftees. "Thus there are three replacements this man had made since 1828: he has made a career of them. He attaches himself to some officer so as to serve no duties and to have his time free to help his wife run a cabaret where the young soldiers go and are lost."[43] But his commanders did not see the gunner himself as the problem. Rather, they decried the bad moral influence of his cantinière wife. To solve their problem, the officers of the company transferred Romieu to another unit on France's Atlantic coast and expelled Madame Romieu from her position as cantinière, since her husband was no longer part of the unit.

Not one to accept defeat easily, the cantinière wrote a letter to the queen, claiming that she was Romieu's wife of seventeen years and had two children, and asked that for the children's sake her husband be transferred back to Toulon. Unluckily for her, the queen forwarded the request to the war minister, who ordered an investigation. The investigation discovered that she was neither Romieu's wife nor the mother of any children. Furthermore, the report stated that "perhaps he will serve better being removed from the influence of this woman who made him spend the prize money from his three replacements." In any case, Gunner Romieu's age of thirty-four years in 1843 meant that he could not enlist again, and the Ministry was content to keep him separate from his wife and in the service, even though "he is of no use as a soldier."[44]

A cantinière of the Forty-seventh Infantry Regiment showed herself to be a bad element of a different sort. When the French attacked the Algerian city of Constantine for a second time in 1837, the bey of Constantine was so confident that he could defeat the French again that he left his harem in the city. After the city fell, the French army was left with more than two hundred women as booty of war. While deciding what to do with them, the French commander placed the Forty-seventh's cantinière in charge of the one door leading to the harem. The assumption was that only a woman could be trusted to guard so many women. One night while the rest of the garrison slept, the cantinière admitted two officers to the harem, probably in return for some bribe. However, "within less than two minutes the frightful uproar caused by two hundred women shrieking at once roused the whole of head-quarters, and our two officers tore full pace back to the guardroom and got the men under arms."[45] Like Madame Romieu, here was a woman who put personal gain before duty, and who betrayed the trust of her superiors.

Likewise, Conneau's encounter with three cantinières in Brest shows an interesting mix of business savvy and personal kindness, as well as potentially serious misbehavior. The jailer's wife arranged for the cantinière of the regiment stationed in the fortress to feed Conneau and his officers, since the official prison ration was so meager. "The cantinière soon appeared with two more females from the same regiment. A bargain was struck with the cantinière for our meals, which should consist of 3 dishes per meal twice a day, at 15 sous each, payable in advance." This represents a fairly extensive kitchen operation, and the prices seem to be in keeping with what cantinières charged soldiers in their regiment. While the French cantinière was all business, the two Spanish cantinières "became our daily visitors, running our errands and procuring for us all those little comforts which women alone can devise."[46] However, Conneau claims that the Spanish cantinières became such good and loyal friends with the ship's Spanish officers that they aided and abetted an escape attempt: a serious charge if true.[47]

Nevertheless, these have to be seen as interesting but isolated examples, recorded precisely because they were so unusual. Most cantinières received respect and admiration from their units, and as in past eras, there is no evidence of prostitution or of similar moral failings. When Englishman Alexander Kinglake visited a canteen in Algeria in September of 1845, he clearly was hoping that the cantinière would be willing to sell more than her drinks. He wrote of the woman that "she had a pretty enticing way of speaking, and was rather nice looking, but the charms of her canteen were confined to *absinthe* and *eau-de-vie*."[48] A clearly disappointed Kinglake continued his voyage, frustrated by the yawning gap between expectation and reality.

It took a certain kind of bravery to be a good cantinière in a war zone, and the war in Algeria attracted an adventurous breed of women. Some of the women serving in Algeria were old cantinières from the First Empire. Catherine Rohmer was born in Colmar in 1783, daughter of a vivandière and a soldier in the Royal Army. She became a vivandière herself at age nineteen, served throughout the campaigns of the Revolution and Empire, and finally lost her husband during the Spanish campaign of 1823. Undeterred, she remarried and accompanied her new husband to Algeria.[49] Thérèse Jourdan was another old campaigner. Born in Besançon in 1768 and a vivandière in 1796, she fought in all of Napoleon's campaigns, and after Waterloo found herself cantinière of the Fourth Infantry Regiment. She served as cantinière in Spain in 1823 and in Algeria until 1834, but stayed with the regiment working odd jobs until her death in 1862.[50] Other cantinières were "old" campaigners even if they were young. Many cantinières in the period 1815–1848 were daughters of cantinières, born in the army and bred to military life. The scarcity of cantinière posts and the relative ease with which a well-liked woman could pass her job on to her daughter made the proportion of hereditary cantinières much higher than in earlier times. These new cantinières, though young, were no strangers to camp life or to battle. Louise Bontemps, a third-generation cantinière of the Nineteenth Infantry Regiment, was born in 1811 in Amiens. She was the daughter of Louis Bontemps, a soldier, and Thérèse Moricours, a cantinière and herself the daughter of a Royal Army vivandière.[51]

This process of inbreeding continued in Algeria at an accelerated pace. From early on, the Algerian war became a "family affair," and it remained so throughout the century. The government had no wish to lower morale by separating soldiers in Africa from their families in France, and from the very beginning it encouraged soldiers' wives and children to accompany them. This encouragement could manifest itself in the free ocean passage accorded in 1831 or in the special allowances for increased numbers of enfants de troupe for units serving in Africa.[52] Although this latter only directly affected boys, there was also a strong preference given to "daughters of the regiment" when choosing cantinières. Already well-versed in army life and in the duties and responsibilities of a cantinière, these young women made ideal candidates for the job, and many girls born in Africa went on to serve there for years. For example, Henriette Gith was born in the Thirtieth Infantry Regiment in 1835, and served as a cantinière in various units in Algeria and in France well into the twentieth century.[53] Similarly, Louise Jean was born in 1839 in the Thirty-sixth Infantry Regiment. Her brothers were both soldiers, her sister married a soldier of the Thirty-sixth, and when she turned nineteen Louise took over her mother's post as cantinière and married a soldier.[54]

Other cantinières came from more or less exotic backgrounds. Marie Monié was born in Nogent la Phaye (Eure-et-Loire) in March 1815. She disappeared from her village as a teenager and resurfaced married to a soldier and serving as a cantinière, much to the surprise of her family.[55] Another story about a runaway could be heard around the campfires of the Second Zouave Regiment. One of the regiment's cantinières, known only as "La Belle Marie," joined the regiment in 1834, and it was said among the soldiers that she came from a prominent and wealthy French family. Supposedly, she loved a common soldier and yearned after a simple life, so she feigned her own death in order to spare the family any embarrassment, and secretly ran off to Algeria, where she lived out the rest of her days as a simple cantinière.[56] A young captain of artillery related a story of more exotic origins. The cantinière of his divisional medical service was "a tall and beautiful wench," kidnapped by an Arab tribe in her youth and rescued by French troops, to whom she attached herself with devotion.[57] Few cantinières perhaps had such adventure-story beginnings, but enough of them did to give continued credence to romantic legends.

Back in Paris, cantinières reached new public prominence at the height of the Romantic movement, when Italian composer Gaetano Donizetti's opera *La fille du régiment* was performed at the Opéra-Comique in 1840. The story of Marie, the adopted daughter and vivandière of the Twenty-first Infantry Regiment, the opera romanticized the life of a vivandière during the Napoleonic period more than it accurately portrayed reality. Marie turns out to be the long-lost daughter of an Austrian noblewoman, but she chooses loyalty to the regiment and to her true love over a life of luxury and privilege. Even the music is unrealistic: the nine high C notes in "Ah! mes amis, quel jour de fête!" are considered impossible for most tenors, reflecting musically the literal unreality of the plot. But what the opera lacked in authenticity, it more than made up for with popular appeal and, if properly cast, musical power. Because of this, the work helped to create the popular nineteenth-century romantic ideal of the cantinière, and it went on to be translated into Italian and English.

The reality of women's lives in the North African wars being fought at the time was less ideal, but it still contained many elements that could appeal to the Romantic sensibility. Part of the romance surrounding the real-life Algerian cantinières came from their fierce independence and inventiveness. Although regulations required them to wear civilian clothing and a large metal identification plaque on their persons, most women chafed at the idea of marching under the hot Algerian sun with such gear. In this regard, cantinières almost universally ignored the regulations. Instead, they painted their tonnelets blue, white, and red, and at one end painted their unit number and insignia, while at the other end they painted their name and sometimes their *patente* number. Since they were never without it, the tricolor brandy tonnelet with the artfully done inscriptions served far more usefully as an identification pass than a metal plaque did, and this tradition continued until the very end of the cantinière corps. Examples of tonnelets preserved in the French Army Museum show a general pattern of white ends, blue and red striped sides offset with polished brass fittings, and black lettering, often accompanied by personalized artwork, though this pattern could vary considerably. The tonnelet thus became not merely a tool of business, but an expression of individuality and a symbol of a certain contempt for impractical military regulations.[58]

Another Algerian innovation that proved to be permanent was the adoption of regimental uniforms for cantinières. The War Ministry never authorized them, but cantinières serving in Algeria quickly adopted female versions of their regiments' uniforms. Prior to the Algerian campaign, cantinières dressed in whatever clothing suited them. This often included a mix of civilian and military clothing, but most often it was the tonnelet and other accouterments that distinguished a woman as a cantinière, not her mode of dress. Even in the 1820s, cantinières continued to dress in essentially civilian clothing.[59] Sometimes this could be quite bizarre. At Antwerp in 1832, Captain Montigny saw a drunken cantinière in a front-line trench dressed in a "waterproof hat, sky-blue nightshirt, and red pants."[60] Even this represented something of an attempt to adopt regulation uniform colors matching the blue tunic and red trousers of the line infantry. While no one is certain why, it is clear that cantinières shifted to a close approximation of regulation military dress in the early and mid-1830s, and it is also clear that the decisive shift occurred in the Army of Africa. One author suggested that the impossibility of finding replacement civilian clothing drove women to fashion military uniforms from readily available materials.[61] However, given the ease of ship-borne commerce between France and Algeria, it is unlikely that scarcity could wholly explain the trend, though there is probably some truth to it. More likely, cantinières in Algeria felt themselves a part of the military society in a stronger sense than those serving in Europe did. Isolated from French civilian society and spending months in hostile territory with small groups of soldiers, cantinières developed a strong sense of group identity with the soldiers with whom they lived and fought. Nothing would seem more natural than that they should dress in a way that explicitly displayed their unit loyalty, and on the distant colonial battlefields women wearing pants did not raise eyebrows as they might have initially done in a garrison town in France. Not everyone approved. An American captain traveling with French troops in 1841 described cantinières as "flauntingly dressed," indicating that he did not approve of their attire. Still, he noted that his unit's cantinière was "the pride and solicitude of her whole corps."[62] The Army of Africa often played fast and loose with regulations, and this is only one example of many. According to Marshal Castellane, this problem with discipline and in particular with uniform regulations came from the top down.[63] However, while some officers scoffed at the uniform innovations, they quickly spread, as the troops returning from Algeria "breathed a new life into the metropolitan army."[64] Once the women returned to France with their units, the uniforms caught on until they became universally accepted. The African influence ran deeply in the French army in the years 1830–1870, and the fact that these women could now walk the streets of Paris in pants proved just how deeply: a small but important and highly visible segment of French women was now wearing trousers, and doing it within the confines of one of the nation's most conservative institutions.

The uniforms themselves developed as logical female extensions of each regiment's male uniform, but they had certain common features. They included a hat, usually a brimmed hat of the type worn by sailors and known as a *marinier,* presumably to protect their complexions from the sun. The hat was often decorated with a feather, and almost always sported a tricolor cockade. Many women also wore their regimental number or crest on their hats as well, as an additional sign of their unit association.[65] Below the hat came a blue or green blouse of the same style and color as the regimental uniform blouse, but tailored to fit the female form. Cantinières used genuine army buttons and trim, and the effect was usually quite striking. Below the waist they wore a knee-length skirt in either red with blue horizontal stripes or blue with red stripes, again depending on the regimental uniform. Under the skirt they wore uniform pants and boots. All this was set off with regulation leather gear and the ubiquitous tonnelet.[66] There were variations, especially in the early days. The Comte de Saint Marie, traveling in Algeria in 1845, admired a passing cantinière and her costume:

> My attention was attracted by her dress. She wore on her head a sailor's old straw hat, beneath which was seen the lace border of a white cap. A blue jacket, fitting tightly to her form, and a petticoat of some kind of red woollen stuff completed her costume. There was a sort of coquettish smartness in every thing about this woman, even down to the little cask of brandy, painted in tri-coloured stripes, which was slung across her shoulder.[67]

The same year, English gentleman Alexander Kinglake visited a canteen in Algeria, and although he was quite smitten with the person of the cantinière, he noted her dress only vaguely, stating that she "wore the costume of her order—trousers, and I think, a sort of jerkin."[68]

The cantinières' unsanctioned adoption of military uniforms once again symbolized their independence and resourcefulness, as well as the contempt they held for codes of dress and conduct that applied to civilian women. Viewing themselves as *militaires* rather than as civilian auxiliaries, they took matters into their own hands when they found themselves far from the watchful eyes of intendants and inspectors. When they returned from Algeria in their new costumes, such was the esteem in which their commanders and soldiers held them that they retained the uniforms, even at a time when French women were subject to ridicule and even arrest for wearing pants. There is no evidence that these cantinières saw themselves as feminists, nor that they identified in any way with the struggles of such women as the Saint-Simonians or the Vesuvians.[69] Rather, they saw themselves as part of an elite military force that won by its victories the right to special treatment. It is also worth noting that while the French popular press stridently attacked feminists for wearing pants, it did not attack cantinières for the same act, since in their case no political or social agenda was directly implied.

Aside from inspiring the first female uniforms, the war in Algeria brought "non-combatants" into danger in the way that all guerrilla wars do. Ambushes, infiltrations of camps and forts, and attacks on moving columns all brought cantinières closer to the danger zone regardless of their own intentions. Because units fought in small detachments against a constantly moving enemy, there were rarely any safe areas, or areas clearly "behind the lines." French tactics after 1841 emphasized the use of small columns of troops mounted on mules and employing quick movement and surprise to catch an elusive enemy in harsh desert and mountain terrain. The goal was to rush forward and close with the enemy, and so deny them the ability to break off combat and flee. In these circumstances, the cantinière would not be out of reach of the enemy at any point in the column of movement in the event of an ambush. Nor could she hang back in the rear if the French brought their enemies to battle. With so few troops, and often facing much greater numbers, the French could ill afford any soldiers to guard the cantinière. Algerian tactics usually included using superior numbers in an attempt to flank and encircle the French, and a cantinière who stayed behind would risk being caught by the Algerians' flanking forces. Instead, cantinières were almost always right in the thick of battle. Most tried to tend to the wounded during fights. As one witness recounted,

> When her husband's battalion is in garrison, the *cantinière* officiates as a laundress; when the battalion is on a march, she puts on her costume and marches along with it. In the event of a charge, she stations herself behind the second platoon; if a square is formed, she takes her place in the centre; and during the action she goes from one wounded man to another, tendering assistance, and distributing glasses of wine or brandy. In Africa, where the French troops have suffered so severely, these women have rendered signal service to humanity, and have frequently performed acts of extraordinary courage. There is not an officer, or private, who does not respect the *cantinière* of the battalion.[70]

But even this was dangerous in close-quarters fighting with an enemy still largely armed with edged weapons such as the *yatagan,* a long sword with a curved blade for maximum cutting ability.

Other cantinières preferred to simply charge forward and fight like soldiers, feeling themselves more secure when surrounded by the living than in the midst of the dying. In either case, cantinières became casualties at a high rate during the wars in Algeria, partly due to the nature of French tactics, partly due to their own attitudes toward battle, and partly because the enemy showed no scruples about deliberately killing French women.

Examples of cantinières in battle in Algeria are legion, despite the fairly limited number of sources for the period. Elisabeth Frache of the Second Engineer Regiment assisted French wounded during their retreat from the disastrous Battle of the Macta River on June 28, 1835. Though five months pregnant, she tended to the wounded rather than looking to her own escape, and she received two yatagan blows to the head and chest. She lost her horse and all her goods in the battle, but escaped with her life, though she spent a month in a military hospital recovering.[71] In a similar situation, Marianne Perrault of the Ninth Artillery Regiment was wounded several times while aiding the wounded. At the battle of Constantine in 1837 she had a leg nearly hacked off by a yatagan while she helped her wounded colonel.[72]

Cantinières often fought more aggressively. Sergeant-Major Claude Roussier of the Twelfth Infantry Regiment recalled an episode in the Kabyle expedition of 1849. His small column came up against a force ten times its size entrenched on a hilltop and barring the route. General St. Arnaud ordered a charge, and the cantinière of a Zouave battalion preferred riding at the head of the attack, next to the general, to hanging back in relative safety. The charge succeeded and the cantinière remained unscathed.[73] Likewise, Catherine Rohmer was "as likely to help the wounded as to fire a gun" in battle, receiving three wounds for her trouble.[74] And at the assault of Constantine, Jeanne Masson of the Sixth Foreign Legion Battalion entered the breach in the city walls with her unit. Carrying a musket like a soldier, she claimed to have saved the life of the Duke of Nemours by killing a defender who was about to shoot the duke at close range. She later claimed to have killed an Arab civilian with her bayonet after he struck and insulted an old French veteran in Algiers.[75] Masson's claims are questionable, as she had no corroborating witnesses, but it is worth noting that no one refuted them either. At the very least, the claims suggest that in the Army of Africa at least, claiming to be a combatant and even a murderer of natives was not unduly harmful to a cantinière's reputation.

Cantinières also saw combat when the French fought a brief campaign in Belgium in 1832, including several sieges. At the siege of Antwerp, Antoinette Mouron, cantinière of the Twenty-fifth Infantry Regiment, rushed forward under fire to help wounded soldiers under the walls of the city. Marshal Gérard cited her in the army's order of the day: "Antoinette Moran [sic], cantinière of the 25th line, affords daily proofs of her courage and devotion; she rescued a wounded miner, who had fallen into the ditch, from under the enemy's fire. She had already had her hat perforated by a ball, in assisting a wounded man: and, amidst a shower of shells and bullets, she brought a bearer to carry off another. She deserves the gratitude of the army."[76] But whereas the cantinières in Algeria were far from the eyes of the king and his ministers, Mouron received high praise. Her division commander was so impressed that he gave her a hundred sous, "which seemed to her to be agreeable."[77] Her case went before the minister of war, who recommended that quick action be taken in striking a gold medal for bravery. King Louis-Philippe himself issued the orders for the award for "this intrepid woman," and decorated her during a postwar review of the regiment: "the celebrated cantinière was presented to the king, when she received a gold medal of 1,000 francs value, and a pension of 250 francs per annum."[78] She soon transferred to the Sixty-first Infantry Regiment and spent time in Algeria, where she was wounded and lost all her goods, including her medal.[79] Nor was Mouron the only cantinière who braved Dutch fire at Antwerp. General Boniface de Castellane, commander of the Third Infantry Division, wrote, "The cantinières of our regiments are really intrepid. One sees them in the most exposed positions; they hear the whistle of the shells and bullets without flinching."[80] This suggests that behavior like Mouron's was commonplace, at least among the thirty to fifty women of Castellane's division. Indeed, Courtois d'Hurbal's painting *Le siège d'Anvers* shows an obviously pregnant cantinière tending a wounded infantryman in a front-line trench under fire.[81] An equally brave but perhaps less useful example comes to us from Montigny. During the siege, he saw a cantinière sitting on a rampart under fire, drinking heavily and saluting each passing cannon ball.[82] Yet another account tells of a bunker being caved in by enemy artillery, burying the occupants. "After a few moments' anxious suspense they were re-assured by hearing the voice of a vivandiere, who, though a second bomb followed close on the heels of the first, killing two and wounding three men, with the utmost coolness walking down, and calling to one of the miners said, 'Here's your dram, but you must drink from your hand, for the cursed shell has broken my glasses.'"[83] This is exactly the sort of coolness under fire that General Castellane admired so much, and it goes a long way toward explaining why the army retained these women for so long: they performed essential services, and they did it with what observers often referred to as "masculine courage."

Given that cantinières risked being killed or wounded fighting for France, it seemed natural to them that the government would provide for their retirement. However, like its predecessors and its successors, the July Monarchy refused to recognize women's service as the equal of men's. Instead, the War Ministry sent women who received pensions a form letter which left room only for their husbands' service. Thus, cantinières who received widows' pensions were given awards "in recompense for the service of their husbands."[84] Although the July Monarchy recognized women like Antoinette Mouron for their courage, it did not consider them to be more than employees. The adoption of uniforms brought cantinières one step closer to being de facto *militaires,* but the War Ministry carefully avoided giving them any statutory encouragement. Even Antoinette Mouron's gold medal was not an army decoration, but a one-of-a-kind item struck by the royal mint especially for the occasion.

Despite these drawbacks, cantinières made progress in the conditions of their service by mid-century. As the French army grew in response to the continuing war in Algeria, the numbers of cantinières grew as well. Their adoption of a quasi-official uniform and its tacit acceptance by the army and the government marked a crucial point in the development not only of their own self-image but also of the way French society as a whole saw them. In both cases, the sight of women in uniform marching with their regiments gave a much more positive impression than had the motley collection of vivandières who traveled with earlier armies. As one British observer remarked on encountering French troops and their cantinière in Oporto during the Portuguese civil war, "There were some few women with the English and the Irish, but they had none of the character about them of La Belle Cantinière."[85] The uniform gave cantinières legitimacy and it reinforced in their own minds the idea that they were members of the military, not camp followers. It henceforth became easy to differentiate between cantinières of the army and mere camp followers or prostitutes, and it may indeed have been for this reason that the War Ministry acquiesced to the new cantinière uniforms. The uniforms and decorative but functional tonnelets became standard equipment for cantinières for the next sixty years, forming part of a deep and long-standing tradition in the French army. Yet for all this, cantinières were still civilians. Despite looking more like soldiers, they continued to hold the official status of *employées* and not *militaires*.

CHAPTER 5

The Second Empire

The "Golden Age" of the Cantinières

IN 1851, PRESIDENT LOUIS NAPOLEON, the nephew of Napoleon Bonaparte, seized power from the short-lived Second Republic with the active aid of the French army. He quickly established a dictatorship, and in 1852 he declared himself Emperor of the French, taking the title of Napoleon III. From the outset, the new emperor showed favoritism toward the army and a strong desire to encourage the growth of the Napoleonic legend. Since cantinières were a part of that legend, their place in the expanded French army was assured. The emperor increased the number of French army regiments, thereby creating more cantinière positions. Later, the military reforms of 1869 doubled the number of cantinières officially allowed to each unit. Thus, the number of cantinières shot up dramatically after 1852. Cantinière uniforms grew more ornate, and became the object of popular interest in the form of color lithographs, books of illustrations, toy figurines, and even advertisements. The cantinières themselves also became popular figures. In their dress uniforms, they often led military parades, and the renewed prestige of the army extended even to these women of low birth. Cantinières also began to receive military decorations, including the coveted *Médaille militaire* (Military Medal) of the Legion of Honor and the less prestigious *Médaille d'honneur* (Medal of Honor). The earning of military decorations marked an important step on the road to official recognition, and some writers have erroneously concluded from this that cantinières were officially part of the army during the Second Empire.[1] In fact, cantinières remained legally only civilian employees, but most cantinières and the general public assumed otherwise; only the bureaucrats of the War Ministry had a full understanding of the cantinières' precarious legal standing.

Even though the Second Empire was in some ways a golden age for cantinières, many of the difficulties and hardships of previous eras persisted.
The French army spent much of the Second Empire on peacetime garrison duty, and this allowed for a flourishing family life. However, despite
Napoleon III's claim that "the empire means peace," France was embroiled
in no fewer than three major European wars and numerous colonial campaigns in Mexico, Algeria, Indochina, Syria, China, and West Africa.[2] In all
of these, cantinières served with their units and suffered losses. The widespread use of relatively accurate modern rifled weapons made combat more
lethal than in the earlier era of smoothbore weapons, making cantinières'
battlefield roles much more dangerous than before. Although their chief
role on the battlefield was not combat but the nursing of the wounded,
this necessarily entailed exposure to enemy fire.[3] In addition, the growing
use of long-range, rifled artillery meant that even well behind the lines,
cantinières were killed and wounded. The catastrophic defeat and collapse
of the French army in 1870 also brought cantinières into added danger. Although English-language histories of the Franco-Prussian War almost universally ignore the presence of cantinières, hundreds of these women were
killed, wounded, or captured in the disastrous campaign that destroyed the
Second Empire. Even off the battlefield, disease continued to be a threat,
and it remained the chief cause of death in all armies of the period. And
although cantinières owned their own businesses and property, in defiance
of the French civil code, once out of the army they faced the same difficult
transition to civilian life that their predecessors had. In theory, they were
taken care of by an efficient pension system that provided money for their
retired husbands, and widows' pensions in case of their husbands' death.
However, informal marriages again became common in the French army
during Napoleon III's reign, and the many cantinières who were not legal
spouses received nothing in their old age. If the cantinières' life during the
Second Empire was in some ways glamorous, publicly acclaimed, and officially recognized, it remained a hard and dangerous one.

By the middle years of the nineteenth century the practical military usefulness of cantinières was waning, though far from gone. Military administration and supply had come a long way since the rough and tumble days
of the First Republic. A relatively efficient supply system provided for soldiers' needs to a degree that would have been impossible even twenty years
earlier. The adoption of the railroad and the telegraph, as well as the industrialization of some manufactured goods, made this possible, and for perhaps the first time in history, the French state could theoretically supply all
its army's needs in the field as well as in garrison. The original rationale for

the cantinière's legalized existence in 1793 had been that she was "absolutely necessary" to the functioning of the army, since the First Republic could not possibly supply its soldiers adequately. By mid-century, factories, railroads, and steamships made it possible for the French government to clothe, equip, and feed its armies even at a great distance from home, as evidenced by the masterful French logistics work in the Crimean War of 1854–1856.

But the theoretical ideal of a fully capable logistical system, while appealing, had yet to be realized in practical wartime experience, and those who assume that cantinières went into a decline in the mid-nineteenth century are wrong. For example, historian Bruno Dufaÿ wrote, "Military administration was better organized, the troops better controlled. Also, the number of cantinières was reduced, and the greatest part of them stayed in the barracks, without going on campaign."[4] While the first part of that statement is true, the second part is patently false—the product of projecting late twentieth-century ideas about the army and warfare backward onto an earlier time. Rather than seeing a reduction of numbers, cantinières saw their numbers doubled by the Second Empire and, for a time at least, were far more publicly visible than ever before. They also routinely went on campaign, and saw service in every campaign up until 1890, and sometimes beyond. The cantinière still proved useful as a distributor of food, supplementing army rations in the Crimea. In Italy in 1859, the French supply system broke down due to poor planning, often leaving cantinières as the sole sources of important supplies. Likewise in Algeria, Mexico, and Indochina, and in other colonial campaigns throughout the Second Empire, the lack of railroads and other modern supply infrastructure continued to make cantinières extremely useful. Since most French units served in the colonies at one time or another, their cantinières stood them in good stead. These campaigns resembled the North African campaigns of the 1830s much more than they resembled the European *grands guerres* of the mid-century. In addition, the Franco-Prussian War of 1870–1871 demonstrated the fragility of the French state and its industrial system. The regular French army was quickly destroyed, and the War Ministry formed ad hoc *bataillons de marche* and called up the poorly armed Mobile Guard, while armed civilians formed paramilitary groups of *francs-tireurs* (partisans) who fought a bitter guerrilla war against the German invaders. These irregular units usually recruited their own cantinières, and in the absence of supply from the government they fended for themselves for food and clothing. These examples demonstrated that if the cantinière's importance in an ideal modern military establishment might be fading, a great power still had many needs for military operations in less-than-ideal conditions. When chaos and primitive conditions prevailed, cantinières were still valuable military auxiliaries, just as they had been in the late eighteenth century.

The regulations of 1832 governing cantinières remained in force under the Second Empire, though they were modified in 1854 and afterward. Early regulations in 1854–1856 extended the scope of cantinières' practice by making every conceivable type of unit associated with the army eligible to have cantinières, including civilian labor detachments under military control, military administration units, and even the firefighters of Paris.[5] During the attempts at military reform in 1869, the War Ministry went further and doubled the number of authorized cantinières, increasing it from four to eight per infantry regiment and from two to four per cavalry squadron.[6] On the whole, however, the reign of Napoleon III is remarkable for its relative lack of cantinière regulations, considering its eighteen-year span and the emperor's intense interest in military affairs. Certainly the Second Empire valued the cantinières for their popular appeal and for their associations with the victories of Napoleon I, and largely refrained from meddling with a proven system. Even so, Napoleon III showed no desire to incorporate women into the French army officially, and despite their improved status, cantinières continued to languish in semi-official limbo.

The cantinières' official military function consisted primarily of selling food, drink, and tobacco to the soldiers in their units. There were no price controls, but the 1832 regulations charged unit commanders with seeing that prices were fair in light of local conditions. In practice, the cantinières of the Second Empire were less likely to overcharge than their predecessors of the Revolution and First Empire. This was partly because the cantinières of the 1850s and 1860s were integrated into the military family far more than earlier cantinières. Regiments served during long periods of peace without the constant turnover of wartime losses, and even in wartime the army of the Second Empire did not suffer casualties on the scale of 1792–1815. Therefore, the regiment became more homelike, and most cantinières' husbands were career soldiers who served twenty to thirty years. Perhaps more important, the Second Empire saw a new function for the cantinière in garrison. She was charged with running a *pension* for the unit's non-commissioned officers in her canteen. This meant that the NCOs ate two meals a day together in the canteen when in garrison. The cantinière cooked the meals and served them, and in recompense she was entitled to a set per diem fee from each NCO. The *pension* became a source of steady income for the cantinières. It also created a domestic sphere for the NCOs in the garrison, further strengthening the sense of the regiment as a family and the role of the cantinière as the symbolic wife and mother of the unit. The canteen thus effectively became the family dining room of the regimental NCOs.

Indeed, by the 1860s, the importance of cantinières as symbols may have outweighed their practical military utility. French soldiers attached as much importance to the cantinières' moral support as they did to the real benefits of a hot meal, a drink, and a smoke, not to mention a comfortable spot on post or in camp to sit and relax. One of the most celebrated cantinières of the Second Empire was Arinda Brun, known to most soldiers as "Mère Ibrahim." A cantinière of the Second Zouave Regiment, she served in Algeria, Mexico, Syria, the Crimea, Italy, and Indochina, and in the Franco-Prussian War. When she died at age seventy-five, she was buried with military honors, and the captain who spoke at her funeral oration summed up the intangible but crucial role of the cantinière:

> You were our mother, our sister, our companion. Everywhere the French flag floated, in defeat as in glory, you followed us, bringing the consolation of your smile, your encouragements in our reverses. They have all come, soldiers of Mexico, old veterans of Italy, young ones of Tonkin, of Sudan, of Dahomey, to accompany you to the field of supreme repose, and to bring you the last goodbye from your military family.[7]

The speaker explicitly painted the cantinière as the player of multiple female roles, mother, sister, and wife, and did so within the symbolic context of the army as family. As the funeral oration suggests, it was not so much the material comforts cantinières brought that French soldiers of the mid-nineteenth century valued, but the unquantifiable female presence in an otherwise male world: a sense of family in an otherwise sterile and uncomfortable existence. This is not surprising considering the changes in military administration that had taken place since the days of the first Napoleon. The soldiers of the First Empire traveled with large numbers of female camp followers, but lived with hunger as their constant companion. Their term of service was often indefinite in practice, and soldiers faced death and privation for years at a time as constant combat wore down their numbers. Soldiers of the Second Empire, however, spent much of their careers in peacetime barracks, received regular if not always adequate supplies, and rarely endured prolonged hunger. The food they purchased from cantinières was usually a supplement to army rations, not a substitute for them. But female company was scarce, since the War Ministry would no longer tolerate the hordes of women who followed earlier French armies. Therefore cantinières, while still very welcome as sources of *eau de vie* and of good meals, became even more valued for their feminine presence within the regimental "family."

The general admiration of the cantinière was also based in part on the legend of bravery and devotion that grew out of the wars of the Revolution and the First Empire. This tradition led many French soldiers and civilians to view all cantinières as heroines to be admired and treasured. Captain Claude Loiseau of the Belgian Volunteer Legion was serving in Mexico in 1865 when one of his cantinières was wounded in battle. He received a letter from E. Masson, an old French veteran, who expressed some of the unconditional emotional attachment many French men had for cantinières as a group. "I have learned that you had a cantinière wounded. Kiss her for me, whether she is pretty or ugly. That means nothing at all. Her courage gives her all the attractions that she will need, and the Cross that she merits will give her even more!"[8] The letter shows the extent to which French soldiers held cantinières to be above normal standards of judgment. Individual character traits seemed less important than cantinières' existence as part of a group, and, at least in the abstract, they all benefited from the deeds of a few heroines. Masson assumed that the cantinière would earn the Cross of the Legion of Honor, a coveted but not uncommon (for men) military distinction. In fact, no cantinière officially received this award during the Second Empire, though many units nominated their cantinières for it, and one cantinière would receive it in 1880 for her actions in the Franco-Prussian War. But many civilians and soldiers alike believed that cantinières received it, providing further evidence that they considered cantinières to be official members of the army.

Becoming a cantinière during the Second Empire continued in theory to be relatively straightforward. The legitimate wife of a soldier could apply to the unit's Council of Administration and receive a *patente* if a position was available. Most units would not give a soldier permission to marry unless a cantinière position was open, since to do otherwise would create an untenable situation for the new couple. In fact, the French army of the Second Empire was marked by moral laxity and a widespread tolerance for informal arrangements. Many women served with French units on campaign without ever marrying their "husbands," and did so even in peacetime garrisons in France. As an American ship captain commented after transporting French troops to the Crimea in 1854–1856, "*femme* is a very convenient French word, and its ambiguity often serves a very desirable purpose."[9] Many women also joined through irregular channels, bypassing the Council of Administration and simply obtaining the consent of a sympathetic officer.

Most of the women did go through proper channels, however. Their stories show a continuing trend toward early marriage, and a strong tendency to remain with the regiment as long as possible. Surviving records suggest that most cantinières of this era married for the first time between fifteen and twenty-three, with the average age at first marriage being nineteen. Those who married at older ages tended to be informal partners who eventually married their soldiers, while those who married at fifteen or sixteen tended to be daughters of the regiment following their mothers' careers. New brides were usually eight to twelve years younger than their husbands, with an average age difference of ten years. French women formed the majority of cantinières, although Germans, Swiss, and Belgians made up a very significant minority. French Algerian women also provided a large proportion of the cantinière corps, especially in the units of the Army of Africa. Elsewhere, the long colonial campaigns did not provide many new local female recruits, but at least one Vietnamese woman became, according to one officer, "an excellent cantinière."[10]

There were far fewer peasant girls among the cantinières of the Second Empire than there had been in earlier periods, and the decline was offset by a growing number of daughters of the urban working class. Most met soldiers who were garrisoned in their hometowns, but many were single women working far from home who married soldiers to escape poverty. Since frontier provinces had more military garrisons than interior provinces, a disproportionate number of cantinières came from these areas. Anna Henriette Thomas represented a typical example. A young woman from Givet (Ardennes), "she fell in love with a handsome drummer corporal of the Ninetieth Infantry Regiment, Henri Busquet." In a 1938 interview with *L'intransigeant,* Anna recalled meeting her husband. Drummer-corporals were known as the peacocks of the French army, and Henri Busquet was no exception. The nineteen-year-old woman was impressed by the "handsome man, with a pretty mustache and a beard à la Napoleon III."[11] When his regiment transferred to Orléans in 1868, Anna followed, marrying him "under the flag" in Orléans and becoming a cantinière. Marie Jarlet had a similar experience with Sergeant Alexandre Delaval when the Forty-seventh Infantry Regiment was stationed in Gueret (Seine-et-Marne). The daughter of a wine merchant, Marie fell in love with the sergeant, though he was seventeen years her senior. The two married in 1866, and she served as cantinière for fourteen years.[12]

Daughters of cantinières formed a large proportion of the cantinière corps, perhaps as much as 25 percent. Because nineteenth-century cantinières tended to live longer and therefore serve longer than their predecessors, some of the Second Empire's hereditary cantinières began their careers in the 1840s, as did Anne Calastroupat. Born Anne Claude Lalouet in 1827 in Gray (Haute-Saône), she married Joseph Calastroupat of the Fourth Dragoons in 1842 when she was only fifteen. She served successively as cantinière of the Fourth Dragoons, the Forty-fifth Infantry, and the 104th Infantry, and was still on active service in 1892.[13] Henriette Gith married at the comparatively advanced age of nineteen. She was born in the barracks of the Twenty-seventh Infantry Regiment, the daughter of cantinière Françoise Castex and musician Joseph Gith. She grew up in the regiment, and in 1855, she married professional soldier Joseph Calvet. She was cantinière to the Twenty-seventh Infantry, the First Zouaves, and the Fourth Chasseurs d'Afrique, and was still on active service in Algeria in 1896.[14] Louise Charlotte was also born in the army, to Sergeant Jean Charlotte and cantinière Marie Albine of the Thirty-sixth Infantry Regiment. When Louise was nineteen, her mother married her to a soldier of the regiment, then gave up her own cantinière position so Louise could have it. Louise stayed with the Thirty-sixth Regiment from her birth to her death, and was still on active service in 1891.[15] Sophie Caroline Lucius was born in Strasbourg (Haut-Rhin) in 1842, the daughter of a soldier and a cantinière. In 1857, she met musician François-Réné Tuvache of the Seventh infantry Regiment when he was garrisoned in Strasbourg, and followed him to Paris when the regiment moved there. Although it was strictly against regulations, she lived in the Reuilly Barracks with her mate while working as a seamstress in Paris. The two finally married in 1859, and Sophie served as cantinière of the Seventh and then the Second Infantry Regiment until 1877, opting for French citizenship in 1872 after her native Alsace became part of Germany.[16]

For the first time since 1815, foreign-born women again provided large numbers of cantinières during the Second Empire. While the French army did not campaign outside of France with anything like the same frequency it had in earlier eras, apparently a much more international and cosmopolitan outlook reigned in the new Imperial era, though it is unclear exactly why this was so. Marie Louise Brändli was one of the non-French women who found a home in the Imperial Army. Born in Zurich in 1842, at age fifteen she married a soldier in the French Eighteenth Infantry Regiment and became a cantinière. When her husband died in 1869, she married Antoine Creste, a drummer in the regiment, and served as cantinière until

1880.[17] The case of Anna Commaret was more unusual. A Prussian subject, she was born Anna Klasen in 1844. In 1867, she married Louis Commaret of the Seventh Artillery Regiment. She served thirty-eight years as a cantinière, fighting against her native Prussia in 1870 and retiring in 1905 decorated with the Military Medal.[18]

Not all cantinières had deep military roots or long careers. Some came from solid petit bourgeois families, but many came from backgrounds that made even a daughter of the regiment seem elevated by comparison. Nathalie Anchin of the Ninth Artillery Regiment was born in 1831 to Blandine de Coninck in Nokère, Belgium. Her father was unknown, and her mother died when Nathalie was only six years old. Nathalie grew up an orphan and eventually moved to Douai, where she worked as a seamstress. There she met Alexandre Anchin, a musician in the Ninth Artillery. Nathalie followed him from garrison to garrison, successively moving from Douai to Nancy, Metz, and Vincennes. She bore a son in 1859, and finally married Anchin in 1861. Upon her marriage she officially became a cantinière and served for ten years.[19] While Louise Graffeuil came from a more stable background, she too had a long affair with her soldier before marriage. Born Louise Joséphine Fédy at Pennesières (Haute-Saône) in 1825, she was the daughter of a coach maker and his wife. In 1845, she began a love affair with Jean Graffeuil, a trumpeter of the Seventy-fifth Infantry Regiment, and followed him to garrisons in Versailles, La Rochelle, and Clermont-Ferrand. She bore two children before marrying him officially in 1849 and serving as cantinière from 1849 to 1864.[20]

One obvious question is whether any of these women served as cantinières before they were married. Nathalie Anchin and Sophie Tuvache were both listed as seamstresses on their wedding licenses, not as cantinières. However, Sophie gave her residence as the Reuilly barracks, so there is little doubt she was living with the regiment, and may have been a de facto cantinière, even if officially she was charged with repairing the men's uniforms. This was common practice on campaign, but some officers tolerated it in peacetime as well. In wartime, commanders tended to be more concerned with their units' fighting efficiency than with regulations, and many officers overlooked unmarried cantinières as long as they performed their duties. Henriette Moutier served as a cantinière of the Seventy-fourth Infantry Regiment during the siege of Sevastopol even though she was unmarried.[21] Likewise, one French artillery officer in the Crimea cynically wrote home in 1855, "I am going to have to play the role of mayor to marry the battery's veterinary sergeant and the cantinière, the former a young lady of virtue who counts fifty springs and who has made fifty thousand men happy."[22] Sometimes, though, Victorian morality could interfere with military laissez-faire. The Catholic chaplain of the Belgian Legion was outraged by the six unmarried cantinières who accompanied the unit to Mexico in 1864. He pressured the commander into ordering that each woman be married to a soldier of her choice, an arrangement that satisfied the chaplain but did not produce happy marriages.[23] Unofficial couples existed in the barracks in France as well. Captain Thoumas of the Seventeenth Artillery described his cantinière in the early 1850s as "the very illegitimate and very unattractive wife of the corporal-farrier."[24]

The large average age difference between cantinières and their husbands meant that husbands often died before their wives, even without the help of enemy fire or disease. The very young age of many cantinières at their first marriage meant that even after a decade or more of married life, a newly widowed cantinière was often quite young. The Swiss cantinière Marie Brändli's case is typical. Married at age fifteen to a man twenty years her senior, she found herself a widow when she was only twenty-six. She had become accustomed to military life and thought of her regiment as her home, so she quickly remarried and served another eleven years until her second husband's retirement.[25] Marie Lambert of the Tenth Chasseurs à Cheval married a man only five years her senior, Bernard Ley, in 1859. However, Bernard suffered from poor health and died in 1869 at the age of thirty-seven, leaving Marie still young and eligible. She married a senior sergeant of the regiment, Pierre Charcot, and served as cantinière until 1884.[26] The career of Marie Ramonède was less typical but hardly uncommon, especially in the rough and tumble conditions in the Army of Africa. Born in 1836 in Vic (Haute-Pyrénées), she settled in Algeria, where she became cantinière to a regiment of Turcos, or indigenous colonial infantry. She stayed with the regiment for more than twenty years, and had at least three husbands, though the legitimacy of all three marriages remained in question.[27]

Many young women from humble backgrounds like Ramonède's had soldier boyfriends who were shipped off to the colonies or to theaters of war like the Crimea. In numerous instances, these civilian women preferred to join their partners illegally rather than face separation, and many went to extraordinary lengths to overcome the obstacles in their way. Upon arriving in the theater of war, they often became cantinières if they could gain the sympathy of commanding officers. Two examples from the Crimean War provide excellent illustrations. Henriette Moutier was "a child of the foundlings' hospice in Grenoble" who took passage to the Crimea in 1855 to join her boyfriend, a gunner in the Eighth Artillery Regiment. The two remained unmarried throughout the war, but the sympathetic colonel agreed to issue Henriette a *patente* as a "civil cantinière."[28] A more dramatic anecdote was told by the captain of a detached battery at Kamiesch outside Sevastopol, also in the Spring of 1855. He wrote that "one morning while I was taking the air in front of my tent with my eyes half closed, I suddenly perceived a young woman in front of me." The woman recounted that she was a cook from Toulouse and that her boyfriend had been sent to Sevastopol as a replacement for the battery. She had stowed away on his ship at Marseilles and hidden under a pile of coal in the ship's hold, living on scraps of food brought by friendly sailors. "She had thus arrived at Kamiesch, from where she had followed her friend to our camp, and she pleaded with me to sign a cantinière's commission for her so she could stay with us." The captain's decision reflected the kind of practical considerations that were often far more important than official regulations when in the field. "I let myself soften, hoping that she would in return repair my socks, through which my toes were beginning to pass."[29] Knowing she was a professional cook probably also influenced his decision. The two lovers lived out the rest of the war together, married when they returned to France, and had long and successful military careers. Most Second Empire cantinières eventually married, whether before accepting a commission (as the regulations required) or several years afterward.

The 1850s and 1860s marked, in many ways, the zenith of the cantinières' history, and the emergence of a new kind of professional military family was one illustration of this. During all periods of history, soldiers and their wives had families of some kind, and cantinières of earlier eras had certainly produced many children who continued their parents' military careers. What made the military family of the Second Empire different was its comfortable, almost bourgeois image in French society. The military family of "the drum-major, the cantinière, and the enfant de troupe" became something of a cliché, but one based solidly on fact. Cantinières' husbands tended to be regimental musicians, and since they were long-service professionals, they tended to rise to the post of drum-major or trumpet-major. In their splendid full-dress uniforms, they cut dashing and colorful figures. French artists at the height of the Second Empire used the military family as subjects for books and popular lithographs as well as for toy figurines. At the same time, cantinière uniforms developed into much more lavish and complicated affairs, and although cantinières often wore simpler versions on campaign, the full dress uniforms that the public saw were truly spectacular, having more in common with the fine dresses of the upper classes than with the rough peasant outfits of eighteenth-century vivandières. Enfants de troupe also wore splendid dress uniforms. In military revues, the cantinières and their children marched in these uniforms along with their regiments, thus lending beauty and glamour to the public's perception of their lives. The sight of such families strolling through garrison towns or down the Parisian boulevards captured the public imagination. It is worth noting that the Baroness de Verly even attended an Imperial costume ball at the Tuileries palace dressed as a cantinière of the Imperial Guard, something that would have been outrageous before 1854 or after 1871.[30]

One of the biggest popularizers of the cantinières and their families was Hippolyte Lalaisse. He did an extensive series of color lithographs covering every type of unit in the French army, and these prints were available widely and cheaply as part of the Images d'Épinal series. No fewer than 135 of these lithographs were of cantinières. The images provided the French public with its most comprehensive view of cantinières and their families, and Lalaisse showed them in scenes of domestic bliss.[31] Always in full dress uniform and in the bloom of health, the men, women and children portrayed seemed to lead happy and fulfilling lives. Couples looked lovingly into each other's eyes, or fathers played with little enfants de troupe while mothers watched joyfully.[32] This portrayal was so definitive that today the French term "Image d'Épinal" signifies a naïve depiction of a subject that shows only its good side. Indeed, an Image d'Épinal of a cantinière found a century and a half later in a Paris flea market had been carefully trimmed from the rest of the original lithograph, then lovingly matted in red velvet and securely sealed into a gilt frame under glass some time in the late nineteenth century. Whoever did so must have held cantinières (or perhaps one cantinière) in very high esteem.[33]

Aside from the mass sales of the Images d'Épinal, Lalaisse's lithographs were published twice in book form, once in 1855 and again in 1861. The first book, *Types militaires,* included only three cantinière plates, including one in which a girl of about eight assisted her mother in selling brandy to gendarmes of the Imperial Guard.[34] However, after cantinières received extensive publicity during the 1859 Italian War, Parisian publisher Gustave Orengo put out a new volume of Lalaisse's work titled *L'armée française et ses cantinières.* The new book consisted of thirty-five color plates, each illustrating a cantinière of a different type of unit. Fourteen of the plates showed cantinières with their husbands, while six of them showed cantinières with children. Only eight showed cantinières alone. The overall impression was one of modest prosperity, good health, happiness, and a light-hearted gaiety, but also a clear emphasis on marriage and family. Children took part in the daily business, but were also portrayed in leisure settings. Whether strolling through parks with their parents or playfully cavorting with their soldier fathers, the children appeared in immaculate and elaborate uniforms like their parents'. The overall effect was to give an impression that cantinières' families lived a happy and contented life.

Orengo's collaboration with Lalaisse was not alone. It was a part of a wave of artwork that portrayed cantinières in family situations and in peacetime. One contemporary lithograph titled "Le tambour-major, la cantinière, et l'enfant de troupe" showed a family in full dress uniform walking along a city street with proud bearing and happy expressions.[35] Another lithograph was published in 1860 in cartoon form as a morality story. It concerned a young Spanish soldier serving in Algeria, Josefo, who was wounded by Arabs and captured. Rescued by another unit, he found that the vivandière who "insisted on caring for him" was really his long-lost mother. After she nursed him back to health, Josefo also found that he was really a nobleman, and the two lived out their days happily on Josefo's Spanish estate.[36] The story epitomized the role of the cantinière/vivandière as a caregiver and mother figure. Making the woman the soldier's actual mother only reinforced the idea that the cantinière's proper role was maternal, and the story's unexpected ending rewarded the proper behavior in a manner reminiscent of eighteenth-century peasant tales. These popular images may have had little to do with actual cantinières' experiences, but they showed a strong public interest in and approval of professional military families. Cantinières' family ties even included royalty. After Princess Charlotte of Belgium became empress of Mexico, she insisted on being the godmother of all daughters born to cantinières serving there. The former curator of the Belgian Army Museum noted that up until 1940, an old woman would surreptitiously decorate the museum's bust of Charlotte with cards and flowers on her birthday, New Year's Day, and Christmas. One card was found with "a dedication written with a trembling hand on the back, 'to my godmother.'"[37] Nor did the cantinières' royal connections stop there. No less a figure than Queen Victoria became enamored of them when she visited French army camps near Boulogne-sur-Mer during her visit to France in August of 1855. Whether it was from nostalgia at leaving France, the glow of moonlight on a summer night, or simply a genuine admiration, the queen wrote, "The moon was rising, like a crimson ball, and giving a beautiful effect to the darkening sky and the dim twilight. I had a cantinière called up to the carriage, and looked at her dress and her little barrel. She was very tidy, clean, and well spoken. I wish we had them in our army."[38]

Since cantinières portrayed in art always had dainty good looks, the real cantinières of the Second Empire found that their own physical beauty or lack thereof was an important element in the health of their business. Often a pretty cantinière would find she had good business even without serving particularly good food and drink, as many young soldiers would pay just to sit near her. This led to "an old trooper's axiom: the quality of the wine is in inverse proportion to the beauty of the cantinière."[39] By extension, other cantinières apparently needed to provide much better victuals if they wanted to retain their customers. One reason for this may have been the very popular lithography that made cantinières into folk heroines for many of the French. Contemporary prints always pictured cantinières with faces of radiant, youthful beauty, ample breasts, and thin waists, often to an exaggerated degree. The cantinières shown in drawings by Lalaisse and others represented a female physical ideal that was beyond the reach of most women, and obtainable only with the aid of corsets and padding by most others. Nevertheless, this popular imagery had a powerful effect on many young men's perceptions of what cantinières should look like, with the result that when they found themselves in the army they gravitated to those cantinières who came closest to fitting the ideal. As one historian wrote, popular imagery "always represented cantinières as adorable *minettes,* the very coquette *femmes soldats* who peopled the dreams of soldiers."[40]

Many cantinières simply ignored this outside influence, content to have solid, hefty bodies suitable for their often hard work. Photographic evidence of such women is easy to find, and they represented a sizable portion of the total cantinière corps.[41] Still, other cantinières worked to conform to the idealized images. Some started out thin, while many others wore corsets, which must have severely limited their ability to carry out their duties.[42] Even during wartime, there was still a high demand among cantinières for corsets and other feminine beauty aids. During the siege of Sevastopol, several civilian merchants made their living selling corsets and other finery to cantinières in the army.[43]

Cantinières also took to increasingly flamboyant costumes in attempts to distinguish themselves. This was particularly common in the Imperial Guard, and was often due more to the initiative of commanders seeking to augment their unit's impressive appearance than to the desire of the women themselves. The emperor's elite bodyguard, the "Cent-gardes," designed a costume for their cantinière that represented the extreme of this trend. It included a blue velour tunic with scarlet satin trim, a fitted vest of silver cloth with gold buttons to simulate the soldiers' iron breastplates, a gold belt, black skirt, white gloves, knee-high leather boots, and a silver and gold cap decorated with a red feather. Though this uniform was for show rather than for combat, the cantinières of the rest of the Imperial Guard went to war in the Crimea in full dress uniform, cutting quite a swath among the battle-weary veterans who saw them. Captain Charles Thoumas was sufficiently impressed to write home after seeing them, though with more than a hint of sarcasm.

> I admired the cantinière of the chasseurs à pied of the Guard, a very chic woman, I beg you to believe, at least for her costume: very short skirt, very baggy pants tucked into her leggings which pinched her calves, a little jacket with short tails and scalloped edges, sword belt and buckle carrying a damasced dagger, a red chechia on her ear with a long tassel falling on her shoulder, a turned-up nose, black hair in braids, and the voice—of a corporal of engineers. Isn't that all very seductive?[44]

Even outside the guard, cantinières could add extravagant or outlandish details. Madame Chevrau of the 137th Infantry Regiment carried a large tonnelet with unusually lavish artwork depicting the regimental crest surmounted by a brace of flags and laurels. More unusual still, her tonnelet had two compartments and two brass spigots, presumably for carrying two types of beverage.[45] Since both wine and absinthe were in high demand among the soldiers in addition to brandy, having more than one drink on tap had obvious advantages. While the double compartment was rare, tonnelets continued to be elaborately decorated expressions of individuality: size, shape, colors, and even materials varied from unit to unit and among cantinières of the same regiment, as evidenced by surviving tonnelets displayed in the French Army Museum. In particular, the two tonnelets belonging to cantinières of the Voltigeurs of the Guard are very different. Madame Froidevaux's tonnelet was made of brass with the regimental crest on white with red and blue stripes on the side. That of Madame Fagot was made of wood and painted overall dark green with the regimental crest on the side. Both followed the standard practice of placing the regimental number at the back end and the cantinière's name at the front above the spigot, but each was lettered in its owner's distinctive style.[46]

The day-to-day reality of the cantinières' existence was less picturesque than the popular images suggest. Certainly, they had their moments in military parades and on their rare days off in garrison, but for most cantinières, life was one long period of work with few breaks and rarely any opportunities for great profit. One mark of this is the fact that the colorful uniforms were generally reserved for campaigning, parades, and public appearances. As one observer wrote, "Glory and noise do not suffice to fill the stomach, so on her return to quarters, the cantinière lays aside her gorgeous apparel and resumes her civilian costume, that is, a skirt and dress, and bestows her attention upon the thousands of details connected with her establishment."[47] Likewise, one English lady on the way to the Crimea by steamship was startled at the discrepancy between a cantinière's daily dress in the canteen and her public attire:

> We had only one Frenchwoman among the troops on board the "Thabor"; and she was a middle-aged Norman, who, in a somewhat dirty cap, orange neckerchief, draggled chintz dress and sabots, was anything but an attractive object. Having seen no other woman however, except our pleasant little Marseilles stewardess, and a *femme de chambre* on her way to Constantinople, I was somewhat startled, the morning we anchored off Smyrna, at the sudden apparition of a brilliant *cantinière,* who, in red trousers, short skirt, and tight jacket, came clanking her spurs down the companion ladder at breakfast, and, strutting with a most self-possessed air into the saloon, touched her casquette to the Colonel, and stated her intention of passing the day at Smyrna. Monsieur le Commandant smiled, bowed, addressed the individual as "Madame," and requested she would have the goodness to be on board again at four. On this, she touched her cap a second time, wheeled round, and re-ascended the "companion" in most military style. Truly dress *is* a great improver of persons, for this dashing *cantinière* was no other than the lady of the sabots, whose chance of creating an impression was entirely the result of this *grande tenue.*[48]

Nevertheless, this example shows how seriously most cantinières took their military appearance. While it was acceptable to work indoors in the female equivalent of fatigue clothing, in public, cantinières took great efforts to look their most impressive and most martial.

Despite the glitter of dress uniforms, the life of the military mother and child remained harsh, though far less so than in earlier periods. The mitigation of the hardships of earlier eras was largely due to the lessened frequency and duration of major conflicts, as well as improved conditions of sanitation, supply, medical care, communication, and transportation. Whereas Napoleon I's cantinières were on campaign almost continuously from 1805 to 1814, the armies of Napoleon III spent much of their time in peacetime French garrisons, and units left enfants de troupe with the regimental depot during wartime. No children accompanied the French

Army to the Crimea, to Italy, or to the frontier in 1870, but children did go to Mexico, and Algeria was full of extended military families. Those families on continuous duty in the Army of Africa suffered greater privations than those in metropolitan France, and infant mortality was highest there. Part of the problem was that terms like "wartime" and "peacetime" had little meaning in Algeria, where wartime conditions always prevailed, but no formal state of war existed. Children could not be left behind in France for years at a time, nor could the children of Zouaves and other African units be sent away. Instead, they traveled with their parents and endured the hardships of campaigning. For example, Louise Bernou's young brother died in Algeria as an enfant de troupe of the Thirty-sixth Infantry Regiment, and she lost two of her own children there to cholera.[49] Despite the perils involved, though, cantinières on campaign bore and raised children in the army, and in the colonies at least, they often faced trials similar to those of their predecessors.

Most cantinières had children, and many had several. However, cantinières in the Second Empire appear to have had fewer children than those of the First, and a good number elected to have no children at all. While by all accounts cantinières of the latter period were emotionally attached to their offspring, increasingly they saw their children as separate from their professional existence as cantinières. In short, they themselves defined two "separate spheres" in their lives: one professional, one private. One reason why it is difficult to determine the number of children cantinières bore during this period is that the women's own letters to the War Ministry rarely mention children. Second Empire cantinières saw themselves as soldiers, not as mothers. Whereas vivandières and cantinières up to about 1840 usually phrased their pension requests in terms of charity for poor widows and mothers of destitute children, pension letters of later cantinières rarely mentioned children at all, and instead based their requests on the cantinières' own service to the nation.

Children of cantinières in this period almost invariably became cantinières or soldiers. Marie-Françoise Bréhaut of the Second Infantry Regiment had only one son during her twenty-four years as a cantinière. Little François-Auguste served as an enfant de troupe, enlisted as a private soldier in 1864 at age seventeen, and by 1900 was the commanding colonel of the Eighty-first Infantry Regiment.[50] Most cantinières' children did not rise to such high rank, but many had impressive careers. Anne Calastroupat of the Forty-fifth Infantry Regiment had three sons, all soldiers who died while on active service. Louis was the *chef de fanfare* of the Third Rifle Regiment, and died in Philippeville in 1887 after eighteen years' service.

Eugène was a musician in the 104th Infantry Regiment, and died in 1881 at Le Mans after eighteen years' service. The youngest, Théophile, reached the rank of sergeant-major in his mother's regiment in only seven years before he fell ill and died in 1873. Anne Calastroupat thus had the common experience of outliving all of her children.[51] Louise Bernou's family also produced a crop of new recruits for the army. One of her brothers died of cholera as an enfant de troupe in Algeria, while her eldest brother retired as a captain. She and her sister both married soldiers of the regiment and became cantinières.[52] Likewise, Anna Commaret's three sons all appear to have entered the service as enfants de troupe and later served as soldiers.[53] And Clémence Mercurin of the Grenadiers of the Imperial Guard had four sons. One became an officer, one a drum-major, and two became private soldiers.[54]

Bearing children was often much less traumatic than in earlier periods, especially if a woman was fortunate enough to be stationed in France. Much of this improvement was due to better standards of medical care as medical science progressed. Part of it also was due to changes in attitudes toward women and childbirth, including the increased prestige of cantinières and the frequent application of more middle-class values to their condition, not so much by the women themselves as by those around them. Thus, when the Belgian Legion took ship for Mexico in October 1864, cantinière Jeannette Van Acker was left behind in St. Nazaire. She was seven months pregnant and the legion's officers wrote in the unit diary that "her state offered dangers for an ocean crossing."[55] This sort of bourgeois solicitude would never have been offered to a cantinière in earlier times. She would have simply been expected to come along on campaign and to give birth as best she could in the field. Jeannette gave birth to a girl in December and immediately embarked for Mexico with her baby to rejoin the unit. Railroads and steamships made it relatively easy for a woman to catch up to her unit after staying behind to give birth, a luxury eighteenth-century vivandières could not afford. But once in combat, birthing conditions could be as primitive as ever. William Russell, the *Times* reporter in the Crimea, witnessed one incident where a cantinière refused to stay out of combat even though she was at full term.

A buxom French cantinière accompanied her battalion to the trenches, there to supply them with their drinks and to brave with masculine courage the storm of shot and shell. Towards the small hours of the morning, she was taken with the pains of maternity and gave birth to twins. Mother and children are doing well.[56]

Far fewer women gave birth in such circumstances than had done so half a century earlier, but wherever cantinières served, new French children came into the world.

Though they wore splendid uniforms and benefited from a public perception that they were soldiers just like the men in the ranks, cantinières continued to suffer from the official denial that they were *militaires*. An example of their daily conditions comes from the 1856 regulation on service in garrison, which greeted troops coming home from their victory in the Crimea: "In the lodgings of blanchisseuses-vivandières [*sic*], the engineer's service will provide nothing but a plank for baggage."[57] In short, cantinières were responsible for all furnishings and other accouterments for their lodgings while in garrison. Considering the many examples of cantinières' aptitude at foraging, however, this regulation was less likely an example of the War Ministry's callousness than an attempt to prevent cantinières from defrauding the government by equipping their homes and canteens at the army's expense. Many cantinières were sharp operators, and only by strictly regulating dispositions of army property could the War Ministry hope to impede fraud even slightly. In some situations the army provided the cantinières with not just a canteen, but accommodations as well. An English engineer officer observing the camp at Châlons-sur-Marne in September of 1861 commented, "The kitchens are in the same building with the canteen, one on either side of it. There are two canteens to each battalion. Each canteen has 3 rooms and a cellar. One is a tap-room, the other two are for the cantiniere, the wife of a soldier. The *sous-officiers* mess in the tap-room; the cantiniere cooks for them." He also noted that "The accommodation for women and children appears limited to 2 cantinières and 2 rooms for washerwomen, per battalion."[58]

The cantinières' greatest business concern continued to be selling alcohol to the troops. In garrison, this occurred in the barracks' canteen, which was run, furnished, and supplied by the cantinière. Arrangements varied, but usually the canteen was a room in the fort with enough space for several tables and many chairs, as well as a bar, storage area, and kitchen. The cantinière worked hard, cooking two meals a day for the NCOs who took their *pension* with her, and selling drinks, meals, and tobacco to everyone else from early morning until late at night. The canteen fulfilled a variety of functions, and it might be compared to a modern American NCO club, post exchange, and franchise restaurant all in one. As one veteran put it in 1870,

The canteen is not what the civilian thinks: it is all at once a restaurant, a bar, a café, an ale house, and a *pension*. It is there that the soldier and sometimes the officer comes to have a morning drink, and the volunteer eats up a bit of the money his family sends him. There the man of good appetite finds a supplement to his rations at a good price, the loafers take their chairs for their parties, and the trooper on duty can savor his *demi-tasse* without leaving the barracks.[59]

In other words, the canteen was both the social center of the regiment and the refuge for the solitary soldier in need of a place to rest. As such it provided a vital psychological boost to the soldiers' morale.

The cantinière was the proprietress, but in peacetime she often employed one or more helpers, depending on the complexity of her operation and the volume of her business. In case of trouble, though, "she herself put the troublemakers out the door."[60] Husbands often took no part whatsoever in the cantinière's business dealings. In the Thirteenth Hussars, the nominal cantiniers showed up only occasionally, and usually for social reasons. There were exceptions, however; Private Antoine Creste of the Eighteenth Infantry Regiment actively assisted his wife Marie in her business affairs, according to legal complaints against the couple.

On campaign, the cantinière sold her wares from a mobile canteen set up in a tent, or from the back of her wagon. The extent of the appointments depended on the nature of the campaign. During the lengthy siege of Sevastopol, cantinières purchased large and colorful Turkish tents that attracted the eye and offered good shelter. In fact, British travelers and soldiers were frequent customers, since the cantinières provided food and drink that the British logistical system failed to deliver. One group of English commented that their fare consisted of "some bread and cheese, and some bad brandy and water," but the group still preferred the canteen to the alternatives in the British camp. "Everybody seemed very jolly and comfortable, especially the cantinière, who had grown fat and aged in the exercise of her calling."[61] In Africa and Mexico, cantinières often did not even have a cart, and their "canteen" consisted of whatever they could carry on a single pack mule. In Italy and in the Franco-Prussian War, cantinières could bring their carts, and could therefore set up tents when the situation warranted, though in 1870 the French army was defeated so quickly and so thoroughly that there was little time to establish a routine. Nonetheless, cantinières remained important and popular among the soldiers. One civilian noted that "each company has, too, its cantinière, and round her cart there is always a crowd."[62]

No matter what the circumstances, the cantinière's livelihood depended on maintaining a supply of goods and on attracting paying customers.

Both required a certain amount of ingenuity, and different cantinières solved their problems in different ways. In garrison in France, the only way to supply the large demands of the canteen and the *pension* was to buy food and drink locally, though some army supplies undoubtedly found their way into the cantinières' stores. This does not mean that cantinières always paid for their goods. For example, Marie and Anton Creste took advantage of their regiment's change of garrison to leave town without paying one of their suppliers 160F. The enraged supplier later wrote to the minister of war, but received no satisfaction.[63] On campaign, a combination of pillage and purchase kept cantinières stocked. Cantinières of the Second Empire were more likely to be deal-makers than looters, but pillage was a source of income, especially in the colonial wars but also in the Crimea. Witnessing one scene of widespread looting at Sevastopol, an officer commented that "the crowd of new arrivals grew at each instant, [and] it was not just the cantinières who provisioned themselves."[64] This suggests that cantinière looting was common and expected; the only thing notable about the incident was that common soldiers were joining in too. On the other hand, Mariette Moerman of the Belgian Legion worked a deal with a German brewer in Mexico City to keep her supplied "with real white beer, a singularly rare item in Mexico and therefore much prized."[65] Another cantinière in Mexico found that her feminine attractions enriched her stock, though she ended up consuming the windfall herself. A French officer tried without success to woo her, finally sending her a basket full of bottles of good wine. That evening he arrived at her tent, thinking he would share the wine with her, and "he had the disappointment to find the knavish woman chaperoned by her brother and four sergeants, all happily guzzling the wine."[66]

Business dealings in a war zone could be quite different from those in garrison, though. Ultimately, toughness and a good head for business were more important than good looks or fancy costumes. One French cantinière in the Crimea showed her mettle in both areas when a party of drunken English officers on horseback decided to have fun at the expense of the cantinière's pet dog, chasing it on horseback as if on a fox hunt. The hunt was "jolly fun, but rather expensive to some of the individuals concerned, as the cur belonged to the proprietor of a French canteen into whose tent we chased it, and [we] had to buy two or three bottles of very bad bordeaux to pacify the irritated female."[67] In this case, the best revenge was to force the offenders to buy a poor product at a high price, no doubt a common tactic. Though the previous scene was somewhat comical, the wartime canteen was also the site of more serious occurrences. An officer

recalled seeing a sergeant of the Twelfth Infantry Regiment, encamped
near Varna in 1854 during a cholera epidemic, "drinking and laughing with
his comrades in front of the canteen, when he suddenly gave out a piercing
cry. . . . fifteen minutes later he was dead," apparently a victim of cholera.[68]
Cantinières on campaign therefore needed to deal not only with the challenges of life, but with sudden death as well, even on their own doorsteps,
and even when the enemy was far off.

Shrewd business dealings could reap large profits in wartime, and many
cantinières were not hesitant to take advantage of the opportunities. A
French military doctor recalled two cantinières who each bought a dozen
ermine pelts in Constantinople for twenty-five francs each, then brought
them back to France to sell at a profit.[69] Buying low and selling high was
a crucial skill for cantinières who wished to rise above their humble stations. A cantinière of the Seventeenth Battalion of Chasseurs à Pied took
part in a successful fight with Russian Cossacks near Chernaya on the last
day of December 1854, and turned the situation to her advantage.

> This day, when we were so cold, wasn't bad for everyone. The cantinière
> of my battalion managed to equip herself with a Cossack officer's horse, for
> which she paid a chasseur 40F. It was a good deal, because the brave canti-
> nière also got a portmanteau well stocked with food, brandy, plus a complete
> officer's uniform and a Bible in good condition. The saddle and bridle were
> perfectly conserved. Many admirers presented themselves to us on our return
> to camp.[70]

Given the number of "admirers" who were interested in the horse, the cantinière most likely sold the horse at a profit, but not before setting aside
the many extras for sale as well. Even bad mounts fetched a very high price
around Sevastopol during the winter of 1854–1855, and a fine officer's horse
was particularly valuable. Through such various wheelings and dealings,
cantinières could sometimes earn large amounts of money.

Even without special deals, cantinières in the Crimea did much of their
profitable business with English soldiers, who were well provided with
pocket money but left to starve by their inept supply service. With no cantinières of their own, and no food or drink arriving from their own country,
they were among the cantinières' best customers.[71] Running a successful
canteen, scavenging, and taking advantage of good purchase opportunities
added up to substantial riches for some. In June 1855, a captain of the Seventeenth Artillery commented disparagingly on the immense profits reaped
by his cantinière and her husband, writing that "these knaves have already

earned 12,000 francs since the start of the campaign," which at that point had lasted only a year.[72] Another ex-soldier working as a guide for English tourists complained that "at a *cafe,* the soldiers could get their cup for 15 centimes, or 20 with liqueur; whereas the *cantiniere* charged a franc, and gave them very bad coffee. Wine, too, which would cost them 60 centimes the kilo in the town, was valued at 2 francs by their grasping enemy."[73]

However, condemnation of cantinières for greed was far from universal. Gaboriau wrote that "the charges are not high, as you see; so cantinieres do not accumulate fortunes as rapidly as the restaurant-keepers on the boulevards." He also noted that "she does not like to give credit; but she is so kind-hearted that she can not bear to see a man suffer, and it is impossible for her to refuse a drop to a really thirsty soldier. Though she censures herself for her weakness, she does not know how to resist an entreaty; but we must admit that she is generally paid, and that she does not lose much by her liberality. . . . Moreover, if a trooper be sick or wounded, though not sufficiently to be sent to the hospital, she nurses him, dresses his wound, and prepares the *tisane,* for which she will never accept any pay."[74]

Cantinières also had military duties to perform on campaign. Self-enrichment and service to the unit were often conflicting goals. Many French officers recognized this, and it contributed later to the growing demand for the elimination of cantinières. The same cantinière who earned twelve thousand francs in a year during the Crimean War was virtually useless as a member of her unit. When typhus struck the camp in 1855, her commander fed barley water to the sick soldiers. He later wrote, "I believe the only service the cantinière rendered for me during the entire campaign was to keep two or three pots full of barley constantly boiling on the fire."[75] On the other hand, some cantinières were more than willing to be of service. When the Second Zouaves landed in the Crimea in 1854, they were short of rations. One of their cantinières, "La Mère Dumont," volunteered to make several trips to Varna on a chartered steamer to purchase supplies with her own money, thus saving the regiment from starvation.[76] Similarly, the commander of the Seventh Artillery Regiment cited Anna Commaret as "a veritable model of a cantinière," who "has always shown a great solicitude for the soldier, even to the detriment of her own interests."[77] One writer noted that "during a campaign she devotes herself to her regiment. More than once in the thickest of the fight she has been seen going from rank to rank to carry a drop to the soldiers, and braving the canister and grape in order to give a little water to the wounded. She keeps no accounts at such times; she does not sell, she gives."[78] Likewise, Anna Busquet of the Ninetieth Infantry Regiment worked as a cook and runner during the battles around Metz in 1870. "Madame Busquet cooked meals in the midst of the battle, and carried pots of soup to the forward positions." While not avaricious, Busquet and her husband were guilty of a breach of a different kind. The two were very passionate, and as Anna later described, Henri accompanied her on her rounds one day while she distributed food to the troops. The two wandered into a little wood and were "driven to madness in the throes of love" when they found themselves accosted by an officer of General MacMahon's staff. "You merit being brought before a court martial for abandoning your post, corporal," he remarked, "but this time I will let it pass."[79] This offers yet another illustration of the willingness of officers to overlook breaches of regulations in the interest of keeping their troops fed, supplied, and content. Cantinières often benefited from this leniency as long as they helped commanders achieve these goals.

Cantinières were useful to the army in a variety of ways, many of them social in nature, some more martial. Part of their appeal to the army was their ability to provide a relatively safe female presence. Male soldiers needed female company, and they were likely to desert or frequent prostitutes if they did not get it. In theory, the cantinière provided non-sexual female company for the entire unit, and took care of only her husband's sexual needs. The drawings of Lalaisse reinforced this social function as primary. Many of his lithographs showed cantinières not only selling drinks to the troops, but chatting and laughing good-naturedly with them.[80] This was indeed the theme of the title page of L'armée française et ses cantinières. While Lalaisse's view was often exaggerated and stylized, socializing remained one of the mid-century cantinières' major functions, especially in camp.

In settled situations such as the siege of Sevastopol, many social events were organized, and cantinières formed almost the entire female contingent. The Second Zouave Regiment created an improvised theater, the famed Théâtre des Zouaves, which produced original plays written by enlisted soldiers. The theater played to huge crowds and donated its proceeds to the ambulance corps.[81] The Zouaves' cantinières played their part by sewing the entire wardrobe for the theater, while the senior cantinière of the regiment acted as cashier and ticket seller, a position of considerable trust.[82]

More traditional social events also occurred, including a number of balls. An English officer wrote home, "Sometimes there are balls at little Kamiesch (the French bazaar near our camp). Ladies are few and far between and chiefly cantinières, sometimes very fat."[83] Apparently, the behavior of the cantinières did not reflect upper-class Victorian ideals, and there was considerable friction between the cantinières and the numerous wives of English officers. At a ball to celebrate the birth of the Prince Imperial, "there were about eight English ladies there at the commencement. Their sense of propriety was very soon shocked when they saw a lot of vivandières coming in with scarlet trousers and shiny hats . . . so you will not be surprised when I tell you the English ladies very soon departed."[84] However the "scarlet trousers and shiny hats" may have appeared to the English ladies, they were in fact the cantinières' uniforms, and perhaps it was less their behavior than their mere presence and the masculinity of their costumes that the English women objected to. Certainly, respectable bourgeois women did not wear trousers in England or in France, but cantinières did, and were proud of it.

Cantinières also provided a social function for officers in the Army of Africa. The extent of the fraternization is entirely open to question, but certainly European women were a scarce commodity in Algeria during the 1850s, and officers as high in rank as general often took consolation in the company of cantinières. Captain Charles Thoumas had never served in North Africa, but found himself attached to a division of *africains* in 1854. His brigade was commanded by General Bouat, who Thoumas implies had an adulterous relationship with a cantinière of the Sixth Infantry Regiment.

> Nothing was more singular than the head of our column. The general was on his large English horse, having at his right the captain of the gendarmerie, his inseparable, and at his left, mounted *en amazone,* a cantinière whose husband, a musician in the Sixth Regiment, walked along behind his wife blowing philosophically into his trombone.[85]

Thoumas was circumspect in his language, but the clear implication was that the cantinière was the general's mistress, and that the husband, as an enlisted man, could only accept the situation with Gallic resignation. Nor was Bouat alone in his admiration for cantinières. The previously cited example of the cantinière in Mexico offers one example of an officer attempting (and failing) to seduce a cantinière. Thirty years earlier General Castellane wrote of cantinière Antoinette Mouron, "My word, she has beautiful eyes!"[86] A less explicit but still telling example comes from a British traveler to Africa in 1854, who found that in order to occupy the men during a quiet spell, a cavalry unit had organized a difficult steeplechase. "The general, as umpire and mayor of the place, was invited, according to ancient custom, to preside at the fête. Every body flocked to it; the exquisites on horseback, and the humble trooper with cane in hand. A cantinière, nominated Queen of Beauty, was to present the winner with a beautiful pair of pistols offered by General Renaud. The stake was worthy of the peril."[87] Thus, the cantinière's role as the surrogate female presence for all the men was even more important in the colonies.

Not all of the cantinières' duties on campaign revolved around commerce and socializing. In many cases, they performed important and sometimes delicate military services for their commanders. During the guerrilla war in Mexico, cantinières came in handy for searching Mexican ladies suspected of smuggling for the Republican forces. An English tourist traveling with a detachment of French chasseurs reported that when the soldiers searched some Mexican women's baggage, "nothing of any importance turned up, although the vivandières of the chasseurs, after a private interview with the lady travelers, discovered some letters from Treviño hid under their petticoats!"[88] Having reliable women available to strip-search local ladies saved the French from making the unpleasant choice between outraging local opinion and allowing unrestricted female smuggling. Likewise, when dealing with important prisoners of war, cantinières were useful ambassadors of goodwill. Near Milan in 1859, the Zouaves of the Imperial Guard captured a number of Austrian officers, but were without time or rations to care for them properly. Captain Luguez "sent them a cantinière with some provisions, to which they did honor."[89]

On the field of battle, cantinières confined themselves mostly to caring for the wounded and bringing drinks to the thirsty troops. Civilian nursing or medical corps along the lines of the Red Cross did not yet exist, and cantinières were the de facto nurses and surgeons' assistants. In fact, it was on the battlefields of Italy in 1859 that Henri Dunant first conceived of the International Red Cross, at the same time French cantinières were risking their lives to save the wounded all around him. As in the past, while women who fought bravely were much valued by their commanders, the women who received official decorations and publicity tended to be those who confined themselves to the more acceptable activities of serving drinks and caring for the wounded. Moreover, the public image of cantinières was more than ever centered on the idea of female caregivers. Those cantinières who routinely fired weapons in anger represented a minority in the army, and during this period, they generally did not gain official recognition.

Nevertheless, cantinières continued to have important combat roles. One prominent English observer commented on the way cantinières led their regiments into battle in the Crimea, particularly during the desperate assaults on the Russian trenches around the "White Works" in the spring of 1855:

The more any regiment was agitated by perturbing emotions, the more its men seemed to contrast with the fair one who rode at their head in her panoply of fearless, calm pride. . . . riding serenely at the head of her regiment in the moments preceding a fight she represents an Idea; and, it being divined, though but dimly, that this march against the Lunette would involve heavy slaughter, she now more than ever seemed one who embodied the spirit of war. You might call her a priestess ordained, and bringing up human sacrifices to lay on the altar of glory; or again might see in her form a conventional image of France nobly leading her sons into action, and commanding them, if need be, to die. Each actress had her own "reading" of the part that she played; so that one corps of troops for example was proudly led down through the gorge by a chieftainess riding in plumes; another by a bright girl attired with all the ineffable comeliness that belongs to the daughters of France when obeying strict laws of costume. The fairest of all was the one at the head of a much-favoured regiment, by our people called the "Green Chasseurs." With infinite grace and composure she led her men down the Ravine to meet the fortune of war. We have—not wrongly—lingered a moment to see the Vivandiere pass; for—always characteristic, and linked with great warlike traditions—the memory of her presence, that day, gathered strength from the slaughter that followed. After an interval of perhaps hardly more than thirty, or thirty-five minutes, the fight was destined to open, and then within one single hour, and within but a few hundred yards of the scenic display we have witnessed, the troops thus led down the Ravine would be falling, and falling by thousands.[90]

While the leading of the troops to battle described above may have been purely ceremonial, there were some who continued to fight in the ranks alongside the soldiers, particularly among the elite regiments of Zouaves. Most cantinières continued to carry daggers or short swords, but by mid-century the industrial revolution had provided a much more useful weapon—the revolver. Many cantinières made use of the compact firepower these weapons provided, though some used military-issue rifles as well. Most fighting cantinières gained their early experience in Algeria, where the use of weapons was often necessary, if only for self-defense. The Zouave regiments, formed in Algeria and continually called upon for the worst combat tasks, produced an inordinately high number of fighting cantinières. Madeleine Trimoreau of the Second Zouave Regiment provides a good example. She joined the regiment at its formation in 1832 and accompanied it to the Crimea in 1854. During the desperate night battle for the Russian "White Works," she received one bullet wound and two bayonet wounds, a testimony to how actively she was involved in the close fighting. Back in Algeria in 1857, she was captured by Kabyle tribesmen while fighting in the ranks, but was rescued by the Zouaves.[91] Annette Drevon was a young cantinière of the Second Zouaves. At the battle of Magenta in 1859, her regiment was involved in fierce hand-to-hand combat when two Austrian soldiers captured the regimental flag. Drevon attacked them armed with a pistol and a saber, killed them both, and brought the flag back under fire. Her colonel took his own Cross of the Legion of Honor from his chest and pinned it on the cantinière. Eleven years later Drevon was captured by the Germans and insulted by a Bavarian officer who tried to take her cross. She responded by pulling out a concealed revolver and shooting him dead.[92] Henriette Calvet was another cantinière who fired shots in anger. She fought in Algeria, the Crimea, Italy, and Mexico, and in the Franco-Prussian War. Fighting with the First Zouaves, she fired a rifle at Solferino and Marignano, but spent much of her time caring for the wounded, including her regimental colonel.[93] She was later awarded the Military Medal for her *belle conduite,* but the award did not mention actual fighting.[94] Louise Bernou was another *africaine* who learned to fight in Algeria. After rigorous campaigns that took the lives of her husband and child, she found herself in barracks at Batna with the Thirty-sixth Infantry Regiment in 1866. However, she had little rest, since Arab prisoners were free to wander around the courtyard of the fort, leading Louise to lock her door and arm herself. "I was afraid every moment of being murdered," she wrote. "The door of my hut was twice broken in and twice I killed the Kabyle dogs."[95] Even elderly and infirm cantinières sometimes showed an irrepressible will to fight. When the Second Zouaves left Algeria for the Crimea, they left behind "La Belle Marie," who was aged beyond reckoning and crippled by arthritis. Rather than accept her pastoral fate, she stowed away aboard a transport in the hope of fighting the Russians.[96] This sort of sentiment gained cantinières the respect of their fellow soldiers, but it did not earn them any official decorations or recognition. It would not be until the disasters of the Franco-Prussian War, and specifically after the end of the Empire, that cantinières would receive decorations for fighting, and even then the awards would be couched in deliberately ambiguous language.

Those cantinières who earned official public praise during the Second Empire were those who nursed the wounded rather than those who fought the enemy, and they certainly represented a majority. By mid-century, the brave examples of previous cantinières had become the new standard for behavior. Commanders and soldiers expected cantinières to expose themselves to enemy fire in order to help the wounded, and these women had in fact become nurses, though they received no medical training or pay. Although originally a cantinière of the First Zouave Regiment, Thérèse Malher transferred to the Thirty-fourth Infantry Regiment and served with it in Italy in 1859. At Melignano and at the bloody fight at Solferino she "showed great energy" in caring for the wounded and was later decorated with the Military Medal.[97] Likewise, Perrine Cros of the Chasseurs of the Guard went into battle at Solferino with the express intention of aiding the wounded. As one witness wrote, "Madame Perrine had taken, in addition to her regulation tonnelet of brandy, a canteen full of cool water, bandages, and strips of cloth. The valiant little cantinière was going to be a sister of charity."[98] She was helping a wounded soldier when she too was hit. On her way to the ambulance, she found a soldier shot through both legs but could not lift him. Instead, despite her wound, she dragged him back to the ambulance, earning her unit's respect and the Military Medal.[99] In a different conflict but under similar circumstances, Anne Lalonne of the Second Battalion of Chasseurs à Pied distinguished herself in caring for the wounded at the battle of Kiloa in Cochinchina. She received a decoration and mention in the *Moniteur officiel.*[100] This role of nurse impressed outside observers much more than did actual fighting because it harmonized better with developing bourgeois ideas about women's roles in the family and society. Photographer Roger Fenton was so interested in portraying cantinières as nurses rather than as barmaids or soldiers that he staged a photograph of a cantinière aiding a wounded soldier near Sevastopol in 1855.[101] Ironically, he chose a cantinière of a Zouave regiment, the very type of unit whose cantinières were most likely to fight in the ranks. Likewise, when Eugène Charpentier painted his *Bataille de Solferino, 24 juin 1859* he included a cantinière of Zouaves bandaging a wounded soldier, but did not include any women firing weapons. Nor did Charpentier's *Bataille de Magenta* include any women, even though Magenta was the site of Annette Drevon's audacious fight.[102] While there were cantinières who received ad hoc decorations on the field of battle for actual fighting, it was the nursing that received praise through official channels. The government praised cantinières who nursed the wounded precisely since it placed these women firmly in a gender role that they all too often transgressed.

One other incident from the mid-century bears discussion, if only because it shows a cantinière not only decorated with the Cross, but decorated for actual combat. As the story goes, a young woman from the tiny village of Epagne (outside Abbeville) fought on the government side in the suppression of the rebellion by the workers of Paris in the bloody June

Days of 1848. The story of Victorine Charlemagne originally appeared in
Le peuple constituent in August 1848. In it, eighteen-year-old Victorine
claimed to have stormed a rebel barricade and cut the flag from the leader
of the defenders' hands. However, she also claimed that this had been done
in extraordinary circumstances, and that she now wished only to be a wife
and mother, and urged French women to fulfill those feminine roles rather
than to take up arms. In addition to various popular songs and folklore,
the story was taken up by Ernest Prarond in an 1854 study of the Abbeville
area. Prarond was equivocal about the story. As he put it, "the story of Victorine Charlemagne is quite difficult to put in its proper light, and we are
left suspended between two impulses: if we keep ourselves in the half-light,
we see too little, and if we demand more clarity, we see too much."[103]
Clearly, Prarond doubted the story, yet just as clearly he did not want to
discount what was after all a brave and heroic deed: an undeniable *beau
geste*. For that reason, he asked readers to suspend disbelief, and then
launched into a story of Charlemagne's life that included a miraculous
childhood ability to reconcile bitter enemies in her village, a fitting trait for
a national symbol in the years after the bitter civil strife of 1848. Prarond
then quoted from the original article, in which General Duvivier "ran to
the young girl, tore off his own Cross, and in tears attached it to the chest
of the heroine. 'France,' he said, 'will never forget you! If God spares me,
as long as you live, you will be happy!'"[104]

The story is problematical for several reasons. The heroine's very name
reeks of a deliberately fabricated patriotic legend, as do the details of the
story. One example among many is the young girl's miraculous salvation
from a volley of point-blank musket fire, as is the fact that as the smoke
dissipated, "Victorine appeared straight and shining on the barricade, the
red flag in her hand, and her hair streaming onto her shoulders, a bullet
having carried away her comb."[105] While this is possible, it is highly unlikely, and the narration smacks of an inspirational, patriotic tale. Moreover, the one man who could without a doubt confirm it (and who had
assured her of his undying gratitude *if* he lived)—General Duvivier—was
already dead of wounds he received in the fighting by the time the story
was published. Conveniently, he could tell no tales. A later investigation
in her village found no trace of her: "We have examined the civil records
carefully, and we can affirm that this heroine was not borne in Epagne, nor
did she even ever live there. She would be sixty-three years old today, but
none of the many persons of that age or of an older age that we spoke to
knew her. It is thus a legend, such as often appear in troubled times."[106]
The records of the Museum of the Legion of Honor also show no record

of Mlle Charlemagne ever receiving an award, so even if the story were true, it would not represent an official award: only a personal and unofficial act of generosity by General Duvivier. Moreover, even the original story makes it clear that Victorine was not an actual cantinière: she was merely a young woman living in an attic room who could not bear to see French troops waver in front of the rebels, and who intervened out of patriotism. Thus, even if the story were true, we could call her a cantinière only in the loosest sense. Just as her award was not official, neither was her status as a cantinière: she became one only by self-proclamation, and in a mythic story at that. Ultimately, the story of Victorine Charlemagne was most likely an effort to convince the public of two things: that the strife of the June Days needed to be put in the past, and that the proper place of women was in the home, except in exceptional cases when they needed to defend the legitimate government of France. Rather than a revolutionary tale of a cantinière taking on a man's role, we have what appears to be a tale designed to discourage civilian women from acting out in daily life.

Even if Victorine Charlemagne was a myth, the extremely active role of real-life cantinières on the battlefield during the Second Empire had a price. The long range and deadly accuracy of the newer generation of rifled small arms and artillery combined with the unwritten code of front-line conduct meant that more cantinières than ever were exposed to danger in European wars. Cantinières became casualties in many locations across the globe over the eighteen years of the Second Empire. Madame Dumont of the Second Zouaves worked herself to exhaustion and died of cholera during the siege of Sevastopol in 1854, while her comrade Madelaine Trimoreau escaped with only three wounds.[107] In December of 1855, William Russell noted that when the French army moved forward into the ruins of Sevastopol, their cantinières did not stay behind, but moved forward as well. The French displayed "great ingenuity in erecting comfortable magazines and shops in out-of-the-way parts of the town, where one can get a cup of coffee and a cigar without much danger. But to the uninitiated the roar of a ball and the twittering hiss of a shell fail to give zest to these luxuries. . . . The whole establishment of a *cantinière* went smash the other day through the operation of a shell, and, although it was tolerably well filled, the only damage done was to the poor proprietress, who lost her hand and an immense amount of crockery, comestibles, and customers."[108]

The fighting in Algeria also cost cantinières their blood. Louise Graffeuil of the Seventy-fifth Infantry was lucky to end her two-year tour of duty there with only a bullet wound through the right hand, but the hand was permanently disabled.[109] Madame Bourget of the First Rifle Regiment served seventeen years in Algeria, and was wounded three different times.[110] Across the Atlantic in Mexico, Juliette Meertz took a bullet in the shoulder at Morelia in 1865, while Catherine Opdemessing of the Belgian Legion was wounded and captured during the siege of Tacambaro.[111] Some captured cantinières fared worse. "Two of them were shot near Orizaba in 1862. Their bodies were mutilated, disfigured, and stripped."[112] Relatively lucky, Mère Ibrahim of the Second Zouaves fought unscathed in every French campaign from 1854 to 1885, only to be wounded in Tonkin toward the end of her career.[113]

Some of the heaviest casualties among cantinières came during the war against Austria in Italy in 1859. For the first time Napoleon III's army faced enemies armed with rifled muskets and modern artillery, and the carnage on the battlefields of Solferino and Magenta sickened even the emperor. Henriette Calvet of the First Zouave Regiment was hit while alternately firing at the Austrians and aiding the wounded at Solferino. At the same battle, Perrine Cros lost her right little finger to an Austrian bullet, and would have lost her ring finger if not for the several rings she wore, which absorbed the impact of the bullet. After the battle she sent the smashed and torn rings to the emperor, as much a gesture of bravado as a token of respect.[114]

While Italy proved to be a costly triumph, the disastrous Franco-Prussian War virtually destroyed the regular French army, and with it the Second Empire. English-language histories of the war have universally ignored the presence of cantinières. One example of the gap in English-language historiography is the comment by Barton Hacker after an extensive search that "I have found nothing written on women with the regular armies during the Franco-Prussian War."[115] French women served in combat with the regular army in large numbers (approximately a thousand), and most of those who survived ended the war as prisoners in Germany. Many French cantinières were inspired by a fierce patriotism and pride in the army, and they refused to quit the struggle even after their units had surrendered. This proved particularly true for battle-hardened women from the elite units of the Army of Africa.

Madame Duchamp of the Third Algerian Rifle Regiment provides a good example. A veteran of twenty-four years' service in Algeria, she fought with her unit in the battle of Froeschwiller, where the regiment was all but destroyed. She retreated with the survivors to Strasbourg, where she was captured along with the rest of the garrison. In the winter of 1871, she managed to escape from her captivity in Germany and return to France via Switzerland. Madame Dutailly of the Third Zouaves also fought at

Froeschwiller, where she killed two German soldiers while rescuing French wounded. Captured at Sédan, she escaped and returned to the besieged city of Strasbourg. She fought in the defense of the city, was wounded, and was captured once again when the city surrendered. She escaped again and this time returned to southern France, where the Government of National Defense was organizing new forces.[116] Henriette Calvet was captured as well. A veteran of Algeria, the Crimea, Syria, Italy, and Mexico, Calvet refused to give up. She escaped captivity, returned to France, and fought out the remainder of the war as a volunteer *ambulancière,* for which she was officially decorated.[117]

Anna Busquet managed to escape capture and showed a bravery and determination of a different kind. German light cavalrymen captured her wagon when she fell behind the regiment near Metz, but she fled on foot. Fortunately, her hometown of Givet was close by, and she was able to seek refuge with her family. Worried about the lack of news from her husband, Henri, she soon set out for Prussian headquarters at Namur, where she found Queen Augusta of Prussia and told her tale. The queen ascertained that Henri was a prisoner in Danzig, thus quieting Anna's worst fears as she returned to Givet to await her husband's homecoming.[118]

Nor were the casualties limited to the field battles. Hundreds of cantinières took part in the defense of Paris, and quite a few paid with their lives. Henry Labouchère participated in the siege and in January 1871 he wrote, "I then went to the Observatory, where according to the *Soir* the shells were falling very freely. . . . In the Rue d'Enfer, just behind, there was a house which had been struck during the night, and close by there was a cantinière, on her way to be buried, who had been killed by one."[119] Likewise, Albert Vandam wrote of a typical cantinière who "was wounded in front of her own *batterie de cuisine*" at the siege of Metz, and who used horse meat, "of which she concocted soups and savoury messes; going about foraging for the smallest scrap of carrot or turnip in order to make the miserable soldier's life a little less hard."[120]

One problem of discussing the Franco-Prussian War in a larger chronological narrative is that the war was started by one French government and continued by another. Thus, any discussion of cantinières in the years 1870–1871 inevitably runs up against the abrupt shift from Empire to Republic. Nevertheless, the real shift in regulations and policies away from those of the Second Empire did not occur until 1875, so to a certain extent the war can be discussed as part of the era of Napoleon III, at least in this context. The bloody defeat of the regular French army in 1870 marked the end of an era for cantinières as well as for many others. The abrupt end of the Second Empire left many career cantinières dead, wounded, or prisoner while a new government with very different agendas from Napoleon III gained control of France. The Third Republic would eventually restrict and then eliminate the military roles of cantinières. Still, many cantinières of the Second Empire continued to serve for extended periods under the new government, and there was much continuity in personnel between the two regimes. Most cantinières' husbands were long-service professional soldiers who served from their early youth until old age. The span of their service was usually longer than the span of the Second Empire, and the long periods of peace combined with a much lower death rate from disease meant that they were more likely to live long lives. Even when they did not, cantinières of the mid-century were very likely to remarry and stay in the army, so that far fewer women left their posts prematurely. Most Second Empire cantinières who applied for pensions therefore did so after 1871, and so their cases are more a reflection of the policies of the Third Republic than of the Second Empire. We will examine them in the next chapter. However, cantinières did retire during the reign of Napoleon III, and their conditions help explain why most preferred to stay with their adopted military family rather than taking their chances in the civilian economy.

Marie Ley of the Tenth Chasseurs à Cheval lost her husband in 1868. She retired to Fresnes-en-Woëvre (Meuse), where she eked out a living on her widow's pension. However, widows' pensions were 50 percent of the husbands' retirement pension, and therefore often not enough to survive on. Ley became increasingly unable to support herself financially, and at age seventy-five, she began a new career running a tobacco concession in a railroad station.[121] Henriette Descombs left the Eighth Artillery Regiment in 1859. She worked the next fifty years as a day laborer in the bleak Parisian industrial suburb of Alfortville. Unable to obtain a pension because she had not been legally married, she passed her old age in poverty and hard work.[122] A similar fate awaited Madame Descours of the Sixty-fourth Infantry Regiment. A veteran cantinière with twenty years' service, she lost her husband in 1868. She stayed on with the regiment until the summer of 1869, but wrote that "the sadness caused by the loss of my husband obliged me to return to my birthplace." However, once out of the army, she found herself impoverished. She had been wounded in the hand in the Crimea, and was missing a finger, making most manual labor impossible. In her own words, she was "totally without resources and had great difficulty even in surviving."[123]

William Blanchard Jerrold related one particularly sad tale of an ex-cantinière's poverty. Investigating the lives of the *chiffoniers* (trash pickers) of Paris, he interviewed a middle-aged woman who lived in the Rue de Grenelle and collected and resold trash for a living. Blanchard wrote, "These rooms consist of two apartments, three and a half metres by two and a half: the walls are whitewashed, but are now dirty. In the first room are the chiffons and other materials collected by the pair [the woman and her male companion], with the two mannequins or baskets, in the centre. All the rags and paper were sorted, and lying in distinct heaps. The inner room contained a broken-down bedstead, a dirty kind of cupboard, and two remarkably rickety chairs. Over the fire-place a piece of broken glass was nailed to the wall. These articles included all the worldly possessions of the pair. When I arrived, the woman had just returned with her heavy basket at her back. She was very dirty, and had the regular chiffonier's handkerchief bound tightly round her head." The woman was reluctant to talk, but Blanchard bribed her with a liter of wine, and, "drinking from two glasses with the feet broken off, and which, consequently, it was impossible to stand anywhere, even if there had been a table to stand them upon, I drew from her the following story of her life."

> I was born "enfant de troupe." My father was a soldier, and my mother was a cantinière. When I was only fourteen years of age, I ran away from them in company with a boy of fifteen. He married me as soon as I had completed my fifteenth year, and I was a mother six months afterwards. My husband became a soldier in the 1st Regiment of Lancers, and I became cantinière in the same regiment. I lived with him twenty years, and had ten children by him. I left him because he had an intrigue with our servant. Afterwards I got my living by selling brandy to the troops on the Champ de Mars, during exercise-time. By this employment I gained a franc for a morning's work.

She remained an honest woman, a fact that gave her a monopoly on trash picking in one wealthy neighborhood, where she "was known to all the housekeepers in the street. They greatly favoured her, because, if by chance, she found any valuables in the rubbish, she knew the house to which it belonged, and returned it to the owners." Nevertheless, she remained a hopeless drunk, and even when her son, an officer in her old regiment, gave her money, she spent it on wine while she wallowed in poverty as part of "perhaps the most drunken and the most brutalised class of workmen in Paris."[124]

Not all women who retired suffered such hardships. Mme Gaspard was a cantinière who participated in the invasion of Algeria in 1830, then participated in the long occupation. Exact dates and details are unclear, but by the 1850s she was something of a celebrity in Algeria as the owner of a hotel and restaurant in Bouffarik, a stopping point on the road from Algiers to Blidah. Louis de Castellane, traveling the road inland, wrote that Bouffarik was a dry and unhealthy place.

> Fortunately we were merely passing through the incipient town, though not without stopping, according to an established usage, at the celebrated cafe of *la Mère Gaspard*. La Mère Gaspard is an Amazon, begrimed in the smoke of many a combat. Landing in 1830, she constantly followed the army, selling her rum and tobacco, until the establishment at Bouffarik. The spot pleased her, and she was tired of following those indefatigable columns; giving up her gipsy life, she took a house, and her tavern soon rose high in renown, so much so, that at the end of a few years she was the possessor of lands and a splendid hotel and cafe. The place was adorned with paintings, marble statues, mirrors, and more especially by a number of fine engravings after Horace Vernet. These engravings were placed there by the hand of the celebrated artist himself. Horace Vernet, dying with thirst, drew up one day at the house of La Mère Gaspard. Drink was offered him, and at the self-same time the purchase of certain meadow lands. He swallowed the drink and bought the meadows; but while signing the bargain, he perceived that the walls were covered with wretched lithograph copies of his pictures. Like a good neighbour, he promised to send her the engravings, and kept his promise. La Mère Gaspard, proud of the fact, never misses an opportunity of relating this grand history.[125]

Anna Busquet and her husband Henri had a less prosperous life after they left the army in 1871, but they still had more than a casual brush with celebrity. They lived a long life in Henri's native village of Maillane (Bouches-du-Rhône), where Henri was good friends with writer Frédéric Mistral.[126] Anna lived a quiet peaceful life and was still active and alert when *L'intransigeant* interviewed her in 1938. She died at age one hundred in December of 1948.[127] The Busquets' case is probably more common than it would seem, since by definition those cantinières who led quiet and prosperous lives in retirement were unlikely to leave a paper trail at the Ministry of War. Never applying for pensions or aid, and not recorded unless they did, many former cantinières must have lived out their lives in relative comfort. Nevertheless, leaving the familiar and supportive military family entailed grave risks, and the willingness of many regiments to care for old cantinières until their deaths meant that cantinières who stayed on as widows were likely better off as a group than those who did not.

One final aspect of the cantinières' existence under the Second Empire had to do with their relative incorporation into the official military world. The Second Empire was in some ways the zenith of the cantinières' long military history, leading Luce Riès to call it "the golden age of the cantinières."[128] The army recognized the right of cantinières to wear uniforms, and although much of the uniform was made from scratch, much of it was standard issue, especially leather gear.[129] There could be no doubt that cantinières who paraded the streets in regimental uniforms with their regiments' brass insignia represented the army to the public as much as or even more than male soldiers did. Furthermore, in 1860, the War Ministry made civilian employees (and therefore cantinières) legally eligible for military decorations, in response to the numerous acts of heroism on the battlefields of Italy. Cantinières had already received the Crimean Campaign Medal, but in 1859–1862 a number of cantinières received the Military Medal, which gave them membership in the Legion of Honor as well as a hundred-franc annual pension. At least four cantinières received the prestigious Military Medal between 1859 and 1861 for actions on the battlefields of Italy, and soon thereafter the War Ministry began awarding the medal for long-term meritorious service.[130] Gaining eligibility for decorations was one of the most visible and psychologically important achievements cantinières made during the period, and it reinforced the view among cantinières and the public that they were in fact members of the army. When Madame Descours wrote to the minister of war in her old age, she asked for a pension not as a widow, but as a "veteran and old warrior who served in the campaigns of Italy, Mexico, Crimea, etc." She asked the War Ministry to find her records that showed "my service as a cantinière, which I always fulfilled with glory and probity because I have always kept for our mother France a love that I will hold until my last breath."[131] This type of sentiment was common among cantinières throughout the Second Empire, and it marked a distinct change from the eighteenth century, when women usually demanded pensions as widows and destitute mothers rather than as veterans.

However, the cantinières, the public, and to a certain extent later historians were deceived by appearances that did not reflect legal realities. The War Ministry was willing to decorate women who performed bravely on the battlefield, but as we have seen, women received official decorations only for nursing the wounded, or for vaguely defined long-term meritorious service. Even Annette Drevon received her Cross of the Legion of Honor only unofficially from her commander. She never received an official decoration for her action at Magenta, nor did any cantinière officially receive a decoration higher than the Military Medal, the lowest grade of the Legion of Honor, during the Second Empire.[132] Actions by cantinières that would have merited the Cross if performed by men received lower decorations or none at all. Likewise, the War Ministry refused to pay cantinières for their services. This was reasonable since cantinières essentially received a concession with a captive clientele, and therefore were expected to earn their pay through commerce. However, lack of army pay further distanced cantinières from "official" membership in the army, and probably encouraged some cantinières to view their commissions as a license to steal. In fact, the cantinières' legal existence depended largely on precedent and tradition. The laws of 1793, 1832, and 1854 that legalized their presence with the army did not stipulate any pay, official uniform, or any other benefits, and cantinières remained classified as civilian employees rather than as soldiers. Still, this was not apparent to most cantinières until they applied for pensions in their old age. Suddenly, they found that the army to which they had devoted their lives did not recognize them as members. To be more precise, while officers and men in the combat units recognized cantinières as members of the unit, the War Ministry's bureaucracy did not. Therefore, most cantinières of the Second Empire went through their careers blissfully unaware of the legal fragility of their military status. They received their *patentes* directly from their unit's Council of Administration, and would deal directly with the War Ministry during their careers only if they received a decoration, an event which would only tend to confirm their own estimation of their military status. The ambiguous legal status of cantinières under the Second Empire left most of them in ignorance until it was too late. As long as they stayed with their units, however, they maintained an enviable status as sisters, mothers, café keepers, and sometimes heartthrobs. This resulted in a growing trend of cantinières remaining with their units until they died—the only assurance that they would be treated as *militaires*.

The Second Empire therefore represents a period full of ambiguities and contradictions, and this in itself makes it a suitable contender for the title of "the golden age of the cantinières," since these women's very existence throughout their history was ambiguous and contradictory. The eighteen years from 1852 to 1870 fixed cantinières in public affection in a way that no previous era had done. The greatest credit for this goes to their uniforms, which combined military elements and contemporary fashion-plate styles to create an attractive and intriguing panoply of female military costumes. The very idea of civilian women in pants was offensive to French public opinion, and French men expended much ink on the evils inherent in such garb.[133] Honoré Daumier among others expressed concern that if women wore trousers there would be serious gender confusion, and he ridiculed the idea that women should wear trousers even under skirts. And yet, the very outpouring of criticism showed that French men were fascinated by female cross-dressing. It was, in fact, illegal for a woman to wear trousers in public, and between 1850 and 1860, only twelve French women received special police permits to do so, one of them in order to facilitate her secret trysts with Napoleon III.[134] Despite this, thousands of cantinières in trousers walked the streets of Paris without permits, without harassment, and without criticism, emphasizing that cantinières lived in a separate world from, and by different rules than, civilian women.

This in itself was probably the most important achievement of cantinières during the Second Empire. In a time when women's rights were not on the public agenda, and when prominent feminists were arrested or exiled, cantinières lived a life free from at least some of the restrictions that hobbled civilian French women. They owned property, ran businesses, wore trousers, traveled widely, and generally lived lives radically different from those of most women. This did not make them proto-feminists, though, nor did it necessarily indicate that they were trailblazers, showing the way for the soon-to-be liberated women of the twentieth century. Rather, a strong argument can be made that they were in fact holdovers: a relatively small group of several thousand women who were allowed certain privileges in exchange for supporting and obeying the military authorities.

Nevertheless, the Second Empire represented an era of unparalleled improvement in the condition of cantinières, and while they did not achieve official status as members of the military, they came as close as women ever would prior to the 1950s. More importantly, they built up a store of goodwill and admiration that would hold off calls for the elimination of the cantinière corps for another four decades.

CHAPTER 6

The Third Republic and the
End of the Cantinières

T HE FRENCH ARMY UNDERWENT profound changes from 1870 to 1914 as industrialization transformed warfare and political turmoil shook the foundations of the nation and the military. While cantinières represented an exception to most social norms over much of their history, at the end of the nineteenth century they fell victim to the same currents that were buffeting the rest of French civil and military society. In particular, the national reappraisals following the defeat of 1870–1871 and the aftermath of the Dreyfus Affair of 1894–1906 both gave birth to reform movements that came to see cantinières not only as expendable, but as detrimental to the efficient functioning of the French army. The War Ministry finally suppressed cantinières altogether in 1905–1906, and women ceased for a brief time to have any role in the French army. The suppression of the cantinières had a number of causes, but ultimately two proved decisive, while a third may have been just as important or even more so. One was the strong drive for reform from within the army in the four decades following the Franco-Prussian War. The other was the desire of Radical Republicans to alter the nature of recruiting in order to democratize and republicanize the army. Neither cause specifically focused on cantinières, but both left cantinières as incidental casualties in the doctrinal and political battles that marked fin de siècle France. Moreover, there is credible evidence that French men felt threatened by the perceived breakdown of gender roles during this period. While no direct evidence exists explicitly linking specific decisions of individual members of the Ministry of War to attempts to enforce gender separation, there is compelling evidence that such sentiments were widespread among French men. The possibility that cantinières were suppressed because men wanted to put women in their place can therefore not be discounted.

The disastrous Franco-Prussian War of 1870–1871 marked the last time cantinières fought in a major conflict. The cantinières of the regular army served in the frontier battles of July–September, but the crushing defeat the invading Prussians inflicted on the French left most of the French army, including its cantinières, either dead, wounded, or captured, and much of the country occupied. However, this defeat opened the way for a new generation of volunteer cantinières who stepped forward to defend France from invasion, and for the last time, large numbers of women suddenly and spontaneously joined military units as cantinières.

The bloody defeat of the main French army at Sedan and the capture of Napoleon III by the Prussians on September 2, 1870, inspired the declaration of the Third Republic in Paris, marking the end of the Second Empire. However, France was still at war with Prussia, and the Government of National Defense set about organizing a new army. The new government hoped that the hastily raised citizen army would repel the invaders just as the army of the First Republic had done at Valmy exactly seventy-eight years earlier. The new army was composed of the shattered remains of the regular army, the National Mobile Guard, and hastily assembled *bataillons de marche* composed of depot troops and recalled veterans. In many departments, bands of armed civilians formed units of *francs-tireurs* (partisans) to harass the enemy in occupied territory or to fight alongside the new army.

As in 1792, a new and unusual breed of volunteer cantinières came forward to defend the country in time of invasion. Some of these women were ex-cantinières whose retired husbands were recalled to service, but most of them were civilians with no prior military experience. They enlisted along with their husbands for the duration of the war, and almost all who survived returned to their homes in the spring of 1871. In a situation where the roads and railways were in chaos, cantinières often sacrificed their own interests to provide valuable transportation to officers or messengers in need of speed, showing that the railroad had not made the cantinière's wagon totally obsolete. The ill-equipped and poorly trained citizen army failed to repel the invaders, but the widespread adoption of cantinières even by partisan bands showed the extent to which the cantinière tradition had permeated French society. Units that wished to associate themselves with professionalism and military efficiency acquired cantinières just like the regular army, and among the National Guard at least, cantinières wore recognizable military uniforms. Although an army medical officer described one cantinière of the Mobile Guard as "very young, very frail, and very pretty to be going on campaign,"[1] the new generation of volunteers was for the most part older than most beginning cantinières, just as the volunteers of 1792–1794 had been significantly older than their professional contemporaries, some being well into their fifties. They were usually already married, some to retired soldiers, some to civilians, and when their husbands received the call to arms, the wives enlisted as well.

The invasion brought women to the colors from all over the French provinces and even beyond. Rose Doucet was typical of former cantinières who returned to the colors in 1870 as volunteers. She married Pierre Guy of the Seventy-third Infantry regiment in 1862 when she was nineteen. She served briefly as a cantinière and retired with her husband to Le Bourget in 1863. In 1870 she was twenty-six when the Republic recalled her husband into the Thirty-ninth Régiment de Marche. In a night battle at Farigné-Levêque on January 8, 1871, a Prussian howitzer shell wounded her, destroying her wagon and all her belongings.[2] Emilie Marot was another example. She was thirty years old and had never left her region of birth when she and her husband Baptiste volunteered for the Francs-tireurs of the Deux-Sèvres. The two were both natives of Niort and had no prior military experience, but were motivated by patriotism. They served for the entire war before returning to civilian life.[3] Patriotism and a desire to be near her husband Pierre when he was drafted in September 1870 inspired Claudine Mallet to enroll as cantinière of the Thirtieth Régiment de Marche, even though she was six months pregnant. As her pregnancy advanced, she marched with her unit from Rouen to Bourges, from Bourges to Orléans, and finally to Besançon, a distance of more than five hundred kilometers. At Besançon the regiment was besieged by the Prussian army, and Claudine gave birth to a son during the siege.[4] Alexandrine Ciret had been married to her husband Jean for less than two years when he was called to the Sixty-ninth Battalion of the Mobile Guard of Ariège. Her baptism of fire came in a four-day battle near Orléans, after which she and her husband escaped from the defeat into the countryside. The mayor of a small village hid them from the Prussians, and the two made their way back to French lines during the winter. She later wrote, "After all the pain and emotion, sleeping in the snow, I fell sick and returned to my home at the beginning of March."[5] Some women came from outside the country in France's hour of need. Hortense Chasseron was living in South America when she and her husband responded to patriotic appeals for volunteers. They left Montevideo for Bordeaux on December 1, 1870, and on their arrival enlisted in the Second Franco-Montevidean Legion. During a rear-guard action near the Swiss frontier, her husband was killed and her wagon and all her possessions captured. After the war, she tried to obtain recompense from the

French government. Although the commander of her unit certified her loss, there is no record that she ever received help from the army.[6]

Paris also provided a large number of volunteer cantinières, many of them serving in combat during the Prussian siege of the city. The most famous example was Louise Michel, the socialist writer who served as cantinière of the Sixty-first Battalion of the National Guard.[7] Less famous and also less fortunate, Étiennette Lechangeur was thirty-nine years old in 1870, and living in the thirteenth arrondissement of Paris. She volunteered for the First Company of Auxiliary Artillery, formed for the defense of the city. On January 20, 1871, she was helping operate the guns at Nogent when a Prussian howitzer shell gave her multiple wounds. She received a special *gratification de réforme* of 125F in 1872, but her health was broken and she died in 1875 at the age of forty-four.[8] Claudine Defurne was another resident of the thirteenth arrondissement who was more fortunate. She volunteered to be cantinière of the Forty-sixth Bataillon de Marche just after her twenty-eighth birthday and survived the siege unhurt.[9]

Despite the heroism of Paris's defenders, the new government decided to surrender to the Prussians in January 1871. Paris was starving, and the prospect of any relief of the siege was dim, since it depended on the newly raised reserve armies fighting their way through the Prussian army to the city. However, the people of Paris—the ones suffering the most from the war—were reluctant to give in, and their anger at the surrender was not diminished by the food supplies that the Prussians allowed into the city following the armistice. Many of the defenders, especially those of the working class, saw the government's decision to surrender as a betrayal, and suspected the government of being secretly in league with the Prussians. They were particularly incensed that the peace agreement included plans for a victory parade of Prussian soldiers through Paris. On top of this, a newly elected national government consisted of two blocs: a conservative rural group of deputies and a radical urban group, largely from Paris. Since the conservatives outnumbered the radicals by two to one, the new government passed a variety of laws that outraged the Parisian working class, particularly laws that called for the immediate payment of all back rent with interest. (Rent had been suspended in September as part of the national emergency.) These grievances led to the open rebellion of the Paris workers and National Guardsmen in March 1871, after the government tried to disarm them.

This uprising of the Paris Commune tainted the official view of the efforts of the Parisian cantinières, despite the bravery they showed during the Prussian siege of the city.[10] A rising of various radical factions and the newly politicized National Guard units stationed in Paris, the Commune became the most violent and costly episode of French civil conflict. The communards disputed the authority of the national government, which had moved to Versailles in order to avoid being held hostage by the Parisian population. The communards championed a variety of radical social and political reforms that the government could not tolerate. The rebellious guardsmen and their civilian co-revolutionaries controlled the city from March until the end of May. The French army stormed the city after an extended siege, and there were atrocities and summary executions on both sides. However, after its victory the French army engaged in wholesale executions that dwarfed the scale of the murders perpetrated by the communards. As many as twenty thousand people were killed in the savage street-to-street fighting and the subsequent government reprisals.

The revolt of the Paris Commune involved hundreds of cantinières fighting on the side of the Commune and on the side of the French government, and there were many casualties, especially among the communards. The National Guard units inside Paris were well supplied with uniformed cantinières, and it is likely that many of the female communards shot out of hand during the Bloody Week were in fact cantinières of the National Guard.[11] Several cantinières of the National Guard are visible in photos of the destruction of the Vendôme column during the height of the Commune, a moment of celebration soon eclipsed by the bloody fighting.[12]

Despite the seriousness of the situation, one officer seemed unable to take his cantinière seriously except as a uniformed decoration, writing, "Madame Boggio would henceforth have the honor of giving drinks to the heroes of the battalion. Coifed in her little Tyrolean felt hat and squeezed into a blue outfit with red stripes that I designed, our cantinière was, I must say, very nice."[13] This echoed much of the anti-Commune popular art produced at the time; it often showed cantinières of the Commune as pretty, young, and utterly naïve and ineffective.[14] The reality was often grimmer. Alexander Thompson recalled one attractive cantinière whose "alluring charms, engaging smile, and captivating revolver" persuaded passersby to allow themselves to be searched at a roadblock on the Boulevard St. Michel, once again highlighting how advances in modern firearms increasingly made cantinières more effective in violent or potentially violent situations.[15] Louise Michel continued to serve as a cantinière and a combatant during the second siege of Paris by French government troops, and was therefore sentenced to deportation for life. During the repression of the Commune in the week of May 21, the communards and the army fought each other mercilessly. One observer saw "a *cantinière* who, while serving out her liquors, had been struck first by a fragment of a shell in the leg, and afterwards, as she lay helpless on the ground, by a bullet through her breast. I could see her as she passed into the cafe, by the light that shone dimly through the open door; and never can I forget her face of agony. She must have been very pretty and *piquante,* but now her face was contorted with pain, and looked ghastly beyond description in the feeble light; her screams were so terrible that I could bear it no longer, and moved away."[16] John Leighton mentioned numerous cantinières who fought actively in the defense of the city. At the start of the attack by government forces, he saw National Guard units moving toward the sound of the fighting, and "the cantinières were carrying guns," but that was only one episode of a more general phenomenon:

It was not enough that men should be riddled with balls and torn to pieces by shells. The women are also seized with a strange enthusiasm in their turn, and they too fall on the battle-field, victims of a terrible heroism. What extraordinary beings are these who exchange the needle for the needle-gun, the broom for the bayonet, who quit their children that they may die by the sides of their husbands or lovers? Amazons of the rabble, magnificent and abject, something between Penthesilea and Théroigne de Méricourt. There they are seen to pass as cantinières, among those who go forth to fight. The men are furious, the women are ferocious,—nothing can appall, nothing discourage them. At Neuilly, a vivandière is wounded in the head; she turns back a moment to staunch the blood, then returns to her post of danger. Another, in the 61st Battalion, boasts of having killed three *gardiens de la paix* and several *gendarmes.* On the plain of Chatillon a woman joins a group of National Guards, takes her stand amongst them, loads her gun, fires, re-loads and fires again, without the slightest interruption. She is the last to retire, and even then turns back again and again to fire. A cantinière of the 68th Battalion was killed by a fragment of shell which broke the little spirit-barrel she carried, and sent the splinters into her stomach.[17]

One unit of the French Second Division reported an encounter in which "the whole post with its cantinière were put to the bayonet without a single man [or woman] being able to escape."[18] Obviously the French government troops saw "enemy" cantinières as combatants to be killed just like enemy soldiers. This may have been in large part because they were. The cantinières of the Commune, motivated perhaps by ideology or by desperation, seem to have fought with rifle in hand far more frequently than did cantinières of the regular army.

After the government crushed the rebellion, it was unwilling to recognize the services of most Parisian women, who were tainted by their association with the Commune. Cantinières not associated with the rebellion received some recognition for their bravery, though, and quite spectacularly in one case. Marie Jarrethout of the Francs-tireurs of Paris fought in three battles and received a permanent cantinière post after the war.[19] In 1880, she also became the first and only cantinière to be awarded the Cross of the Legion of Honor, for bravery under fire during the siege of Châteaudun.[20] Jarrethout was fifty-three when her husband and sons joined the *francs-tireurs,* and she signed up as well to serve as a cantinière to their battalion. There is every reason to believe that she was in fact a retired ex-cantinière of the regular army returning in the nation's hour of need, since she was listed on the battalion's rolls as "widow of Pélicot, former non-commissioned officer," and her son was listed as "ex-enfant de troupe of the forty-seventh regiment."[21] To my knowledge, no one who has written of Mme Jarrethout has yet made this connection, and it again suggests that far more of the volunteer cantinières of the Franco-Prussian War may have been experienced old campaigners than has previously been thought. If this is the case, then their extraordinary devotion to duty, bravery under fire, and defiance of defeat and even capture by the enemy may have had more to do with a lifetime of military service than it did with naïve and exuberant patriotism. Though mostly serving in the traditional cantinière roles of nurse and sutler, Mme Jarrethout took up arms on several occasions, most notably when she dressed as a man and fought the Prussians from the walls of Châteaudun. Ten years later, she was awarded the Cross for "her courage and her devotion," the award coming in time for her to wear it in the parade marking the tenth anniversary of the siege of Châteaudun.[22]

This singular example of a Cross being awarded to a cantinière merits further exploration. Many cantinières had performed similar feats of heroism, yet none ever received the Cross, despite a popular belief that some had. In 1880, though, France was still smarting from a humiliating defeat, and the need for stirring and inspiring patriotic symbols was strong. As the movement for *revanche* against Germany gathered momentum, Marie Jarrethout became a symbol for all the women of France. Rather than pass out awards to the many cantinières who had distinguished themselves, the government gave one award, and made Mme Jarrethout the personification of patriotic French womanhood in general and of cantinières in particular. Examining how that personification played out is most instructive. Newspaper and popular accounts of Jarrethout's combat exploits tended to downplay her firing a rifle at the enemy. Rather, they focused on either nursing or vague statements about her "courage." For example, Anatole Alès' 1886 book on decorated women described her story in a way that was just ambiguous enough to avoid having her perform masculine actions:

> A Breton, . . . Madame Julienne-Marie-Jarrethout, called "The Volunteers' Mother," earned the Cross in 1870–71, but it was not awarded until July 12, 1880. Madame Jarrethout, née Biohain, widow of M. Pellicot, was born in Ploermel on June 30, 1817. In 1870, she signed up as cantinière with the *francs-tireurs* of Châteaudun (called the *francs-tireurs* of the Turgot School); it was in this capacity that she could offer military service that twice could have cost her her life. She distinguished herself the first time in the fight at Ablis, where 120 *francs-tireurs* succeeded in capturing two enemy squadrons; the second time was at the defense of Châteaudun. Under Prussian fire, she had the *sang-froid* and courage to supply the combatants with ammunition. Other trains of bravery and devotion figure in Madame Jarrethout's dossier: she bandaged the wounded, assisted in the defense of Le Mans, the Battle of Alençon, was taken prisoner at Saint-Péravy, and escaped to return to the French ranks. Finally, she saved the lives of M. Marsonlan, municipal council member, and M. Maillet, Mobile Guard commandant.[23]

Alès deftly dodged the question of Mme Jarrethout's actual fighting in combat. She "distinguished herself" in the skirmish at Ablis, but Alès gives no details. Likewise, she "assisted" in the defense of La Mans and at the Battle of Alençon, but is worth noting that in French, the verb *assister* can mean either "to aid or assist" or, alternatively, "to be present," and the second is by far the more common usage. Therefore, Alès cleverly presented readers with an ambiguous *double entendre*. Anyone who wanted to believe that Mme Jarrethout had fired shots in anger could interpret *assister* as "aiding in" the battles, but anyone who wished to see her as merely an angel of mercy could interpret it as having the more common meaning of "being present." In this way, both the truth and the gendered myth could be preserved. The only statements about specific actions concerned carrying ammunition to the (male) combatants, nursing the wounded, and escaping Prussian captivity. None of these was terribly remarkable: virtually all cantinières in 1870 did the first two deeds, and many others accomplished the third. In short, in many popular accounts there seemed no particular reason why Mme Jarrethout, and not some other cantinière, had been awarded the Cross.

As time went on, Jarrethout's deeds became even more benign. In 1900, as part of the Paris Olympic Games and the Universal Exposition, Jarrethout was honored by being included in a parade of dignitaries following the lifesaving competitions. The official report of the games is telling in the way it is very carefully framed to completely sanitize the historical record. The 1900 games were an important moment for France, for the modern world, and for the future of women. Since these were only the second modern Olympic games (and the first held outside Greece), there was a reasonable expectation that they would set a trend for the future. For the first time, women would be competing, meaning that many eyes would be focused on the way gender was portrayed. Moreover, impressive modern icons were created for the exposition, including the first line of the Paris Metro. In short, this was in several ways a defining moment. And so, as the lifesaving competition ended, a special parade of honor took place:

> With all the events ended, the societies, flags deployed, parade with their equipment: the effect on the eye is truly beautiful; our lifesavers, all old soldiers, many of whom wear on their chests the glorification of their bravery, had not forgotten their military uniforms, and, to see their glorious and brave expressions, one thinks that more than one quit their first aid post in time of war to go fire shots at the enemy. Next come the delegations of Women of France, the French Ladies, then our Ambulance Women and Madame Jarrethout, Knight of the Legion of Honor, ex-cantinière of the siege of Châteaudun. Hail to you, Woman of France! We are nothing compared to you, because, if we give our life, our strength, and our devotion for glory and the greater good, you, you are the modest flower who knows only trials and tribulations. Daughter, mother, or spouse, tears are your lot, and, while all these brave men throw themselves forward into battle, thinking only of the glory and grandeur of the Fatherland, you, simple and collected, you will pray and prepare your care and your consolations for those who suffer.[24]

Madame Jarrethout had indeed become not a decorated cantinière, but "the French Woman," a symbolic and sanitized hero who firmly fit into the gender role that the French state expected of women. French men might leave their ambulances to fight the enemy, but French women did not, even if they were cantinières. Instead, they only comforted the wounded, prayed, and shed tears for the brave men of the army.

Of course, these examples do not encompass every public discussion of Mme Jarrethout's deeds; the map of gender in France was far more complex than that, even for cantinières. However, there was a marked tendency to turn cantinières from rough and tumble military heroines into feminine angels of mercy, and these examples show this very well. Even though it was well known in some circles that Mme Jarrethout had fought actively in combat, most popular press coverage focused either on her nursing or more vaguely on "her courage and devotion," while avoiding any mention of specifics.[25] One article written three years after her death even focused on the fact that she falsified her age when she enlisted: not out of "coquetterie," but out of genuine fear that she would be denied the right to serve her country if she was viewed as too old.[26] Interestingly, one source that did mention her combat exploits in detail was an American newspaper: the *New York Times*. An obituary for Jarrethout appeared under the title "Female Soldier Dead," and that alone must have drawn many viewers' eyes. The *Times* stated that

> Mme Jarrethout went through the whole campaign as cook, as nurse, and sometimes as a soldier too, for she could use a rifle and did so on occasions. At Ablis, in October 1870, she took two prisoners. . . . At Alençon, in the following January, she was severely wounded, but tied up her wound and went on caring for the wounds of "her children," as she called the soldiers. Finally, during the siege of Chateau d'Un [*sic*], she dressed herself in a man's uniform, took her turn on the walls with the defenders of the town, and when her work there was done threw a loose gown over her uniform and went to do what she could for the sick and wounded in the hospital.[27]

Even here, each instance of battlefield combat is linked directly to an act of nursing: Jarrethout might be a "female soldier," but she was one who only fought "on occasion," and balanced her martial deeds with those of motherly nursing.

One further aspect of Jarrethout's award needs comment. Many cantinières fought on the field of battle over the years, yet this did not earn them decorations. They won awards either for lifesaving, for nursing, for long-term meritorious service, or for more generalized "courage and devotion" (always paired). However, France has a long history of turning women into heroes for fighting in defense of their homes. These "defenders on the walls" fought by necessity against invaders to protect their castles or their towns or cities. Jeanne Hachette was the semi-legendary military woman best known for such action. She prevented enemy troops from scaling the walls of Beauvais in 1472 by attacking them with a hatchet when the men proved unable to stem the enemy assault. She became a legendary heroine in France, but she is only one of many such heroines—some historical, some dubious—revered by French folklore.[28] While women who deliberately marched away to war were often (though not always) seen as aberrant, women who defended their homes in extraordinary times of invasion invariably came off as heroes: they were fighting in defense of hearth and home, not in transgression of gender norms.[29] They were in effect fighting out of desperation, because they had no choice if they wished to preserve their lives and their honor. As Dominique Godineau wrote, in medieval and early modern times, "it was the duty of women to replace a husband to manage and in case of need to defend the family patrimony. . . . in case of necessity, ladies could replace men, or participate in the protection of a besieged city by repairing the walls, encouraging the combatants, even taking up arms."[30] This is precisely the role Jeanne Hachette supposedly took. In a sense, the desperate struggles of 1870 can be viewed as an extended defense of hearth and home, and to a large extent, French society viewed the volunteer women of 1870 with respect precisely because they were acting in desperate and expedient defense of their homes. Significantly, Mme Jarrethout received her Cross for her actions at Châteaudun, where she manned the walls in defense of the town—a parallel to the Jeanne Hachette legend, as well as a more metaphorical parallel with Madeleine Kintelberger, who was also rewarded for defense of her family in extraordinary circumstances. The fact that Jarrethout continually nursed the wounded as well only strengthened the case that this was properly female behavior. This is only an exploratory argument, but the idea certainly bears further examination, particularly in combination with non-military women like Legion of Honor winner Juliette Dodu.

Despite the Cross awarded to Mme Jarrethout, several authors have made arguments that the participation of women as cantinières in the Commune resulted in a generally negative and deprecatory image of cantinières in late nineteenth-century France, but this is not true. While it is clear that cantinières of the Commune were subjected to ridicule, no such ridicule was attached to the many women who were cantinières of the regular army, and who faced their socialist sisters across the barricades in May 1871. Nor were all volunteer cantinières subject to ridicule. Rather, the scorn and ridicule leveled at the cantinières of the Commune was reserved solely for those women who fought against the new government in what many saw as an attempt to establish a "red republic," even though the women of the Commune saw their battle as legitimate defense of their homes.[31] The anger directed at them was based at least as much on class and on social and economic ideology as it was on gender. It is significant that Mme Jarrethout was a volunteer cantinière from Paris, but one who did not participate in the uprising of the Commune. It is also highly significant that the French army retained cantinières for another thirty-five years after the Commune:

hardly the act of a society that saw cantinières in general in a negative light. One problem with current interpretations of cantinières and the Commune is that some historians seem ignorant of the extent of cantinières' prior service in the regular French army. For example, while Gay Gulickson correctly notes that "these women were a customary part of the nineteenth-century warfare and were easily identified," her discussion focuses mostly on the comparatively new position of *ambulancière,* and includes no discussion at all of the presence of cantinières with the regular French army, or of their long tradition of service.[32] More troubling is Carolyn Eichner's comment that "communardes' trespasses onto the battlefield would have been intensified by the connection between an outdated, less professional version of France's army, and the appearance of 'unofficial' working-class women on the field of battle. After 1840, the wives of rank-and-file soldiers were barred from traveling with armies as camp followers. In their place, the military hired nuns to act as nurses, and unmarried women, wearing officially assigned uniforms, to serve as cooks."[33] Incorrect on every count, this statement shows the extent to which historians need to rethink ideas about gender, popular conceptions of women, and warfare in late nineteenth-century France in the light of the thousands of women serving very publicly and visibly (at least in their own time) as cantinières.

While Madame Jarrethout remained the only cantinière to receive such a prestigious award, Thérèse Vialar might have been the first cantinière to receive the Cross of the Legion of Honor had it not been for the events of the Commune. She was a retired cantinière who had served in the Crimea and who joined the Fifth Battalion of the Mobile Guard of Finistère in 1870. She fought bravely at the battles of Villejuif, L'Hay, and Hautes-Bruyères, after which General Petit called her "the first cantinière of France" while recommending her for the Cross.[34] However, the communards set fire to the legion's Grand Chancellery, and Vialar's recommendation burned with it. Madame Petitjean of the 127th Régiment de Marche was one of the few cantinières to actually receive a decoration for the war. She earned the Military Medal in January 1871 after saving two wounded officers from the Prussians near Buzeval.[35] On the whole, however, the volunteer cantinières of 1870–1871 suffered under harsh wartime conditions and received little postwar recognition. Marie Jarrethout, the glaring exception with her prestigious Cross, merely highlighted the overall scarcity of decorations for the hundreds of cantinières who served under desperate conditions where bravery was routine.

Nevertheless, the Franco-Prussian War was an important event for the many volunteer cantinières. Hundreds of women who had never had any military experience walked away from their homes and their work in order to defend the nation from invasion as the Government of National Defense raised emergency armies. The existence of cantinières as an accepted and normal military institution in the regular army opened a path for civilian women to defend their country without transgressing accepted feminine roles. Since they marched away in defense of the new Republic, their service challenged at least implicitly the idea that only men were full citizens because military service made them so. However, this idea remained implicit, and even the suffragist feminists of the late nineteenth century never made an explicit connection between cantinières' military service and the vote. Despite this, many women who volunteered as cantinières remained convinced that they were veterans of the French army and, as such, entitled to decorations and pensions.

The full implications of the war for the regular army's cantinière corps were more far-reaching and ominous, although they became clear only in retrospect. For reasons both valid and suspect, the Third Republic looked on 1870 as a defeat not of France but of the Napoleonic system. Therefore, politicians and officers blamed the defeat on the lighthearted, frivolous, and ostentatious nature of the Imperial Army. As Paul de la Gorce later wrote, "Studying the causes of the defeat of 1871, parliamentarians and journalists, moralists and military thinkers all believed they saw intellectual and moral reasons. . . . What was needed, after the defeat, was a return to austerity, to discipline, to seriousness, and to passionate work and effort."[36] Douglas Porch paints a more complex picture, arguing that the various reformers presented a "supermarket of military theories" as cures. Nevertheless, almost everyone agreed that the root cause of defeat was the Empire's decadence: "a combination of ridiculous luxury, shameless speculation, and dubious customs."[37] In that context, the cantinières of the Imperial era, with their elaborate uniforms and their questionable morals, were hardly the model for the new army of the Republic. There was an active search at all levels for improvements to remedy the defects of 1870, and "the problems of the organization of transport, of movement, of supply and resupply impassioned the army's departments and headquarters. Thus the management of an army on campaign appeared like that of a giant industrial enterprise."[38] Indeed, influential officers like Colonel Lewal argued that "1870 revealed that bravery was no substitute for efficiency"; they approached army reform with a positivist spirit that attempted to change war from an "art" into a "science."[39] Uniformity was paramount, and irregularities and inefficiencies had to be found and corrected. What was more, the French political elite was beginning to see the army not just as a means of national defense, but as a tool for national identity-building and as a school for good citizenship. The Duke of Audiffret-Pasquier expressed this view in a speech to the National Assembly after the defeat, arguing that the army was "the school where we must send those who seem to have forgotten, to learn how one serves and loves one's country. Therefore let all the children go there and let compulsory service be the great school of future generations."[40] In 1872, such sentiments did not directly threaten cantinières' existence. France was a republic in name only, and the idea of a professional long-service cadre of NCOs and musicians was not repugnant to the French government. Therefore, the goal of a true citizen army remained unrealized. By the end of the century, though, the idea of the army as school would lead Republican politicians to abolish the strongholds of monarchist and imperial sentiment in the army, and to create an environment morally acceptable to the bourgeoisie whose sons would now serve.

For the first four years after the defeat, however, army life continued much as it had under the Empire, and cantinières were governed by the same rules promulgated by Napoleon III. A new recruitment law in 1872 brought in compulsory universal service in theory, but in reality just half of each year's recruits served a five-year term and the rest served only one, while many young men were exempted from service altogether. This was because the conservative and monarchist right distrusted universal military service, seeing it as a means of weakening discipline and arming the workers. The regular army alone had stood between revolution and reaction in 1848 and in 1871, and the French right wanted to maintain the long-service and professional nature of enlisted service, in order to maintain the army as a symbol and tool of order. Some conservatives also remembered the coup of December 2, 1851, and wished to preserve the army as a possible tool for political intervention.

The political left held an opposite opinion. It saw a regular professional army as a tool not for national defense but for domestic repression. It too remembered the June Days of 1848 and the Bloody Week of 1871, as well as Napoleon III's army-supported coup in 1851. In all these cases, soldiers insulated from the public by long service had acted on the orders of their officers against democratic and republican movements. In general, Republican politicians wished for universal short-term military service in order to strengthen the ties between the army and the people, and thus reduce the possibility that the army would be used for a coup. The law of 1872 represented a compromise, but one that leaned heavily toward the conservative conception of a professional army, since the conservatives still controlled the government.

But although cantinières thrived in the long-service professional army, the maintenance of long-term enlistments was not for their benefit, nor was the War Ministry in general sympathetic toward them. From 1875 onward, the War Ministry subjected cantinières to a series of efficiency-related regulations that made their jobs more difficult and less profitable. That year, the War Ministry launched a major reorganization of the cantinière corps. It established new guidelines for cantinière selection and service and cut the number of cantinières per unit in half, effectively restoring their numbers to the levels prior to the reforms of 1869. This marked the beginning of a long and steady decline in cantinières' fortunes under the Third Republic, as a growing number of senior officers and members of the government came to view cantinières as impediments to the efficient functioning of the new army. The 1875 cuts were part of a much larger effort to streamline military administration and the War Ministry itself, and while these efforts were only partly successful against more powerful entrenched interests, in the long run the streamlining of the cantinière corps was successful and irreversible.[41]

The new regulations required cantinières to run a canteen and to provide a *pension* for non-commissioned officers at a fixed price as before. However, the regulations also ordered commanding officers to set prices in the canteen as well as in the *pension,* thus limiting cantinières' ability to act as independent businesswomen and bringing them under stricter military control. Another element that restricted their freedom was the prohibition "under any pretext" of granting credit to soldiers.[42] This prevented soldiers from spending more money in the canteen than they earned, a common problem during the Second Empire. It also led to an increase in the abusive practice of *"payer sa goutte,"* in which older soldiers forced recruits to buy them drinks in the canteen as a rite of initiation. While this tradition had a long history going back at least as far as the eighteenth century, universal conscription brought in a more affluent group of recruits, so the *anciens* were able to exploit this new source of wealth in order to circumvent the credit prohibition.[43]

In addition to price controls and the prohibition on credit, the regulation subjected cantinières to supervision by the medical corps. Each unit's medical officer would monitor the quality of food and drink served in the canteen. For the first time, the War Ministry gave specific guidelines for dismissal of cantinières in case of "notorious misconduct"—a term that was left undefined—while any cantinière found giving credit to soldiers was to be dismissed immediately. The regulation focused on control, surveillance, and punishment rather than on any positive benefits cantinières provided, setting the tone for the demise of the cantinière corps thirty years later. Although the new regulation halved the number of cantinières per battalion from two to one, it specifically provided for cantinières to accompany their units to war, and even provided a requisitioned horse and its fodder in wartime, so it de facto acknowledged their continued importance.

In 1879, only four years after the first cuts in cantinière numbers, the War Ministry announced that "the number of cantinières-vivandières has been recognized as exceeding the real needs of the service." In consequence, the minister reduced the number of authorized cantinières in infantry regiments from six to four: one per infantry battalion, but none for the depot or headquarters troops. The regulation also established two further principles. One was that in circumstances of special need, units could issue provisional commissions either to women who met all the requirements to be cantinières, or *to any man* as a "civil cantinier." The appearance of the civilian male cantinier as an acceptable substitute marked a major milestone in the decline of cantinières. Once it was established in principle, the way was open for cantinière posts to be converted into patronage positions for retired soldiers and civil servants. The next twenty-five years saw a steady decline in the numbers of cantinières and a steady increase in the numbers of civil cantiniers. The fact that female cantinières had to meet strict eligibility requirements but male cantiniers' only requirement was that they be men made it much easier to hire men than women. The other enduring principle was the idea of elimination through attrition. Any move to throw out cantinières would have damaged army morale and raised public outcry: women like Louise Bernou and Mère Ibrahim who had devoted their lives to the army could not be tossed aside casually. Instead, the new law ordered that "in infantry regiments where the number of commissioned cantinières-vivandières currently exceeds four, that number will be reached by way of extinction."[44] In other words, old cantinières could remain, but the army would not replace them. Since retirements would no longer automatically create new openings, there were few chances for young women to begin careers as cantinières. This, combined with the 1875 ruling allowing widows to continue to serve after their husbands' deaths, resulted in a steady and perceptible aging of the cantinière population.

Even so, the French high command was still uncertain about the future role of cantinières. An illustration of this confusion came in a circular to brigade and division commanders from Minister of War André Berthaut in December 1876. It showed a continuing intention to use cantinières in active wartime roles, while also illustrating the increasing regimentation and mandated expenditures that reduced the cantinières from independent and

flamboyant entrepreneurs to virtual non-entities during the last quarter
of the century. The circular reminded commanders that "these women are
required to procure their wagon and their horse at their own expense. . . .
All this gear must be maintained in good condition in order to be of immediate useful service in case of mobilization." This concern that cantinières'
wagons be properly harnessed and pulled represented a long tradition of
blaming road congestion and march delays on non-military transport, and
Berthaut brought it to a new level of concern for uniformity. He argued
that cantinières' wagons were "sometimes heavy and unmaneuverable
vehicles," and in order to bring "a very desirable uniformity," he ordered
that the artillery department design and build standard-issue cantinière
wagons, and ordered all cantinières to purchase one to replace their current vehicles.[45] Furthermore, Berthaut ordered that since space for storage
was short in most garrisons, all cantinières would have to store their vehicles outside government property, at their own expense. This represented
a serious contradiction in goals. If the object of the circular was to ensure
that cantinières' wagons were at maximum readiness for operations, then
storing them on base was a necessity. For cantinières to contract privately
for garage space in cities and farms would necessarily prevent them from
maintaining their vehicles and harness properly, since to do so required
them to leave the barracks and their canteens. This movement to improve
and regularize all army equipment and procedures was army-wide. Charles
de Gaulle later summarized this period using the army engineers as an
example. "There is not one tool, caisson, or boat for which, between 1875
and 1900, the army did not adopt a new model."[46] However, for the army's
cantinières, this movement had the effect of increasing their expenses and
responsibilities at the same time it reduced their income.

Like earlier regulations, however, this one proved less effective in practice than in theory. In May 1881, General Blois, chief of the Army General
Staff, complained that only "a very small number of cantinières have asked
the artillery service" for the regulation cantinière wagon, and reminded
commanders "that cantinières *will be required to provide themselves with
wagons of this type* as replacements for their existing vehicles. Only regulation vehicles can be employed by cantinières in case of mobilization."[47]
The message ended with a stronger-than-usual call for rigorous enforcement of the regulation and demanded detailed reports on the number of
cantinières in each unit and the status of their equipment. Commanders
henceforth enforced these regulations more rigorously, but as late as 1909,
a fire in a military barracks destroyed the wagon of a cantinière stored there
against army regulations. The resulting inquest brought a sharp note of

reprimand from Undersecretary of State for War Henri Chéron, reminding commanders that cantinières "must provide themselves at their own expense for the garaging of their horses and rolling stock in buildings not belonging to the Department of War."[48] Nor is there any evidence that the reforms, when carried out, were beneficial. One American observer noted in 1888 that the official cantinière vehicles were "huge, solidly built wagons drawn by two and sometimes four horses," hardly an improvement in mobility over the light carts favored by most cantinières when allowed to choose for themselves.[49]

Despite an apparent lack of success, the passion for controlling even minute details continued under the ministry of General Thibaudin, and cantinières once again felt the negative effects. In 1883, Thibaudin wrote to all corps commanders, "I have decided that all cantinières' wagons will, in time of war, be pulled by two horses." Since this conflicted with current requirements that cantinières' wagons be pulled by only one horse in peacetime, the minister advised them, "I am looking at present for a device permitting at the same time the harnessing of two horses at the front, without augmenting the total length of the wagon, and the harnessing of one horse in case one of the horses is missing. I will send to you separately, under the cover of the Directorate of Artillery, the description of the device adopted."[50] Once this harness was invented and produced, cantinières would be required to purchase it at their own expense. Although there is no evidence that the new harness was ever produced, this incident illustrates the extent to which a mania for detailed and impractical intervention in all aspects of army operations infected the French high command in the late nineteenth century, and ultimately made it harder for cantinières to do business.

The era of attacks on cantinières motivated by a desire for efficiency and uniformity peaked in the years immediately preceding the Dreyfus Affair, when the army high command was still in the hands of relatively conservative, tradition-minded men. But many other officers rejected tradition and argued for a new scientific approach to war and to military administration.[51] In 1888, War Minister Freycinet reinstituted the defunct Supreme War Council, with the minister of war as president and all wartime field army commanders as members. Its purpose was to act as a consultative body on "all measures which could affect the organization of the army or its mission," but in reality it became "a de facto high command."[52] In June 1888, the Council met to discuss the complete and simple suppression of cantinières. Once again, the issue at hand was the reduction of army supply trains to a manageable level in order to facilitate mobilization and movement on campaign. The discussion centered on the fact that an army corps on campaign possessed

> 2065 vehicles of every type, and this figure does not include the 100 ammunition wagons that will soon be added to the infantry regiments nor the 300 wagons of the auxiliary convoys. This enormous extension of rolling stock could, in certain circumstances, become the source of true dangers and compromise the success of operations. It is to be feared that these immense columns of wagons will be a constant encumberment, will hinder or slow the march of the troops, and will pose an almost insurmountable obstacle to the mobility of the armies.[53]

At Freycinet's request, the Council studied ways to reduce the number of wagons accompanying the army, and it decided that cantinières represented an area where reductions were possible. Despite the fact that the total number of cantinières authorized to follow each corps was small, the Council voted to eliminate the vehicles of cantinières and cantiniers.[54]

Nevertheless, it was not an easy decision, and "the discussion was lively."[55] The officers of the infantry were willing to suppress the cantinières, while those of the cavalry and artillery were not. The arguments against them reflect not only the strong influence of the "army as industrial enterprise" metaphor, but France's growing fear of spies.[56] The official report of the Ministry's study group read,

> The canteens generally render very few services to the unit. On the contrary, they present numerous inconveniences. With their wagons usually badly pulled and too heavily loaded, they are a permanent cause of hindrance in the columns. They easily escape the surveillance of the authorities and offer a convenient refuge to enemy spies. Moreover, they are, for the most part, now run by civil cantiniers, who probably will not march in case of mobilization. In these conditions, there would be every advantage to suppress, purely and simply, the canteens of the army corps.[57]

In retrospect, there is a certain irony in the French high command's concern for spies among the cantinières, considering that the Germans were at the time receiving information from a highly placed and as yet undetected male source. Nevertheless, the fear of spies among the cantinières had more to do with the fear of the irregular and the unconventional than with any real threat. French military leaders of the fin de siècle wanted the army to be neat, uniform, efficient, and regular. Cantinières, by their very nature, smacked of ambiguity and irregularity. They served in uniform with the army, but they were not soldiers. They were non-combatants, but they often fought. They were required to be soldiers' wives, but were often unmarried. In short, cantinières fit into neither the category of soldiers nor into that of civilians, and that sort of ambiguity was unacceptable.

Nevertheless, the vote to suppress cantinières passed "by a very feeble majority," and the minister of war did not feel he had a mandate to carry out the policy.[58] This supports Porch's assertion that Freycinet's reorganization of the high command created multiple power centers, none of which had the ability to easily push through strong reforms.[59] However, the fears expressed in the Council's meeting found expression in the 1890 revision of the military police service instructions. A wide range of powers helped to confine, regulate, and control the activities of cantinières, and the Ministry assigned these powers not to unit commanders but to the military police. Many commanders were too sympathetic with their cantinières to effectively enforce the numerous War Ministry rulings, so it now became the responsibility of the gendarmerie, not the commanders, to police cantinières. The new police regulations made an explicit connection between the presence of cantinières and the presence of spies, despite the fact that no cantinière had ever been accused of being a spy, let alone convicted of espionage. "*Patentes* must be the object of severe examinations on the part of the gendarmerie. It will require their presentation and assure the identity of the individuals holding them. This measure is of the highest importance in hindering or preventing espionage." The regulation further required all cantinières to visit police headquarters once a month to have their *patentes* verified and stamped. To ensure hygiene, the gendarmerie would supervise surprise inspections of canteens by military doctors, who would "verify the quality of liquids and comestibles."[60] The gendarmes, on their part, would verify weights and measures and punish offenders with fines and imprisonment of up to twelve months for falsification. For any offense, the police could rescind a cantinière's *patente:* temporarily for the first offense, and permanently for the second.

But these police instructions represented only a partial step. One of the main issues for many senior officials was the ambiguous status of cantinières. Although they were not members of the army per se, they wore army uniforms with official insignia, and this reinforced a common perception that they were in fact soldiers. In August 1890, the War Ministry ordered that henceforth all male cantiniers would wear a simple gray uniform, but that female cantinières "will not wear any special military attire. They will wear prominently on their left arm, in the circumstances where

they must follow the unit, the regulation plaque discussed in the instruction of 18 April 1890 [sic] on the service of military police."[61] At one blow
this removed the most visible outward indication that cantinières were
members of the armed forces. It firmly and publicly signaled that they
were in fact civilian employees of the War Department. But while reformers in the War Ministry were not willing to let matters rest, neither were
defenders of the cantinières willing to see them go. A strong current of
support and admiration for cantinières existed, based largely on personal
experience, but also on tradition. As one former soldier wrote in 1891,
"That picturesque uniform was so valiantly and so dearly honored! The
French cantinière deserved better than the gray and lusterless garb of a
housewife!"[62]

The repetition of the 1888 debate in July of 1892 provides yet another
illustration of the divergence between the reformers and the traditionalists.
The reformers' attacks on cantinières rested ultimately on rhetorical strate-
gies that emphasized the irregularity and non-uniformity inherent in the
practice of maintaining female sutlers. They saw the elimination of cantinières as a step toward creating a perfectly uniform and rational army.
On the other hand, the traditionalists argued for the maintenance of the
cantinières based on their utility, on their legendary place in French military history, and on the disciplinary problems units would suffer without
cantinières.

Ostensibly, the reason the Army General Staff asked the Council to "re-
consider the question" in 1892 was that there were irregularities between
regular and reserve forces' cantinière complements. In the event of mobilization, only cantinières with regulation wagons could travel with the troops,
but the report stated that "regular army corps are supplied with 41 cantinière wagons, while supplementary army corps only have 13 of them. . . .
It seems that this difference has no reason for being." Additionally, there
was talk of adding a cantinière wagon to certain corps artillery batteries,
which would push their total equipment over the maximum regulation
weight limit. "For all these reasons, the Army General Staff thought it
had reason to reexamine the question." The director of infantry, the Duke
of Auerstadt, argued for suppressing cantinières and using the resulting
wagon space to carry some of the soldiers' equipment, thus reducing their
loads by three to four kilograms per soldier, calling this measure "an indispensable easing of their burden if one wants to conserve the necessary
mobility for our infantry."[63] However, since the ostensible reason for suppressing cantinières was to reduce the number of wagons in the military
train, Auerstadt's proposal made no sense. Replacing cantinières' wagons

with an equal number of other wagons would not alleviate the alleged problem, though it might lighten the individual soldier's burden.

General Gallifet argued for "the maintenance of cantinières, even though it is not possible to give them to all formations on campaign." But Gallifet also suggested that after observing the next practice mobilization the Council could judge the question again. General Ferron asked "that the cantinière be maintained if she cannot be replaced by some other organ capable of rendering the same services," while General Berge of the artillery argued, "It is necessary to maintain the cantinière, because she is the sole legal intermediary between the soldier and civilian suppliers for the purchase of diverse items that can ameliorate his nourishment." In an argument that recalled the ideas and policies of the Old Regime, Berge argued that "if there are no cantinières, one will have to authorize the men to buy in the villages, and from that can come inconveniences from the point of view of good order and discipline." In other words, the presence of the cantinières allowed commanders to keep their men on a short leash, and their abolition would lead to disorder. General Auerstadt countered that "there are no cantinières in the German army, but a special service is organized under the direction of a non-commissioned officer to sell certain goods to the men."[64] The comparison to the German army was a common theme—since 1870 the Germans had become the new standard for military efficiency, especially among the defeated French.[65] The outpouring of literature comparing the German and French armies began after the Franco-Prussian War and continued for some time. The main current of thought was that Prussian organization and administration, particularly in supply, was superior, and that was the explanation for France's defeat. Though rarely discussed explicitly, cantinières suffered implicitly from this comparison, since the Prussian army had no female auxiliaries, and General Auerstadt's explicit connection is an important example.[66]

But Auerstadt did not carry his point. General Saussier pointedly argued that "it is not necessary to copy foreign organizations. Our army has its own mores and habits that we must take into account, and without attaching to this question more importance than it merits, it is preferable to maintain that which exists in conserving the cantinière, who has her legend in our regiments."[67] Saussier's arguments were a model for traditionalism and conservatism for their own sake, despite his progressive political credentials. He did not see the question of cantinières to be worth arguing too much about, but he did think that France should maintain its cantinières for the sake of their traditional place in the army. The minister put the issue to a vote, and the Council voted to maintain cantinières, but previous regulations had already stripped them of much of their privileges and popular appeal. Moreover, the debate showed that those who favored cantinières did so either conditionally, like Gallifet, or solely because of tradition and precedent, like Saussier. In the first case, these supporters would be willing to abandon cantinières if pressed, and in the second case traditionalists were bound eventually to retire or die. Only Berge and Ferron argued to maintain cantinières based on their utility, yet Ferron was willing to see them go if they could be replaced, while Berge had shown in his 1871 book on army reform that he was strongly in favor of suppressing cantinières under certain circumstances.[68] Defenders of the cantinières among the high command were few in number, and most were not particularly staunch in their convictions.

Despite their setbacks, however, many cantinières continued to serve, and some even thrived. Active campaigning was now limited to only a very few cases, in Indochina in 1884–1885 and in various parts of Africa on a sporadic basis. For most cantinières, life revolved around the peacetime routines of barracks, marches, parades, and maneuvers. The increased regimentation and control placed on cantinières hindered business, but most still found army life to be preferable to life in the civilian economy. Many cantinières ran up service records of more than thirty years, and some served for more than forty. But the tenacity with which they stuck to their jobs, the new ruling that allowed them to stay on even as widows, and the overall rapidly decreasing number of cantinière posts all combined to exclude younger women, creating a rapidly aging cantinière population. Therefore, few new cantinières began careers during the period, and the popular image of the cantinière became that of a mother more than that of a sex object. Traveling with the French army in 1887, American artist Rufus Zogbaum compared the old cantinières unfavorably to the popular images of the 1860s:

> Alas for the picturesque vivandière of by-gone times, the traditional "daughter of the regiment!" Where is she now? Can this fat old woman, her white cap fastened on her head by an old shawl passing under her chin, and a much-worn private's overcoat thrown over her shoulders . . . can she be the descendent of the lace-coated, scarlet-trousered Hebes we have read of in novels and applauded at the Opera?[69]

Ironically, the old woman of 1887 had more likely than not also been the "flauntingly dressed" young cantinière of forty years earlier, though Zogbaum missed this obvious point. Many cantinières served for decades in their positions, and grew old and died in them, so the fetching young woman of the mid-century was still in service long after, but was now an older woman, and one gradually stripped of her functions by increasingly hostile regulations. Even in their decline, however, cantinières remained for the most part popular, respected, and fully integrated into the extended military family of their regiments.

One illustration of this respect was the fact that the regulations called for elimination of excess cantinières by attrition. Most units therefore started out with an excess of cantinières above the new complement, so as older cantinières retired or died, the unit simply did not replace them. This resulted in a long period of closed opportunities for newcomers, more so than if the army had simply turned out all the excess women immediately. In addition, some progressive-minded officers voluntarily limited their cantinière compliment even further in order to increase mobility. Thus, while the director of cavalry lobbied for the maintenance of cantinières in 1892, seven of his seventy regimental commanders limited themselves to only one cantinière rather than the two that regulations allowed.[70] Since new regulations continued to reduce the allowable numbers of cantinières, it was almost impossible during the period 1875–1900 for a woman to break into the cantinière profession. Some few women did manage to gain cantinière posts, however. Often they were retired cantinières returning to military life, cantinières marrying into a different regiment, or women with family connections.

Eugénie Girod was one of the last women to become a cantinière before the 1875 reductions. Born in 1846 in Viry (Haute-Savoie) to a peasant family, she moved to Lyon and worked as a cook. In 1873, she met and married Ferdinand Lenoir of the 105th Infantry Regiment while he was stationed in Lyon. At age twenty-seven, she was much older than the typical beginning cantinière of earlier times, though true to form she was eleven years younger than her husband. She served as a cantinière for nine years, retiring with her husband in 1882.[71] More typical of earlier times, Angeline Cottard was born March 9, 1862, in Dauclay (Loiret). She married Jean Foulet of the Thirteenth Infantry Regiment when she was nineteen, and served as a cantinière until 1909, remarrying Joseph Prun in 1887 after her first husband's death.[72] Marie Tobi was a peasant woman from Faures (Puy-de-Dôme) and represented an unusual case, since she was able to become a cantinière after 1875. She married into the Thirty-sixth Artillery Regiment in 1879 at age twenty-six and was still on active service in 1912.[73] Claudine Boyaud also managed to beat the odds and gain a cantinière post, marrying musician Pierre Dubief of the Second Zouave Regiment in 1877 in Algeria, though regulations were more loosely enforced in North African units.[74] However, these women remained the exception, and few cantinière posts were filled after 1875.

A result of this lack of new blood was that most cantinière marriages during the Third Republic were second marriages. Remarriage of widows was no longer strictly necessary to retain cantinière posts after the 1875 regulation authorizing widows to serve, and many women chose to remain widows rather than to remarry. This trend was not universal, though, and younger women especially tended to remarry. Thus when Angeline Foulet's husband died unexpectedly in 1884, the twenty-two-year-old cantinière promptly remarried within her regiment.[75] Likewise, Madeleine Kréher remarried in 1876 when she was thirty-eight. A Bavarian, she began her service with the Third Cuirassier Regiment under the Second Empire and fought against Germany in 1870–1871: she had no home to return to after the death of her husband, since the new German state would see her as a traitor.[76] Adelaïde Favrolles followed a similar though more mobile career path. Born Adelaïde Leblanc in Dunkirk (Calais) in 1839, she married Christophe Favrolles of the First Regiment of Voltigeurs of the Guard in 1857. In 1871, the Imperial Guard was disbanded and the Favrolles were incorporated into the 109th Infantry Regiment, where they served four years. They then passed successively into the 48th, 130th, and 103rd Infantry Regiments before Christophe died in 1880. Although she was no longer young at forty-one, Adelaïde remarried almost immediately and served with the Twenty-ninth Battalion of Chasseurs à Pied. She was still active in December of 1897 after forty years of service.[77] Some cantinières took widowhood as an opportunity to change to new regiments. Catherine Dumas was an eighteen-year-old woman from the Gironde when she married Charles Dutailly of the Second Hussar Regiment in 1863. She served as a cantinière of the regiment until Charles's death in Algeria in 1877, then switched to the Third Zouave Regiment, where she married Private Abel Laurin in 1879.[78] Anne Calastroupat had begun serving with the Fourth Dragoons in 1842 at age fifteen, and when her husband Joseph retired in 1859 she retired as well. But Joseph died in 1872, and four years later the restless Anne acquired a position as cantinière of the 104th Infantry Regiment, where her son Eugène was a musician. She outlived her entire family and was still on active service in 1892, fifty years after she first became a cantinière.[79]

Anne Calastroupat's case illustrates a phenomenon that could only occur under the Third Republic, when widows were allowed to serve and many units expected more of a mother figure than a young woman. Many cantinières who had married men much older than themselves found themselves doomed to inactivity at an early age when their elderly husbands retired.

Bored with civilian life, they found that when their husbands died they were free and relatively young, so they returned to the army once again as cantinières. Anne Calastroupat was only thirty-two when her husband retired, and was still only forty-nine when she returned to the army after his death.

Henriette Calvet had an even more adventurous life. The daughter of a military musician and a cantinière, she was born in the barracks of the Twenty-seventh Infantry Regiment in 1835. In 1855 she married Joseph Calvet of the Twenty-seventh Regiment. She served in the Twenty-seventh and in the First Zouaves in every campaign of the Second Empire, and as a volunteer *ambulancière* after escaping from a German prison in 1870. Her husband retired in 1872 when Henriette was only thirty-two, and the two lived quietly in Paris for twenty-four years until his death in 1896. Thereupon, fifty-six-year-old Henriette promptly sold her belongings, wrote to the Ministry of War asking that her widow's pension be sent to her care of the Fifth Chasseurs d'Afrique in Mustafa, Algeria, and proceeded to enroll as cantinière of the unit where her sons were serving.[80] She was sixty-one years old. Louise Bernou was another daughter of the regiment who could not endure civilian life. Born into the Thirty-sixth Infantry Regiment in 1839, she left the army in 1869 when her husband died of cholera in Algeria. She returned to France with three children, but soon found herself unable to support them on her widow's pension, which did not make allowances for child support. In 1873, she returned to the regiment, where her sister, brother-in-law, and eldest son were still serving. Undoubtedly her status as a daughter of the regiment helped her secure such an unusual appointment, as did the large number of family and friends she had in the unit. She served another twenty years as cantinière to the Thirty-sixth, dying as she had been born in its close-knit military family.[81]

One reason cantinières preferred the military to civilian life was that survival often became a struggle, especially after husbands died. The pensions allotted to retired soldiers were adequate, but widows' pensions were usually 50 percent of the retirement pension. This meant that many women found widows' pensions to be a useful supplement, but not a sufficient sum to live on. This was especially true for those women who lived in Paris or other large cities where the cost of living was high. Robert Sherrard was at the hotel where General Boulanger was holding court in late 1888 when "there came a ragged old woman" who "had walked twelve miles that morning" in order to plead her case to Boulanger.

It appeared that she had been a *cantinière* in the war, had had her sons killed and her house burned, and for nineteen years had in vain demanded compensation from the Government. Joseph [Boulanger's page boy] was absent but a minute, and when he returned it was to announce, not that General This or Deputy That was to pass the desired portal, but that "Madame Aubert was to be so kind as to enter," which she, in rags, did amidst the envy of the hundreds who were waiting. She was inside the room for twenty minutes, and when she returned she was radiant. "He has taken all my papers," she said to me, "and has promised immediate attention. I have got in five minutes from him what from others I failed to obtain in twenty years. And look here!" With these words she opened her hand and showed me three gold pieces.[82]

This illustrates one reason why Boulanger was so popular, but it also illustrates the depths to which ex-cantinières could sink in the absence of real government financial support: homeless, alone, and in rags.

Even Mme Jarrethout, with her fame and her Cross of the Legion of Honor, fell on hard times. Her obituary reported that "she died in poverty and her burial yesterday was of 'the eighth class' only. But a picket of soldiers followed the poor coffin to the grave."[83] Some ex-cantinières worked as common laborers to make ends meet, while many more were forced to work as street vendors selling food, tobacco, newspapers, or souvenirs to passers-by. One American tourist musing on the valor of cantinières wrote, "I know of one, poor thing! who proudly wore her cross, and eked out a living by selling catalogues at a panorama in the Rue St. Honoré at Paris."[84] Nor was she alone. Annette Drevon of Magenta fame worked for years as a seller of vegetables in a Paris market. Jeanne Bonnemère, who was wounded and decorated in the Crimea, served in Italy in 1859 and again in 1870. She won fame for chewing and swallowing an army message she was carrying rather than turning it over to the Prussians, then ended up "making and selling bouquets in a small florist's shop at one of the entrances to the Louvre."[85] The case of Louise de Beaulieu was tragic. A woman of some means, she volunteered at age thirty to be a cantinière of volunteers. She spent twenty thousand francs of her own money to supply the troops with food, drink, and medical supplies, then faced execution as a spy by her own army when soldiers believed her to be "too aristocratic" to be a cantinière. She escaped execution and went on to rescue the wounded in numerous battles around Paris, losing her right arm to a gunshot wound at Champigny on December 2. Refusing to give up, she returned to the battlefield and "during the fights at Grospay and on the plain of Drancy she carried the wounded in her left arm, affixed the bandages with her uninjured hand, and used her teeth to help make the ligatures."[86] She suffered frostbite in her left foot that night, but continued to aid the wounded. After the war, decorated with nine medals including the Military Medal, but broken in body and impoverished, she sold matches on the streets of Paris. One reporter wrote, "I have been to see her in the dingy street near the Central Markets in which she has lived for several years. She has been earning a living by 'knocking up' market people in the small hours of the morning, being paid a small fee by each."[87] In other words, Mme Beaulieu worked as a human alarm clock in addition to selling matches. The reporter noted that "one is at once aware that she must have seen better days. Though weather-beaten and bearing the traces of twenty years of hardship, she is not a 'mannish' woman. She says she is fifty and looks her age, and she is decently though coarsely dressed. Louise de Beaulieu was a lady who had independent means." Mme Beaulieu also was authorized to distribute flyers, but a national outcry over her situation was raised in 1891, and she eventually received a tobacco shop as a means of supporting herself.[88]

In fact, one of the most common forms of state welfare for old and indigent cantinières was to give them a *bureau de tabac* in a railroad station or other public place, but to receive one, a woman had to show proof of her service. This was not always easy. Angeline Prun wrote to ask the minister of finance for a *bureau de tabac* in 1911, two years after she left the Fifth Dragoons. Told to provide proof of service, she wrote to the War Ministry, which informed her that it had no records of her service.[89] Similarly, Gabrielle François, formerly of the Fifth Battalion of the Mobile Guard, tried to get a tobacco concession in 1904 when she was forty-six. However, the War Ministry could find no records of her service, and she was left to fend for herself.[90] There is the possibility that these women were lying in an attempt to gain pensions they did not deserve. However, while this might explain a query to the minister of finance, it seems unlikely that these women would then write to the War Ministry when told they needed to do so, unless they believed the War Ministry held such records. They had nothing to gain by asking for records they knew did not exist.

Louise Graffeuil had more luck in her old age, though not with a *bureau de tabac*. Her husband had retired in 1866, and the two lived on his military pension and his salary as an *ouvrier* until he died in 1893. At age seventy-two, she asked the war minister for a widow's pension. She wrote, "I run a little boutique that serves me as a lodging, where I sell newspapers and earn my living with difficulty." With the extra 375F a year she received as a widow's pension, she was able to improve her standard of living, though she still applied for (and received) a special permission for a boutique in the Jardin des Tuileries in 1897. She was able to obtain this permission because she could present proof of her service as a cantinière to the Ministry of Beaux-Arts, but only because she was lucky enough to receive her service records from the Ministry of War.[91]

Louise Graffeuil's case was fairly unusual in its happy outcome. Because she wanted a widow's pension and not a *bureau de tabac,* she was not required to prove her status as an ex-cantinière, only that she was her husband's legal wife. Nevertheless, the search for her husband's records also turned up proof of her own service, so she was doubly lucky, which stood her in good stead four years later when she applied to another ministry. But since the War Ministry did not systematically keep cantinières' records, it appeared that only a lucky chance in a search of the army archives turned up her records. Women who themselves kept scrupulous records of their own service fared the best. The rest had to hope that someone at the War Ministry had kept their records, and that a thorough enough search to find them would be made years later. Women who had never married, who were divorced or separated, or whose husbands had not earned substantial pensions were left with no hope but an appeal to the minister of finance. This inevitably involved writing to the War Ministry to ask for proof that they had served as cantinières.

However, the situation at the War Ministry was such that even if an honest attempt were made, it was often impossible to find any proof of service. All decisions regarding individual cantinières were made at the regimental level by Councils of Administration and commanding colonels, and many units did not record these details in their daily unit journals. Decades later, most cantinières found that no one could confirm their service. For those who served in the ad hoc forces raised in 1870–1871 the situation was worse. The War Ministry did not retain any records for units of *franc-tireurs* or Mobile Guards. Instead these were retained by the Recruitment Bureau in the military district where the units were raised. For many desperately poor ex-cantinières, the process of obtaining proofs became a frustrating process of writing back and forth to several entities. For example, Aglaée Massey of the Fiftieth Regiment of the Mobile Guard was wounded at Champigny during the Franco-Prussian War. When she later wrote to the War Ministry, she was told that she had to address the Bureau of Recruitment, which advised her to write to the War Ministry.[92] Another volunteer of 1870, Clotilde Cherié, had served as a cantinière to the Francs-tireurs of the Alpes-Maritimes. In 1904, she sought admission to the Hospice général de Lille, but was unsuccessful because no records existed of her service as a cantinière.[93]

Most women accepted the rejections passively, but some reacted with anger. Alexandrine Ciret, an ex-cantinière of the Sixty-ninth Battalion of the Mobile Guard of Ariège, wrote a sharp letter to the minister of war in 1904 after being referred back and forth several times. "I am very astonished," she wrote, "that the commander of recruitment at Bourges can not find my commission, especially since it was made at Bourges on the 26th of September 1870." She demanded that the minister order further searches, and made it plain that she not only needed, but merited, additional assistance.[94] Rose Guy of the Thirty-ninth Régiment de Marche was even stronger in her criticism. In 1903 she wrote in exasperation to the minister of war, "I cannot believe that my service in the army during that unhappy period has left no trace in the records of the Thirty-ninth Regiment, nor in the War Ministry archives. My valorous conduct had to have merited the most eulogistic attestations from General Bourdilon, Lieutenant Colonel Sombret, and Commandant Gigon, under whose orders I served." Mme Guy used language that suggested she had served her country as a member of the military, and that she merited by her own service the help and understanding of the government. However, she only received the same formal reply that all such applicants received with minor variations: "There exists no document at the Ministry of War permitting us to state that you exercised the profession of cantinière."[95]

But the most scathing riposte came from Aglaée Massey, who was infuriated by her treatment at the hands of the army. In 1887, she wrote to request a certificate of service, and the War Ministry referred her to the Bureau of Recruitment. The Bureau was unhelpful, and in her third letter to the minister of war in April 1887, she lost her temper. The letter contained no honorific greeting or closing, used short, angry sentences, and *tutoyed* the minister. "I am told that my papers have wandered by chance into the Bureau of Recruitment of Rouen. I am told I am of so little importance and of such low origin I have no right to anything: I understand it too late. We lost everything during that miserable war, property and health. Now today when I need a little help no one knows me any more."[96] In subsequent letters she returned to a more respectful tone, and after almost a year of regular communications, she inspired the War Ministry to make a thorough search, including the interviewing of former officers and soldiers of the Thirty-seventh Regiment: a highly unusual step. They confirmed her claim, and the minister sent her eight copies of a certificate of her services just before Christmas, 1887.

Sometimes persistence paid off, but in other cases former cantinières only alienated the War Ministry employees by badgering them, as in the case of Claudine Mallet. Mallet served as a cantinière for the Thirtieth Régiment de Marche in 1870–1871, and twenty-four years later she found herself widowed and destitute, her "failing sight and rheumatism" making her unemployable. In her attempt to gain a *bureau de tabac* from the Finance Ministry, she wrote six letters to the minister of war over a twelve-year period asking for proof of service. The War Ministry's internal memos showed that "there is no doubt that Pierre Mallet was the husband of the petitioner," but there were no records to show she had served as a cantinière. Claudine Mallet did provide her son's birth certificate, which showed that young Antoine had been born in Besançon during the siege of the city. The certificate listed her husband as "cantinier of the 30th Régiment de Marche" and Claudine as "marchande and legitimate wife." This clearly indicated that she was a cantinière, but the first response from the War Ministry was negative, and all others echoed its conclusion: no unit journal entry, no certificate. Rather than initiate new searches, War Ministry officials invariably referred back to previous negative replies each time Madame Mallet wrote pathetically to "clarify" her request. Fearful of offending, she never lost her temper or demanded a more thorough search. She simply provided new information or explained yet again some small details of her service. In 1907, the War Ministry warned her not to write again, and stated that it would in no case consider further appeals.[97]

Some former cantinières were lucky. Their units had recorded their presence in the unit journal and the army officials concerned made genuine efforts to find the relevant entries. This rarely gave a complete picture of a cantinière's service, but it helped some widows to receive assistance. Thus when Anne-Justine Rivière wrote in 1904 to ask for her service record, the War Ministry was able to verify her service with the Second Regiment of Chasseurs d'Afrique from 1858 to 1865, and her receipt of the Italian Campaign Medal, but not her eligibility for the Colonial Medal.[98] Émilie Marot was even more fortunate, since she was the cantinière for the Company of Francs-tireurs of the Deux-Sèvres from October 1870 until March 1871. Thirty-five years later she was in need of assistance, and army researchers found her inscribed in the unit's records, a rarity for regular army units, let alone irregular units raised in time of crisis and therefore little given to official recordkeeping.[99] And Félicie Fournery, who served a mere four years as cantinière of the Third Algerian Rifle Regiment from 1870 to 1874, wrote in 1908 for a certificate of her services and received one because the regiment kept fastidious records.[100]

For other women, survival into old age and widowhood took on different forms. Alexandrine Delaval and her husband Alexandre of the Forty-seventh

Infantry Regiment retired quietly to his birthplace of Châtelet-en-Brie in 1878, living on his generous pension until his death in 1910. The pension, though reduced when it passed to Alexandrine, proved sufficient to keep her alive among her husband's family.[101] Anna Commaret, the Prussian cantinière of the Seventh Artillery Regiment, adopted a different strategy. When her husband Louis died in 1898, she continued serving as cantinière until 1905, collecting her widow's pension at the same time.[102] Commaret's case may have been unusual. She could not return to her native Prussia after serving for thirty-eight years with the French army. Nor would she find herself necessarily welcome in French civil society, where the law courts still held that to call someone a "Prussian" was defamatory, "given the state of opinion in France concerning the Prussian nation."[103] Therefore, Commaret's best option was to remain in the bosom of the only family she had left, her regiment.

Foreigners were not the only ones who preferred to stay in the ranks. Many French cantinières chose to die at their posts rather than to submit to the poverty and obscurity of civilian life. Adelaïde Favrolles served from age fifteen until her death, receiving the Military Medal in 1889 after thirty-one years of service and two campaigns, including the Franco-Prussian War.[104] And Thérèse Malher chose to serve until "she died under the flag, March 8, 1901, at Fort-National, Algeria."[105] Likewise Anne Calastroupat and Louise Bernou were both daughters of the regiment who chose to die, as they had been born, in the army. Even relative latecomers such as Marie Tobi, who started as a cantinière at age twenty-seven in 1879, chose to live out their old age in the army.[106] In civilian life, former cantinières were often poor, lonely, and unrecognized, while in the army old cantinières were surrounded by friends, gainfully employed, and could look forward to a brisk social life, sometimes even to honors and decorations. Small wonder then that many women chose to stay even after the War Ministry took away their uniforms and limited their activities.

One extraordinary case of a woman with few financial difficulties appeared in 1905, when Madame Hofer, cantinière of a cavalry regiment, won a million francs in the first modern Press Lottery in France. Hofer was forty years old, a widow, and childless. The *Petit journal illustré*, an illustrated news and adventure journal for schoolchildren, reported that "there is thus one more millionaire present on our planet. The 'lucky winner' is appropriately one of those brave cantinières to whom we consecrate today's issue: Mme Hofer, cantinière of the 28th Dragoons at Sedan."[107] Paul Bluysens, writing a Parisian news column, was less generous as he jealously wrote, "A cantinière! What strange places chance finds to nest? We had to resign ourselves to fate." But Bluysens changed from envy to grudging admiration as he recounted that "the reporters and photographers fell like whirlwind on the canteen of the 28th Dragoons, where the good woman had never stopped selling sausages."[108] Even though she was officially a millionaire, the widowed cantinière continued to work as she always did, and apparently gave no thought to leaving the regiment. As Bluysens recounted, "one anecdote among many will show her set on wisdom. When she was certain of having won, she finally went to town to do her grocery shopping and she went into a dress shop to buy a slip. She chose one that cost fifteen francs. Meanwhile, she told her good fortune to the shopkeeper, who was unaware of it. She was struck dumb, then cried out, 'But it's not a slip costing fifteen francs that you need now!' 'Why not?' replied the cantinière. 'I'm not going to throw money out the window.' And carrying her modest purchase, she went placidly about her daily occupations and continued to receive more reporters." According to the article, she received two thousand proposals of marriage, "but the cantinière remained 'La Bonne Lorraine'—a widow."[109] Mme Hofer's case can hardly be considered representative, yet her reaction to her good fortune shows common traits of late nineteenth-century cantinières: devotion to her regiment, lack of great pretension, and a desire to continue to serve the army regardless of the larger circumstances of her life.

However, her story did not end with her good fortune. One of the first things she said to reporters when asked what she planned to do with the money was "I am going to make some people happy."[110] Indeed, she quickly adopted each of the orphans who had drawn the winning lottery numbers, according to one account, while another claimed she gave them ten thousand francs.[111] What followed was a veritable deluge of fortune-seekers. In addition to the marriage offers, even more letters arrived asking for money in various amounts for various reasons. A local doctor calculated that if one totaled all the demands for money, they would equal four million francs: four times her original winnings.[112] These ranged in tone and amount from a young boy who wanted her to buy him a bicycle because his parents could not afford it, to a man who wanted a tenth of her fortune. He wrote, "You have a million, so you are rich, very rich. You would still be rich if, instead of a million, you had only 900,000 francs. You could still live very comfortably and you could send me 100,000 francs. . . . What sacrifice is it for you to make me a present?"[113] There was such interest in her fortune that a publisher sorted through the ten thousand letters she received and published a selection as a book.[114]

Under pressure of the intense publicity, which drew everything from marriage proposals to pleadings, to threats, Mme Hofer was forced to leave her regiment. She moved to Paris, where she indulged her taste in antique furniture, bought an automobile, hired a domestic staff, and invested or loaned money out generously. By 1921 she was broke, and the story of her lawsuit to reclaim some of her fortune made news around the world. It is interesting to see how badly the foreign press muddled her story. They referred to her as a "barmaid" or as a "small café keeper," completely missing the true nature of her prior career, just as they got dates wrong or badly compressed the sixteen years of her celebrity into as little as twenty days.[115] Her court case went badly, though, and neither her debtors nor her financial adviser were held accountable. Madame Hofer died in poverty shortly thereafter, in 1922.[116] The million-franc lottery prize had after all only been a means of prying her away from her regimental family, and she ended as did many other cantinières of her generation.

Madame Hofer's sad story stands in contrast to the relatively active and comfortable lives that most cantinières managed to lead in the 1880s and 1890s. After they lost their right to wear uniforms they continued to march in parades, to accompany troops on maneuvers, and to run their canteens. Their duties still included active campaigning in case of war, though no war came. And although the cantinière corps was rapidly aging, many cantinières still served as lightning rods for the love, requited or not, of young soldiers. Daily life in barracks was similar in some ways to life under the Second Empire. A typical cantinière kept the NCOs' *pension* and ran her canteen, where she "reigned as sovereign" while her husband stayed out of the way.[117] She and her canteen remained the center of social life, and soldiers of all ranks came to her for tobacco, alcohol, hot coffee, and good meals. The somewhat exaggerated claim by one soldier that "there are cantinières who are cordon bleu emeriti" notwithstanding, some cantinières of the era were professional cooks before marriage, and most of them learned to cook well as a matter of necessity.[118] One soldier recalled that in contrast to the disgusting regimental kitchens with their poor fare and filthy, blackened pots, the cantinière of the Tenth Infantry offered "sparkling casseroles, and her cauldrons mirrored the chandeliers that themselves reflected the light of the matches. . . . she served us a nice, hot soup, rare veal cutlets, poured us a good glass of wine, and for fifteen or twenty sous, we were so happy we didn't dare talk about it, for fear of making others jealous."[119] Twenty years later, not much had changed. As Albert Vandam wrote,

> Truth to tell, the regimental kitchen, with its greasy flagstones; its black iron boilers, encrusted with thick layers of soot; its warrior amateur cooks in linen overalls that were once white, and large clogs that were once black, but

are now hidden beneath several coatings of coagulated bouillon, is not an appetizing sight. Nevertheless, the recruit would lift the lid of his kettle and take a peep at its contents, but for the money rattling in his pocket. But inasmuch as with that money carefully husbanded he can have cleanliness and *decent* food, a basin of smoking hot soup, a juicy cutlet, and a glass of wine to boot, at the rate of about tenpence, it is not very wonderful that young hopeful staves off the crucial gastronomic experiment until the want of cash compels him to give in. Not that the *cantinière*—a buxom matron if ever there was one—would refuse him credit. She generally knows "who's who;" for, contemporaneously with the arrival of each batch of recruits, she has not only their several family pedigrees, but, above all, their financial status, whether *in posse* or *in esse,* at her fingers' ends. Apart from this faculty of making assurance doubly sure, she is the kindest, most motherly woman on earth. The exceptions to this are rare indeed.[120]

In fact, soldiers of some financial means who were trapped into serving one-year terms in the early days of conscription found that the cantinière could provide them with a way to avoid army fare altogether. As the German Karl Hillebrand wrote, "they are expected to eat out of the same dish as their comrades, and clean their own boots; but they know how to 'arrange matters;' and even in the land of equality the *cantinière* is ready for a tip to cook an extra dish for the 'sons of gentlemen.'"[121]

Aside from its culinary attractions, the canteen continued to serve as a vital psychological center of the soldiers' world. By the late nineteenth century, most recruits could write, and communication had improved to the point that homesickness could often be ameliorated if not cured by exchanges of letters with loved ones. Cantinières under the Third Republic sold writing paper, envelopes, and stamps to an increasingly literate soldiery, and since barracks rooms were furnished in a spartan manner, the canteen's comfortable tables and chairs provided an excellent spot to compose letters home, perhaps warmed by a cup of coffee or a shot of brandy. Vandam wrote that

her canteen is by a long way the most enjoyable spot in the barracks, and, perhaps, outside of them; not excepting even the gaudy but stuffy cafés with which every garrison town and military centre swarms. In the former, the young soldier feels at home; the benches and tables are snowy white, thanks to the cantiniere's husband, a soldier, who has the scouring of them every morning. Her saucepans and boilers, her candlesticks and platters, shine like looking-glasses.[122]

The fact that the canteen was heated and the barracks were not made for a strong additional incentive for soldiers to pass their time with the cantinière, especially at night and in winter. Because it was a regimental social center, the canteen was vital as a place to form bonds. "There one exchanged information and rumors formed. It was therefore a place that was completely essential in the daily life of the soldier and a place which he had to frequent if he wanted to be integrated into the group of men he had joined."[123]

On marches, maneuvers, and firing exercises, which occurred more than ever in the years 1871–1914, cantinières continued to accompany their regiments. In the early years, they rode in their light wagons and carts, but in later years they plodded along in their mandatory large, boxy wagons. At rest stops and in the evening they did a brisk business, supplementing the poor fare of the soldiers' rations with sausage, cheese, wine, and brandy. A British officer observing French army maneuvers in 1883 wrote that

> the canteen arrangements are capitally conducted by the *cantinière,* who has a light two-wheeled cart placed at her disposal, also two large pack-mules carrying each a pair of strong wooden boxes. Plenty of the necessaries and even luxuries of life were to be had from this good woman, who supplied both officers and men for hard cash. From what I could gather, there are no canteen accounts kept with the regiment, and no canteen committee, an arrangement which saves a good deal of trouble to the officers, and appears to answer admirably. The *cantinière* is a successor to the *vivandière,* and acts as a sort of provisioner, always accompanying the regiment, in peace and war, and of course, in her own interest, supplying it as cheaply and plentifully as possible.[124]

A few years later, an American observer noted that the wagons "were soon surrounded by chaffing, pushing throngs of soldiers," while each cantinière "strove with scolding voice and authoritative gestures to maintain a little order among her thirsty customers."[125] And in 1894, author Matilda Betham-Edwards watched maneuvers in Arcis-sur-Aube and was impressed by the women of the regiment.

> The *cantinières* and their equipages formed an important feature of the show. The gaily-dressed "Filles du Regiment" of former days are now replaced by sober matrons, the name of each being affixed to her heavy vehicle. This change dates from the Franco-Prussian war. Until 1870 the *cantinière* wore a semi-military uniform, and was ornamental as well as useful. Her successor

is a portly *bourgeoise* in neat bonnet and dress of hodden grey. Each is accompanied by an equally decorous assistant of her own sex. Very important looking were Madame This and Madame That of such and such regiments, as seated in their semi-open carriages, they acknowledged the cheers of the crowd.[126]

It is worth noting that the officers depended on the cantinières for sustenance on the march just as much as, if not more than, the men did. Expatriate English artist Philip Gilbert Hamerton encountered a French column outside his home. "On a fearfully hot day in August he overheard a *cantinière* who, talking to her husband from the top of a wagon which had just stopped near La Tuilerie, was lamenting her inability to find a shady place for the *déjeuner* of the officers, who would shortly arrive." Hamerton offered the woman his shaded lawn for the officer's luncheon, which she accepted with relief. When the regiment arrived, "the Colonel began to swear and scold at sight of the white, dusty, sultry road where the *cantinière* had stopped, and for a few moments refused to listen to her explanations; but when he saw Mr. Hamerton coming out of the garden gate to invite him inside with his brother officers, he dismounted to salute him, and stood fixed in a state of ecstasy before the inviting white tablecloth, looking so fresh and cool between the green grass of the lawn and the green leaves of the trees."[127] This shows that on the march at least, the officers of the regiment depended on the cantinière for their meals. It also shows they had high standards, and expected comfort if not luxury. They most likely assumed that the cantinière would find a way to *se débrouiller* and to provide a reasonable facsimile of the comfortable barracks canteen, even on the march. In this case, at least, they were not disappointed.

The cantinières' position had good potential for profits before the War Ministry began to regulate prices strictly. One soldier's song pointed out that "the cantinière has diamonds / at the expense of lieutenants / the cantinière buys mittens / out of the purse of captains."[128] But if some cantinières took advantage of their customers, many others worked selflessly for their units. For example, Marie Tobi's regimental commander, Colonel Fayolle, wrote of her "great generosity."[129] The colonel of the 104th Infantry Regiment noted that Anne Calastroupat voluntarily fed and cared for the regiment's sick without charge, actions that won her the Medal of Honor in 1892. Her normal business dealings led the colonel to write on her nomination form, "Her selflessness is cited throughout the regiment, because she is always busier serving the NCOs than in making a profit from them."[130] And Louise Bernou summed up her own selfless attitude in a letter to the minister of war in 1891. "I believe I have rendered service to my country and have given to my regiment proof of my devotion, because if I had been after personal gain, after thirty-two years of service, I wouldn't still have to work today."[131]

Cantinières also served as objects of desire for the young soldiers in their regiments. The soldiers' barracks song "The Cantinière" had a ribald passage that alluded to cantinières' business savvy as well as their unattainability by young recruits. "The cantinière does not get hot / for the blue eyes of a poor private / when she gives looks of encouragement / it's usually for a good sergeant / and if she decides to go for a roll / to the quartermaster she will go!"[132] The song "The Corporal's Wife" suggested that cantinières were far from paragons of virtue. "Ah! if the corporal knew about that / tra la la / He would say *Sacré nom de Dieu!* / One, two, three! / Hou!"[133] Certainly these songs and images represented the male soldiers' view, and they are perhaps more instructive about soldiers' fantasies than about cantinières' sexuality. As Émile Gaboriau pointed out, the soldiers' violent crushes on the cantinières were usually unrequited.[134] However, they show soldiers' continuing amorous attraction to the few women who remained in their midst, and illustrate some of the attitudes and pressures with which cantinières contended. They also illustrate a continuing fascination in popular culture with the sexual possibilities of a woman living among thousands of men.[135] Indeed, cantinières were condemned to listen endlessly to the sexual bragging of the soldiers, since the canteen was the primary meeting place for soldiers to engage in such talk.[136] Not surprisingly in this context, physical beauty or lack thereof was an important element in the health of cantinières' business, but ultimately not decisive.

There was another side to the cantinières' existence, though, and that was the respect, admiration, and appreciation they received from their units. Rufus Zogbaum, despite his dismay at one cantinière's lack of youth, chic, and beauty, conceded that the men of her unit were well served. "I doubt whether the prettiest vivandière that ever existed—if she ever did exist, and is not wholly a creature of romance—could have been more popular, or have administered more fully to the comfort of her comrades, than did this obese old creature."[137] This was an important point, because in an army where results counted, cantinières were ultimately there to serve, not to look pretty. And while many soldiers still venerated the beautiful young cantinières, the army itself gave its respect and recognition to those women with long and distinguished service. Many elderly cantinières of the Third Republic earned decorations for meritorious service, not on the battlefield but in the long day-to-day routine of barracks and maneuvers. In this, the Third Republic was unique, as no previous regime

had decorated women for anything other than battlefield heroics, and even
those decorations were extremely rare and usually extra-legal.[138]

Beginning in 1886, civilian employees of the War Ministry became eligible for the Military Medal and the Medal of Honor for meritorious service of more than thirty years. Many cantinières received the awards,
which marked both an increase in status and a confirmation of their civilian nature, since they received them under the 1886 civilian statute, not the
1852 military regulation. The medals were therefore an ambiguous legacy.
They rewarded distinguished service and represented a real and tangible
advance, while at the same time they confirmed the cantinières' status
as non-military personnel. Several cantinières had received the Military
Medal during the Second Empire for their actions in Italy, but the Third
Republic was reluctant to decorate women at all. Civilians' new eligibility
for decorations was intended to benefit not cantinières, but male civilian
employees. The War Department eventually awarded decorations to women
because it had maintained all along that they were employees, not *militaires;*
in effect, the War Ministry was forced reluctantly to decorate women because the arguments it had created over the years to prevent cantinières
from claiming pensions or wages placed them firmly and unequivocally in
the same category as male civilian employees. Many of the women who
received the medals had combat records left over from the Second Empire
or from colonial adventures, but none was decorated for specific actions
on the battlefield. This denied their martial roles, but it also emphasized
their long-term contributions to the army's subsistence and highlighted
the matronly respect in which their units held them.

For example, Marie Tobi of the Thirty-sixth Artillery Regiment received
her Military Medal in 1911, after almost thirty-two years of service to the
unit. Her regimental commander, Colonel Fayolle, wrote that she was a
"brave woman and a woman of heart, of an exemplary probity and great
generosity. Application very highly recommended." And if the commanding general of her army corps could only write "no observations to make,"
the corps artillery commander, Colonel Vidal, wrote that she was "an
excellent woman, held in great esteem by all."[139] Anna Klasen's 1905 nomination for the Military Medal contained similar notations, suggesting that
soldiers and commanders valued those cantinières most who served for the
sake of serving rather than for any pecuniary advantage.

Many cantinières received the coveted Military Medal, and if anything
this only reinforced their own conception of themselves as members of the
military, even though they received it under a statute that explicitly opened
the award to civilian employees. However, despite the precedents and the

regulations, many French officers and even War Ministry officials were often reluctant to believe that women could receive the Military Medal, which brought with it a small stipend and membership in the Legion of Honor. Whether cantinières received it or not depended largely on their own willingness to be assertive, the relative knowledge and attitude of their commanders (who had to recommend them), and even the whims of the minister of war. Louise Bernou's case provides an interesting example. In 1891 she wrote to her colonel asking for a Military Medal, stating that "with 32 years of service and 5 campaigns, I would be very proud now to end my career by being able to see the Military Medal gleaming on my chest."[140] The colonel passed the request on to General Pesme, the commander of the Fifth Infantry Division. At this point, things began to go wrong. General Pesme did not believe that cantinières could receive the Military Medal. "Despite the good service rendered for many years to the 36th Regiment by Madame Bernou, I doubt that it is possible to accommodate her request," he wrote in a letter to the minister. Nevertheless, he sent on an official nomination for the less prestigious Medal of Honor with "a very favorable recommendation." At the Ministry of War, a secretary brought the matter to the attention of the minister, writing that "*in principle* there is nothing opposed to the award of a Military Medal to this cantinière. In effect, this distinction has already been accorded to: Mesdames Vialar, 24 June 1886; Boyer, 28 December 1888; Teyssier, 30 December 1890."[141] The secretary then asked if the minister would like to follow the letter of the nomination, despite the ignorance of General Pesme, and award a Medal of Honor, or whether he would like to award the higher and more prestigious Military Medal, which was, after all, the original intention of her colonel. Louise Bernou had longer and more distinguished service than other cantinières who had received the Military Medal, and the secretary pointed this out, but the minister decided on the lesser Medal of Honor, and that only in bronze. Determining the minister's motivation is difficult. Granting a Military Medal would have entailed asking for a new nomination form, and would have resulted in a considerable delay. It is possible that the minister simply wished to avoid any delay in recognizing Louise Bernou, but it is also possible he wished to avoid any extra paperwork. However, this was also the same Minister Freycinet who was in the midst of lobbying for the complete elimination of cantinières from the army, so recognizing one with exemplary service might have fueled the arguments of his critics on this issue. In any case, Louise Bernou did not argue the point, though she had a friend with fewer years of service who had received the Military Medal and therefore she knew full well that she qualified for the higher decoration. Never one to cause trouble, she finished her career with bronze rather than gold gleaming on her chest.

Louise Bernou was the victim of ignorance and perhaps even willful obstruction. But many soldiers and civilians alike were unsure of just who qualified for what medal, and few understood that cantinières could receive the various decorations of the Legion of Honor, such as the Military Medal. Although many women received the Military Medal, and later, some (including one cantinière) even received the Cross of the Legion of Honor, published lists tended to omit them. For example, a book purporting to list all the recipients of the Legion's various decorations failed to mention even one woman, stating only that "the Military Medal was instituted by decrees of 22 January and 29 February 1852; it counts today 40,000 members."[142] This paralleled the army's unfortunate tendency to lose or to fail to keep records on cantinières.

In at least two cases, former cantinières tried to obtain decorations directly from the Legion of Honor, and in both cases the Legion's chancellor took their requests seriously. However, requests that the Legion sent to the War Ministry for service records invariably met with unhelpful or even prejudicial replies, and the Legion was dependent on the Ministry for records confirming service. For example, Catherine Laurin served as cantinière of the Third Hussars from 1863 until 1879, and for the Third Zouaves from 1879 to 1899. She received the Military Medal on July 12, 1890, and retired in 1899 at age sixty-four. In 1911, she applied for the Cross of the Legion of Honor, but the War Ministry archives held no record of her service, and the Bureau of Infantry could not find her nomination dossier for the Military Medal. By 1911, cantinières had become irrelevant to most army functionaries, and the records were no doubt thrown away as unnecessary. The army could only reply to the grand chancellor of the Legion of Honor that "the War Ministry can not furnish any information on the service of Madame Laurin as a cantinière."[143] Another cantinière who asked the grand chancellor for the Cross was Madame Lematte, formerly of the Twenty-second Infantry Regiment. The War Ministry replied to the grand chancellor's request for verification in such a way as to cast doubt on Madame Lematte's claim to have been a cantinière at all, let alone to have merited an award. "There does not exist at the Ministry of War the slightest trace of a proposition for this distinction in favor of Madame Lematte, nor a single document that can permit the establishment of her service record."[144] Neither woman received the Cross.

These letters, in which the War Ministry and the ex-cantinières seemed to speak different languages, show the extent to which the women considered themselves to be members of the army, and the extent to which the War Ministry did not. When Lilie Muller was seventy years old in 1903, her daughter wrote to the minister to obtain her mother's service record "to be attached to a pension application I am putting together for my mother."[145] Both mother and daughter believed that the mother's service as a cantinière entitled her to a retirement pension, and the War Ministry did nothing to correct their error, again simply telling them that there were no records on cantinières because individual units handled cantinière paperwork. Therefore, the Mullers found themselves blocked from obtaining a pension because they lacked certain information, but even if they had the necessary information, it would have done them no good, since cantinières were not eligible on their own for pensions. The War Ministry did not tell them this, so they continued to believe that cantinières held official status as members of the armed forces. While many former cantinières, like Aglaée Massey, were firmly disabused of this belief, many others, like Lilie Muller, never realized the full extent of their error. The status of the cantinières continued to be ambiguous even in retirement.

Actions taken by the War Ministry soon made the question of cantinières' status irrelevant. Practical military grounds for suppressing cantinières were simultaneously reinforced by political and moral grounds. The Three-Year Law of 1889, by closing many loopholes and vastly extending the breadth of military service, brought many more sons of the bourgeoisie into the army. The army thus came much closer to achieving the Republican ideal of a national army serving as a school of citizenship for France's youth. And yet these young men, serving among long-service regular soldiers, were exposed to bad moral examples that led all too often to venereal disease and alcoholism. As Odile Roynette has observed, "With the putting into effect of the recruitment law of 1889 and the influx of men from all the social classes, the fears tied to the perversion of youth during their regimental stay grew stronger."[146] The answer to syphilis was simple: keep the soldiers in the barracks by denying them access to towns. However, this was not entirely possible, and in any case confining soldiers to barracks merely left them to drink in the canteen. By the turn of the century the War Ministry was moving toward the total suppression of cantinières, in part because a drive against alcoholism in the army gave new impetus to regulations against them. The beginnings of this change occurred under the ministry of General Gallifet, a traditionalist who was nonetheless willing to let the cantinières go if necessary. Gallifet had adopted a wait-and-see attitude toward the suppression of cantinières in 1892, but by 1899 he was no longer interested in preserving what he saw as an anachronistic female institution. A strong drive for the moral reform of army life inevitably placed cantinières in a vulnerable position.

Cantinières already suffered from being strongly associated with the Napoleonic tradition, and particularly with the pomp and glitter of the Second Empire. Since most Frenchmen saw the moral laxity of the Second Empire as a chief cause for the defeat of 1870, there was a strong intellectual current within the army that argued for moral as well as physical strength, and alcohol detracted from both, according to the thinking of the time. As the chief vendors of alcohol to the soldiers, cantinières became a target of many reforming officers. Some limited the hours and conditions under which cantinières could sell alcohol, some banned alcohol sales in their units altogether, while others wrote about the problem of alcoholism. One of the officers who wrote extensively on the question of alcohol use was Captain Auguste Richard. Born in 1860, he did not experience the decadence of the Empire, and was only a child in 1870. Nevertheless, Richard was a strong voice for reform. The author of six books on military theory and history, he was obsessed with finding and remedying the reasons for France's humiliation. Toward the turn of the century, he focused on the problem of alcohol and alcoholism as a major force undermining the army's morale and fighting strength. Much like the more celebrated Colonel Ardant du Picq, Richard argued that moral strength was absolutely necessary in order to fight and win the next war with Germany.[147] For Richard, and for many others, alcohol represented a primary moral corrosive. In 1901, Richard published *Livret antialcoolique du soldat,* a thirty-six-page work in which he outlined the evils of alcohol and the need for young soldiers to reject the easy life of the canteen. The pamphlet proved so popular that Richard expanded its ideas to almost a hundred pages and reissued it the same year.[148] But Richard represented as much a symptom as a cause. His ideas were already widely held, and the proponents of an anti-alcohol policy included the ministers of war Freycinet and Gallifet. Freycinet decried alcohol consumption as corrosive of discipline, believing that the soldier "loses, with this unhealthy behavior, respect for authority, a sense of duty, and a spirit of sacrifice."[149] Indeed, on several occasions rebellious soldiers gathered in the canteen to sing the communist anthem, "The Internationale," lending credence to Freycinet's claim.[150]

Gallifet ordered the suppression of liquor sales in all army canteens in May 1900, "in order to protect the troops from the dangers of alcoholism." He remarked that there already existed a wide variety of restrictions on the sale of alcohol, each one implemented independently by local commanders concerned about the moral strength of their troops. In the name of uniformity, he strengthened the restrictions and extended them to the entire army, again showing a strong desire for standardization in all aspects of army life.

> It is important from the point of view of hygiene and of discipline to stop these divergences, to standardize the prescriptions relative to the prophylaxis of alcoholism and to extend to the entire army a beneficial action, which should not be localized to only certain units. In consequence I have decided on the total prohibition of the sale in canteens of all brandy or liquor with an alcohol base.

The elimination of hard alcohol sales in the army damaged cantinières' business, and even called their existence into question. Gallifet's order did leave cantinières able to sell beer, wine, and cider, in addition to "all the usual beverages (coffee, tea, milk, chocolate, etc.) not containing alcohol."[151] However, hard alcohols like brandy and absinthe were the cantinières' best-selling items, and the prohibition had disastrous effects on their profits, though it probably had positive effects on soldiers' health.

Gallifet did not last long as minister, and in 1900, General Louis André took over the post of minister of war. André was a committed Republican who resented his long service in a conservative army where "it would not do to show oneself as a Republican if one did not want to be banished, abandoned even by one's comrades."[152] André was determined to republicanize the army, and he ruthlessly carried out reforms aimed at breaking the conservatives' hold.[153] His first act relating to cantinières was the suppression of the fourth battalion in many infantry regiments, and thus incidentally the elimination of several dozen more cantinière posts.[154] More damaging to cantinières' ability to survive were his attempts to provide alternatives to the canteen. He authorized the establishment of NCO mess circles, effectively replacing the *pension* that provided cantinières with their steady income. In the words of General Véron, these would allow NCOs to "avoid the canteens where they find themselves mixing with corporals and soldiers," yet another attempt to separate the young recruits from the long-service NCOs, and thus to protect them from bad influences.[155] He also authorized the creation of soldiers' cooperatives in the form of recreation halls, which served drinks and sold tobacco and various sundries at cost, providing soldiers with a place to sit and write, read, engage in sports, or socialize. In short, they provided all the services that cantinières provided, and did so at a lower price since they were not for profit. Indeed, any profits made were sometimes paid back as dividends to the soldiers, but more often used to fund ameliorations of the soldiers' condition, allowing the cooperatives to seize the moral high ground in comparison with the profit-seeking cantinières.[156] André fell from his post in November 1904 due to revelations that he spied on officers and kept secret dossiers on their personal habits, family affairs, and religious and political leanings, but his fall did nothing to alleviate the plight of the army's cantinières.

The final straw for cantinières was the Two-Year Law of March 21, 1905. This law democratized military service by mandating universal two-year service with no exemptions. By shortening the term of service to two years, the government brought the army's rank and file much closer to French civilian society, and the ideal of a national army seemed finally realized. As Richard Challener noted, Republicans concluded that "if the army underwent such reform, then it could become not merely a school in which the raw recruit learned the basic military arts but also an educational establishment in which he could discover the way to become a better citizen. . . . The army was a school, and as such it could perform an important social role in French life."[157] The Dreyfus Affair, in which conservative officers railroaded the conviction of an innocent Jew named Alfred Dreyfus for espionage, had convinced Republican politicians that the army was a hotbed of anti-Republican sentiments, and by 1905, they were able to implement their plans for a true citizen army. War minister Maurice Bertaux wanted the Two-Year Law to turn the army into "a school of civic duty" for France's youth.[158] As sellers of alcohol, cantinières represented a bad moral influence within the "school," and as matrons of the very type of professional military family the Two-Year Law was meant to eliminate, they had no place in the new army. The law laid the groundwork for their elimination by requiring that certain posts be reserved for retired soldiers, and canteens were among them. Only former soldiers with at least four years of service were entitled to be cantiniers of combat units, and only retired NCOs with at least ten years of service were allowed to hold sedentary canteens in military forts.[159] The immediate effect was that no new female cantinières could gain employment. Their total extinction was therefore only a matter of time.

Bertaux's replacement, Eugène Étienne, took the provisions of the law much further and embarked on an active attempt to eliminate many existing cantinières. His first step was to drastically curtail the number and activities of cantinières. Writing that "the functioning of the canteen service has been the cause in all times of numerous critiques," Étienne ordered that in all units where such soldiers' cooperatives "existed *or could exist*," army corps commanders could reduce the number of authorized cantinières accordingly (emphasis added). In effect, this meant that each new cooperative would replace a canteen rather than simply competing with it. In fact, even the theoretical possibility of a cooperative's existence would, according to the letter of the regulation, eliminate a cantinière post. By placing the authority to eliminate cantinières with the corps rather than regimental commanders, Étienne created distance between those ordering reductions and the cantinières affected by them, since regimental commanders were known to protect their own cantinières from War Ministry regulations, while corps commanders had no daily contact with regimental cantinières and could be counted on to be more ruthless. Furthermore, cantinières were no longer authorized to travel with their units "on exercises, firing matches, and military marches," meaning their incomes were reduced even further. In another serious blow to their incomes and to their central social role in the regiment, cantinières also lost the right to feed the NCOs, who were now required to eat in the formerly optional mess circles. Finally, Étienne forbade cantinières to sell alcoholic beverages of any kind, including beer and wine. He also set up a special system for commanders to report to the minister on their progress in eliminating canteens, and through which they could request special envoys from the minister to handle any difficult situations on site. Étienne ended on an optimistic note, arguing that "those cantinières who are maintained, no longer having to feed the NCOs and benefiting from not having to pay rent, should find it possible to reduce the prices on the items they sell to the soldiers."[160] His logic was curious: now that cantinières had essentially no steady income, were severely limited in their inventory, and were faced with serious competition, they could afford to charge less. The loss of the *pension* was, for most cantinières, not a benefit but a serious detriment. The lack of an assured, steady monthly income forced cantinières to rely entirely on their canteens for their livelihood at a time when the War Ministry was universally mandating the new soldiers' cooperatives. The banning of alcoholic beverages and the prohibition on accompanying their units on marches and maneuvers merely worsened what was already a bad situation by limiting their ability to fill existing demands.

In October 1906, Étienne issued a final circular that accelerated the suppression of cantinières. He argued that the law of March 21, 1905, authorized him to replace all existing cantinières and cantiniers immediately with candidates who qualified under the new law.

This has not been done in order to avoid compromising the interests of those concerned by a decision too brusque and unforeseen. The rule applied

up to now has therefore been to replace cantinières and cantiniers named
before the law of 21 March 1905 only by way of attrition. But this tolerance
should not be maintained except with reservations scrupulously observed.
These reservations are as follows: 1. Irreproachable service and honorability.
2. The holder of the canteen runs it him- or herself; managers are not per-
mitted. 3. A person can only have title to one canteen; the pretext of annexes
for the detached parts of a unit is not acceptable; nor can the husband and
the wife each hold title to a canteen. 4. If the husband of a cantinière is
named cantinier under the new law, the cantinière is ipso facto considered
to have resigned.[161]

In a symbolic move, the order even mandated that a cantinier gaining his
position under Title 4 should receive his wife's former canteen, thus revers-
ing the traditional role of cantinières and their husbands and stripping
cantinières of their property. Henceforth cantinières' legal status in regard
to property would be more in line with that of civilian French women.
After 116 years of being property owners and businesswomen in a country
that forbade women these roles, cantinières finally faced reintegration into
the Napoleonic Code. This raised another issue: the cantinière as threat to
male dominance. Cantinières had, for more than a century, operated as
strong, independent women in a man's world. They were an important
exception to the laws that firmly subordinated women to men in French
society. Their suppression came at a time when feminist activity in France
was on the rise, and many men felt threatened. With civilian feminists
increasingly successful in making their demands heard, many French men
felt a need to strike back. As historian Margaret Darrow noted, "At the
turn of the century, when gender norms seemed increasingly under attack,
the cantinière or *femme soldat* was a much more disturbing figure that she
had been forty years earlier."[162] Likewise, Gil Mihaely has argued that popular representations of cantinières increasingly focused on gender role reversals and the emasculation of men, including older women who cuckolded
their husbands by sleeping with young recruits.[163] While no "smoking gun"
evidence that this perception directly influenced Étienne's decision is likely
ever to be found, it seems probable that it did. However, a connection
between popular songs and plays on the one hand and the official decisions
of the minister of war on the other is difficult to prove, and the popular
image of cantinières was complex. While some elements of popular culture
portrayed them as immoral or as threatening gender roles, other elements
focused on their heroism, devotion, patriotism, and "proper" maternal

gender roles.[164] This question merits further research, yet by its very nature it seems unlikely ever to be wholly resolved. One thing that the negative popular imagery most certainly did do was to reduce the popular outcry against the suppression of cantinières. It is clear that the War Ministry had been working toward the suppression of these women for decades, but by the early twentieth century, it had a variety of playwrights, cartoonists, and song writers as allies in the fight for public opinion. As long as cantinières remained a universally revered, cherished, and respected group among the public, their suppression was problematical. Once they became marginalized and suspect, at least in the eyes of many Frenchmen, their suppression could proceed with little opposition.

Regardless of the state of public opinion, Étienne's circular contained one last crucial provision. He ordered all military authorities "to inform him before December 15 of all cantiniers and cantinières whose service has not been exempt from reproach and whom, for this reason *or for any other,* they wish to replace [emphasis added]."[165] This effectively created an open season on all cantiniers and cantinières, since few could be said to be totally exempt from reproach. Even the venerable and highly decorated Henriette Gith of the First Zouave Regiment once had her *patente* pulled by an angry colonel in Mexico.[166] In any case, the clause that allowed officers to dismiss cantinières "for any other reason" meant that henceforth those cantinières and cantiniers not holding their positions by virtue of the new law were totally at the mercy of their commanders.

The Two-Year Law and its subsequent ministerial interpretations marked the end of the cantinières as a significant part of the French army. Already, changes in army organization and recruitment had damaged their positions. In addition, improvements in transportation and supply, particularly the widespread availability of canned rations, the modern, efficient postal service that allowed soldiers' families to send them care packages, and the increasingly sedentary nature of French army postings, made the remaining cantinières increasingly superfluous. The association of regiments with particular geographical areas also increased the importance of long-term economic ties between soldiers and local business owners, which must have resulted in widespread but hard-to-quantify pressure for the suppression of cantinières. A number of women stayed on in their posts, but their numbers were steadily dwindling and there were no new replacements. By 1914, there were few cantinières still with the army, and since they were no longer allowed to accompany units to war, those few who remained sat out their final years in barracks behind the lines as a new and incomprehensible kind of war raged. The French government would soon mobilize young women for war work when manpower shortages appeared during the First World War, and in many respects these women would fulfill the same roles as the cantinières had done. However, the army would be very careful to avoid giving them the same status and privileges that cantinières had enjoyed for more than a century.

Conclusion

THE SUPPRESSION OF CANTINIÈRES IN 1906 did not end the story of the army's canteens, nor did it end the story of women's association with the French army. A few cantinières served out the rest of their lives with their units, but exactly how many is unclear. Certainly, there were a number of women still on active duty in 1912–1913, especially but not always in Algeria. It is likely, though difficult to prove, that some cantinières continued to serve during the First World War. The male cantiniers who replaced cantinières continued to serve through the war years of 1914–1918, and their numbers were later supplemented by many of the disabled veterans generated by the Great War. However, the army soon became dissatisfied with the cantiniers as well, claiming in the mid-1920s that they were greedy, insensitive to the needs of their customers, and taking up space that could be put to better use.[1] The army moved toward the complete elimination of independent civilian contractors for auxiliary rations and recreation, instituting mess circles and soldiers' cooperatives to fill these needs, a transition that was complete by 1940.

Thus the demise of the cantinières was part of a larger movement of professionalization and militarization of all aspects of army life, especially in the areas of supply and recreation. This movement also masculinized these roles, since the army and the War Ministry could not accept the idea of female soldiers. The army's conception of its role in soldiers' lives thus became total—no aspect of military life would be left to civilians, except the role that French men deemed feminine: nursing.

The appearance of women trained to nurse soldiers was a late nineteenth-century phenomenon that helped to doom cantinières. Nursing societies sent women who had medical training to tend sick or injured soldiers, thus taking away one of the cantinières' most important and highly valued roles.[2] Though the army generally replaced cantinières as nurses by assigning male solders as *infirmiers,* female civilian nurses increasingly served in theaters of war, especially in North Africa. As private nursing societies became more widespread and prominent, one of the key remaining justifications of cantinières' existence disappeared. Thanks to a steady stream of deleterious regulations that restricted cantinières' ability to function, these women became mere bartenders at the same time that public and governmental concern over soldiers' health led to strong anti-alcohol campaigns. Thus the belief that the army and government must look after the health of their soldiers resulted in both the usurpation of the cantinières' nursing role and the belief among many officers that, as providers of alcohol to the soldiery, cantinières had to be eliminated.

By 1906, the cantinières' apparent military value had become minimal, and in some ways, they were harmful to the health and smooth functioning of the army. On the surface at least, their suppression was beneficial, or at least benign in terms of French military effectiveness, given that all of their vital material functions had already been taken over by other providers. Yet cantinières arrived at this low point gradually, as a result of decisions over which they had no control and with which they strongly disagreed. Ultimately, the army forced cantinières to give up their usefulness slowly over four decades, then blamed them for being useless. Therefore, a true assessment of their military effectiveness needs to look at their contributions over time, not just at the moment of their dissolution, when they had been artificially reduced to irrelevance. Moreover, any attempt to judge their military effectiveness also requires a look at what happened to the French army after it cashiered its cantinières. It is particularly important to consider the roles cantinières might have played in World War One, and the roles that other women did play in that conflict, as well as the supply and morale problems that plagued the army late in the war. On the whole, did the French army's performance in World War One vindicate the decision to eliminate cantinières, or condemn it?

Vivandières and cantinières were valuable parts of the French military system of the eighteenth and early nineteenth centuries. They supplemented the army's rudimentary logistics system, provided essential laundry and sewing services, and in the old Royal Army at least, helped to prevent desertion by providing in camp what soldiers might otherwise desert to obtain: food, drink, tobacco, and female companionship. (It is worth noting that among members of the Supreme War Council, this was still a strong argument in favor of retaining cantinières as late as 1892.)

Cantinières' willingness to dispense alcohol to soldiers under fire in the years 1793–1815 also had a real military benefit. Since the chief role of the infantry in particular was often simply to stand firm under cannon fire, the ready availability of brandy helped keep soldiers steady when they probably preferred to flee. Cantinières also bore and raised children accustomed to army life, children who almost always followed their parents' footsteps into military careers. Especially in times when new soldiers were scarce, this contribution of high-quality recruits was indispensable to the army, and the War Ministry rightly valued these enfants de troupe. However, the enfant de troupe's value was most pronounced in a long-service professional army with limited manpower resources. In such an environment, the cantinières' young sons provided a numerically significant manpower pool, and one whose lifetime familiarity with military life made them valuable stiffeners to the inexperienced volunteers and draftees who made up the common soldiery. Once the army moved to universal conscription with short terms of service, essentially unlimited manpower became available. Enfants de troupe were no longer necessary, and indeed they represented the old professional, hereditary, and anti-Republican army that the government wished to reform. Therefore, while cantinières provided a valuable resource to the army in the form of their children for more than a century, by the late nineteenth century the army no longer wanted enfants de troupe, and they were transferred from their regiments to separate preparatory boarding schools in 1885, a process that was completed the following year.[3] Although the new students were (and still are) referred to as "enfants de troupe," the real enfant de troupe institution died when the boys were removed from their regiments and transformed from soldiers-in-training into boarding school students.[4] Thus, under pressure from the War Ministry, the hereditary military family was already in serious decline two decades before its final elimination, yet cantinières outlasted enfants de troupe as regimental fixtures by more than twenty years; apparently, cantinières were far less expendable to the army than their sons were.

Cantinières not only provided their children as combatants, they themselves fought alongside the soldiers as well, and while this did not greatly augment the firepower of a given unit, it did provide a morale boost to those soldiers tempted to run from the enemy, and it showed a fierce devotion to duty beyond what was legally expected of cantinières. This was an excellent example to the soldiers: how could they flee when women who were not duty-bound to fight did so anyway? Thus, Alexander Kinglake's observations of deep symbolism in the role of cantinières in the Crimea are perhaps more perceptive than they at first appear, particularly when we consider the propaganda regarding cantinières that became common around the turn of the twentieth century. Finally, cantinières and their children provided a genuine family atmosphere in their regiments, which undoubtedly helped foster unit cohesion and build morale. Soldiers did not need to be reminded of remote, long-forgotten families that they were fighting for; their families (or those of their comrades) were right there on the battlefield. Official propaganda often stresses the defense of hearth and home as a reason for soldiers to fight. It has often been argued, though, that soldiers in all times and places fight not for such remote reasons, but for their comrades immediately around them. The presence with the regiment of cantinières and their children neatly combined both motivations, and therefore undoubtedly stiffened the morale of the French troops in a doubly effective way.

Taken together, these contributions to French military effectiveness were significant, especially in the earlier periods of this study. There is no doubt that vivandières represented valuable assets for eighteenth-century field commanders, even if their unruly side presented some problems. Cantinières continued to be important and valued parts of the army during Napoleon's wars, and in Algeria as well as in the European campaigns of the Second Empire they distinguished themselves repeatedly. As long as France maintained a long-service, professional army, there was always a shortage of manpower, and a subsequent need to farm out support roles to non-military personnel. The same was true of periods of intense warfare even with mass conscription, such as in the years 1789–1814. This allowed cantinières and their children to flourish and to perform useful work. The common soldiers of the long-service, professional army also had weak connections with French civil society, and in particular with the privileged classes, so concern among the elite for their moral rectitude and health was not great.

Once France began moving toward a short-service conscription army, cantinières' usefulness began to decline, though this was more a matter of perception and political expediency in the War Ministry than it was real and of practical import. The first cuts in cantinière complements occurred in 1875, the same year that a nominal form of universal military service was introduced. Over the next three decades, the French army moved toward true universal conscription at precisely the same time it eliminated cantinières and enfants de troupe. Universal conscription gave the French army the surplus manpower it needed to fully militarize support and logistics functions, apparently eliminating the need for cantinières. The entry into the army of so many sons of the middle class also engendered more concern among the bourgeoisie about the living conditions of the soldiers, and a concomitant drive against alcoholism, already given impetus by reform-minded officers. The result was that cantinières found themselves squeezed out by forces beyond their control.

Cantinières' roles as women also need to be examined. Their status was so ambiguous, and their privileges so sweeping, that it is surprising they have not already figured prominently in histories of the period. After all, cantinières owned property and ran businesses without their husbands' permission, traveled widely and engaged in "masculine" activities, and wore trousers at a time when it was considered outrageous and even illegal for civilian women to do so.[5] In these ways, cantinières seem at first glance to be on the forefront of the women's movement of the nineteenth century.

However, cantinières and feminists seem to have remained largely ignorant of one another's existence. Cantinières attracted neither the praise of French feminists nor the damnation of anti-feminists. They also did not see themselves as feminists or as advocates of women's rights. Why the women's movement missed noticing cantinières remains uncertain, though the movement's rejection of the military and militarism in general may explain it. Through their writings and the writings of those who knew them, cantinières identified themselves as soldiers rather than as women, and may indeed have held advocates of women's rights in contempt. They certainly do not give them any notice whatsoever in surviving sources. In any case, since cantinières already enjoyed some of the rights French feminists were demanding, there was little incentive for them to join in the struggle for the larger idea of women's rights. Voting rights, for example, seem to have exercised little or no fascination for cantinières. Immersed as they were in the hierarchical and undemocratic society of the army, cantinières in general apparently did not think of such things. Their minds were on their businesses, their families, their regiments, and increasingly on their own devotion to the nation. Rather than be concerned with civil emancipation, if cantinières sought any rights, it was the right to be called *militaire* and to earn full recognition as members of the army, and their efforts to obtain them usually occurred only after their retirement, when they suddenly realized they did not in fact have these rights.

Nevertheless, cantinières' experience paralleled that of the women's movement in some ways. Old Regime vivandières asked for and received compensation based on their own service, without referring to their husbands' records, but the revolution, while making their *patentes* their own personal property, firmly subsumed them to their husbands when it came to pensions. Thus, cantinières gained unusual independence during their working years, but lost virtually all of it in their old age unless widowed. Still, the experience of vivandières and cantinières during the years 1793–1815 suggests that the First Republic's and First Empire's restraints on women were not as monolithic as the literal texts of their laws made them appear. For a select few at least, these regimes brought new opportunity and increased independence.[6] During the late eighteenth and early nineteenth centuries, cantinières portrayed themselves in pension requests as wives and mothers, but as their positions solidified and as their rights and privileges increased over time, cantinières began to argue for decorations and retirement benefits solely on the grounds of their own service. This trend was especially marked after 1875, when the civilian women's movement was starting to recover from the repression of the Commune, and when cantinières demanded respect and recognition for the work they were doing, a movement paralleled in civilian society of the 1880s and 1890s. This does not mean that cantinières were actively or consciously engaging in a struggle for "women's rights"; it does suggest, though, that, consciously or not, they were absorbing larger ideas from the society around them. If this is true, their suppression by the men in the government may indeed have had more to do with anti-feminism than with military efficiency. Given the surviving records, this is impossible to prove definitively. However, Margaret Darrow makes an excellent case for a masculine French ideal of war that grew out of the defeat of 1870 and reached its peak in the 1890s and early 1900s: exactly the time that the War Ministry eliminated cantinières.[7] While she does not explicitly mention cantinières, her argument for a widespread cultural movement to define war and the military as purely masculine bears further exploration, especially as it bears on the personal beliefs of the ministers of war and members of the Supreme War Council.

Even though the army succeeded in suppressing cantinières, their legend continued to have an influence on French military tradition, and their very existence reminds us that the period of time in which women were totally excluded from European armies was short and historically highly unusual. After 1906, the army did not do without female auxiliaries; it simply replaced cantinières with civilian women from the nursing societies and, during World War One, with female civilian employees in a wide variety of jobs, not to mention the many volunteer functions women were encouraged to provide. It would be easy to argue that though this move was a blow to individual cantinières, it was a positive one for women in general since it changed the status of women working with the army. Rather than being all-purpose, unskilled camp followers, the new nurses were trained professionals who opened the way for a more official and professional female presence in the army. Likewise, the female civilian volunteers expanded their actions into a more public and vital sphere—the military defense of the nation—and thus arguably laid stronger claims for full citizenship rights for all women. Eventually, the French army trained women to fill a variety of non-combat roles, a common trend in western armies of the twentieth century, especially during and after the two world wars.

However, this transition was not easy or rapid, especially in France. While most of the great powers of World War One formed uniformed female military auxiliaries to make up for manpower shortages, the French army strongly discouraged female participation of any kind, and successfully avoided militarizing women. Nevertheless, the French high command's own inept handling of the war resulted in massive and unprecedented casualties that had to be made good from a limited manpower pool. Throughout 1915, a vigorous debate raged in France over the place of women in the defense of the nation. From 1916 to 1918, despite intense hostility from many generals, the French army grudgingly employed 120,000 female civilian employees as nurses, clerical workers, telephone operators, cleaners, and even in a limited capacity as drivers. However, they were not allowed uniforms or any military privileges such as housing, meals, transportation, or free postage.[8] Even though these privileges were routinely granted to cantinières in the eighteenth and nineteenth centuries, French generals insisted on preventing female employees from receiving them during World War One, for fear that they would blur the lines between male soldiers and women. In fact, French women serving in World War One faced all of the restrictions that cantinières' status as employees brought upon them, yet shared absolutely none of the benefits that cantinières enjoyed. Because of this, the years of the Great War actually marked a large step backward for French women who wished to defend their country.

And yet, despite the War Ministry's insistence on eliminating cantinières as useless, and despite its long protestations that women and war had nothing in common, the role of French women in World War One closely paralleled that of cantinières in the preceding centuries. In brief, while the French government insisted that women be *employées* (or even *volontaires*) and not *militaires*, it asked them to fulfill four major roles: to provide the troops with supplies that the army could not or would not provide; to encourage the soldiers to fight hard to defend France; to nurse the wounded; and to fill in for jobs that men could not be spared for. In all of these roles, French civilian women were essentially fulfilling the same functions as cantinières had, with only some minor updating of the place, means, and details of their work. For example, from the very start of the war, women began spontaneously acting as surrogate cantinières. As the war began and the troops headed for the front, "women and girls gathered at the train stations and along the roadsides to cheer the passing troops and to hand out fruit, coffee, sandwiches, chocolate, and cigarettes." In other words, thousands of French women did exactly what cantinières would have done had they not been suppressed in 1906, with the caveat that the new volunteers did it far less efficiently and in only a very ephemeral way, since they did not travel with and live with the regiments. Perhaps more importantly from the soldiers' point of view, alcohol was noticeably absent from their list of provisions. However, before long, women began to organize volunteer canteens in the locations most likely to see military traffic. The Duchesse de Gramont wrote, "In all the train stations, canteens are springing up; girls spend the night in the station, the mothers knit and oversee the stove while their daughters supply the convoys of wounded."[9] If one substitutes a regimental camp or marching column for the train station, and wagons for trains, this could describe a mother-daughter canteen that any nineteenth-century cantinière would be familiar with. Likewise, by 1916, "feminist groups were being singled out for their patriotic work, for doing everything from sewing for soldiers to sustaining 'morale' throughout Paris." Cooking and doing other chores in military installations also became the norm, to the extent that a French newspaper could "praise such women serving the army for 'doing the housekeeping of France.'"[10]

Even women who did not come in direct contact with the troops were recruited into the "surrogate cantinière" role. Many women engaged in soldiers' charities that sent care packages to the troops at the front, including such items as "writing paper, soap, flea powder, cigarettes, and chocolate." These are all items (among others) that would have been readily available within the regiment had cantinières not been suppressed. According to Margaret Darrow, French women were even told that "it was their duty, rather than that of the Army supply department, to keep their men at the front as comfortable as possible. Moralizing fiction and propaganda encouraged women and children to skimp on their own food to send treats to their men at the front."[11] Again, the role of all French women became that of the cantinière: to provide those extra special items that the army would not so that the soldiers' lives would be more comfortable. It is worth noting that in 1897, Georges Montorgueil personified France as a cantinière in an updating of the Marianne image for a children's history of the nation since 1789.[12] His book was extremely popular and went through many printings. Now, only two decades later, all French women were being asked to serve as surrogate cantinières—in effect, to *be* the female incarnation of

France in the hour of need. However, in this case, the real cantinières were gone, and French women were asked to play the role of a fictional and symbolic character: a fitting commentary on the nature of the work they were allowed to perform. Still, as limited and symbolic as this work was, it reflected an ongoing need for the work the cantinières had formerly performed, and it highlighted again that the all-male military machine was not as smooth nor as self-sufficient as the cantinières' detractors had claimed. As Frédéric Masson wrote in 1915, women should "disregard government assurances that supplies for the soldiers were sufficient. Only French women could give to the soldiers the little personal touches so necessary to morale."[13] This was essentially the same argument that Françoise Verier made in her 1819 letter to the minister of war, and this was the same function cantinières had performed for so many years.

All of the above roles included providing for the soldiers' sustenance, but they also spilled over into the second major role women played: encouraging the troops. Since the misery of the trench stalemate was particularly hard on the "soldierly spirit," various French entities promoted schemes for buoying up the morale of the front-line troops. One of the most popular and widespread of these was the *marraine de guerre* (war godmother) program that paired concerned women at home with young soldiers at the front. The *marraines* acted as adoptive mothers of soldiers, especially those who had lost their families. The *marraine* would send packages of foodstuffs, cigarettes, and personal essentials to her adoptive "godson," who would presumably be encouraged to fight to the death.[14] Once again, French women were called on to supply the soldiers with items necessary to their comfort, just as cantinières had done. The key differences were that now women did this from a distance (which protected them from the "defeminizing" effects of the battlefield) and at their own expense rather than for a profit. In addition, since *marraines* were often young and attractive, they also filled another cantinière role: that of sexual fantasy for the soldiers. Just as the cantinière had served as the object of soldiers' crushes and fantasies in the nineteenth century, during the Great War, French popular fiction made much of the potential for romance, real or imagined, between young soldiers and their *marraines*.[15] In a sense, then, the French army and government were able to retain (at least to a limited degree) the function of cantinières while simultaneously denying women the right to earn a living while providing it. In fact, they demanded that women pay for the privilege. This represented a major setback for women's independence.

The status of army nursing in 1914 also suggests that the French army erred badly when it eliminated cantinières before the war. Three years after the suppression of cantinières, the army began training women to be military nurses, but the male hierarchy was so resistant, and the high command's predictions of the need so catastrophically understated, that by 1914 the army had trained only a hundred women. When the war began, therefore, the army issued mobilization orders for twenty-three thousand Red Cross volunteer nurses, but even these proved totally inadequate for the massive casualties of the opening weeks of the war. The existing hospital system was utterly overwhelmed, and many soldiers died or suffered unnecessarily because of a lack of adequate first aid and hospital facilities. The French army eventually utilized sixty-three thousand volunteer Red Cross nurses as well as thirty thousand female civilian employee nurses. However, if cantinières had still been a part of the organization of French regiments, there would have been thousands more women already stationed with combat units and ready to act as battlefield nurses. While cantinières could not claim to have the medical expertise of the highly trained prewar nurses, according to Margaret Darrow, "once the war began, training became much speedier and focused on dressing wounds," tasks for which cantinières were fully qualified, and which they had indeed practiced for more than a century on battlefields around the world.[16] In the end, the suppression of cantinières left the army with multiple unfilled needs when the test of battle arrived. Nursing was perhaps the most crucial.

One unique woman illustrated all three of the above lacunae that the suppression of cantinières had exacerbated, and that were keenly felt by the common soldier throughout the war: lack of supplies, lack of moral encouragement, and lack of adequate nursing staff. Madame Ricaux appeared on the cover of the November 16, 1916, issue of *Les annales politiques et litteraires,* a weekly illustrated review, billed as "the only frontline cantinière of the French army."

> She is named Mme Ricaux; she is popular in the region of Compiègne where she lives. At the start of the war she conducted herself so valiantly and cared for the wounded with such devotion that the doctors who utilized her services gave her certificates full of admiration. Touched by these testimonials, the military authorities gave her a privilege refused up to now to all other women, that of provisioning the soldiers of the front lines. Every day, whether it rains, snows, or is windy, one sees Mother Ricaux's cart passing through the streets of Compiègne, pulled by her little grey donkey, and loaded with everything the troops could want: tobacco and food. The modern vivandière, helmeted like Minerva, gives them an example of courage and good humor.[17]

This brief paragraph shows that Madame Ricaux combined the two roles of supplier and morale booster, and she did it right in the Zone of the Army. However, it is worth noting that she was not really a cantinière; she was a civilian woman who lived in the war zone and who was allowed the "privilege" of supplying the troops at her own expense. The newspaper gave her the title of "cantinière," but in reality she was merely another civilian volunteer. Photos show her, a stout, middle-aged woman wearing a black dress and an Adrian helmet, smiling and surrounded by happy soldiers. She had a helmet and permission from local authorities to move about among the troops, but apparently no official sanction beyond that. Moreover, while the article describes her as a front-line cantinière, the photos tell a different story. The land all around her is unscathed, still in cultivation, and with undamaged trees and structures. Of all the soldiers gathered around her little cart, only one wears a helmet; the others wear kepis or side caps, and all have immaculate uniforms. While Madame Ricaux operated in the Zone of the Army, she was nowhere near the actual front, but well out of the range of even long-range artillery, and she neither supplied nor encouraged the men who needed it most: the front-line soldiers in the trenches. The article praised Madame Ricaux for her nursing, her provisioning of the troops, and her work as a morale booster, but it avoided the question of why the army needed civilian women to step into these roles, and it never mentioned that the real cantinières who had fulfilled those roles for so long had been suppressed only eight years before the war. Instead, it merely recounted the facts without addressing issues that a critical reading and a cursory knowledge of recent history would have raised. Like Victorine Charlemagne and Madame Jarrethout, Madame Ricaux served as a symbol to a nation ignorant of the true situation but hungry for assurance and inspiration. If anything, she shows that the French nation itself was in need of "an example of courage and good humor" as it approached, in late 1916, the nadir of the war. The article also illustrated once again the army's continuing need for the services that cantinières provided, even if the War Ministry denied it.

Women filled a variety of other non-combat roles during the war, but always as non-military employees. While the army's female drivers eventually received uniforms in 1917, this measure was purely practical in nature, and the army rushed to reassure people that this in no way "militarized" the women involved.[18]

On the whole, then, even the brief history of women's employment by the French army during World War One suggests that the functions that cantinières provided (and that the army claimed were unimportant or capable of being filled by male soldiers) remained and indeed grew greatly in importance during the First World War. Ultimately, the French army reinvented the cantinière in ways that kept most French women firmly in the domestic sphere, and forced those women to bear the financial costs of the army's own failures. Those women who were allowed to step into the male world of warfare were still kept carefully segregated from the real participation in war and battle that cantinières had routinely engaged in. Nevertheless, the price the army paid for this segregation was the drastically reduced effectiveness of the "surrogate cantinières" as compared to the real ones, and therefore an unquantifiable but real reduction in the effectiveness of the army as a whole.

Moreover, the role of women in the war does not fully explain the merits of the army's decision to suppress cantinières. The massive and widespread mutinies that shook the French army in the spring of 1917 also bear some examination. While it is true that the senseless slaughter of repeated and futile offensives was a key factor in sparking the mutinies, the soldiers also demanded better and more plentiful food and drink, decent rest facilities, and adequate home leave: all important factors in the morale of any group of soldiers. Hunt Tooley argues that the French troops "got no food at all in the trenches, and hardly any food when in reserve," while also asserting that when the troops were fed, the "food was terrible."[19] Likewise, John Morrow argues that while the slaughter at the front was a key factor in the mutinies, when asked what they wanted, the troops complained of "inadequate time for leave, abysmal living conditions in general, and poor food and wine in particular."[20] Albert Fyfe also cites "the poor food, the lack of leave, the wretched medical services" as key complaints of the soldiers of 1917.[21] On only a slightly less basic level, the soldiers missed the shelter that the cantinières and their canteens had provided. As David Englander points out, "Apart from questions concerning food and drink, soldiers were exercised by issues respecting pay allowances, clothing and comforts, shelter, warmth and rest."[22] Except for the pay issues, all of these were part of the duties of the cantinières before their suppression. Had cantinières and their canteens been available with combat units at nineteenth-century levels, they would have provided front-line soldiers with good food and drink as well as a warm and comfortable shelter where they could thaw out, dry off, write letters home, and socialize.[23] Perhaps most importantly, they would have provided a sympathetic female ear, a domestic environment, and a touch of home: literally for the cantinières' husbands, and figuratively (but far more tangibly than the *marraines de guerre*) for the rest.

That the presence of cantinières might have propped up army morale is supported by the sociological research on aberrant collective military behavior done by Bruce Watson. In his study of various mutinies, massacres, and collapses, Watson argues that in each army, "doubt was enhanced by the belief that the group was isolated—that no one cared about them anymore—and by anxieties concerning the army's inability to provide adequate food, clothing, and medical aid, and worries about the safety of their families." More specifically, Watson wrote that "a variety of events, feelings, and perceptions can bring a group to despair. But among the examples discussed in this study, there was one complex factor that stood out: the feelings within the various groupings that no one cared about them, that no one listened, that they were somehow cut off, alone."[24] Thus, the very real psychological benefits of having family with the regiment, and of having female members of the regiment who would listen, commiserate, and comfort as well as provide good food and drink and a warm, comfortable, and inviting place to rest and relax, were precisely what was missing from the French army in 1917. General Pétain's own actions in ending the mutinies speak particularly loudly: he did end the senseless offensives, but he also made sure that French troops had adequate home leave, mobile field kitchens, a regular liquor ration, and "clean facilities and good food."[25] In short, "in terms of day-to-day life, Pétain's reforms restored dignity to the soldier" by providing some of the comforts once routinely provided by the cantinière, even if the reforms were not always implemented quickly enough.[26]

Leaving aside the issues of patriotism and devotion to husbands and sons within the regiment, free-market forces alone would have compelled cantinières to supply most of the soldiers' unfulfilled needs on their own during the war, and at no cost to the French government. It is likely that had cantinières still been present during World War One, the increased availability of good food and drink within the regiment would have improved morale and ameliorated soldiers' other complaints. Moreover, since the canteen during the Third Republic played such a vital role as a social center and a refuge from the elements and the pressures of duty, it seems likely that cantinières' continued presence with the regiment would have been psychologically very beneficial to the troops, and might well have helped them cope with the stresses of the battles of 1917. Certainly it is clear that their absence was keenly felt. In addition, the presence in the regiment of soldiers' wives and the easy accessibility of a sister or mother figure in the canteen might well have made soldiers feel their separation from home and family less sharply: evidence shows that this was clearly the case with the draftees of the 1890s and 1900s, and the army seemed to recognize this, if only half-heartedly, during the First World War. After all, wasn't that the whole point of the *marraine de guerre* campaign? This discussion must remain speculative, but it is worth considering that a continuance of the cantinière corps might indeed have improved the French army's ability to carry on a prolonged and bloody struggle by reducing or eliminating the soldiers' perception that "they had been treated like animals."[27] Certainly, the verifiable and undeniable historical record of the French high command's handling of the war could hardly be more dismal: inadequate numbers of nurses, poor or non-existent rations, and a brutal and insensitive treatment of private soldiers combined with an almost surreal ignorance of modern tactics all led within three years to the mutiny of perhaps half of the army. This does not speak well of the handling of the war or of the War Ministry's prior decision to militarize and masculinize all support functions. If nothing else, the timing and execution of the decision were extremely poor.

Therefore, it seems clear that while cantinières may have presented some problems for the War Ministry, their usefulness over time was undeniable. What is more, their suppression was premature, and had severe consequences for individual French soldiers, the French army, and the French nation during World War One. French women went through a difficult and prolonged period in which their desire to serve their country was rebuffed and ridiculed, even as the country desperately needed their help. Because of this, from 1909 until the 1950s, French women underwent a process of training and professionalization in order to show that they were capable of fulfilling important roles in the defense of the nation. Eventually, this paved the way for women to serve not as auxiliaries, but as soldiers in their own right. Cantinières were an important part of this overall transition. They were not the clandestine women soldiers of the eighteenth century who fought disguised as men, nor were they the professional women soldiers of the late twentieth century. Cantinières (and their First World War stand-ins) were the essential link between the two, and their roles, both on and off the battlefield, give testimony to the rich variety of women's experience in the modern era.

Notes

1. Lettre du Général Rapp au ministre de la guerre, 26 juillet 1806; Extrait des minutes de la Secrétairerie d'état au palais des Tuileries, 3 mars 1809; Lettre de Madeleine Kintelberger au Ministre de la Guerre Berthier, 6 février 1806, in "Muller née Kintelberger," Xs12, Service historique de l'Armée de terre, Vincennes (hereafter referred to as AT).

2. For a recent study of this phenomenon, focused mainly on the seventeenth century, see Lynn, *Women, Armies, and Warfare in Early Modern Europe.*

3. Hacker, "Women and Military Institutions in Early Modern Europe." Hacker's description of cantinières and their history was inaccurate on many points, and the details he provides should be handled with care. However, this is understandable, since the article was meant to stimulate more research on a hitherto neglected topic, not to serve as a definitive history of these women. Based mostly on published sources, this was a survey, not a history. Much later trouble has come from an ambiguous statement Hacker made concerning French women: "In 1840, the French army barred army wives from serving as *vivandières,* who were now issued uniforms and assigned regular duties; no other women followed the French army to the Crimea in 1854, save some nursing sisters" (666). Several later historians have read this as meaning that vivandières/cantinières were banned in 1840, and this is clearly false. However, even the literal meaning of this statement is false, and in fact totally contradictory to reality. Army regulations required vivandières/cantinières to be the wives of soldiers—in theory at least, one could not obtain a post without being married to a soldier, so the idea that "army wives" were banned from serving is false. Hacker is probably referring to the 1839 regulation forbidding sergeants' wives from serving as "vivandières or blanchisseuses." However, this regulation did not apply to private soldiers, and in any case it was never enforced and was universally ignored. (See chapter 4.) Unfortunately, Hacker's mistake has been picked up and used by a variety of historians over the last three decades, resulting in a variety of unfortunate misinterpretations.

4. Lynn, "The Strange Case of the Maiden Soldier of Picardy"; Hacker, "Where Have All the Women Gone?"; for a larger study, though one based entirely on Anglophone

folklore, see Dugaw, *Warrior Women and Popular Balladry.* Noel St. John Williams covers the British army in *Judy O'Grady and the Colonel's Lady,* while Elizabeth Salas covers Mexico's female soldiers in *Soldaderas in the Mexican Military.* Women traveling with the armies in the American War of Independence are covered in Holly Mayer, *Belonging to the Army.* Myna Trustram wrote a study that focuses very narrowly on the British army, with no real transnational comparisons: *Women of the Regiment.*

For a more contemporary history, see Margaret Darrow's excellent study, *French Women and the First World War.* Two relatively recent works on *femmes soldats,* or female soldiers, are Steinberg, *La confusion des sexes,* and Godineau, "De la guerrière à la citoyenne." Both ignore cantinières in favor of the few women who served in the ranks. Popular accounts of women in the military across all periods include Jones, *Women Warriors,* and Dever and Dever, *Women and the Military.* In what is perhaps the most encouraging sign for the growing vitality of the field, noted military historian John Lynn recently published *Women, Armies, and Warfare in Early Modern Europe,* an excellent study that combines a sweeping knowledge of military history with an impressive understanding of issues of women's history and of gender studies. Hopefully, this will lead to a growing collaboration between historians of women and historians of armies and war. My own book was written and accepted for publication before Lynn's book was released (and in any case deals mostly with a later era), but I have still profited as much as possible in the editing and revision process from his insights.

5. For example, John Lynn devoted two short paragraphs to them in *Giant of the Grand Siècle,* 341–342; Elting, *Swords around a Throne,* contains a short chapter titled "Vivandières, enfants, et bric a brac," 605–621. The very title suggests the marginal nature of the subjects. In France, Luce Larcade (née Riès) wrote two pieces using information from the French army archives and the Musée de l'armée: Larcade, "Les cantinières," and Riès, "Les cantinières ou les 'dessous' de la gloire," parts 1 and 2. More recently, Gil Mihaely has written a piece arguing that fear of gender disorder was the sole cause of the suppression of cantinières: "L'effacement de la cantinière ou la virilisation de l'armée française au XIXe siècle." Interestingly, the most accurate brief representation of cantinières in a larger work on military history was also one of the earliest: Rothenberg, *The Art of Warfare.*

6. In fact, John Lynn argues convincingly that the real reduction in the number of women with European armies took place around 1650, when states moved from "aggregate contract armies" to more professional (and controllable) "state commission armies." Lynn, *Women, Armies, and Warfare,* 19, 221–228.

7. Lynn, *Giant of the Grand Siècle,* 338.

8. Although the records were completely uncatalogued and undisturbed when I first visited Vincennes, they have since been catalogued by the archives' staff. It is therefore much easier now to find records of individual cantinières.

9. Beaunis, *Impressions de campagne;* Roussier, "Un soldat d'Afrique"; Villeneuve, *Mes années militaires.*

10. Montesquiou-Fezensac, *Souvenirs militaires de 1804 à 1814;* Montigny, *Souvenirs anecdotiques d'un officier de la Grande armée;* Cadet de Gassicourt, *Voyage en Autriche, en Moravie, et en Bavière;* Thoumas, *Mes souvenirs de Crimée.*

11. Gaboriau, "Military Sketches," in Gaboriau and Mérimée, *A Thousand Francs Reward . . . and Carmen,* 19.

12. Farge argues that the women in Watteau's *Le camp volant* are there as symbols, missing the altogether straightforward and practical consideration that they are there because vivandières and blanchisseuses always traveled with armies, and were indeed an essential part of them. Farge, *Les fatigues de la guerre*, 59.

13. Even a cursory glance at the bibliography of this work will note many unconventional sources, quite a few of which would not readily leap to mind as a source for researching French military women. While many of these were tracked down the tediously slow, old-fashioned way, quite a few more were found only through the good offices of the newly digitized collections noted above.

14. Those without a knowledge of modern French history may wish to consult a general history of France before proceeding. The standard (and excellent) source remains Gordon Wright, *A History of Modern France* (New York: Norton, 1995). A less detailed but still strong treatment can be found in Jeremy Popkin, *History of Modern France*, 3rd ed. (Upper Saddle River, N.J.: Prentice Hall, 2005). Those wishing for the briefest of treatments may consult Lisa Neal, *France: An Illustrated History* (New York: Hippocrene, 2001).

15. Of course, another interpretation is possible: that the Second Republic's early demise was due to its own failure to republicanize the army through a ruthless program of legislation, regulation, and selective promotion.

16. Larcade, "Les cantinières," 55.

17. Gosselin, *D'un révolution à l'autre*, 33.

1. An Uncertain Existence

1. For France see Babeau, *La vie militaire*, 1:327–328. For examples from several countries, see Gooch, *Armies in Europe*.

2. Parker, *The Military Revolution*, 47–49; Rothenberg, *The Art of Warfare*, 12.

3. Redlich, *The German Military Enterpriser and His Work Force*, 2:202.

4. Lynn, *Giant of the Grand Siècle*, 324. For a detailed discussion of social background, see Corvisier, *L'armée française*, 1:473–506.

5. Kennett, *The French Armies in the Seven Years' War*, 72–73.

6. Mention, *L'armée de l'ancien régime*, 37; Société historique de Rueil-Malmaison, *Les Gardes suisses et leurs familles*, 16.

7. "Extrait du journal du baron Gabriel Albert d'Erlach," reprinted in Société historique de Rueil-Malmaison, *Les Gardes suisses et leurs familles*, 25, 27.

8. Chagniot, *Paris et l'armée au XVIIIe siècle*, 423, 527–528. Mention, *L'armée de l'ancien régime*, 59–66, provides discussion and illustrations of capital and corporal punishments.

9. Scott, *The Response of the Royal Army*, 43.

10. This disparity much impressed French soldiers during the Empire, who called out lotto numbers using brief aphorisms for each number, rather than the number itself. For thirty-one, they used "Jour sans pain, misère en Prusse" (Day without bread, misery in Prussia). Blaze, *Souvenirs d'un officier de la Grande armée*, 46. This aphorism was still in use at the dawn of the twentieth century: see Vandam, *French Men and French Manners*, 123–124.

11. Scott, *The Response of the Royal Army*, 43. For a clear statistical study of how badly soldiers' pay and the overall military budget deteriorated in the final years of the Old Regime, see Sturgill, "The French Army's Budget in the Eighteenth Century," 123–134.

12. Morvan, *Le soldat impérial,* 1:364–365.

13. Chagniot, *Paris et l'armée au XVIIIe siècle,* 438–447; Béla, *Mémoires militaires,* 30.

14. Redlich, *The German Military Enterpriser and His Work Force,* 2:206.

15. Béla, *Mémoires militaires,* 30–32; Duffy, *The Military Experience,* 171–172; Scott, *The Response of the Royal Army,* 39–40.

16. Mathe, *Dix-huitième siècle,* 328.

17. Rothenberg, *The Art of Warfare,* 13; Duffy, *The Military Experience,* 249.

18. Parker, *The Military Revolution,* 57–58; Kennett, *The French Armies in the Seven Years' War,* 84.

19. Duffy, *The Army of Frederick the Great,* 67.

20. Martin Van Creveld tried erroneously to show that eighteenth-century armies in fact lived off the land. However, his argument supports only the obvious: that they foraged for fodder because it was impossible to supply the necessary quantities from the rear. Rations were still supplied from magazines, since foraging for rations involved a much greater dispersion and loss of control than did foraging for fodder. Van Creveld, *Supplying War,* 26–39. See John Lynn's excellent critique in *Giant of the Grand Siècle,* 140–145.

21. Babeau, *La vie militaire,* 1:333–334; Kennett, *The French Armies in the Seven Years' War,* 85.

22. Mopinot de la Chapotte, *Sous Louis le bien-aimé,* 25–55.

23. Mention, *L'armée de l'ancien régime,* 57.

24. Thoumas, *Les transformations de l'armée française,* 2:222.

25. Babeau, *La vie militaire,* 2:205.

26. Fox-Genovese, "Women and Work," 116.

27. Cartons XS11 and XS12, "Femmes militaires," AT; Lebrun, *La vie conjugale sous l'ancien régime,* 31–32.

28. Extrait des registres de mariage de la municipalité de Thionville, 16 juillet 1793, in "Pain, née Gaudin," XS12, AT; Commune d'Arte, Certificat de naissance, 23 janvier 1767, in "Sabatier, née Campagne," XS12, AT; Extrait du registre des baptêmes de la ville de La Bassée, 6 novembre 1750, in "Sauger, née Liénard," XS12, AT.

29. Corvisier, *L'armée française,* 2:763. See also Scott, *The Response of the Royal Army,* 10–11.

30. Lettre du Conseil d'administration de la 142e Demi-brigade au Citoyen Collé, chef de l'état-major de la Grande division de l'ouest, 6 messidor An IV, in "Eulen née Sauvart," XS11, AT.

31. Extrait du registre de mariage de la cidevant paroisse Suisse, 11 juillet 1778; 3e Régiment de Hussards, Conseil d'administration, Certificat de service de Joseph Bisetky [*sic*], 9 messidor An IV, in "Pisetky, née Boos," XS12, AT.

32. Delasselle, "Les enfants abandonés," 189.

33. Extrait des registres des actes de naissance de la cidevant paroisse St. Gennet deposés au secretariat de la mairie d'Avignon, 29 juin 1757; 48e Régiment d'infanterie de ligne, Certificat de non-divorce, 9 janvier 1811, in "Hoccard, née Pierrette," XS12, AT.

34. Extrait des actes de marriage, canton de St. Pierre (Pas de Calais), 26 novembre 1792; Lettre de Marie Roche à l'empéreur Napoléon, 24 mai 1810, in "Roche, née Lepère," XS12, AT.

35. Lettre du baron Baurot au Bureau des pensions des veuves, 30 janvier 1815; Lettre de Catherine Sabatier au ministre de la guerre, 30 janvier 1815, in "Sabatier, née Campagne," Xs12, AT.

36. Montigny, *Souvenirs anecdotiques d'un officier de la Grande armée*, 326–327.

37. Corvisier, *L'armée française*, 2:763.

38. Lebrun, *La vie conjugale sous l'ancien régime*, 33.

39. The 123 individual files in cartons Xs11 and Xs12, AT, provide a snapshot view, but do not give an accurate picture of fertility over time. Unfortunately, the records to do so simply do not exist, given the limited nature of the War Ministry's interest.

40. Corvisier, *L'armée française*, 2:764.

41. Ibid.

42. For a representative picture of family life and children's activities in camp, see Charles Cozette, *Vue du Camp du havre en 1756*, oil on canvas, the anonymous *Un camp de cavalerie*, lithograph from the collection of General Vanson, n.d., and Pierre l'Enfant, *Vue du Camp de Calais en 1756*, oil on canvas, all in the Musée de l'armée, Paris.

43. Hennet, *Regards en arrière*, 6–8, 10.

44. De Saugeon, *Collection des ordonnances militaires*, 53, 66, 67.

45. Corvisier, *L'armée française*, 2:761, 767.

46. Conseil d'administration du 4e Régiment de chasseurs à cheval, Armée d'Angleterre, Certificat de mort d'Antoine Leytier, in "Leytier, née Delforge," XS12, AT; Conseil d'administration du 3e Régiment de Hussards, Certificat d'indigence, 9 messidor An VII, in "Pisetky, née Boos," XS12, AT; Lettre du baron Baurot au Bureau des pensions des veuves, 30 janvier 1815; Lettre de Catherine Sabatier au ministre de la guerre, 30 janvier 1815, in "Sabatier, née Campagne," Xs12, AT.

47. D'Erlach, cited in Société historique de Rueil-Malmaison, *Les Gardes suisses et leurs familles*, 27; Duffy, *The Military Experience*, 169.

48. Mopinot de la Chapotte, *Sous Louis le bien-aimé*, 295–296.

49. Ibid., 296.

50. Rothenberg, *The Art of Warfare*, 14.

51. Mopinot de la Chapotte, *Sous Louis le bien-aimé*, 296.

52. For examples from Normandy and Champagne (both areas of heavy military activity), see Vallez, "Cartographie des régimes et des circonscriptions des gabelles" and Clause, "La contrabande du sel."

53. Corvisier, *L'armée française*, 1:94–96.

54. De Bonnelles, *Ordonnances militaires* (Paris, 1724), 237 (uncatalogued manuscript), AT.

55. Ibid., 352.

56. "Ordonnance du roy pour faire condamner les filles de mauvaise vie qui se trouveront avec les soldats . . . ," cited in Lynn, *Giant of the Grand Siècle*, 343; Babeau, *La vie militaire*, 2:201.

57. De Bonnelles, *Ordonnances militaires*, 352–353.

58. Chagniot, *Paris et l'armée au XVIIIe siècle*, 580.

59. L'Enfant, *Vue du Camp du havre*, Musée de l'armée, Paris.

60. Lynn, *Women, Armies, and Warfare*, 47.

61. Dumonchelle, *La vivandière*, oil on canvas, Musée de l'armée, Paris.

62. Lynn, *Women, Armies, and Warfare*, 46–47.

63. "Ordonnance du roi pour régler le service dans les places et dans les quartiers du 1er mars 1768," in *Ordonnances militaires* (Paris, 1768–1769), 4:14.

64. De Bonnelles, *Ordonnances militaires*, 374.

65. Mopinot de la Chapotte, *Sous Louis le bien-aimé*, 79.

66. Kennett, *The French Armies in the Seven Years' War*, 123.

67. Deschard, *L'armée et la Révolution*, 211.

68. Certificat de service de Michel Daunay, 14 nivôse An IV, in "Daunay, née Bracq," Xs11, AT. Daunay joined the Régiment de Lorraine (deserted 1761), the Régiment de Montreville (deserted 1762), the Bataillon de Rennes (deserted 1763), the Régiment du roi (deserted 1769), and the Gardes françaises (deserted 1773). He took advantage of a general amnesty for deserters on December 12, 1775.

69. Mopinot de la Chapotte, *Sous Louis le bien-aimé*, 400.

70. Mention, *L'armée de l'ancien régime*, 65.

71. Babeau, *La vie militaire*, 2:207.

72. Mopinot de la Chapotte, *Sous Louis le bien-aimé*, 287.

73. Babeau, *L'armée de l'ancien régime*, 2:207.

74. Lettre du Comte de St. Germain à M. de Clugny, controlleur général, 20 septembre 1776, in "Andierne," Xs11, AT.

75. Hennet, *Regards en arrière*, 11–12; Corvisier, *L'armée française*, 2:765.

76. Flandrin, *Familles*, 182.

2. "Absolutely Necessary"

1. Rothenberg, *The Art of Warfare*, 98.

2. Scott, *The Response of the Royal Army*, 102–103, 109–113.

3. Marquant, *Carnet d'étapes du dragon Marquant*, 145. For a more measured and more nuanced view of this phenomenon, see Forest, *Soldiers of the French Revolution,* esp. 189–197. For an actual example from 1790, see Scott, *The Response of the Royal Army,* 39.

4. Rothenberg, *The Art of Warfare*, 134. For practical examples of this played out in real life as late as 1809, see Jean Chevillet, *Ma vie militaire,* passim.

5. Rothenberg, *The Art of Warfare*, 35.

6. Décret no. 804 de la Convention nationale, 30 avril 1793: Pour congédier des armées les femmes inutiles, Xs11, AT.

7. 7e demi-brigade, Certificat du service, 30 frimaire An X, in "Horr, née André," Xs11, AT; 68e Demi-brigade, Certificat de blanchisseuse, 29 messidor An VI, in "Donnet, née Peter," Xs11, AT; Patente de blanchisseuse-vivandière, in "George, née Rost," Xs12, AT.

8. Blaze, *Souvenirs d'un officier de la Grande armée,* 112.

9. For examples of this trend see Armée du Rhin, Permission de vivandière et blanchisseuse, 26 brumaire An VIII, in "Bertinet, née Dimel," Xs11, AT; 23e Demi-brigade, Armée du Rhin, Permission de blanchisseuse et vivandière, 25 brumaire An IX, in "Billers, née Conrad," Xs12, AT; 1er Régiment de carabiniers, Certificat de service, 14 thermidor An X, in "Bory, née Peter," Xs11, AT (this summary for the Pension Bureau gives Mme Bory's title as "vivandière et blanchisseuse"); 7e Bataillon de Paris, Certificat de service de Charlotte Daunay, 12 juillet An II [*sic*], in "Daunay, née Braque," Xs12, AT (this document, which also mixes old- and new-style dates, simply states that Daunay was "attached to the battalion"); Compagnie des cannoniers du

4e Bataillon des Ardennes, Certificat de blanchisseuse-vivandière, 6 août 1793, in "George, née Rost," Xs12, AT; Extrait de register des délibérations du district de Fougères: séance publique du 29 floréal, 3e année républicaine, in "Sicard, née Gourau," Xs12, AT.

10. For examples of patriotic women serving their country as combat soldiers during the Revolution, see Xs49, AT ("Femmes soldats": thirty-one dossiers); Caire, *La femme militaire des origines à nos jours;* Klein-Rebour, "Les femmes soldats à travers les ages," 3–20; Roquet, "Les femmes soldats dans la Sarthe sous la Révolution"; Godineau, "De la guerrière à la citoyenne." Sylvie Steinberg's study *La confusion des sexes* suggests a complex variety of motives.

11. 1er Régiment de carabiniers, Certificat de service, 14 thermidor An X, in "Bory, née Peter," Xs11, AT.

12. Various documents in "Donnet, née Petry," Xs11, AT.

13. Various documents in "Boyer, née Ressouce," Xs11, AT.

14. Commune de Dix, Certificat de mariage, Sept. 1791; Hôpital ambulant du Cateau, Certificat de mort, 13 fructidor An II, in "Dionkre, née Hequette," Xs11, AT.

15. Lettre du ministre de la guerre au ministre des finances, 30 October 1820, in "Billers, née Conrad," Xs11, AT.

16. Lettre du préfet de l'Ourthe au ministre de la guerre, 2 messidor An X, in "Horr, née André," Xs12, AT.

17. Delasselle, "Les enfants abandonés," 189. For a case study of a nearby city, see Fairchilds, *Poverty and Charity in Aix-en-Province,* 84.

18. Paroisse de St. Genet (Avignon), Certificat de naissance; Certificat de mariage, in "Hoccard, née Pierrette," Xs12, AT.

19. Certificat de naissance; Certificat de mariage, 15 nivôse An II; Lettre du Sophie Bachelet au ministre de la guerre, 26 messidor An V, in "Bachelet, née Barrau," Xs12, AT.

20. Extrait du registre des mariages de commune de Craön, in "Sicard, née Gourau," Xs12, AT.

21. Extrait du registre des délibérations du district de Fougères: séance publique du 29 floréal, 3e année républicaine, in "Sicard, née Gourau," Xs12, AT.

22. Various documents in "Boldevin, orphelin," Xs11, AT.

23. Various documents in "Langlet, née Bathis," Xs12, AT.

24. 21e Demi-brigade d'infanterie de ligne, Certificat no. 48, 10 thermidor An X, in "Moulin, née Bailleul," Xs12, AT.

25. Gosselin, *D'un révolution à l'autre,* 25.

26. Lettre de Jeanne Delforge au ministre de la guerre, 2 messidor An III, in "Leytier, née Delforge," Xs12, AT.

27. François, *Journal du capitaine François,* 1:30–31.

28. Lettre de Marianne Boyer au 6e Commission, 9 messidor An III, in "Boyer, née Ressouce," Xs11, AT.

29. Various documents in "Roche, née Lepère," Xs12, AT.

30. Lettre du 1er Compagnie, 68e Demi-brigade au 4e Division militaire, 13 ventôse An IX, in "Donnet, née Petry," Xs11, AT.

31. Certificat de marriage, commune de Cassé, département de la Mayence, 30 brumaire An VII; Certificat de naissance, commune de Houden, département de Seine-et-Oise, 9 nivôse An VII, in "Boulanger, née Tyronneau," Xs11, AT.

32. In his study of the French army of this period, Alan Forrest wrote that "in the opinion of most soldiers it was not cold or even disease which sapped their strength most damagingly, but the shortage of food and nourishment. Nothing was more likely to create unrest in the ranks than the threat of starvation." Forrest, *Soldiers of the French Revolution*, 174. Clearly, the authorities had a strong incentive to retain vivandières, and to extend their use to the volunteer battalions that often started without them.

33. Brice, *La femme et les armées*, 287.

34. Various documents in "Martin, née Jumier," Xs12, AT.

35. François, *Journal du capitaine François*, 1:108.

36. Ibid., 1:107–108.

37. For a fictional but accurate account of this revenge phenomenon and its rationales, see Erckman-Chatrian, *Madame Thérèse: ou les volontaires de '92* (New York: Holt, 1886), 21–24.

38. Patente de vivandière, in "Simon née Bathis," Xs11, AT.

39. Conseil d'administration du Grand parc d'artillerie, Certificat de cantinière, 19 fructidor An II, in "Leroux, née Longrais," Xs12, AT.

40. Ibid. The culture of corruption and war profiteering pervaded the army's supply services, in stark contrast to the patriotic rhetoric of the time.

41. See for example Forrest, *Conscripts and Deserters*, 95, 172.

42. Gunther Rothenberg, for example, argues that these "hordes" were short-term expedients and were largely replaced by more conventional tactics by 1795. Even after that, however, the French tended to adopt more open and flexible formations than their enemies did. Rothenberg, *The Art of Warfare*, 67, 114–115.

43. Keegan, *The Face of Battle*, 184–185.

44. Picard, *Au service de la nation*, 172.

45. Canard, "Le général Debrun," 509.

46. Lettre de Meurisse, officer de santé et chef de l'Hôpital militaire de Lorient, 9 messidor An II, in "Brévilier, née Pélletier," Xs12, AT.

47. Baron Milius, commandant de Cologne, Passe datée 5 juin 1794, in "Corcellier, née L'Abbé," Xs11, AT.

48. Smith, *The Prisoners of Cabrera*, 44.

49. Various documents in "Chauvet, née Bonnet," Xs12, AT.

50. Inspection générale du Service de santé des armées, Certificat de visite, 18 brumaire An VI [marginal note by Delacroix], in "Brévilier, née Pélletier," Xs12, AT.

51. Lettre du capitaine du *Cazira*, 2 prairial An II, in "Girard, née Deluille," Xs12, AT.

52. Kryn, *Le petit tambour d'arcole*, 267.

53. See, for example, "Femmes dans la guerre," in *Le petit journal militaire et colonial*, December 13, 1903.

54. Extrait du registre des décès de la commune de Nord Libre, premier jour sansculottides An II, in "Gauthier, née ———," Xs11, AT. ("Nord Libre" was the new, Revolutionary name for the old city of Condé. It is now Condé-sur-l'Escaut.)

55. "Lettre de Gand du Député Delacroix à la Convention, 22 mars 1793," Carnot, *Correspondance générale*, 2:117n.

56. "Lettre de Lille de J. Defrenne à Bouchotte, 27 avril 1793," ibid., 1:135.

57. "Lettre de Dunquerque de Pierre Gadolle à Ministre LeBrun, 27 avril 1793," ibid., 2:117.

58. "Lettre de Carnot et Duquesnoy à la Convention, 16 avril 1793, ibid., 2:116–117.

59. "Lettre de 22 avril 1793," ibid., 2:232. According to John Lynn's recent work, "whores" should be understood to refer not to prostitutes, but to the unmarried but usually monogamous permanent or semi-permanent companions of soldiers. Lynn, *Women, Armies, and Warfare,* 67, 75–78.

60. Décret de la Convention nationale no. 804, 30 avril 1793, Xsii, AT.

61. Carnot, *Correspondance générale,* 2:117; Gosselin, *D'un révolution à l'autre,* 25.

62. Forrest, *Soldiers of the French Revolution,* 150.

63. Armée d'Italie, Certificat d'utilité à l'armée, 12 vendémiaire An III, in "Bertaux, dit Chopard," Xsii, AT.

64. Poisson, *L'armée et la Garde nationale,* 2:340. For an example of a woman forced to leave the army by the law, see "Chabre, née Pierrard," Xsii, AT.

65. "Arrêté de Carnot, Delbrel, et Desacy, Arras, 9 juillet 1793," Carnot, *Correspondance générale,* 2:390–391.

66. "Ordre à l'armée du Nord pour rétablir la discipline, 2 septembre 1793," Carnot, *Correspondance générale,* 3:62–63.

67. Herlaut, *Le colonel Bouchotte,* 1:245–246.

68. Pétigny, *Un bataillon de volontaires,* 87–88.

69. Napoléon I, *Correspondance,* nos. 38, 49, 161.

70. Coignet, *Les cahiers,* 72–73.

71. Pétigny, *Un bataillon de volontaires,* 86.

72. 7e Bataillon de Paris, États de service, in "Daunay, née Bracq," Xsii, AT.

73. Woloch, "War-Widows' Pensions," 238.

74. Poisson, *L'armée et la Garde nationale,* 3:153.

75. Woloch, "War-Widows' Pensions," 240.

76. Lettre de Marguerite Pain au Bureau des pensions, 21 ventôse An II, in "Pain, née Gaudin," Xs12, AT.

77. Lettre de Jeanne Leytier au ministre de la guerre, 4 messidor An VII, in, "Leytier, née Delforge," Xs12, AT.

78. Poisson, *L'armée et la Garde nationale,* 3:153.

79. Various documents in "Eulen, née Sauvart," Xsii, AT.

80. Various documents in "Leytier, née Delforge," Xs12, AT.

81. Lettre au Citoyen Lamarke, 14 ventôse An V, in "Leytier, née Delforge," Xs12, AT.

82. Various documents in "Branche, née Petit," Xs12, AT.

83. Lettre de Leroux, commissaire-ordonnateur chargé des dépenses de la guerre, au ministre de la guerre, 2 vendémiaire An VIII, in "Leroux, née Longrais," Xs12, AT.

84. Lettre de Madame Ressouce au ministre de la guerre, 3 vendémiaire An III, in "Boyer, née Ressouce," Xsii, AT.

85. Bureau des veuves, Rapport, 16 messidor An III, "Boyer, née Ressouce," Xsii, AT.

3. Expanded Opportunities

1. All these terms were used in official regulations and correspondence during the course of the nineteenth century, and none can be considered definitive. "Cantinière" was used most often, though, both in regulations and in common usage, as the century wore on. During the Napoleonic era it was common to see and hear all the terms used interchangeably, with no clear pattern except that "cantinière" was gaining

ground on the others. By the mid-century, it was rare to hear anyone but an Anglophone refer to one of these women as anything but a "cantinière." Nonetheless, I will treat the terms as largely interchangeable, except where they have certain connotations or nuances that are important to the understanding of the topic.

2. Armée du Rhin, Patente de vivandière, 25 brumaire An IX, in "Billers, née Pauli," XsII, AT; Armée du Rhin, Permission de vivandière et blanchisseuse, 26 brumaire An VIII, in "Bertinet, née Dimel," XsII, AT.

3. Colonel Petri au duc de Feltre, 19 novembre 1810, in "Angot," XsII, AT.

4. "Arrêté relatif aux enfans de troupe, et aux femmes à la suite de l'armée," *Journal militaire,* 2e semestre, An VIII, 751.

5. Certificat de naissance; Certificat de mariage, in "Bory, née Peter," XsII, AT.

6. Certificat de mariage; Lettre du colonel Voutier au Ministre de Guerre Clark, 2 septembre 1808, in "Léger, Marguerite (Boldevin, orphelin)," XsII, AT.

7. Ministre de finance à Latour-Maubourg, 28 novembre 1820, in "Billers, née Pauli," XsII, AT.

8. Extrait des minutes de la Secrétairerie d'état, 25 mars 1811, in "Hoccard, née Pierrette," Xs12, AT.

9. Various documents in "Gerard, née Demonay," XsII, AT.

10. Relevé des services (Haros, Louis); Lettre du Bureau des lois et archives à la veuve Cornet, 6 février 1863, in "Haros, née Scherre," Xs12, AT.

11. Bourgogne, *The Memoirs of Sergeant Bourgogne,* 126–127.

12. Ibid., 128.

13. Ibid., 277.

14. Lettre de la veuve Cornet au ministre de la guerre, 26 juillet 1864, in "Haros, née Scherre," Xs12, AT.

15. Bourgogne, *The Memoirs of Sergeant Bourgogne,* 4.

16. Bonneval, *Mémoires anecdotiques,* 53–54.

17. Lettre du colonel Petri au duc de Feltre, 19 novembre 1810, in "Angot," XsII, AT.

18. Lettre de Depouthou au ministre de la guerre, 18 mai 1817; Veuve Daubigny au ministre de la guerre, 8 mai 1817, in "Daubigny, née ———," XsII, AT.

19. Lettre du Conseil d'administration, 48e Régiment d'infanterie de ligne, au ministre de la guerre, 9 janvier 1811, in "Hoccard, née Pierrette," Xs12, AT.

20. 3e Division de l'armée d'Espagne, Patente de cantinière, in "Sabatier, née Campagne," Xs12, AT.

21. Bourgogne, *The Memoirs of Sergeant Bourgogne,* 62.

22. Conneau, *A Slaver's Logbook,* 1. Mme Conneau was probably a cantinière, but the author does not use that word to describe his mother. His father was a "Captain Paymaster" by the time of Waterloo, but given the long span of his career and the high casualties and consequent rapid promotion in the French army during this time, it seems almost certain that he was an enlisted man in 1799 when he met his Italian wife. Sixteen years of campaigning as a captain would have been almost unthinkable, especially for a veteran of the 1799 campaign. What is remarkable is that he did not rise higher in rank in such a long time.

23. See, for example, Guillemard, *Mémoires de Robert Guillemard,* 1:185.

24. Elting, *Swords around a Throne,* 611.

25. Pelet, *The French Campaign in Portugal,* 313.

26. Romand, *Mémoires de ma vie militaire*, 72.

27. Montesquiou-Fezensac, *Souvenirs militaires de 1804 à 1814*, 320.

28. Schrafel, *Merckwürdige Schicksale des ehemaligen Feldwebels*, 50–51.

29. Paris, "Souvenirs du 14e léger," 121.

30. Girault, *Mes campagnes sous la république et l'empire*, 60–62, 65.

31. Biot, *Souvenirs anecdotiques et militaires*, 32–33, 58.

32. Blaze, *Souvenirs d'un officier de la Grande armée*, 50–51.

33. Quennevat, *Les vrais soldats de Napoléon*, 158. Quennevat's assertions have some basis in fact, but not universally. The famous "Madame Sans-Gêne" was probably not a cantinière, and various stories attribute this title to the laundress wife of Marshal Lefebvre or to a cross-dressing female soldier. See Cere, *Madame Sans-Gêne et les femmes soldats,* and Gribble, *Women in War*, 14–17.

34. Smith, *The Prisoners of Cabrera*, 122, 184, 20.

35. "Arrêté relatif aux enfans de troupe, et aux femmes à la suite de l'armée," *Journal militaire*, 2e semestre, An VIII, 751.

36. Bourgogne, *The Memoirs of Sergeant Bourgogne*, 51.

37. Paris, "Souvenirs du 14e léger," 121.

38. Bourgogne, *The Memoirs of Sergeant Bourgogne*, 279.

39. Lettre de Kellerman, duc de Valmy, au ministre de la guerre, 21 mai 1808, in "Muller, née Kintelberger," Xs12, AT.

40. For example, Heinrich-Christian von Geißler [Christian Gottfried Heinrich Geißler], *Ankunft der Franzosen in Leipzig, 1806,* watercolor, #19463, Musée de l'armée, Paris; Leopold Beyer, untitled watercolor, Musée de l'armée, Paris.

41. Montigny, *Souvenirs anecdotiques d'un officier de la Grande armée*, 326.

42. Norvins, *Souvenirs d'un historien de Napoléon*, 3:193.

43. Blaze, *Souvenirs d'un officier de la Grande armée*, 50; Bourgogne, *The Memoirs of Sergeant Bourgogne*, 66–67.

44. Adam, *Voyage pittoresque et militaire*, 23.

45. Bourgogne, *The Memoirs of Sergeant Bourgogne*, 66–67, 72.

46. Langeron, *Mémoires de Langeron*, 92–93.

47. Ducor, *Aventures d'un marin*, 1:212.

48. Lecointe de Laveau, *Moscou, avant et après l'incendie*, 146.

49. Montesquiou-Fezensac, *Souvenirs militaires de 1804 à 1814*, 320.

50. Lecointe de Laveau, *Moscou, avant et après l'incendie*, 150. Castellane also saw a cantinière (perhaps the same one) holding up her baby to be saved, but was unable to help her. Castellane, *Journal du maréchal de Castellane*, 1:196.

51. "Circulaire no. 163—Enfants de troupe: Ils doivent être réunis au dépôt de leurs corps," 9 mars 1809, Xs195, AT.

52. Cadet de Gassicourt, *Voyage en Autriche, en Moravie, et en Bavière*, 76.

53. "Arrêté relatif aux enfans de troupe, et aux femmes à la suite de l'armée," *Journal militaire*, 2e semestre, An VIII, 750–751.

54. Lettre de Berthier aux Conseils d'administration des Corps d'infanterie de ligne et légère, 11 nivôse An XI, Xs195, AT.

55. "Arrêté relatif aux enfans de troupe, et aux femmes à la suite de l'armée," *Journal militaire*, 2e semestre, An VIII, 750–751.

56. Rapport du sécrétariat général, 1 frimaire An XI; L'inspecteur aux revues au Citoyen Dabbadie, 8 frimaire An XI, MR 2214, AT.

57. "Arrêté relatif aux enfans de troupe, et aux femmes à la suite de l'armée," *Journal militaire*, 2e semestre, An VIII, 750–751.

58. Schneid, *Soldiers of Napoleon's Kingdom of Italy*, 80.

59. Girault, *Mes campagnes sous la république et l'empire*, 77.

60. Ibid., 68.

61. Parquin, *Souvenirs du commandant Parquin*, 305.

62. Norvins, *Souvenirs d'un historien de Napoléon*, 193.

63. Levavasseur, *Souvenirs militaires*, 61.

64. Blaze, *Souvenirs d'un officier de la Grande armée*, 49.

65. Parquin, *Souvenirs du commandant Parquin*, 280.

66. Bourgogne, *The Memoirs of Sergeant Bourgogne*, 17.

67. Blaze, *Souvenirs d'un officier de la Grande armée*, 96; Albrecht Adam, untitled sketch, Musée de l'armée, Paris.

68. Christian Wilhelm von Faber du Faur, *In der Gegend von Semlewo den 28. August 1812*.

69. Cadet de Gassicourt, *Voyage en Autriche, en Moravie, et en Bavière*, 74–75.

70. Montigny, *Souvenirs anecdotiques d'un officier de la Grande armée*, 87.

71. Blaze, *Souvenirs d'un officier de la Grande armée*, 49.

72. Bourgogne, *The Memoirs of Sergeant Bourgogne*, 279.

73. Grisaille, *Arrivée des conscrits au camp vers 1796–1799*, lithograph, Service photographique #K10379, Musée de l'armée, Paris.

74. Blaze, *Souvenirs d'un officier de la Grande armée*, 103–104.

75. Chuquet, *Human Voices from the Russian Campaign of 1812*, 78.

76. Bourgogne, *The Memoirs of Sergeant Bourgogne*, 311.

77. Roos, *Avec Napoleon en Russie*, 127–128.

78. Blaze, *Souvenirs d'un officier de la Grande armée*, 46.

79. Keegan, *The Face of Battle*, 182–183. See also the constant references to "butin" (booty) in Chevillet, *Ma vie militaire*.

80. Cadet de Gassicourt, *Voyage en Autriche, en Moravie, et en Bavière*, 77.

81. Richard, *Cantinières et vivandières françaises*, 21. See also Heinrich-Christian von Geißler, *Ankunft der Franzosen in Leipzig, 1806*, which shows soldiers and cantinières rushing to sell looted articles to stereotypical Jewish merchants in a Leipzig square. Watercolor, #19463, Musée de l'armée, Paris.

82. 1er Bataillon républicain, Autorisation de procuration, in "Simon née Bathis," XSII, AT.

83. Brice, *La femme et les armées*, 289.

84. Quennevat, *Les vrais soldats de Napoléon*, 158; Elting, *Swords around a Throne*, 609.

85. Blaze, *Souvenirs d'un officier de la Grande armée*, 46.

86. Bourgogne, *The Memoirs of Sergeant Bourgogne*, 135–136.

87. Roeder, *The Ordeal of Captain Roeder*, 89–92.

88. Combe, *Mémoires du colonel Combe*, 62–63.

89. Cadet de Gassicourt, *Voyage en Autriche, en Moravie, et en Bavière*, 76.

90. Bourgogne, *The Memoirs of Sergeant Bourgogne*, 56, 5.

91. Biot, *Souvenirs anecdotiques et militaires*, 155–156.

92. Chevillet, *Ma vie militaire*, 91–92. See also "Peasants Tell Tales: The Meaning of Mother Goose," in Darnton, *The Great Cat Massacre*.

93. Bourgogne, *The Memoirs of Sergeant Bourgogne,* 51.

94. Barrès, *Memoirs of a Napoleonic Officer,* 176.

95. Lagneau, *Journal d'un chirurgien de la Grande armée,* 219.

96. Pelet, "Le combat de Krasnoë et la retraite de Ney," 627.

97. Ibid., 552.

98. Parquin, *Souvenirs du commandant Parquin,* 250.

99. Blaze, *Souvenirs d'un officier de la Grande armée,* 50.

100. Paris, "Souvenirs du 14e léger," 121.

101. Biot, *Souvenirs anecdotiques et militaires,* 141.

102. Pelet, "Le combat de Krasnoë et la retraite de Ney," 632.

103. Patente de blanchisseuse; Lettre de la veuve Chauvet au duc de Feltre, janvier 1812, in "Chauvet, née Bonnet," Xs12, AT.

104. Montigny, *Souvenirs anecdotiques d'un officier de la Grande armée,* 327–328.

105. Quartermaster François Robert described her in his memoirs as "a tough woman" who always carried a pistol. Guye, *Le bataillon de Neuchâtel au service de Napoléon,* 199.

106. Thirst was a key factor in the surrender of an entire French army at Bailén in Spain: fatigued from marching on dusty roads, and forced to give battle under a hot sun with only a muddy stream as a water source, the French collapsed. Esdaile, *The Spanish Army in the Peninsular War,* 101.

107. Blaze, *Souvenirs d'un officier de la Grande armée,* 49–50.

108. Quennevat, *Les vrais soldats de Napoléon,* 158.

109. Lejeune, *Memoirs of Baron Lejeune,* 2:69.

110. Blaze, *Souvenirs d'un officier de la Grande armée,* 50.

111. Maurer, "Une cantinière du terrible 57e," 414.

112. Combe, *Mémoires du colonel Combe,* 143.

113. Nicolas Antoine Taunay, *L'armée française traversant le grand Saint-Bernard,* oil on canvas, Musée national du Château de Versailles; Maurer, "Une cantinière du terrible 57e," 416.

114. Dedem van de Gelder, *Un général hollandais sous le premier empire,* 280.

115. Bourgogne, *The Memoirs of Sergeant Bourgogne,* 279.

116. Romand, *Mémoires de ma vie militaire,* 72.

117. Bourgogne, *The Memoirs of Sergeant Bourgogne,* 11–12.

118. Cere, *Madame Sans-Gêne et les femmes-soldats,* 273.

119. Marbot, *Mémoires du baron Marbot,* 2:395.

120. Lettre de Kellerman au ministre de la guerre, 21 mai 1808, in "Muller, née Kintelberger," Xs12, AT.

121. Ducor, *Aventures d'un marin,* 1:89–90.

122. François, *Journal du capitaine François,* 2:719.

123. Ducor, *Aventures d'un marin,* 1:90.

124. Ibid., 1:212–213.

125. Billon, *Souvenirs d'un vélite de la garde,* 187.

126. Ibid., 231.

127. Guillemard, *Mémoires de Robert Guillemard,* 185. There is some question as to the authenticity of Guillemard's book. "Robert Guillemard" is a pseudonym, and English sources especially have disputed the book's accuracy on the Battle of Trafalgar in particular.

128. Brice, *La femme et les armées,* 297.

129. Elting, *Swords around a Throne,* 613.

130. Patente de boulangère-cantinière, 13 mars 1810, in "Sabatier, née Campagne," Xs12, AT.

131. For a detailed discussion of guerrilla warfare in Italy, but sadly not a single mention of cantinières, see Finley, *The Most Monstrous of Wars.* For a superb description of guerrilla war in Spain, including welcome accounts of women camp followers, see Esdaile, *Peninsular Eyewitnesses.*

132. Parquin, *Souvenirs du commandant Parquin,* 205.

133. François, *Journal du capitaine François,* 2:664.

134. Barrès, *Memoirs of a Napoleonic Officer,* 186.

135. Blaze, *Souvenirs d'un officier de la Grande armée,* 107.

136. "Loi additionelle à celle relative aux secours accordés aux veuves et enfans de militaires—Du 14 fructidor, an 6," *Journal militaire,* 2e semestre, An VI, 912.

137. Woloch, "War-Widows' Pensions," 244.

138. "Rapport sur l'armée morte par Lacuée," Archives nationales, AF IV 1075, cited in ibid., 245.

139. Woloch, "War-Widows' Pensions," 244, and statistical analysis of Xs11, Xs12, AT. In comparison, Silvain Larreguy de Civrieux earned seventy francs a *month* as a minor employee of the Imperial customs service when he was only sixteen years old in 1812; *Souvenirs d'un cadet,* 61.

140. "Notes sur la liquidation des pensions dictés par l'empereur, 13 Juin 1810," Archives nationales, AF IV 909, cited in Woloch, "War-Widows' Pensions," 246.

141. 5e Division, Bureau de section C, Rapport fait au ministre, in "Muller, née Kintelberger," Xs12, AT.

142. Pensions, rapports, in "Veuve Rigollet" and in "Veuve Monthion," Xr6, AT.

143. Various documents in "Chauvet, née Bonnet," Xs12, AT.

144. Extrait des minutes de la Secrétairerie d'état, 25 mars 1811, in "Hoccard, née Pierrette," Xs12, AT.

145. Décret impérial du 29 November 1809; Rapport de pension, in "Huin, née Toulouse," Xs12, AT.

146. Balzac, *Old Goriot,* 46.

147. Lettres de 2 messidor An X, 15 vendémiaire An XI, et 11 fructidor An XI, in "Horr, née André," Xs12, AT.

148. Lettre du colonel Petri au duc de Feltre, 19 novembre 1810, in "Angot, née ————," Xs11, AT.

149. Cadet de Gassicourt, *Voyage en Autriche, en Moravie, et en Bavière,* 76.

150. Castellane, *Journal du maréchal de Castellane,* 1:74.

151. Blaze, *Souvenirs d'un officier de la Grande armée,* 112.

152. Montigny, *Souvenirs anecdotiques d'un officier de la Grande armée,* 330–331.

153. Thoumas, *Mes souvenirs de Crimée,* 54.

4. "Useful and Necessary"

1. Oudinot, *Récits de guerre et de foyer,* 359–360; Saint-Chamans, *Mémoires du général comte de Saint-Chamans,* 277.

2. Peyrusse, *Mémorial et archives de m. le baron Peyrusse,* 291. ("We have apples / for the king of Rome." Obviously, the song loses quite a bit in the translation.)

3. Brett-James, *The Hundred Days*, 3.

4. Larreguy de Civrieux, *Souvenirs d'un cadet*, 151.

5. 92e Régiment de ligne, Certificat de service, 18 Septembre 1815, in "L'Archevêque," Xs12, AT; Brice, *La femme et les armées*, 307. For a fictionalized account based on fact and written by an eyewitness, see Stendhal, *The Charterhouse of Parma*.

6. Montigny, *Souvenirs anecdotiques d'un officier de la Grande armée*, 330–333.

7. Ministère de la guerre, Bureau du personnel, Décision du 18 juin 1815, Xr6, AT.

8. Resnick, *The White Terror and the Political Reaction after Waterloo*.

9. Lettre du 6e Division militaire au ministre de la guerre, 24 septembre 1815; Lettre du col. Marion au ministre de la guerre, 28 décembre 1815, in "Charlet, née ———," Xs11, AT.

10. Various documents in "Daubigny, née ———," Xs11, AT.

11. Lettres du Mme Meynier au ministre de la guerre, 6 juillet 1816, 27 fevrier 1819, in "Meynier, née Dieulevant," Xs12, AT.

12. Various documents in "Bory, née Peter," Xs11, AT.

13. Various documents in "Sabatier, née Campagne," Xs12, AT.

14. For examples, see "Bernou, née Charlotte," Xs11; "Calastroupat, née Lalouet," and "Calvet, née Gith," Xs12, AT.

15. Lettre de Mme L'Archevêque au ministre de la guerre, 30 novembre 1818; Lettre du ministre de la guerre au Comte Despinois, 20 décembre 1818, in "L'Archevêque," Xs11, AT.

16. Lettre de Gouvion St. Cyr au colonel de la Légion du Tarn et Garonne, 1 juillet 1818, in unmarked dossier (the thirteenth folder in the carton), Xs11, AT. This folder was an anomaly, and it shows the extent to which cantinière records were ignored for a century. It may well have been marked and catalogued since I did my initial research, but at the time it simply sat there, unmarked, and unread since its placement in the archives. No one in the archives could explain it to me, and whoever originally failed to organize it is long dead. It appeared to contain various cantinière records from the Restoration period that for some reason were never organized by name. I refer to it hereafter as "Dossier 13."

17. Note du ministre au Mme Bouquet, 11 avril 1820, in "Dossier 13," Xs11, AT.

18. Various documents in "Billers, née Conrad," Xs11, AT.

19. Conneau, *A Slaver's Logbook*, 225.

20. Lettre de Mme Decker au ministre de guerre, in "Dossier 13," Xs11, AT.

21. Lettre de Mme Bouquet au ministre de guerre, 21 mars 1820, in "Dossier 13," Xs11, AT.

22. Lettre de Femme Petier au ministre de guerre, 1 avril 1819, in "Dossier 13," Xs11, AT.

23. Lettre de Celestine Prevost, Femme Gressier, au ministre de guerre, 2 Septembre 1819, in "Dossier 13," Xs11, AT.

24. Sullivan, *Thomas-Robert Bugeaud, France, and Algeria*, 117, 119.

25. Kearny, *Service with the French Troops in Africa*, 21.

26. Julien, *Histoire de l'Algérie contemporaine*, 125–132.

27. Thoumas, *Les transformations de l'armée française*, 1:305.

28. Sullivan, *Thomas-Robert Bugeaud, France, and Algeria*, 77–93.

29. "Ordre: Le passage gratuit pour Alger est accordé aux femmes et enfans des militaires . . . ," *Journal militaire*, 1831, 1:369.

30. "Dispositions relatives à l'éxecution de l'Ordonnance royale du 14 de ce mois (I), concernant les Enfans de troupe, et les Femmes à la suite des Corps de toute arme," *Journal militaire*, 1831, 1:284.

31. "Ordonnance du Roi relative aux Enfans et Femmes de troupe de toute arme, 14 avril 1832," *Journal militaire*, 1831, 1:276–277.

32. Bulwer, *The Monarchy of the Middle Classes*, 283.

33. "Dispositions relatives à l'exécution de l'ordonnance royale du 14 de ce mois . . . ," *Journal militaire*, 1831, 1:286.

34. "Ordonnance sur le service des armées en campagne," *Journal militaire*, 1832, 1:1–95.

35. Ibid., 79–80.

36. Ibid., 80.

37. Ibid. This highlights another ongoing issue: confusion over what to call these female auxiliaries. The official terminology for the period after 1832 was "blanchisseuse-vivandière," but common usage remained "cantinière," as it had since the Empire. Indeed, this term was so common that it crept into official regulations without eliciting the slightest comment or correction. On the other hand, English speakers insisted on referring to the women as "vivandières" even after the official term was finally changed to "cantinière."

38. Ibid., 80–81.

39. Julien, *Histoire de l'Algérie contemporaine*, 316–319.

40. "Instruction sur l'exécution du Service des convois militaires," *Journal militaire*, 1836, 1:49–50. However, the Belgian army, which also used cantinières, apparently provided forage for their horses, at least in cavalry regiments. Sherburne, *The Tourist's Guide*, 125.

41. "Décision ministérielle portant que les Femmes de sous-officiers ne pourront plus recevoir l'autorisation d'exercer la profession de blanchisseuse ou de vivandière dans les corps," *Journal militaire*, 1839, 2:235. This regulation is most likely the source of Barton Hacker's confusion over when cantinières stopped serving in the French army. Unfortunately, that confusion transformed to certainty with a number of later authors who wrongly read 1840 as the end of the institution. Even this regulation was universally ignored, as evidenced by the many wives of NCOs who continued to serve as cantinières.

42. The military systems of most nineteenth-century nations, including France, allowed men who were drafted to avoid service by purchasing a "replacement." The draftee paid the replacement a cash fee, and in exchange the replacement served the draftee's time. This often resulted in bitter recriminations against those who avoided service in this fashion, and replacements were usually viewed with suspicion by their superiors. Clearly, Gunner Romieu's superiors found his repeated enlistments as a replacement to be distasteful and suspect. Lettre du M. Defresne au ministre de la guerre, 30 mars 1843, in "Romieu, née ———," X512, AT.

43. Ibid.

44. Ibid.

45. Joinville, *Memoirs of the Prince de Joinville*, 89–90.

46. Conneau, *A Slaver's Logbook*, 225.

47. Ibid., 232, 235. Conneau has to be treated carefully as a source. There are clear attempts to embellish the narrative, and he was after all an impoverished ex-slaver

writing an adventure tale for public consumption as a way of repairing his fortunes. Still, the idea of Spanish cantinières aiding fellow Spaniards in an escape from a civil prison is at least plausible. While this was criminal, it did not involve any action against the French army or their own regiment; it did involve action against the French state and against the civil authorities, but it does not suggest disloyalty to the regiment. Had Conneau and his crew been held in a military prison, this situation might have been very different.

48. De Gaury, *Travelling Gent,* 175.

49. Larcade, "Les cantinières," 58.

50. Klein-Rebour, "Les femmes soldats à travers les ages," 20–21.

51. Certificat de mariage, in "Dufour, née Bontemps," Xs11, AT.

52. *Journal militaire,* 1836, 1:332.

53. État civil, 19 juin 1890, in "Calvet, née Gith," Xs12, AT.

54. Inspection générale de 1891, 36e Régiment d'infanterie, Mémoire de proposition pour la Médaille militaire, in "Bernou, née Jean," Xs11, AT.

55. Lettre d'Emile Lecot au ministre de la guerre, 23 août 1896, in "Monié," Xs12, AT.

56. Cler, *Reminiscences of an Officer of Zouaves,* 113.

57. Thoumas, *Mes souvenirs de Crimée,* 54.

58. For examples, see "Tonnelet de vivandière du 9ème dragons," #15266, and "Tonnelet-bidon modèle 1832, compagnie des voltigeurs," #10929, Musée de l'armée, Paris.

59. See, for example, M. Cottreau, *Capitaine de fusiliers du 28e de ligne, 1821–1828,* watercolor, #Ec269, Musée de l'armée, Paris.

60. Montigny, *Souvenirs anecdotiques d'un officier de la Grande armée,* 365.

61. Riès, "Les cantinières I," 6.

62. Kearny, *Service with the French Troops in Africa,* 21–22.

63. Castellane, *Journal du maréchal de Castellane,* 3:406.

64. Margerand, *L'armée française en 1845,* 8, 17.

65. See, for example, the anonymous painting of a cantinière of the Seventh Infantry Regiment, *La cantinière,* oil on canvas, The Vail Corporation Museum, Atlanta, Georgia.

66. See, for example, Horace Vernet, "Madame Bru, cantinière du 7e Hussards," 1837 Inv. 1482, #Ea292, oil on canvas; Eugène Lami, "Collection des armes de la cavalerie française en 1834: Chasseurs d'Alger," color lithograph; M. Levert, "Cantinière du 1er Léger vers 1835," statuette in wood, #5146, Musée de l'armée, Paris.

67. Saint Marie, *Algeria in 1845,* 250–251.

68. De Gaury, *Travelling Gent,* 175.

69. See Moses, *French Feminism in the 19th Century.*

70. Saint Marie, *Algeria in 1845,* 251.

71. Declaration du chirurgien aide-major Perotte, 18 janvier 1837, in "Frache, née ————," Xs11, AT.

72. Larcade, "Les cantinières," 58.

73. Roussier, "Un soldat d'Afrique," 52.

74. Klein-Rebour, "Les femmes soldats à travers les ages," 22.

75. Lettre de Mme Masson à l'empéreur Napoléon III, 1 février 1853, in "Masson, née Chevreux," Xs11, AT.

246 Notes to pages 124–133

76. "The French Moll Flagons, or Vivandières," 196.
77. Castellane, *Journal du maréchal de Castellane,* 3:44.
78. Ibid.
79. Lettre du ministre de la guerre au ministre de commerce et des travaux publiques, 5 janvier 1833, in "Mouron, née ———," Xs12, AT.
80. Castellane, *Journal du maréchal de Castellane,* 3:44.
81. Oil on canvas, Musée de l'armée, Paris.
82. Montigny, *Souvenirs anecdotiques d'un officier de la Grande armée,* 365.
83. "The French Moll Flagons, or Vivandières," 196.
84. Lettre du ministre de guerre à la veuve Alloux, 29 décembre 1838, in "Alloux, née Blanchard," Xs11, AT.
85. Bollaert, *The Wars of Succession of Portugal and Spain,* 1:150.

5. THE SECOND EMPIRE

1. See, for example, Lacau-Mougenot, "Des femmes dans l'armée," 102.
2. The three major European wars were the Crimean War (1854–1856), fought against Russia, the Italian War (1859), fought against Austria, and the Franco-Prussian War (1870–1871), fought against Prussia and its German allies.
3. While rifled muskets were used in small numbers by specialized troops during the era of the French Revolution and the Napoleonic wars, these early rifles were extremely slow to reload and were used only by a few soldiers. Napoleon dispensed with them altogether as not worth the trouble. It was only in the mid-nineteenth century that rifled muskets and ammunition (such as the Minié bullet) were mass-produced that would allow rapid fire and therefore the widespread use of rifles by normal infantrymen. The effects on the battlefield were horrifying as accuracy and range dramatically increased. The French army armed with rifled muskets faced a Russian army armed with antiquated smoothbore muskets in the Crimea in 1854–1855, giving the French a decided advantage. In 1859 and 1870, France's opponents were armed with modern rifles, resulting in a much more even fight.
4. Dufaÿ, "Les cantinières."
5. "Décision ministérielle concernant la nomination des enfants de troupe et les autorisations de mariage dans les sections d'ouvriers militaires d'administration, 2 août 1855," *Journal militaire,* 2e semestre, 1854, 238. Though few records remain of the cantinières of the *sapeurs-pompiers,* fragmentary evidence suggests that they were fairly widespread throughout the country. This is a subject that calls for considerable further research. (See http://www.cantinieres.com for research updates.)
6. "Décision ministérielle fixant, pour chacun des corps des différentes armes, le nombre des cantinières admises à profiter des dispositions de la circulaire ministérielle du 28 juillet 1854," *Journal militaire,* 2e semestre, 1869, 145–147.
7. *France militaire,* 25 juillet 1896.
8. Lettre de M. E. Masson au capitaine Loiseau, 21 October 1865, quoted in Albert Duchesne, "Petit enquête au sujet des cantinières,"
9. Codman, *An American Transport in the Crimean War,* 140.
10. Villeneuve, *Mes années militaires,* 130.
11. "Madame Busquet, cantinière," 7J6, Archives départementales des Ardennes (hereafter referred to as ADA).
12. Various documents in "Delaval, née Jarlet," Xs11, AT.

13. 104e Régiment d'infanterie, Relevé des services de Madame Calastroupat, in "Calastroupat, née Lalouet," Xs12, AT.

14. Various documents in "Calvet, née Gith," Xs12, AT.

15. Inspection générale de 1891, 36e Régiment d'infanterie, Mémoire de proposition pour la Médaille d'honneur, in "Bernou, née Charlotte," Xs11, AT.

16. Various documents in "Tuvache, née Lucius," Xs12, AT. Interestingly, Sophie Tuvache surfaced again in 1927, when the eighty-five-year-old ex-cantinière received the Military Medal for her past services. According to the London *Times,* Tuvache was working as the "*concierge* of an orphanage" and had a perfect memory. However, while every detail of the *Times* article can be confirmed from Tuvache's War Ministry file, the article claims that she, "like her mother, was a *cantinière* in the French Army. Her mother was a corporal shoemaker in the 7th Infantry Regiment of the Line." Her mother could not have been a *caporal cordonnier,* since that was a male military rank; the author must have meant that her father was a corporal shoemaker. "A Cantinière of the Second Empire: Award of the Médaille Militaire" (from our Paris Correspondent), *Times* (London), June 17, 1927.

17. Various documents in "Creste, née Brändli," Xs11, AT.

18. 7e Régiment d'artillerie de la 19e Division, Mémoire de proposition pour la Médaille militaire, 5 octobre 1904, in "Commaret, née Klasen," Xs11, AT.

19. Various documents in "Anchin, née de Coninck," Xs12, AT.

20. Various documents in "Graffeuil, née Fédy," Xs12, AT.

21. Lettre de Henriette Moutier au ministre de la guerre, 18 février 1895, in "Decombe, née Moutier." Xs11, AT.

22. Thoumas, *Mes souvenirs de Crimée,* 204.

23. Duchesne, "Petit enquête au sujet des cantinières," 129.

24. Thoumas, *Mes souvenirs de Crimée,* 25.

25. Various documents in "Creste, née Brändli," Xs11, AT.

26. Various documents in "Ley, née Lambert," Xs12, AT.

27. Various documents in "Dénis, née Ramonède," Xs11, AT.

28. Various documents in "Descombs, née Moutier," Xs11, AT.

29. Thoumas, *Mes souvenirs de Crimée,* 223–224.

30. Verly, *Souvenirs du Sécond empire,* quoted in Riès, "Les cantinières I," 6–7.

31. "Imagerie d'Épinal," 48J, Archives départementales des Vosges.

32. See, for example, the Images d'Épinal "Dragons," "Lanciers," and "Lanciers de la Garde impériale," Series 48J, "Imagerie d'Épinal," Archives départementales des Vosges.

33. Author's collection. See illustrations.

34. Lalaisse, *Types militaires,* plate 9. This is #Oa 126. Fol. in the collection of the Bibliothèque nationale, Cabinet des estampes, Paris (hereafter referred to as BN Estampes).

35. "Le tambour-major, la cantinière, et l'enfant de troupe," color lithograph, c. 1860, in the carton "Tc mat. 2a boite 4: contes de Grimme, de Mme Aulnay, divers, légendes," BN Estampes.

36. "Le fils de la vivandière," black and white lithograph, Metz: Fabrique d'estampes de Gangel et Didion, c. 1860, in the carton "Tc mat. 3 boite 5: historiettes," BN Estampes. Oddly enough, this story parallels to a degree the history of Theophilus Conneau, though his story is less romantic. The son of a First Empire cantinière,

Conneau was succored many years later by two Spanish women who had become can-tinières in the French army. See chapters 3 and 4.

37. Gerard, *Belles gisantes,* 158–159.

38. Martin, *The Life of His Royal Highness the Prince Consort,* 3:288.

39. Gaboriau, *Le 13e hussards,* 283.

40. Riès, "Les cantinières II," 7.

41. For examples, see the photograph of Madame Pelloux of the Zouaves of the Imperial Guard and the photo of three cantinières of the Second Infantry Regiment reproduced in Riès, "Les cantinières II," 7–8.

42. See, for example, the photograph of Perrine Cros, Ga.175, Musée de l'armée, Paris, the photos of three cantinières reproduced in Larcade, "Les cantinières," 56 and 60, and the excellent photograph of the cantinière of the Forty-sixth Infantry Regiment reproduced in Lacau-Mougenot, "Des femmes dans l'armée," 102.

43. Thoumas, *Mes souvenirs de Crimée,* 171.

44. Ibid., 163.

45. "Tonnelet de cantinière, 1870," Gb.587, Musée de l'armée, Paris.

46. See, for example, Ga.171, Gb.584, and Gm.1, Ga.211, Ga.170, Musée de l'armée, Paris. Another example is provided by the photograph of three cantinières of the Sec-ond Infantry Regiment reproduced in Riès, "Les cantinières II," 8. All three tonnelets are of different size, shape, and material.

47. Gaboriau, "Military Sketches," in Gaboriau and Mérimée, *A Thousand Francs Reward . . . and Carmen,* 19.

48. Young, *Our Camp in Turkey,* 154–155.

49. Lettre de Louise Bernou au commandant du 36e Régiment d'infanterie, 28 mai 1891, in "Bernou, née Charlotte," X511, AT.

50. Riès, "Les cantinières II," 8.

51. Ministère de la guerre, Relevé des services de Madame Calastroupat, in "Calas-troupat, née Lalouet," X512, AT.

52. Lettre de Louise Bernou au commandant du 36e Régiment d'infanterie, 28 mai 1891, in "Bernou, née Charlotte," X511, AT.

53. 7e Régiment d'artillerie de la 19e Division, Mémoire de proposition pour la Médaille militaire, 5 Octobre 1904, in "Commaret, née Klasen," X511, AT.

54. Riès, "Les cantinières II," 7.

55. Gerard, *Belles gisantes,* 159.

56. William Russell, "The Siege of Sebastopol," *Times* (London), 23 August 1855.

57. "Règlement sur le service du casernement, 30 juin 1856," *Journal militaire refon-due,* 1856, 7:243.

58. Martindale, "Notes on the Camp of Châlons-sur-Marne," 133. Martindale noted that the combined kitchen/canteen buildings cost five thousand francs each to con-struct, and that the latrines were "very dirty" and there were no urinals, meaning women would have equal access to the toilet facilities, even if their cleanliness left something to be desired. Ibid., 142, 133.

59. Gaboriau, *Le 13e hussards,* 278.

60. Ibid., 280.

61. *Inside Sebastopol,* 231.

62. Labouchere, *Diary of the Besieged Resident in Paris,* 237.

63. Lettre au ministre de la guerre, 24 février 1881, in "Creste, née Brändli," X511, AT.

64. Thoumas, *Mes souvenirs de Crimée,* 244.

65. Duchesne, "Petit enquête au sujet des cantinières," 131.

66. Loiseau, *Le Mexique et la légion belge,* 62–63.

67. Reid, *Soldier-Surgeon,* 67.

68. Thoumas, *Mes souvenirs de Crimée,* 101.

69. Villeneuve, *Mes années militaires,* 30–31.

70. Luguez, *Crimée-Italie,* 27–28.

71. Cler, *Reminiscences of an Officer of Zouaves,* 239–240.

72. Thoumas, *Mes souvenirs de Crimée,* 204.

73. Browne, *Ice Caves of France and Switzerland,* 233. In fairness, it should be noted that the Reverend found his guide to be a bit of a cheat and a scoundrel himself, trying when he could to skimp on accommodations and to pocket the difference himself. Therefore, his accusations against the cantinière may be less than ingenuous.

74. Gaboriau, "Military Sketches," in Gaboriau and Mérimée, *A Thousand Francs Reward . . . and Carmen,* 20–22.

75. Thoumas, *Mes souvenirs de Crimée,* 168.

76. Cler, *Reminiscences of an Officer of Zouaves,* 197–198.

77. 7e Régiment d'artillerie de la 19e Division, Mémoire de proposition pour la Médaille militaire, 5 Octobre 1904, in "Commaret, née Klasen," Xs11, AT.

78. Gaboriau, "Military Sketches," in Gaboriau and Mérimée, *A Thousand Francs Reward . . . and Carmen,* 22.

79. "Madame Busquet, cantinière," 7J6, ADA.

80. Lalaisse, *L'armée française et ses cantinières,* plates 15, 17, 22.

81. Bapst, *Le maréchal Canrobert,* 2:425–427.

82. Laurencin, *Nos Zouaves,* 109; Bapst, *Le maréchal Canrobert,* 2:426.

83. Reid, *Soldier-Surgeon,* 128–129.

84. Ibid., 136.

85. Thoumas, *Mes souvenirs de Crimée,* 54.

86. Castellane, *Journal du maréchal de Castellane,* 3:44.

87. Morrell, *Algeria,* 190.

88. Elton, *With the French in Mexico,* 133. Treviño was one of the leaders of the anti-French opposition.

89. Luguez, *Crimée-Italie,* 104.

90. Kinglake, *The Invasion of the Crimea,* 8:104–105.

91. Klein-Rebour, "Les femmes soldats à travers les ages," 3–20, 58.

92. Ibid., 60.

93. Various documents in "Calvet, née Gith," Xs11, AT.

94. Alès, *Les femmes décorées de la Légion d'honneur,* 61.

95. Lettre de Madame Bernou au commandant du 36e Régiment d'infanterie, 28 mai 1891, in "Bernou, née Charlotte," Xs11, AT.

96. Cler, *Reminiscences of an Officer of Zouaves,* 113–114.

97. Ministère de la guerre, États de service de Thérèse Malher, in "Malher, née Lévy," Xs12, AT.

98. Riès, "Les cantinières II," 8.

99. Exhibit Ga.175, Musée de l'armée, Paris.

100. États de service, in "Lalonne, née Blois," Xs12, AT.

101. Gernsheim and Gernsheim, *Roger Fenton,* 34–35.

102. Eugène Charpentier, *Bataille de Solferino, 24 juin 1859* and *Bataille de Magenta,* oil on canvas, Musée de l'armée, Paris.

103. Prarond, *Notices historiques, topographiques, et archéologiques,* 194.

104. Ibid., 195.

105. Ibid.

106. *Mémoires de la Société d'émulation d'Abbéville,* 21, Abbeville: F. Paillart, 1906, 176.

107. Cler, *Reminiscences of an Officer of Zouaves,* 198–199.

108. Russell, *The War,* 396.

109. Lettre de Mme Graffeuil au ministre de la guerre, in "Graffeuil, née Fédy," Xs12, AT.

110. Klein-Rebour, "Les femmes soldats à travers les ages," 58.

111. Duchesne, "Petit enquête au sujet des cantinières," 132; Loiseau, *Le Mexique et la légion belge,* 200, 148.

112. Salas, *Soldaderas in the Mexican Military,* 35.

113. Lettre du Professeur Gandolphe au directeur des archives du Ministère de la guerre, 27 février 1939, in "Ibrahim, née Brun," Xs12, AT.

114. Exhibit Ga.175, Musée de l'armée, Paris.

115. Hacker, "Women and Military Institutions in Early Modern Europe," 666.

116. Larcade, "Les cantinières," 60.

117. Various documents in "Calvet, née Gith," Xs12, AT.

118. "Madame Busquet, cantinière," 7J6, ADA. This was not the only time the strong-willed and independent Augusta interceded on behalf of French prisoners, much to the annoyance of some Prussian officers. See Herre, *Wilhelm I,* 401.

119. Labouchere, *Diary of the Besieged Resident in Paris,* 237.

120. Vandam, *French Men and French Manners,* 116.

121. Various documents in "Ley, née Lambert," Xs12, AT.

122. Various documents in "Descombs, née Moutier," Xs11, AT.

123. Lettre de Mme. Descours au ministre de la guerre, 4 mars 1903, in "Descours, née Aubertin," Xs11, AT.

124. Jerrold, *Imperial Paris,* 181–182, 183, 184, 186. The woman's use of the term "enfant de troupe" in describing herself is interesting. Legally, only boys could be enfants de troupe; female children of soldiers and cantinières had no legal status as members of the regiment until such time as they became cantinières themselves. However, this woman used the term for herself, suggesting that cantinières viewed themselves as much more fully (and equally) integrated into their regiments than the War Ministry did, even as children. For more on enfants de troupe, see Thomas Cardoza, "Stepchildren of the State: Educating Enfants de Troupe in the French Army, 1800–1845," *Paedagogica Historica* 37, no. 3 (2001): 551–568; Thomas Cardoza, "These Unfortunate Children: Sons and Daughters of the Regiment in the French Army, 1789–1815," in *Children and War: An Anthology,* ed. James Marten (New York: New York University Press, 2002), 205–215.

125. Castellane-Novejan, *Military Life in Algeria,* 1:6–7.

126. "Madame Busquet, cantinière," 7J6, ADA.

127. Mathieu, "Derniers vétérans." The information on Mme Busquet's death was given to M. Mathieu by one of Mme Busquet's descendants.

128. Larcade, "Les cantinières," 55.

129. Riès, "Les cantinières II," 6.

130. Alès, *Les femmes décorées de la Légion d'honneur,* 61–62.

131. Lettre de Mme Descours au ministre de la guerre, 4 mars 1903, in "Descours, née Aubertin," Xs11, AT.

132. The staff of the Musée du Légion d'honneur confirm that there is no record of Annette Drevon ever being nominated for or receiving the Cross. This remains one of several cases where public belief in the Cross being awarded to a cantinière is inaccurate. These stories remain, at best, accounts of spontaneous, unofficial, and unauthorized action by officers on the spot, or, at worst, fabrications.

133. See, for example, the series of prints by Edouard de Beaumont titled *Les Vésuviennes,* reproduced in Moses, *French Feminism in the 19th Century,* 123–126. Feminist writers themselves often disapproved of women wearing trousers (130).

134. Steele, *Paris Fashion,* 163–164.

6. The Third Republic and the End of the Cantinières

1. Beaunis, *Impressions de campagne,* 75.

2. Various documents in "Guy, née Doucet." Xs12, AT. For a contemporary medical view of the terrible nature of wounds from modern howitzer shells, see Beaunis, *Impressions de campagne,* 46.

3. Ministère de la guerre, Certificat de service, 15 juin 1905; Lettre de Émilie Marot au ministre de la guerre, 28 mai 1905, in "Marot, née Ruet," Xs12, AT.

4. Lettre de Claudine Mallet au ministre de la guerre, 27 mai 1895; Mairie de Besançon, Acte de naissance, 1 février 1871, in "Mallet, née Boitier," Xs12, AT.

5. Lettre d'Alexandrine Ciret au ministre de la guerre, 22 août 1904, in "Ciret, née Alexandrine," Xs11, AT.

6. Lettre de Mme Chasseron au ministre de la guerre, 22 février 1871, in "Chasseron, née ———," Xs11, AT.

7. Michel, *The Red Virgin,* xiv; Moses, *French Feminism in the 19th Century,* 192.

8. Ministère de la guerre, Gratification de réforme #17.752; 37e Régiment d'artillerie, Demande pour une gratification, 22 juin 1872, in "Lechangeur, née Richard," Xs12, AT.

9. Ministère de la guerre, Questionnaire à remplir pour obtenir un certificat de services, in "Defurne, née ———," Xs11, AT.

10. For a discussion of just how virulent official attacks on these women became, see Gulickson, *Unruly Women of Paris.*

11. Detailed and complete records of the summary executions are of course nonexistent. Most historians of the Commune have either misunderstood the presence and roles of cantinières or ignored them completely. Works of art history are particularly weak on this topic, analyzing art and photos of the Commune but failing to note that many of the women were in fact part of a long tradition in the French military, and not something new and radical produced by the Commune. The communards had cantinières because the regular army had them, not because they were redefining gender roles in radical new ways.

12. "Commune de Paris: Groupe des fédérés au pied de la Colonne Vendôme," photograph, Salle Chanzy, Musée de l'armée, Paris.

13. Commandant de Comminges, quoted in Delpérier, *De la Crimée à la Grande guerre,* 67.

14. See, for example, Gulickson, *Unruly Women of Paris,* 91, 93. Another example of a cantinière presented as an overly sexualized and incompetent onlooker, though unnoticed by an author who appears not to know what a cantinière was, is in Milner, *Art, War and Revolution in France, 1870–1871,* 155. The other (completely contradictory) propaganda image was of stout, stern, masculine women who threatened to blur gender lines. Gulickson, *Unruly Women of Paris,* 93.

15. Thompson, *Here I Lie,* 22.

16. "A Victim of Paris and Versailles," part 1, 403.

17. Leighton, *Paris under the Commune,* 87, 152–153.

18. Rapport, 2ème division, 2ème corps, 22–27 mai, 1871, Lu7, AT. Originally cited in Tombs, *The War against Paris, 1871,* 152.

19. Klein-Rebour, "Les femmes-soldats a travers les ages," 60.

20. LH/1355/49, "Jarrethout," Archives nationales, Paris.

21. Laut, "Les femmes de 1870."

22. "Revue de la semaine," *L'indicateur de la Savoie,* October 30, 1880.

23. Alès, *Les femmes décorées de la Légion d'honneur,* 41–42. The book went through several editions and was quite popular. Alès is incorrect about the origins of Jarrethout's unit, which was in fact from Paris, not from Châteaudun. The École Turgot was also located in Paris. It is possible that Alès was confused by the fact that Jarrethout earned her Cross for her actions at Châteaudun, but is also possible that he was deliberately distancing this heroine from the unacceptable actions of the volunteer cantinières of the Paris Commune, who were portrayed in the press as monstrous and unnatural amazons. Any irregular unit from Paris would have been suspect in the public eye.

24. Ministère de commerce, de l'industrie, des postes et des télégraphes, *Exposition universelle internationale de 1900 à Paris,* 2:108.

25. "Revue de la semaine," *L'indicateur de la Savoie,* October 30, 1880.

26. Laut, "Les femmes de 1870."

27. "Female Soldier Dead: French Heroine of the Conflict of 1870—Speeches at Grave," *New York Times,* September 8, 1905.

28. For a survey of these women going back to biblical times, see Klein-Rebour, "Les femmes soldats à travers les ages." For Hachette, see page 11.

29. For an excellent look at this phenomenon in the early modern period, see Lynn, *Women, Armies, and Warfare,* 202–208.

30. Godineau, "De la guerrière à la citoyenne," 4.

31. For accounts of these attacks and some illustrations, see Gulickson, *Unruly Women of Paris,* especially the chapters "The Symbolic Female Figure," and "Unruly Women and the Revolutionary City."

32. Gulickson, *Unruly Women of Paris,* 89.

33. Eichner, *Surmounting the Barricades,* 105–106. Eichner cites De Pauw, *Battle Cries and Lullabies,* but no page number (the relevant page number is 144). De Pauw took this erroneous information from Hacker's "Reconnaissance" article in *Signs:* a good example of how misinformation can work its way down into a variety of contexts over time. For a balanced critique of De Pauw's work, see Lynn, *Women, Armies, and Warfare,* 3, esp. note 7.

34. Riès, "Les cantinières II," 8.

35. Klein-Rebour, "Les femmes soldats à travers les ages," 61.

36. De la Gorce, *La République et son armée,* 15.

37. Porch, *The March to the Marne*, 33.

38. De la Gorce, *La République et son armée*, 22.

39. Porch, *The March to the Marne*, 38; Bernède, "Relecture des écrits du général Jules Louis Lewal," 9, 14.

40. De la Gorce, *La République et son armée*, 15.

41. Porch, *The March to the Marne*, 48–49.

42. "Arrêté ministériel relatif aux cantinières-vivandières des corps de troupe," 22 juillet 1875, *Journal militaire officiel*, 2e semestre, 1875, 60.

43. Roynette, *"Bons pour le service,"* 261.

44. "Arrêté ministériel concernant les cantinières-vivandières dans les régiments d'infanterie, 10 janvier 1879," *Journal militaire officiel*, partie réglementaire, 1er semestre, 1879, 13.

45. "Dispositions à prendre au sujet des voitures, des harnais et du cheval dont doivent être pourvues les cantinières-vivandières," *Journal militaire officiel*, partie supplementaire, 2e semestre, 1876, 815–816.

46. De la Gorce, *La République et son armée*, 19.

47. État-major général, Organisation et mobilisation générales, 21 mars 1881, 7N10, AT (emphasis in original).

48. "Circulaire relative au logement des chevaux et du matériel roulant employés par les cantiniers ou cantinières, 24 avril 1909," *Bulletin officiel du Ministère de la guerre*, partie réglementaire, 1er semestre, 1909, 725.

49. Zogbaum, *Horse, Foot, and Dragoons*, 26.

50. État-major Général, Organisation et mobilisation générales, 7 août, 1883, 7N10, AT.

51. De la Gorce, *La République et son armée*, 22.

52. Porch, *The March to the Marne*, 52–53.

53. Conseil supérieure de guerre, Registres des délibérations, procès verbaux des séances, 8 juin 1888, 1N4, AT.

54. General Blois' circular of May 21, 1881, claimed that on war footing each corps would have ten cantinière wagons in the field, and the entire French army would have a total of only 276 cantinière wagons. 7N10, AT. However, the Supreme War Council gave different figures in 1892: forty-one cantinière wagons per corps. 1N5, AT. The latter appears to be more accurate.

55. Conseil supérieure de guerre, Registres des délibérations, procès verbaux des séances, 8 juin 1888, 1N4, AT.

56. For a brief description of the spy mania of 1887–1894, see Weber, *France: Fin de Siècle*, 121. For a more in-depth discussion see Baumont, *Au coeur de l'affair Dreyfus;* Johnson, *France and the Dreyfus Affair.*

57. Conseil supérieure de guerre, Registres des délibérations, procès verbaux des séances, janvier–juin 1892, 1N5, AT.

58. Conseil supérieure de guerre, Régistres des délibérations, procès verbaux des séances, 8 juin 1888, 1N4, AT.

59. Porch, *The March to the Marne*, 53. See also Ralston, *The Army of the Republic*, 189–192.

60. "Instructions sur le service prévôtal de la gendarmerie aux armées, 14 avril 1890," *Bulletin officiel du Ministère de la guerre*, partie réglementaire, 1er semestre, 1890, 929, 931.

61. "Note ministérielle relative à la tenue des cantiniers civils et des cantinières-vivandières, 3 août 1890," *Bulletin officiel du Ministère de la guerre,* partie réglementaire, 2e semestre, 1890, 167–168.

62. Dufaÿ, "Les cantinières," 100. He used the term *accoutrement,* implying bizarre or ridiculous clothing, further emphasizing the dishonor cantinières had suffered.

63. Conseil supérieure de guerre, Registres des déliberations, procès verbaux des séances, janvier–juin 1892, 1N5, AT.

64. Ibid.

65. Ralston, *The Army of the Republic,* 50.

66. See, for example, Baratier, *L'intendance prussienne comparée à l'intendance française.* For a more general expression that the defeat represented a superiority of German science over French science, and by extension resulted from a less scientific approach in all areas of French life, see Beaunis, *Impressions de campagne,* 6. Finally, General Charles Thoumas, who was strongly anti-cantinière, made the Prussian comparison and the search for answers to the debacle of 1870 recurring themes in his *Les transformations de l'armée française.*

67. Conseil supérieure de guerre, Registres des délibérations, procès verbaux des séances, janvier–juin 1892, 1N5, AT.

68. Berge, *Études sur la réorganisation des forces militaires de la France,* 105–106, 167–168.

69. Zogbaum, *Horse, Foot, and Dragoons,* 26–27.

70. Conseil supérieure de guerre, Registres des délibérations, procès verbaux des séances, janvier–juin 1892, 1N5, AT.

71. Various documents in "Lenoir, née Girod," Xs12, AT.

72. Lettre d'Angeline Cottard au ministre de la guerre, 21 mai 1910; Lettre du Bureau des archives au Mme Cottard, 4 juin 1910; Relevé des services (Jean Foulet et Joseph Prun), in "Prun, née Cottard," Xs12, AT.

73. 36e Régiment d'artillerie, Mémoire de proposition pour la Médaille militaire; Ministre de la guerre, Note de service, 27 février 1912, in "Tobi, née Saint-Royre," Xs12, AT.

74. Ministère de la guerre, États de service: Dubief, 31 août 1905, in "Dubief, née Boyaud," Xs11, AT.

75. Relevé des services (Jean Foulet et Joseph Prun), in "Prun, née Cottard," Xs12, AT.

76. Relevé des services #4688.4, in "Kréher," Xs11, AT.

77. Ministre de la guerre, Note pour le service intérieure, 10 décembre 1897, in "Favrolles, née Chelle [*sic*]," Xs11, AT.

78. Relevé des services, in "Laurin, née Dumas," Xs12, AT.

79. Archives de la guerre, Relevé des services de Madame Calastroupat, in "Calastroupat, née Lalouet," Xs12, AT.

80. Various documents in "Calvet, née Gith," Xs12, AT.

81. Various documents in "Bernou, née Charlotte," Xs11, AT.

82. Sherrard, *Twenty Years in Paris,* 279–280.

83. "Female Soldier Dead: French Heroine of the Conflict of 1870—Speeches at Grave," *New York Times,* September 8, 1905. The dateline on the story was "Paris, August 25," so the actual date of her funeral would have been August 24.

84. Zogbaum, *Horse, Foot, and Dragoons,* 28.

85. Gribble, *Women in War,* 32.

86. Ibid., 36.

87. "A True Heroine Now Reduced to Selling Matches for a Living—Her Record," *New York Times,* November 3, 1891. The story originally appeared in the *London News,* and was reproduced with only minor changes in the *Nursing Journal,* October 22, 1891, 210–211. The "dingy street" the article refers to was in fact the Rue Quincampoix, where Beaulieu lived at number 63, close to Les Halles. "Knocking someone up" is an Anglicism meaning to wake them in the morning by knocking on the door, though it has a drastically different meaning in American usage.

88. Gribble, *Women in War,* 35–37.

89. Lettre de Mme Prun au ministre de la guerre, 21 mai 1910; Lettre du Ministère de la guerre à la veuve Prun, 4 juin 1910, in "Prun, née Cottard," Xs12, AT.

90. Lettre de Mme François au ministre de la guerre, 19 août 1904; Lettre du Bureau des archives au Mme François, 28 août 1904, in "François, née Mouty," Xs11, AT.

91. Various documents in "Graffeuil, née Fédy," Xs12, AT.

92. Various documents in "Massey, née Busquet," Xs12, AT.

93. Lettre de Clotilde Cherié au ministre de la guerre, 23 mars 1904; Lettre des Archives administratifs à Mme Cherié, 7 avril 1904, in "Cherié, née ————," Xs11, AT.

94. Lettre de Mme Ciret au ministre de la guerre, 22 décembre 1904, in "Ciret, née Ambroziewicz," Xs11, AT.

95. Lettre de Rose Guy au ministre de la guerre, 12 février 1908; Lettre du Bureau des archives à Rose Guy, 24 février 1908, in "Guy, née Doucet," Xs12, AT.

96. Various documents in "Massey, née Busquet," Xs12, AT.

97. Various documents in "Mallet, née Boitier," Xs12, AT.

98. Cabinet du ministre, Note pour la service intérieure, in "Rivière, née Corbière," Xs12, AT.

99. Lettre du 3ème Bureau à Mme Marot, 15 juin 1905, in "Marot, née Ruet," Xs12, AT.

100. 3ème Bureau, Certificat de service, 13 novembre 1907, in "Fournery, née ————," Xs11, AT.

101. Various documents in "Delaval, née Jarlet," Xs11, AT.

102. Note de service: 7e Régiment d'artillerie au ministre de la guerre, 8 mars 1906, in "Commaret, née Klasen," Xs11, AT.

103. Weber, *France: Fin de siècle,* 106.

104. Various documents in "Favrolles, née Leblanc," Xs11, AT. Almost four decades later she was mentioned in a retrospective piece as one of the many cantinières who were "modest heroines" of 1870: Laut, "Les femmes de 1870."

105. Lettre de Madame Renaut au ministre de la guerre, 5 novembre 1902, in "Malher, née Lévy," Xs12, AT.

106. Conseil d'administration du 36e Régiment d'artillerie au ministre de la guerre, 28 février 1912, in "Tobi, née Saint-Royre," Xs12, AT.

107. "Le tirage de la loterie de la presse," *Le petit journal illustré,* August 13, 1905.

108. Bluysens, "La vie parisienne," 654.

109. Ibid.

110. Doctor Gueillot, "Madame Hofer: La cantinière au million," 7J6, Archives départementales des Ardennes.

111. "Informations: France," *L'indicateur de Savoie,* August 5, 1905; Claretie, *La vie à Paris—1905,* 311.

112. Doctor Gueillot, "Madame Hofer: La cantinière au million," 7J6, Archives départementales des Ardennes.

113. Claretie, *La vie à Paris—1905,* 308–310.

114. Sattler, *A l'assaut du million.*

115. See, for example, the untitled paragraph in the Melbourne, Australia, newspaper *The Argus,* May 7, 1921; "Rich from Lottery Is Poor in 20 Days: French Woman Sues to Recover Part of 1,000,000 Francs Lent Indiscriminately," *Oswego Daily Palladium,* March 23, 1921.

116. Doctor Gueillot, "Madame Hofer; la cantinière au million," 7J6, Archives départementales des Ardennes.

117. Gaboriau, *Le 13ème hussards,* 280.

118. Ibid., 279; Mairie du premier arrondissement de la ville de Lyon, Acte de mariage no. 252, 31 mai 1873, in "Lenoir, née Girod," Xs12, AT.

119. Vallery-Radot, *Journal d'un volontaire d'un an,* 40.

120. Vandam, *French Men and French Manners,* 115.

121. Hillebrand, *France and the French,* 90.

122. Vandam, *French Men and French Manners,* 115–116.

123. Roynette, *"Bons pour le service,"* 384–386.

124. Chawner, "What I Saw in the French Maneuvers," 71.

125. Zogbaum, *Horse, Foot, and Dragoons,* 26.

126. Betham-Edwards, *Anglo-French Reminiscences,* 222–223. Betham-Edwards was incorrect on the timing of the switch from colorful uniforms to the plain gray dress. It had in fact been mandated only ten years earlier in 1890, not in 1870. She also incorrectly assumes that the "gaily dressed" young women of former times had been "replaced" by a different set of "sober matrons." In fact, they were the same women later in life, and stripped of their finery by new regulations.

127. Hamerton and Hamerton, *Philip Gilbert Hamerton,* 468–469.

128. Vingtrinier, *Chants et chansons des soldats de France,*

129. Mémoire de proposition pour la Médaille militaire, octobre 1910, in "Tobi, née Saint-Royre," Xs12, AT.

130. État major du 7e Division d'infanterie, Proposition pour une Médaille d'honneur, 1 août 1892, in "Calastroupat, née Lalouet," Xs12, AT.

131. Lettre de Madame Bernou à Monsieur le Colonel Commandant le 36e Régiment d'infanterie, 28 mai 1891, in "Bernou, née Charlotte," Xs11, AT.

132. Vingtrinier, *Chants et chansons des soldats de France,* 255.

133. Ibid., 249.

134. Gaboriau, *Le 13e hussards,* 276–282.

135. For more on popular representations of cantinières in plays and songs, see Mihaely, "L'effacement de la cantinière." Mihaely takes his argument on the suppression of cantinières further than his evidence will really support, but he does prove that fascination with cantinières' sexuality, and particularly with gender confusion and role reversals, was fairly widespread in popular entertainment.

136. Roynette, *"Bons pour le service,"* 386.

137. Zogbaum, *Horse, Foot, and Dragoons,* 27–28.

138. Marianne Dauranne (1796), Antoinette Mouron (1832), and Madeleine Trimoreau (1859) were all celebrated and decorated cantinières, but none received recognition through normal military channels.

139. 36e Régiment d'artillerie, Mémoire de proposition pour la Médaille militaire; Ministre de la guerre, Note de service, 27 février 1911, in "Tobi, née Saint-Royre," Xs12, AT. It should be noted that Mme Tobi was on active service and being decorated five years after cantinières had been abolished, and only three years before World War One.

140. Lettre de Louise Bernou au commandant du 36e Régiment de ligne, 28 mai 1891, in "Bernou, née Charlotte," Xs11, AT.

141. Lettre du Général Pesme au ministre de la guerre, 31 juillet 1891; Cabinet du ministre, Note pour le ministre, 21 octobre 1891, in "Bernou, née Charlotte," Xs11, AT. The minister's secretary was ignorant of numerous other cantinières who had also received the Military Medal, both under the old regulations of the Second Empire in 1860–1875 and under the new regulations. See, for example, "Favrolles, née Leblanc," Xs11, AT, for the case of Adelaïde Favrolles, and Klein-Rebour, "Les femmes soldats à travers les ages," 60, for the case of Madame Tajan of the Second Algerian Rifle Regiment.

142. Lamathière, *Panthéon de la Légion d'honneur: Dictionnaire biographique des hommes du XIXe siècle.* The very title gives us a clue as to the author's agenda: this book deals only with men.

143. Lettre du Ministère de la guerre au grand chancelier de la Légion d'honneur, 20 avril 1891, in "Laurin, née Dumas, veuve Dutailly," Xs12, AT.

144. Lettre du Ministère de la guerre au grand chancelier de la Légion d'honneur, 25 septembre 1896, in "Lematte, née ———," Xs12, AT. Some cantinières received their Military Medals after very long delays. Sophie Tuvache, who served in Italy, Mexico, and the 1870 campaign, received her medal at age eighty-five in 1927 (see note 16 to chapter 5). Mme Goucla, described as "the 100-year-old *doyenne* of cantinières," received the Military Medal on May 21, 1936, "in recognition of her services, which date back to the Franco-Prussian War of 1870." By this time, however, aged ex-cantinières represented mere symbols of France's heroic past, not concrete examples of current and troubling social issues. They had, in effect, become "safe" subjects for official praise and recognition. "A Cantinière of the Second Empire: Award of the Médaille Militaire" (from our Paris Correspondent), *Times* (London), June 17, 1927; "Centenarian Cantinière Decorated" (from our own correspondent), *Times* (London), May 21, 1936.

145. Lettre de Mlle Muller au ministre de la guerre, 17 janvier 1903, in "Muller, née Henriot," Xs12, AT.

146. Roynette, *"Bons pour le service,"* 156.

147. Richard, *L'armée et les forces morales.*

148. Richard's *Livret antialcoolique du soldat* was expanded as *La lutte contre l'alcoolisme.*

149. Undated newspaper clipping, carton 11, #6, correspondence, MSS153, The Aristide Rieffel Collection, Davidson Library Special Collections, University of California, Santa Barbara.

150. Porch, *The March to the Marne,* 117, 130.

151. "Circulaire interdisant d'une façon absolue la vente de toutes boissons alcooliques dans les cantines," *Bulletin officiel du Ministère de la guerre,* 1er semestre, partie réglementaire, 1900, 588–589.

152. De la Gorce, *La République et son armée*, 72.

153. Ralston, *The Army of the Republic*, 262–263.

154. "Circulaire concernant les cantinières des 4e bataillons qui ont été supprimés dans certains regiments d'infanterie," *Bulletin officiel du Ministère de la guerre*, 2e semestre, partie réglementaire, 1903, 1560.

155. Roynette, *"Bons pour le service,"* 155.

156. Porch, *The March to the Marne*, 126.

157. Challener, *The French Theory of the Nation in Arms*, 64.

158. Porch, *The March to the Marne*, 126.

159. Emploi des cantiniers, no. 9141C, 23 juillet 1906, Xs11, AT.

160. "Circulaire relative à la réduction des cantines," *Bulletin officiel du Ministère de la guerre*, 2e semestre, partie réglementaire, 1906, 857–858.

161. "Circulaire indiquant la règle qui sera appliquée à l'avenir pour la nomination des cantiniers," *Bulletin officiel du Ministère de la guerre*, 2e semestre, partie réglementaire, 1906, 1348.

162. Darrow, "The Eclipse of the *femme soldat*," 10.

163. Mihaely, "L'effacement de la cantinière," 42.

164. See, for example, Mihaely's discussion of the 1897 play *La fille de la cantinière*, his discussion of Georges Montorgueil's illustrated 1899 children's history book *La cantinière: France, son histoire* (in which France herself is personified by a cantinière: the modern image of Marianne), and his discussion of the 1880s "Sais-tu" images from Pellerin that caused cantinières to "constitute a feminine model for the girls of the bourgeoisie." Ibid., 45.

165. "Circulaire indiquant la règle qui sera appliquée à l'avenir pour la nomination des cantiniers," *Bulletin officiel du Ministère de la guerre*, 2e semestre, partie réglementaire, 1906, 1349.

166. Notes pour état de services, Ministère de la guerre, Service intérieur, 3e Bureau, Archives d'administration, juillet 1890, in "Calvet, née Gith," Xs12, AT.

CONCLUSION

1. "Situation des cantiniers," 8N161, AT.

2. Caire, *La femme militaire des origines à nos jours*, 34.

3. Décret portant exécution de la loi du 19 juillet 1884, ayant pour objet la suppression des enfants de troupe dans les regiments et la création de six écoles militaires préparatoires, *Journal militaire officiel*, partie réglementaire, 1885, 229–237.

4. See Richard, "Des enfants de troupe aux lycéens militaires."

5. John Lynn speaks of a sixteenth-century "battle for the pants" between early modern soldiers and their female companions, suggesting that the tough, masculine aspects of camp followers' personalities created gender tensions that often erupted into violence as men sought to maintain dominance in the armies. While this is no doubt true for the earlier period, cantinières seem to have engendered no such "battle for the pants" in the mid-nineteenth century: they wore pants *and* skirts, and so neatly straddled the fine line of gendered costume. The extent to which the suppression of their uniform in 1890 represented a new front in the "battle for the pants" remains unclear. Lynn, *Women, Armies, and Warfare*, 94–104.

6. See also Heuer, *The Family and the Nation*; Hesse, *The Other Enlightenment*.

7. Darrow, *French Women and the First World War*, 1–15.

8. Ibid., 255, 257.

9. Ibid., 72–73.

10. Grayzel, *Women's Identities at War,* 203.

11. Darrow, *French Women and the First World War,* 73, 78.

12. Montorgeuil, *La cantinière.*

13. Darrow, *French Women and the First World War,* 95 note 104.

14. Ibid., 81.

15. Grayzel, *Women's Identities at War,* 30–32.

16. Darrow, *French Women and the First World War,* 137–141.

17. "L'unique cantinière du front de l'Armée française," 514. The article was also accompanied by a half-page retrospective article titled "Les vivandières." This article was sweeping in its generalizations, and it explicitly misstated history when it claimed that the cantinières' ornate costumes had been "bequeathed by the vivandières of the Grand Army." (See chapter 4.) Nevertheless, it was mostly positive in tone, discussing the recently suppressed women with nostalgia: "There were also brave women, many of whom made striking figures on the battlefield, where they were stingy with neither devotion nor charity." Rousset, 514.

18. Ibid., 258–259.

19. Tooley, *The Western Front,* 184.

20. Morrow, *The Great War,* 186–187.

21. Fyfe, *Understanding the First World War,* 259.

22. Englander, "Mutinies and Military Morale," 201.

23. One question that arises is where would these women have been stationed. Modern military practice suggests they would set up their canteens in rest areas inside the Zone of the Army but outside the actual combat zone. Historical precedent suggests they would have had permanent canteens in the second or third trench lines, but that they would have spent a good deal of time in the first. During the mobile phases early and late in the war, they would most likely have traveled with their regiments as they always had.

24. Watson, *When Soldiers Quit,* 159, 163.

25. Tooley, *The Western Front,* 185. Nor did the army's half-hearted ameliorative efforts solve the problem of psychological alienation. Four decades later, Jean-Pierre Léaud's character Paul could still strike a chord with his lament that military service consisted of "sixteen months of life that lacks comfort, money, love, leisure. . . ." Godard, *Masculin/Féminin,* 1.

26. Clayton, *Paths of Glory,* 157. It is worth noting, also, that Pétain's actions were a reaction to a crisis already in existence; had the army retained cantinières, the crisis might well not have occurred, or at least it might have been less severe. Even if it did, having the cure to the problem already in place is always infinitely better than having to create the cure from scratch once the problem has become unmanageable. Complaints about the slowness with which the reforms were implemented lingered for some time.

27. Fyfe, *Understanding the First World War,* 258.

Bibliography

ARCHIVAL SOURCES

The Service historique de l'Armée de terre (AT) at Vincennes provided the bulk of archival materials for this work. In particular, series Xr (Non-combatants), Xs (Cantinières), 1N and 7N (Deliberations of the Superior War Council), and the Mémoires and Reconaissances (MR) series were crucial to this study, as were the Archives de l'Artillerie. Many other documents, as well as artwork, published and unpublished books, and official journals from the rest of the collection were also extremely helpful. In 2005, the archives of the various service branches were consolidated administratively into a single Service historique de la Défense: the army archives now form the Département de l'Armée de terre.

The Musée de l'armée at the Hôtel des Invalides furnished a great deal of useful material in the form of art, artifacts, and uniforms. The Museum's extensive library also provided access to several rare books and a collection of military history journals.

The Bibliothèque nationale's Cabinet des estampes (BN Estampes) was the source of a great deal of art on the subject of cantinières, including the published works of Gustave Orengo and Hippolyte Lalaisse. The BN's main reading room also furnished a number of primary and secondary published sources.

The Archives départementales du Doubs, de Maine-et-Loire, and du Val d'Oise provided limited but important documents.

The Archives départementales des Ardennes provided information from their J series on two cantinières: Madame Hofer and Henriette Busquet.

The Archives départementales des Vosges' series 48J contains the most complete selection of "Images d'Épinal," over one hundred of which feature cantinières, and which were important to my study of popular lithographs of cantinières.

PERIODICALS

Bulletin officiel du Ministère de la guerre
Echo de Paris
France militaire
L'intransigeant

Journal militaire
Le matin
New York Times
Le petit journal illustré
Le petit journal militaire et colonial
Le temps
Times (London)

PUBLISHED PRIMARY SOURCES

Adam, Albrecht. *Voyage pittoresque et militaire de Willenberg en Prusse jusqu'à Moscou fait en 1812, pris sur le terrain meme.* Munich: Hermann & Barth, 1828.

Adolphus, F. *Some Memories of Paris.* London: Blackwood, 1895.

Adrien, Henri. "La campagne de Crimée, d'après les lettres du Commandant Adrien au Capitaine Joppé." *Carnet de la sabretache* 16 (1907): 209–224.

Alès, Anatole [Jean Alesson, pseud.]. *Les femmes décorées de la Légion d'honneur et les femmes militaires.* Paris: Melet, 1891.

"Aspects of French Military Life." *Hibernian Magazine,* July–December 1864, 59–64.

Audouin, Xavier. *Histoire de l'administration de la guerre.* 4 vols. Paris: P. Didot, 1811.

Balzac, Honoré de. *Old Goriot.* New York: Penguin, 1951.

Baratier, Anatole. *L'intendance prussienne comparée à l'intendance française.* Paris: Taneru, 1873.

Barrès, Jean-Baptiste. *Memoirs of a Napoleonic Officer.* London: Allen and Unwin, 1925.

Beaunis, Henri. *Impressions de campagne (1870–1871).* Paris: Berger-Levrault, 1887.

Béla, Jean Philippe de. *Mémoires militaires du Chevalier de Béla.* Bayonne: Lamaignère, 1896.

Belleval, René. *Un capitaine au régiment du roi.* Paris: Lechevalier, 1894.

Bellune, Claude Victor Perrin, duc de. *Mémoires de Claude Victor Perrin, duc de Bellune, pair et maréchal de France.* Paris: Dumaine, 1847.

Berge, Henri. *Études sur la réorganisation des forces militaires de la France.* Tarbes: Telmon, 1871.

Bernède, Alain. "Relecture des écrits du général Jules Louis Lewal (1823–1908), fondateur de l'École supérieure de la guerre." *Révue de la société des amis du Musée de l'armée* 2 (2001): 6–15.

Betham-Edwards, Matilda. *Anglo-French Reminiscences, 1875–1899.* Leipzig: Bernhard Tauchnitz, 1900.

Billon, François-Frédéric. *Souvenirs d'un vélite de la garde sous Napoléon Ier.* Paris: Plon-Nourrit, 1905.

Biot, Hubert-François. *Souvenirs anecdotiques et militaires du Colonel Biot.* Paris: Vivien, 1904.

Blaze, Elzéar. *Souvenirs d'un officier de la Grande armée.* Paris: Fayard, n.d.

Bluysens, Paul. "La vie parisienne." *La grande révue,* 9ème année, no. 9 (September 15, 1905): 648–661.

Bollaert, William. *The Wars of Succession of Portugal and Spain, from 1826 to 1840.* 2 vols. London: E. Stanford, 1870.

Bonneval, Armand Alexandre Hippolyte de. *Mémoires anecdotiques du général marquis de Bonneval (1786–1873).* Paris: Plon-Nourrit, 1900.

Boulart, Jean François. *Mémoires militaires du général baron Boulart sur les guerres de la république et de l'empire.* Paris: Librairie illustrée, 1892.

Bourgogne, Adrien Jean Baptiste François. *The Memoirs of Sergeant Bourgogne, 1812–1813.* Trans. Paul Cottin and Maurice Hénault. New York: Hippocrene, 1979.

Brookbank, Arthur. *Letters from the Crimea by a Subaltern Officer.* York: Sotheran, 1873.

Browne, G. F. *Ice Caves of France and Switzerland: A Narrative of Subterranean Exploration.* London: Longman's, Green, 1865.

Browne, Thomas Henry. *The Napoleonic War Journal of Captain Henry Browne, 1807–1816.* London: Army Records Society, 1987.

Bulwer, Henry Lytton. *The Monarchy of the Middle Classes, or France: Social, Literary, Political.* Paris: Baudry, 1836.

Cabolan. "Le convoi funebre." *The Celt: An Irish Catholic National Monthly Magazine* n.s. 1, no. 1 (August 1859), 48.

Cadet de Gassicourt, Charles-Louis. *Voyage en Autriche, en Moravie, et Bavière: Fait a la suite de l'armée française, pendant la campagne de 1809.* Paris: L'Huillier, 1818.

Canard, Capitaine. "Le général Debrun." *Carnet de la sabretache* 14 (1905): 355–370, 486–511, 551–576.

Carnot, Lazare. *Correspondance générale de Carnot.* 2 vols. Paris: Imprimerie nationale, 1894.

Caron, Pierre. *Les papiers des comités militaires de la constituente de la législative, et de la convention (1789–An IV).* Paris: Cornély, 1912.

Castellane, Boniface Esprit de. *Journal du maréchal de Castellane, 1804–1862.* 7 vols. Paris: Plon, 1895–1897.

Castellane-Novejan, Louis Charles Pierre de. *Military Life in Algeria.* 2 vols. London: Hurst and Blackett, 1853.

Chawner, Lieutenant H. "What I Saw in the French Maneuvers." *Army and Navy Magazine,* November 1883, 69–81.

Chevalier, Jean-Michel. *Souvenirs des guerres napoléoniennes.* Paris: Hachette, 1970.

Chevillet, Jean. *Ma vie militaire, 1800–1810.* Paris: Hachette, 1906.

Chuquet, Arthur. *Human Voices from the Russian Campaign of 1812.* London: Melrose, 1994.

Claretie, Jules. *La vie à Paris—1905.* Paris: Biblothèque Charpentier, 1906.

Clausewitz, Carl von. *The Campaign of 1812 in Russia.* London: Academic International, 1970.

Cler, Jean Joseph. *Reminiscences of an Officer of Zouaves.* New York: Appleton, 1860.

Codman, John. *An American Transport in the Crimean War.* New York: Bonnell-Silver, 1896.

Coignet, Jean Roche. *Les cahiers du capitaine Coignet.* Paris: Hachette, 1968.

Combe, Michel. *Mémoires du colonel Combe sur les campagnes de Russie 1812, de Saxe 1813, de France 1814 et 1815.* Paris: Plon, 1896.

Conneau, Theophilus. *A Slaver's Logbook or 20 Years' Residence in Africa: The Original Manuscript.* Englewood Cliffs, N.J.: Prentice-Hall, 1976.

Davout, Léopold Claude Étienne Jules Charles, duc d'Auerstaedt. *Projet de réorganisation militaire.* Paris: Didot, 1871.

Dedem van de Gelder, Antoine. *Un général hollandais sous le premier empire.* Paris: Plon, 1900.

De Saugeon. *Collection des ordonnances militaires.* Paris: n.d.

Ducor, Henri. *Aventures d'un marin de la Garde impérial.* 2 vols. Paris: Dupont, 1833.

Elton, J. F. *With the French in Mexico.* London: Chapman and Hall, 1867.

Erckman-Chatrian. *Madame Thérèse: ou les volontaires de '92.* New York: Holt, 1886.

Faber de Faur, Christian. *Napoleons Feldzug in Russland, 1812.* Leipzig: Schmidt & Günther, 1897.

Fantin des Odoards, Louis-Florimond. *Journal du général Fantin des Odoards.* Paris: Plon, 1895.

Faucher de Saint-Maurice, Narcisse. *De Québec à Mexico: Souvenirs de voyage, de garnison, et de bivouac.* 2 vols. Montréal: Duvernay, 1874.

"Femmes dans la guerre." *Le petit journal militaire et colonial,* December 13, 1903.

Fleury, Émile Felix, Comte de. *Souvenirs du général Comte Fleury,* 2 vols. Paris: Plon, 1908.

François, Charles. *Journal du capitaine François dit le dromedaire d'Égypte.* 2 vols. Paris: Tallandier, 1984.

"The French Moll Flagons, or Vivandières." *The Schoolmaster and Edinburgh Weekly Magazine* 2, no. 35 (March 30, 1833): 196.

Gaboriau, Émile. *Le 13e hussards: Types, profils, esquisses et croquis militaires.* Paris: Dentu, 1870.

Gaboriau, Émile, and Prosper Mérimée. *A Thousand Francs Reward, by Emile Gaboriau, Translated from the French by Miss M. J. Stafford; and Carmen: The Power of Love, by Prosper Merimee.* New York: George Munro, 1887.

Gautier, Théophile. *Voyage pittoresque en Algérie.* 1845. Paris: Droz, 1973.

Girault, Phillipe. *Mes campagnes sous la république et l'empire, 1791–1810.* La Rochelle: Siret, 1884.

Guillemard, Robert [pseud.]. *Mémoires de Robert Guillemard, sergent en retraite, suivis de documents historiques, la plupart inédits, de 1805 à 1823.* 2 vols. Paris: Delaforest, 1826.

Hamerton, Philip Gilbert, and Eugénie Hamerton. *Philip Gilbert Hamerton: An Autobiography, 1834–1858, and a Memoir by His Wife, 1858–1894.* London: Seeley, 1896.

Hazen, William B. *The School and the Army in Germany and France, with a Diary of Siege Life at Versailles.* New York: Harper, 1872.

Hillebrand, Karl. *France and the French in the Second Half of the Nineteenth Century.* Translated from the third German edition. London: Trübner, 1881.

Hodge, Edward Cooper. *"Little Hodge": Being Extracts from the Diaries and Letters of Colonel Edward Cooper Hodge Written during the Crimean War, 1854–1856.* London: Cooper, 1971.

Inside Sebastopol, and Experiences in Camp. London: Chapman and Hall, 1856.

Jacquemont, Porphyre. "Carnet de route d'un officier d'artillerie (1812–1813)." *Souvenirs et mémoires* 8 (February 15, 1899): 7–121.

Jerrold, William Blanchard. *Imperial Paris: Including New Scenes for Old Visitors.* London: Bradbury & Evans, 1855.

Joinville, François de. *Memoirs of the Prince de Joinville.* London: Heinemann, 1895.

Kearny, Philip. *Service with the French Troops in Africa, by an Officer in the United States Army.* New York, 1844.

Kinglake, Alexander. *The Invasion of the Crimea: Its Origin and an Account of Its Progress down to the Death of Lord Raglan.* 8 vols. London: Blackwood, 1887.

Kryn, Jacques. *Le petit tambour d'arcole, 1777–1837.* Cadenet (Vaucluse): Chez l'auteur, 1987.

Labouchere, Henry. *Diary of the Besieged Resident in Paris.* 3rd ed. London: Macmillan, 1872.

Lagneau, Louis-Vivant. *Journal d'un chirurgien de la Grande armée, 1803–1815.* Paris: Émile-Paul, 1913.

Lalaisse, Hippolyte. *L'armée française et ses cantinières: Souvenir de 1859.* Paris: Orengo, 1861.

———. *Types militaires.* Paris: Morier, 1855.

Lalo, Désiré-Joseph. *Cahiers inédits du capitaine Lalo.* Paris: Belfond, 1988.

Lamathière, T. *Panthéon de la Légion d'honneur: Dictionnaire biographique des hommes de XIXe siècle.* Paris: Dentu, 1900[?].

Langeron, Alexandre Louis. *Mémoires de Langeron: Général d'infanterie dans l'armée russe.* Paris: Picard, 1902.

Larousse, Pierre. *Grand dictionnaire universel.* Paris: Larousse, 1860.

Larreguy de Civrieux, Silvain. *Souvenirs d'un cadet, 1812–1823.* Paris: Hachette, 1912.

Laurencin, Paul. *Nos Zouaves.* Paris: Rothschild, 1888.

Laut, Ernest. "Les femmes de 1870." *Le petit journal illustré,* September 6, 1908.

Lecointe de Laveau, G. *Moscou, avant et après l'incendie.* Paris: Gide, 1814.

Legrande-Girarde, Émile Edmond. *Un quart de siècle au service de la France.* Paris: Presses littéraires de France, 1954.

Leighton, John. *Paris under the Commune: or, The Seventy-Three Days of the Second Siege with Numerous Illustrations, Sketches Taken on the Spot, and Portraits (from the Original Photographs).* London: Bradbury, Evans & Co., 1871.

Lejeune, Louis. *Memoirs of Baron Lejeune.* 2 vols. London: Longmans, 1897.

"Lettres interceptées par les russes durant la campagne de 1812." *Carnet de la sabretache* 21 (1913): 19–27.

Levavasseur, Octave. *Souvenirs militaires d'Octave Levavasseur, officier d'artillerie et aide de camp du Maréchal Ney (1802–1815).* Paris: Plon, 1914.

Luguez, François. *Crimée-Italie, 1854–1859: Extraits de la correspondance d'un officier avec sa famille.* Nancy: Crépin-Leblond, 1895.

Marbot, Marcellin de. *Mémoires du baron Marbot.* 2 vols. Paris: Plon, 1892.

Marquant, François-Étienne. *Carnet d'étapes du dragon Marquant.* Edited by Georges Vallée. Paris: Berger-Levrault, 1898.

Martin, Theodore. *The Life of His Royal Highness the Prince Consort.* New York: Appleton, 1878.

Martindale, Captain. "Notes on the Camp of Châlons-sur-Marne." In *Papers on Subjects Connected with the Duties of the Corps of Royal Engineers,* n.s. 11, ed. Captain C. S. Hutchison, 128–142. Woolwich: W. P. Jackson, 1862.

Mathe, Charles de, Marquis de Valfons. *Dix-huitième siècle: Souvenirs de Marquis de Valfons, 1710–1786.* Paris: E. Dentu, 1860.

Maupassant, Guy de. *Lettres d'Afrique: Algérie, Tunisie.* Paris: La boite à documents, 1990.

Michel, Louise. *The Red Virgin: Memoirs of Louise Michel.* University: University of Alabama Press, 1981.

Ministère de commerce, de l'industrie, des postes et des télégraphes. *Exposition universelle internationale de 1900 à Paris: Concours internationaux d'exercices physicaux et de sports; Rapports.* Vol. 2. Paris: Imprimerie national, 1902.

Montagnac, Lucien-François de. *Lettres d'un soldat: Neuf années de campagnes en Afrique*. Paris: Plon, 1885.

Montesquiou-Fezensac, Raymond de. *Souvenirs militaires de 1804 à 1814*. Paris: Dumaine, 1863.

Montigny, Louis. *Souvenirs anecdotiques d'un officier de la Grande armée*. Paris: Gosselin, 1833.

Mopinot de la Chapotte, Antoine-Rigobert. *Sous Louis le bien-aimé: Correspondance amoureuse et militaire d'un officier pendant la Guerre de sept-ans*. Paris: Calmann-Lévy, [1905?].

Morrell, John Reynell. *Algeria: The Topography and History, Political, Social, and Natural, of French Africa*. London: Nathaniel Cooke, 1854.

Napoléon I. *Correspondance de Napoleon I: Publiée par ordre de l'empereur Napoleon III*. Paris: Plon, 1858–1870.

Norvins, J. de. *Souvenirs d'un historien de Napoléon: Mémorial de J. de Norvins*. 3 vols. Paris: Plon, 1896–1897.

Ordinances militaires. 4 vols. Paris: Imprimerie royale, 1768–1769.

Orengo, Gustave. *L'armée française et ses cantinières: Souvenir de 1859*. Paris: Orengo, 1861.

Oudinot, Eugénie de Coucy. *Récits de guerre et de foyer: Le maréchal Oudinot, duc de Reggio*. Paris, 1894.

Paris, Pierre-Auguste. "Souvenirs du 14e léger (1805–1812)." *Carnet de la sabretache* 13 (1904): 103–127.

Parquin, Denys Charles. *Souvenirs du commandant Parquin*. 1843. Paris: Tallandier, 1979.

Paulin, Jules Antoine. *Les souvenirs du général baron Paulin (1782–1876)*. Paris: Plon, 1895.

Pelet, Jean-Jacques. *The French Campaign in Portugal, 1810–1811*. Minneapolis: University of Minnesota Press, 1973.

———. "Le combat de Krasnoë et la retraite de Ney sur le Dneiper (extrait des carnets du général Pelet sur la campagne de Russie en 1812)." *Carnet de la sabretache* 15 (1906): 519–552, 626–640.

Peyrusse, Guillaume, *Lettres inédites du baron Guillaume Peyrusse écrites à son frère André pendant les campagnes de l'Empire*. Paris: Perrin, 1894.

———. *Mémorial et archives de m. le baron Peyrusse, trésorier général de la couronne pendant les centjours*. Carcassonne: Labau, 1869.

Picard, Ernest, ed. *Au service de la nation: Lettres de volontaires (1792–1798) recueillies et publiées*. Paris: Alcan, 1914.

Pils, François. *Journal de marche du grenadier Pils (1804–1814)*. Paris: Ollendorff, 1895.

Pion des Loches, Antoine. *Mes campagnes (1792–1815)*. Paris: Firmin-Didot, 1889.

Ponchalon, Henri de. *Souvenirs de guerre, 1870–1871*. Paris: Limoges, 1893.

Porter, Robert Ker. *Letters from Portugal and Spain, Written during the March of the British Troops under Sir John Moore*. London: Longman, 1809.

Pouget, Baron. *Souvenirs de guerre du général baron Pouget*. Paris: Plon, 1895.

Prarond, Ernest. *Notices historiques, topographiques, et archéologiques sur l'arrondisement d'Abbéville*. Abbeville: T. Jeunet, 1854.

Puget-Barbantane, Hilarion Paul. *Mémoires du lieutenant-général Puget-Barbantane*. Paris: Pichon-Béchet, 1827.

Puybusque, Louis de. *Souvenirs d'un invalide.* 2 vols. Paris: Dentu, 1841.

Reid, Douglas A. *Soldier-Surgeon: The Crimean War Letters of Dr. Douglas A. Reid, 1855–1856.* Knoxville: University of Tennessee Press, 1968.

Richard, Auguste-Jean-Charles. *L'armée et les forces morales.* Paris: Plon-Nourrit, 1902.

———. *Cantinières et vivandières françaises.* Paris: Flammarion, 1887.

———. *Livret antialcoolique du soldat.* Paris: Chapelot, 1901.

———. *La lutte contre l'alcoolisme.* Paris: Chapelot, 1901.

Roeder, Helen. *The Ordeal of Captain Roeder.* New York: St. Martin's, 1960.

Röhrig, Karl. *Im Kampf um Freiheit und Vaterland, 1806–1815.* Leipzig, 1912.

Romand, Louis-Jacques. *Mémoires de ma vie militaire, 1809–1815, manuscrit inédit de 1819.* Besançon: Charlin, 1981.

Roos, Heinrich Ulrich Ludwig von. *1812: Souvenirs d'un médecin de la Grande armée.* Paris: Perrin, 1913.

———. *Avec Napoleon en Russie: Souvenirs de la campagne de 1812.* Paris: Chapelot, 1913.

Rousset, Lieutenant-Colonel. "Les vivandières." *Les annales politiques et litteraires,* November 19, 1916, 514.

Roussier, Claude-Nicolas. "Un soldat d'Afrique: Journal du sergent-major Roussier, du 12e de ligne." *Carnet de la sabretache* 13 (1904): 46–62.

Russell, William Howard. *The War: From the Death of Lord Raglan to the Evacuation of the Crimea.* London: G. Routledge, 1856.

Saint-Chamans, Alfred Armand Robert, comte de. *Mémoires du général comte de Saint-Chamans, ancien aide-de-camp du Maréchal Soult, 1802–1832.* Paris: Plon, 1896.

Saint Marie, Comte de. *Algeria in 1845: A Visit to the French Possessions in Africa.* Trans. T. Ross. London: Richard Bentley, 1846.

Sallmard de Peyrins, Charles de. *Combats et colères d'un dragon de l'empire (1783–1858).* Nice: Serre, 1983.

Sattler, Édouard. *A l'assaut du million, les tapeurs de la cantinière, quelques-unes des 10.000 lettres authentiques reçues par Mme Hofer, . . . et publiées par Édouard Sattler et Lucien Klotz.* Paris: F. Juven, 1905.

Schrafel, Joseph. *Merckwürdige Schicksale des ehemaligen Feldwebels im Königl: Bayern 5ten Linien-Infanterie-Regiment.* Nürnberg: Bäumler, 1835.

Sherburne, John H. *The Tourist's Guide, or Pencillings on England and on the Continent.* Philadelphia: Zieber, 1847.

Sherrard, Robert. *Twenty Years in Paris.* 2nd ed. London: Hutchinson, 1906.

Stendhal. *The Charterhouse of Parma.* Trans. C. K. Scott Moncrieff. London: Zodiac, 1980.

Thompson, Alexander M. *Here I Lie: Memorial of an Old Journalist.* London: G. Routledge & Sons, 1937.

Thoumas, Charles Antoine. *Les transformations de l'armée française: Essais d'histoire et de critique sur l'état militaire de la France.* 2 vols. Paris: Berger-Levrault, 1887.

———. *Mes souvenirs de Crimée.* Paris: Librairie illustrée, 1892.

"A True Heroine Now Reduced to Selling Matches for a Living—Her Record." *New York Times,* November 3, 1891.

"L'unique cantinière du front de l'Armée française." *Les annales politiques et litteraires,* November 19, 1916, 514.

Vallery-Radot, René. *Journal d'un volontaire d'un an.* Paris: Hetzel, 1874.

Vandam, Albert. *French Men and French Manners.* London: Chapman and Hall, 1895.

Verly, Albert. *Souvenirs du Second empire: L'escadron des cent-gardes.* Paris: Ollendorff, 1894.

"A Victim of Paris and Versailles." *MacMillan's Magazine.* Parts 1 and 2. No. 143J (September 1871): 384–408; no. 144J (October 1871): 487–496.

Villeneuve, A. Symon de. *Mes années militaires (1856–1867): Souvenirs anecdotiques d'un ex-médecin aide-major de 1ère classe.* Angers: Siraudeau, 1907.

Vingtrinier, Joseph. *Chants et chansons des soldats de la France.* Paris: Méricant, 1902.

Walter, Jakob. *The Diary of a Napoleonic Foot Soldier.* New York: Penguin, 1993.

Weber, Eugen. *France: Fin de siècle.* Cambridge, Mass.: Harvard University Press, 1986.

Wedel, Carl Anton. *Geschichte eines Offiziers im Kriege gegen Russland, 1812, in russischer Gefangenschaft, 1813 bis 1814, im Feldzug gegen Napoleon, 1815.* Berlin, 1897.

Wilkin, Anthony. *Among the Berbers of Algeria.* London: Unwin, 1900.

Young, Marianne. *Our Camp in Turkey and the Way to It.* London: Richard Bentley, 1854.

Zogbaum, Rufus Fairchild. *Horse, Foot, and Dragoons: Sketches of Military Life at Home and Abroad.* New York: Harper, 1888.

Published Secondary Sources

Ageron, Charles. *Histoire de l'Algérie contemporaine (1830–1970).* Paris: Presses universitaires, 1970.

Applewhite, Harriet, and Darline Lévy. *Women and Politics in the Age of the Democratic Revolution.* Ann Arbor: University of Michigan Press, 1993.

Babeau, Albert. *La vie militaire sous l'ancien régime.* 2 vols. Paris: Firmin-Didot, 1889–1890.

Baldet, Marcel. *La vie quotidienne dans les armées de Napoléon.* Paris: Hachette, 1964.

Bapst, Constant Germain. *Le maréchal Canrobert: Souvenirs d'un siècle.* 3rd ed. 6 vols. Paris: Plon-Nourrit, 1989–1911.

Baroli, Marc. *La vie quotidienne des Français en Algérie, 1830–1914.* Paris: Hachette, 1967.

Barral-Gasparin, Rose. *Thomas-Augustin de Gasparin, officier de l'armée royale et conventionnel (d'après sa correspondance et ses papiers inédits), Orange: 1754–1793.* Marseilles: Laffitte, 1982.

Baumont, Maurice. *Au coeur de l'affair Dreyfus.* Paris: Del Duca, 1976.

Beard, Mary R. *Woman as Force in History: A Study in Traditions and Reality.* New York: Macmillan, 1946.

Becker, Jean-Jacques. *The Great War and the French People.* Oxford: Berg, 1993.

Bertaud, Jean-Paul. *La vie quotidienne des soldats de la révolution, 1789–1799.* Paris: Hachette, 1985.

———. *The Army of the Revolution: From Citizen-Soldiers to Instrument of Power.* Trans. R. R. Palmer. Princeton, N.J.: Princeton University Press, 1988.

Black, Jeremy. *European Warfare, 1660–1815.* New Haven, Conn.: Yale University Press, 1994.

Boime, Albert. *Art and the French Commune: Imagining Paris after War and Revolution.* Princeton, N.J.: Princeton University Press, 1995.

Brégeon, Jean-Joël. *L'Égypte française au jour le jour, 1798–1801.* Paris: Perrin, 1991.

Brereton, J. M. *The British Soldier: A Social History from 1661 to the Present Day.* London: Bodley Head, 1986.

Brett-James, Anthony. *Europe against Napoleon: The Leipzig Campaign*. London: Macmillan, 1970.

———. *The Hundred Days*. New York: St. Martin's, 1964.

Brice, Raoul. *La femme et les armées de la Révolution et de l'Empire*. Paris: Ambert, 1913.

Caire, Raymond. *La femme militaire des origines à nos jours*. Paris: Lavauzelle, 1981.

Cere, Émile. *Madame Sans-Gêne et les femmes soldats*. Paris: Plon, 1884.

Chagniot, Jean. *Paris et l'armée au XVIIIe siècle: Étude politique et sociale*. Paris: Economica, 1985.

Challener, Richard D. *The French Theory of the Nation in Arms, 1866–1939*. New York: Columbia University Press, 1955.

Chandler, David G. *The Campaigns of Napoleon*. New York: Macmillan, 1966.

Clause, G. "La contrabande du sel entre Lorraine et Champagne à la fin de l'ancien régime." In *Le roi, le marchand, et le sel*, ed. Jean-Clause Hoquet, 187–206. Lille: Presses universitaires de Lille, 1987.

Clayson, Hollis. *Paris in Despair: Art and Everyday Life under Siege (1870–71)*. Chicago: University of Chicago Press, 2002.

Clayton, Anthony. *Paths of Glory: The French Army, 1914–1918*. London: Cassell, 2003.

Coetzee, Frans, and Marilyn Shevin-Coetzee, eds. *Authority, Identity, and the Social History of the Great War*. Oxford: Berghahn, 1995.

Compton, Piers. *Colonel's Lady and Camp Follower: The Story of Women in the Crimean War*. New York: St. Martin's, 1970.

Conner, Susan P. "Les Femmes Militaires: Women in the French Army, 1792–1815." *Proceedings of the Consortium on Revolutionary Europe* 12 (1983): 291–302.

Corvisier, André. *L'armée française de la fin du XVIIeme siècle au ministère de Choiseul: Le soldat*. 2 vols. Paris: Presses universitaires de France, 1964.

———. *Armies and Societies in Europe, 1494–1789*. Trans. Abigail Siddall. Bloomington: Indiana University Press, 1979.

———, ed. *Dictionnaire d'art et d'histoire militaires*. Paris: Presses universitaires, 1988.

———. *Sources et méthodes en histoire sociale*. Paris: SEDES, 1980.

Dabbs, Jack Autrey. *The French Army in Mexico, 1861–1867*. The Hague: Mouton, 1963.

Darnton, Robert. *The Great Cat Massacre and Other Episodes in French Cultural History*. New York: Basic, 1984.

Darrow, Margaret. "The Eclipse of the *femme soldat*: Women in the French Army from 1870–1914." Paper presented at the annual meeting of the French Historical Association, 2002.

———. *French Women and the First World War: War Stories of the Home Front*. New York: Berg, 2000.

De Gaury, Gerald. *Travelling Gent: The Life of Alexander Kinglake, 1809–1891*. London: Routledge and Kegan Paul, 1972.

Dekker, Rudolf, and Lotte C. van de Pol. *The Tradition of Female Transvestism in Early Modern Europe*. New York: St. Martin's, 1989.

De la Gorce, Paul-Marie. *La République et son armée*. Paris: Fayard, 1963.

De la Motte, Dean, and Jeannene M. Przyblyski. *Making the News: Modernity and the Mass Press in Nineteenth-Century France*. Amherst: University of Massachusetts Press, 1999.

Delasselle, Claude. "Les enfants abandonés à Paris au XVIIIe siècle." *Annales: Économies, sociétés, civilisations* 30, no. 4 (January–February 1975): 187–218.

Delpérier, Louis. *De la Crimée à la Grande guerre: L'armée française devant l'objectif, 1854–1914.* Paris: Charles-Lavauzelle, 1985.

De Pauw, Linda. *Battle Cries and Lullabies: Women in War from Prehistory to the Present.* Norman: University of Oklahoma Press, 1998.

Déprez, Eugène. *Les volontaires nationaux (1791–1793): Étude sur la formation et l'organization des bataillons d'après les archives communales et départementales.* 1908. Geneva: Slatkine, 1977.

Desan, Suzanne. *The Family on Trial in Revolutionary France.* Berkeley: University of California Press, 2004.

Deschard, Bernard. *L'armée et la Révolution: Du service du roi au service de la nation.* Paris: Desjonquères, 1989.

Dever, John, and Maria Dever. *Women and the Military: Over 100 Notable Contributors, Historic to Contemporary.* Jefferson, N.C.: McFarland, 1995.

De Watteville, H. *The British Soldier: His Life from Tudor to Modern Times.* New York: Putnam, 1955.

Duchesne, Albert. "Petit enquête au sujet des cantinières du corps des volontaires belges au Mexique (1864–1867)." *Carnet de la fourragère,* 1956, 123–151.

Dufaÿ, Bruno. "Les cantinières." *Revue historique des armées* 2 (1980): 95–107.

Duffy, Christopher. *The Army of Frederick the Great.* London: David & Charles, 1974.

———. *The Military Experience in the Age of Reason.* London: Routledge and Kegan Paul, 1987.

Dugaw, Dianne. *Warrior Women and Popular Balladry, 1650–1850.* Cambridge: Cambridge University Press, 1989.

Duplessis, Gérard. *Les marriages en France.* Paris: Colin, 1954.

Eichner, Carolyn J. *Surmounting the Barricades: Women in the Paris Commune.* Bloomington: Indiana University Press, 2004.

Elting, John. *Swords around a Throne: Napoleon's Grande Armée.* New York: Free Press, 1988.

Enders, Victoria L., and Pamela Beth Radcliffe, eds. *Constructing Spanish Womanhood: Female Identity in Modern Spain.* Albany, N.Y.: SUNY Press, 1999.

Englander, David. "Mutinies and Military Morale." In *World War I: A History,* ed. Hew Strachan, 191–203. New York: Oxford University Press, 1998.

Esdaile, Charles. *Fighting Napoleon: Guerillas, Bandits, and Adventurers in Spain, 1808–1814.* New Haven, Conn.: Yale University Press, 2004.

———. *Peninsular Eyewitnesses: The Experience of War in Spain and Portugal, 1808–1813.* London: Pen and Sword, 2008.

———. *The Spanish Army in the Peninsular War.* New York: Manchester University Press, 1988.

Fairchilds, Cissie C. *Poverty and Charity in Aix-en-Province, 1640–1789.* Baltimore, Md.: Johns Hopkins University Press, 1976.

Farge, Arlette. *Les fatigues de la guerre.* Paris: Gallimard, 1996.

Finley, Milton. *The Most Monstrous of Wars: The Napoleonic Guerilla War in Southern Italy, 1806–1811.* Columbia: University of South Carolina Press, 1994.

Flandrin, Jean-Louis. *Familles: Parenté, maison, sexualité dans l'ancienne société.* Paris: Hachette, 1984.

Forrest, Alan. *Conscripts and Deserters: The Army and French Society during the Revolution and Empire.* New York: Oxford University Press, 1989.

————. *Soldiers of the French Revolution.* Durham, N.C.: Duke University Press, 1990.

Fox-Genovese, Elizabeth. "Women and Work." In *French Women and the Age of Enlightenment,* ed. Samia I. Spencer, 111–127. Bloomington: Indiana University Press, 1984.

Fridenson, Patrick. *The French Home Front, 1914–1918.* Oxford: Berg, 1992.

Fyfe, Albert J. *Understanding the First World War: Illusions and Realities.* New York: Peter Lang, 1988.

Gerard, Jo. *Belles gisantes.* Brussells: Delrue, 1965.

Gernsheim, Helmut, and Alison Gernsheim. *Roger Fenton, Photographer of the Crimean War: His Photographs and His Letters from the Crimea, with an Essay on His Life and Work.* London: Secker & Warburg, 1954.

Glover, Richard. *Peninsular Preparation: The Reform of the British Army, 1795–1809.* Cambridge: Cambridge University Press, 1963.

Godard, Jean-Luc. *Masculin/Féminin: 15 faits précis.* Paris: 1966.

Godineau, Dominique. "De la guerrière à la citoyenne: Porter les armes pendant l'ancien régime et la Révolution française." *Clio* 20 (2004): 1–20.

Gooch, John. *Armies in Europe.* London: Routledge and Kegan Paul, 1980.

Gosselin, Louis. *D'un révolution à l'autre.* Paris: Flammarion, 1932.

Grayzel, Susan. *Women's Identities at War: Gender, Motherhood, and Politics in Britain and France during the First World War.* Chapel Hill: University of North Carolina Press, 1999.

Gribble, Francis. *Women in War.* New York: E. P. Dutton, 1917.

Gulickson, Gay. *Unruly Women of Paris: Images of the Commune.* Ithaca, N.Y.: Cornell University Press, 1996.

Guye, Alfred. *Le bataillon de Neuchâtel, dit le Canaris, au service de Napoléon, 1807–1814.* Neuchâtel: La Baconnière, 1964.

Hacker, Barton C. "Where Have All the Women Gone? The Pre–Twentieth Century Sexual Division of Labor in Armies." *Minerva* 3 (Summer 1985): 107–148.

————. "Women and Military Institutions in Early Modern Europe: A Reconnaissance." *Signs* 6, no. 4 (Summer 1981): 643–671.

Hennet, Léon. *Regards en arrière.* Paris: Chapelot, 1911.

Herlaut, August Philippe. *Le colonel Bouchotte, ministre de guerre en l'An II.* Paris, 1946.

Herre, Franz. *Wilhelm I: Der letzte Preuße.* München: Heyne, 1980.

Hesse, Carla. *The Other Enlightenment: How French Women Became Modern.* Princeton, N.J.: Princeton University Press, 2003.

Heuer, Jennifer. *The Family and the Nation: Gender and Citizenship in Revolutionary France, 1789–1830.* Ithaca, N.Y.: Cornell University Press, 2005.

Hoquet, Jean-Claude, ed. *Le roi, le marchand, et le sel.* Lille: Presses universitaires de Lille, 1987.

Howard, Michael. *The Franco-Prussian War.* New York: Macmillan, 1962.

Johnson, Douglas. *France and the Dreyfus Affair.* New York: Walker, 1966.

Jones, David E. *Women Warriors: A History.* Washington, D.C.: Brassey's, 1997.

Julien, Charles-André. *Histoire de l'Algérie contemporaine.* Paris: Presses universitaires de France, 1964.

Keegan, John. *The Face of Battle.* New York: Penguin, 1976.

————. *The First World War.* New York: Knopf, 1999.

Kennett, Lee. *The French Armies in the Seven Years' War.* Durham, N.C.: Duke University Press, 1967.

Klein-Rebour, F. "Les femmes soldats à travers les ages." *Révue historique de l'armée* 16, no. 2 (1960): 3–20; 16, no. 3 (1960): 57–62.

Kryn, Jacques. *Le petit tambour d'arcole, 1777–1837.* Cadonet: Kryn, 1987.

Lacau-Mougenot, Marie-Thérèse. "Des femmes dans l'armée aux sous-officiers féminins." *Revue historique des armées,* 1987, no. 163: 100–107.

Lapouge, Gilles. *The Battle of Wagram.* London: Hutchison, 1988.

Larcade, Luce. "Les cantinières: Ces dames du champs d'honneur." *Révue des amis du Musée de l'armée* 96 (1987): 53–61.

Lebrun, François. *La vie conjugale sous l'ancien régime.* Paris: Colin, 1975.

Lechartier, Georges. *Les services de l'arrière à la Grande armée en 1806–1807.* Paris: Chapelot, 1910.

Lemaitre, Jean-Loup. "Nécrologes et obituaires des religieuses en France." In *Les religieuses en France au XIIIe siècle,* ed. Michel Parisse, 163–198. Nancy: Presses universitaires de Nancy, 1985.

Loiseau, Claude Joseph Desiré. *Le Mexique et la Légion belge, 1864–1867.* Bruxelles: De Cocq, 1870.

Lynn, John A. *The Bayonets of the Republic.* Chicago: University of Illinois Press, 1984.

———. *Giant of the Grand Siècle: The French Army, 1610–1715.* Cambridge: Cambridge University Press, 1997.

———. "The Strange Case of the Maiden Soldier of Picardy." *MHQ: The Quarterly Journal of Military History* 2, no. 3 (Spring 1990): 54–56.

———. *Women, Armies, and Warfare in Early Modern Europe.* Cambridge: Cambridge University Press, 2008.

Margerand, J. *L'armée française en 1845.* Paris, 1945.

Martin, Paul. *European Military Uniforms.* London: Spring, 1967.

Mathieu, Frédéric. "Derniers vétérans: Guerre de 1870–1871." *Derniers vétérans des guerres.* http://derniersveterans.free.fr/1870.html.

Mauguin, Georges. *Les grognards de la Grande armée.* Vichy: Wallon, 1960.

Maurer, Louis. "Une cantinière du terrible 57e." *Feuilles d'histoire* 6 (1911).

Mayer, Holly. *Belonging to the Army: Camp Followers and Community during the American Revolution.* Columbia: University of South Carolina Press, 1996.

McMillan, James. *France and Women, 1789–1914.* New York: Routledge, 2000.

———. *Housewife or Harlot: The Place of Women in French Society, 1870–1940.* New York: St. Martin's, 1981.

Mention, Léon. *L'armée de l'ancien régime de Louis XIV à la revolution.* Paris: Société française d'éditions d'art, 1900.

Mihaely, Gil. "L'effacement de la cantinière ou la virilisation de l'armée française au XIXe siècle." *Revue d'histoire du XIXe siècle* 30 (2005), http://rh19.revues.org/index 1008.html.

Mills, H. Sinclair. *The Vivandiere: History, Tradition, Uniform and Service.* Collinswood, N.J.: C. W. Historicals, 1988.

Milner, John, Art, *War and Revolution in France, 1870–1871: Myth, Reportage and Reality.* New Haven, Conn.: Yale University Press, 2000.

Ministère de l'instruction publique et des beaux-arts. *Catalogue général des manuscrits des bibliothèques publiques de France: Bibliothèques de guerre.* Paris: Plon, 1911.

Montagnon, Pierre. *La conquête de l'Algérie, 1830–1871.* Paris: Watelet, 1986.

Montorgueil, Georges (pseud.). *La cantinière (France: son histoire).* Paris: Boivin, 1897.

Morrow, John H., Jr. *The Great War: An Imperial History.* New York: Routledge, 2004.

Morvan, J. *Le soldat imperial.* 2 vols. Paris: Plon-Nourrit, 1904.

Moses, Claire Goldberg. *French Feminism in the 19th Century.* Albany, N.Y.: SUNY Press, 1984.

Muir, Rory. *Tactics and the Experience of Battle in the Age of Napoleon.* New Haven, Conn.: Yale University Press, 1998.

Müller, Klaus Jürgen. "The Military and Society in France and Germany between 1870 and 1974," in *The Military in Politics in France and Germany in the Twentieth Century,* 27–41. Washington, D.C.: Berg, 1995.

Pachonski, Jan. *Poland's Caribbean Tragedy: A Study of Polish Legions in the Haitian War of Independence, 1802–1803.* New York: Columbia University Press, 1986.

Parker, Geoffrey. *The Military Revolution: Military Innovation and the Rise of the West, 1500–1800.* New York: Cambridge University Press, 1988.

Pétigny, Xavier de. *Un bataillon de volontaires (3eme bataillon de Maine-et-Loire), 1792–1796.* Angers: Germain et Grassin, 1908.

Poisson, Claude. *L'armée et la Garde nationale.* 4 vols. Paris: Durand, 1858.

Porch, Douglas. *The French Foreign Legion.* New York: Harper, 1991.

———. *The March to the Marne: The French Army, 1871–1914.* New York: Cambridge University Press, 1981.

Prior, Robin, and Trevor Wilson. *The First World War.* London: Cassell, 2001.

Quennevat, Jean-Claude. *Les vrais soldats de Napoléon.* Paris: Sequoia-Elsevier, 1968.

Ralston, David B. *The Army of the Republic: The Place of the Military in the Political Evolution of France, 1871–1914.* Cambridge, Mass.: MIT Press, 1967.

Redlich, Fritz. *The German Military Enterpriser and His Work Force.* 2 vols. Wiesbaden: Steiner, 1965.

Resnick, Daniel P. *The White Terror and the Political Reaction after Waterloo.* Cambridge, Mass.: Harvard University Press, 1966.

Richard, Jean-Roch. "Des enfants de troupe aux lycéens militaires: L'évolution d'une institution (1766–1985)." *Revue historique des armées* 159 (June 1985): 4–39.

Riès, Luce. "Les cantinières ou les 'dessous' de la gloire, I: Des origines à la fin du premier empire." *Uniformes: Les armées de l'histoire,* no. 67 (May–June 1982): 8–12.

———. "Les cantinières ou les 'dessous' de la gloire, II: De la restauration à la troisième république." *Uniformes: Les armées de l'histoire,* no. 68 (July–August 1982): 6–11.

Roeder, Helen. *The Ordeal of Captain Roeder.* New York: St. Martin's, 1960.

Roquet, Henry. "Les femmes soldats dans la Sarthe sous la Révolution." *Bulletin du comité départemental de la Sarthe pour la recherche et la publication des documents économiques de la Révolution française* 19 (January–June 1924): 5–23.

Ross, Steven T. *French Military History, 1661–1799: A Guide to the Literature.* New York: Garland, 1984.

Rothenberg, Gunther E. *The Art of Warfare in the Age of Napoleon.* Bloomington: Indiana University Press, 1978.

Roynette, Odile. *"Bons pour le service": L'expérience de la caserne en France à la fin du XIXe siècle.* Paris: Belin, 2000.

Salas, Elizabeth. *Soldaderas in the Mexican Military: Myth and History.* Austin: University of Texas Press, 1990.

Schneid, Frederick. *Soldiers of Napoleon's Kingdom of Italy.* Boulder, Colo.: Westview, 1995.

Scott, Samuel F. *The Response of the Royal Army to the French Revolution: The Role and Development of the Line Army.* Oxford: Clarendon, 1978.

Seidler, Franz W. *Frauen zu den Waffen? Marketenderinnen, Helferinnen, Soldatinnen.* Koblenz: Wehr und Wissen, 1978.

Smith, Denis. *The Prisoners of Cabrera: Napoleon's Forgotten Soldiers, 1809–1814.* New York: Four Walls Eight Windows, 2001.

Société Henry Dunant. *Aux sources de l'idée Croix-Rouge.* Genève: Croix-Rouge, 1984.

Société historique de Rueil-Malmaison. *Les Gardes suisses et leurs familles aux XVIIe et XVIIIe siècles en région parisienne.* Rueil-Malmaison: Société historique de Rueil-Malmaison, 1989.

Steele, Valerie. *Paris Fashion: A Cultural History.* New Haven, Conn.: Yale University Press, 1988.

St. John Williams, Noel. *Judy O'Grady and the Colonel's Lady: The Army Wife and Camp Follower since 1660.* London: Brassey's Defence, 1988.

Steinberg, Sylvie. *La confusion des sexes: Le travestissement de la Renaissance à la Révolution.* Paris: Fayard, 2001.

Strachan, Hew. *The First World War.* New York: Simon and Schuster, 2003.

Strieter, Terry W. "The French Army's Cadre, a Mirror of French Civilian Society? Some Aspects of the Family among the Professional Cadre, 1848–1895." In *Proceedings of the Seventh Annual Meeting of the Western Society for French History, 1–3 November 1979,* 1981, 79–89.

Sturgill, Claude C. "The French Army's Budget in the Eighteenth Century: A Retreat from Loyalty." In *The French Revolution in Culture and Society,* ed. David Troyansky, 123–134. Westport, Conn.: Greenwood, 1991.

Sullivan, Antony Thrall. *Thomas-Robert Bugeaud, France, and Algeria: Power, Politics, and the Good Society, 1784–1849.* Hamden: Archon, 1983.

Tombs, Robert. *The War against Paris, 1871.* Cambridge: Cambridge University Press, 1981.

Tooley, Hunt. *The Western Front.* New York: Palgrave, 2003.

Trustram, Myna. *Women of the Regiment: Marriage and the Victorian Army.* Cambridge: Cambridge University Press, 1984.

Tuetey, Louis. *Catalogue général des manuscrits des bibliothèques publiques de France: Archives de la guerre.* 3 vols. Paris: Plon-Nourrit, 1912.

Vallez, J. M. "Cartographie des régimes et des circonscriptions des gabelles en Normandie." In *Le roi, le marchand, et le sel,* ed. Jean-Clause Hoquet, 187–199. Lille: Presses universitaires de Lille, 1987.

Van Creveld, Martin. *Supplying War: Logistics from Wallenstein to Patton.* Cambridge: Cambridge University Press, 1979.

Vignaud, Jean. *Notre enfant, Algérie.* Paris: Flammarion, 1947.

Vinde, François. *L'affaire des fiches, 1900–1904: Chronique d'un scandale.* Paris: Éditions universitaires, 1989.

Waksman, P., Philippe Shillinger, and M. A. Corvisier. *État des fonds privés (dépots, donations, successions, achats).* 2 vols. Vincennes: Service historique de l'Armée de terre, 1981.

Watson, Bruce Allen. *When Soldiers Quit: Studies in Military Disintegration.* Westport, Conn.: Praeger, 1997.

Weber, Eugen. *France: Fin de siècle*. Cambridge, Mass.: Harvard University Press, 1986.

Western, J. R. *The English Militia in the Eighteenth Century.* London: Routledge and Kegan Paul, 1965.

Weygand, Maxime. *Histoire de l'armée française*. Paris: Flammarion, 1961.

Wilson, Kathleen. *The Island Race: Englishness, Empire and Gender in the Eighteenth Century.* London: Routledge, 2003.

Woloch, Isser. "War-Widows' Pensions: Social Policy in Revolutionary and Napoleonic France." *Societas* 6, no. 4 (Autumn 1976): 235–254.

Index

Page numbers in italics indicate illustrations.

Thomas Cardoza is the author of numerous articles on French military women. He holds a master's degree in military history from Purdue University, where he studied under Gunther Rothenberg, and a Ph.D. in French history from the University of California, Santa Barbara. He has taught at the Santa Barbara and San Diego campuses of the University of California, and he is currently Professor of Humanities at Truckee Meadows Community College in Reno, Nevada.

www.ingramcontent.com/pod-product-compliance
Lightning Source LLC
Chambersburg PA
CBHW070401100426
42812CB00005B/1595